The Sit Room

The Sit Room

In the Theater of War and Peace

DAVID SCHEFFER

OXFORD
UNIVERSITY PRESS

The Sit Room: In the Theater of War and Peace. David Scheffer.
© Oxford University Press 2019. Published 2019 by Oxford University Press.

OXFORD
UNIVERSITY PRESS

Oxford University Press is a department of the University of Oxford. It furthers the
University's objective of excellence in research, scholarship, and education by publishing
worldwide. Oxford is a registered trademark of Oxford University Press in the UK
and certain other countries.

Published in the United States of America by Oxford University Press
198 Madison Avenue, New York, NY 10016, United States of America.

Library of Congress Cataloging-in-Publication Data

Names: Scheffer, David.
Title: The sit room : in the theater of war and peace / David Scheffer.
Description: New York : Oxford University Press, 2019. | Includes bibliographical references
and index.
Identifiers: LCCN 2017059881 | ISBN 9780190860639 (hardback)
Subjects: LCSH: United States—Foreign relations—1993–2001. | United States—
Foreign relations—Decision making. | Yugoslav War, 1991–1995—
Participation, American. | Yugoslav War, 1991–1995—Atrocities. | Yugoslav War,
1991–1995—Bosnia and Herzegovina.
Classification: LCC E885 .S347 2018 | DDC 327.73009/049—dc23
LC record available at https://lccn.loc.gov/2017059881

1 3 5 7 9 8 6 4 2

Printed by Sheridan Books, Inc., United States of America

Note to Readers

This publication is designed to provide accurate and authoritative information in regard
to the subject matter covered. It is based upon sources believed to be accurate and
reliable and is intended to be current as of the time it was written. It is sold with the
understanding that the publisher is not engaged in rendering legal, accounting, or other
professional services. If legal advice or other expert assistance is required, the services of
a competent professional person should be sought. Also, to confirm that the information
has not been affected or changed by recent developments, traditional legal research
techniques should be used, including checking primary sources where appropriate.

*(Based on the Declaration of Principles jointly adopted by a Committee of the
American Bar Association and a Committee of Publishers and Associations.)*

You may order this or any other Oxford University Press publication
by visiting the Oxford University Press website at www.oup.com.

Situation Room

They gather during the day,
They assemble in the night,
These men and women of war and peace.
Invested with "intelligence" briefings, dire forecasts of
    military brass, and scheming of politicians.
They act as diplomats and generals on the fields of reality.
Look! Down there in the Situation Room, of the West Wing, at
    the White House, the dungeon below all the fun,
The Deputies and Principals roll the dice with every ruling of
    their minds.

DAVID SCHEFFER, 2018

This book is dedicated to the American Academy in Berlin and the staff and fellows "on deck" during fall 2013.

Contents

Cast of Characters

(alphabetically)

Madeleine Albright, U.S. Permanent Representative to the United Nations

Yasushi Akashi, Special Representative of the United Nations Secretary-General for the Former Yugoslavia

Kofi Annan, United Nations Under Secretary-General for Peacekeeping Operations

Diego Arria, Venezuela's Permanent Representative to the United Nations (1991–1993)

Les Aspin, Secretary of Defense (1993–1994)

Milan Babić, Minister of Foreign Affairs, so-called Republic of Serbian Krajina

Reginald Bartholomew, U.S. Special Envoy for the Balkans (1993) and U.S. Ambassador to Italy (1993–1996)

Samuel ("Sandy") Berger, Deputy National Security Adviser

Jeremy Boorda, Admiral, U.S. Navy, and Commander in Chief, U.S. Naval Forces, Southern Europe and Commander in Chief, Allied Forces Southern Europe and Commander in Chief, Operation Provide Promise (1993–1994)

Boutros Boutros-Ghali, United Nations Secretary-General

George H.W. Bush, the 41st President of the United States

Warren Christopher, Secretary of State

Vitaly Churkin, Russia's Ambassador to Belgium (1994–1998)

Wesley Clark, Lieutenant General, U.S. Army, and Director of Strategic Plans and Policy (J5), Joint Chiefs of Staff (1994–1996)

William ("Bill") Clinton, the 42nd President of the United States

Ivo Daalder, staff, National Security Council (1994–1995)

John Deutch, Deputy Secretary of Defense (1994–1995); Director of the Central Intelligence Agency (1995–1996)

Tom Donilon, Secretary of State Warren Christopher's Chief of Staff

Nelson Drew, Colonel, U.S. Air Force, and European Affairs Staff Director, National Security Council (1995)

Robert Frasure, Deputy Assistant Secretary of State for European and Canadian Affairs (1994–1995)

Leon Fuerth, National Security Adviser to Vice President Al Gore

Peter Galbraith, U.S. Ambassador to Croatia

David Gergen, Counselor to President Clinton (1993–1994)

Al Gore, Vice President of the United States

Mate Granić, Croatia's Minister of Foreign Affairs

Christopher ("Chris") Hill, U.S. Foreign Service Officer

Richard Holbrooke, U.S. Ambassador to Germany (1993–1994); Assistant Secretary of State for European and Canadian Affairs (1994–1996)

Karl ("Rick") Inderfurth, U.S. Representative for Special Political Affairs at the United Nations and U.S. Deputy Representative on the U.N. Security Council and USUN Deputy on the Deputies Committee of the National Security Council

Alija Izetbegović, President of the Republic of Bosnia and Herzegovina

Bernard Janvier, French Army General and Commander of UNPROFOR (1995)

David Jeremiah, Admiral and Vice Chairman of the Joint Chiefs of Staff (1990–1994); Acting Chairman of the Joint Chiefs of Staff (October 1993)

George Jouwan, Commander in Chief, United States European Command and Supreme Allied Commander

Radovan Karadžić, President of Republika Srpska (1992–1996)

Donald Kerrick, Director of European Affairs, National Security Council (1994–1995) and Lieutenant General, U.S. Army

Klaus Kinkel, Minister of Foreign Affairs and Vice Chancellor of Germany

John Kornblum, Assistant Secretary of State for European Affairs and Special Envoy to the Balkans, U.S. Department of State (1995–1997)

Andrei Kozyrev, Minister of Foreign Affairs of Russia

Momčilo Krajišnik, First Speaker of the National Assembly of Republicka Srpska (1991–1996)

Joseph ("Joe") Kruzel, Deputy Assistant Secretary of Defense for European and NATO Affairs and Captain, U.S. Air Force

Anthony ("Tony") Lake, National Security Adviser

Sergey Lavrov, Russia's Permanent Representative to the United Nations (1994–2004)

Jan Lodal, Principal Deputy Under Secretary of Defense for Policy

Barry McCaffrey, U.S. Army General, Director of Strategic Plans and Policy, Joint Chiefs of Staff (1993–1994)

John Menzies, U.S. Foreign Service Officer, U.S. Embassy in Sarajevo

Slobodan Milošević, President of Serbia

Ratko Mladić, Commander of the Main Staff of the Army of Republika Srpska

James O'Brien, U.S. State Department Lawyer and Adviser to Ambassador Albright, and Special Presidential Envoy for the Balkans

David Owen, European Union Co-Chair of the Conference for the Former Yugoslavia (1992–1995)

Roberts ("Bob") B. Owen, Senior Adviser to U.S. Delegation in Bosnia Peace Talks (1995)

William Owens, Admiral, U.S. Navy, and Vice Chairman of the Joint Chiefs of Staff (1994–1996)

William Perry, Deputy Secretary of Defense (1993–1994); Secretary of Defense (1994–1997)

Colin Powell, General, U.S. Army, and Chairman of the Joint Chiefs of Staff (1989–1993)

Charles E. Redman, U.S. Special Envoy to the Balkans (1993–1994); U.S. Ambassador to Germany (1994–1996)

Malcolm Rifkind, British Secretary for Defence

Alice Rivkin, Director of the White House Office of Management and Budget (1994–1996)

Hugh Michael ("Mike") Rose, British Army General, Commander of UNPROFOR (1994–1995)

Muhamed ("Mo") Sacirbey, Bosnian Permanent Representative to the United Nations (1992–2000), Foreign Minister (1995)

David Scheffer, Senior Adviser and Counsel to U.S. Permanent Representative to the United Nations, Dr. Madeleine Albright, and her representative on the Deputies Committee of the National Security Council

Norman Schindler, Chief, Director of Central Intelligence Interagency Balkan Task Force

John Shalikashvili ("Shali"), U.S. Army General and Chairman of the Joint Chiefs of Staff (1993–1996)

John Sheehan, General, U.S. Marine Corps, and Supreme Allied Commander Atlantic for NATO and Commander in Chief for the U.S. Atlantic Command (1994–1997)

Haris Silajdžić, Minister of Foreign Affairs (1990–1993); Prime Minister (1993–1996) of Bosnia and Herzegovina

Walter ("Walt") Slocombe, Deputy Under Secretary of Defense for Policy (1993–1994); Under Secretary of Defense for Policy (1994–2001)

Leighton W. ("Snuffy") Smith, Jr., Admiral, U.S. Navy, Commander in Chief, U.S. Naval Forces Europe and NATO Commander in Chief Allied Forces Southern Europe (1994–1996); Commander of IFOR (1995–1996)

Rupert Smith, British Army Lieutenant General and Commander of UNPROFOR Bosnia (1995)

James Steinberg, Director of Policy and Planning, U.S. Department of State (1994–1996)

George Stephanopoulis, Senior Adviser to President Clinton

Thorvald Stoltenberg, Special Representative of the [U.N.] Secretary-General (1993); Co-Chair of the Peace Negotiations on Behalf of the United Nations (1994–1995)

William Studeman, Admiral, U.S. Navy, Deputy Director of the Central Intelligence Agency (1993–1995)

Gojko Šušak, Minister of Defense of Croatia

Strobe Talbott, Deputy Secretary of State (1994–2001)

Peter Tarnoff, Under Secretary of State for Political Affairs

Franjo Tudjman, President of Croatia

Cyrus Vance, United Nations Special Envoy to Bosnia (1993)

Alexander ("Sandy") Vershbow, Special Assistant to the President and Senior Director for European Affairs, National Security Council (1994–1997)

Yuli Vorontsov, Russia's Permanent Representative to the United Nations (1991–1994)

John P. White, Deputy Secretary of Defense (1995–1997)

Frank Wisner, Under Secretary of State for International Security Affairs (1992–1993); Under Secretary of Defense for Policy (1993–1994)

R. James ("Jim") Woolsey Jr., Director of the Central Intelligence Agency (1993–1995)

Boris Yeltsin, President of Russia

Entities and Actions

(alphabetically)

BTF	Interagency Balkan Task Force (Central Intelligence Agency)
CAS	close air support
CIA	Central Intelligence Agency
EC	European Community
EU	European Union
FYROM	Former Yugoslav Republic of Macedonia (as of 2018 the Republic of Northern Macedonia)
ICRC	International Committee of the Red Cross
IFOR	Implementation Force
JNA	Yugoslav National Army
MASH	Mobil Army Surgical Hospital
Medevac	emergency evacuation of sick or wounded, typically from a combat area
NAC	North Atlantic Council
NATO	North Atlantic Treaty Organization
NSC	National Security Council
OPLAN 40104	operational plan to extract UNPROFOR from Bosnia and Croatia under cover of NATO protection
OSCE	Organization for Security and Cooperation in Europe
PIF	Peace Implementation Force
RRF	Rapid Reaction Force
SACEUR	Supreme Allied Commander for Europe
SFOR	Stabilization Force
SICOR	Senior Implementation Coordinator
SVTS	Secure Video Teleconference System
UNCRO	United Nations Confidence Restoration Operation in Croatia
UNHCR	United Nations High Commissioner for Refugees

UNPA	United Nations Protected Area (UNPROFOR)
UNPREDEP	United Nations Preventive Deployment Force
UNPROFOR	United Nations Protection Force
UNSC	United Nations Security Council
USUN	United States Mission to the United Nations

Introduction

I always felt I was entering the most important room in Washington, indeed sometimes the world, when I walked through the Sit Room door.

DAVID SCHEFFER

JANUARY 20, 2018: THERE was nothing particularly remarkable about the day, but precisely 25 years earlier, when one corner of the globe—the Balkans in southeast Europe—was consuming itself with hatred, I stepped into the middle of that war and its atrocities. I was neither soldier nor humanitarian worker. No act of valor catapulted me. I was an international lawyer, age 39, who found himself entering the halls of power in Washington and being thrust into the Balkans conflict from afar with a daily tasking: How does the great and powerful United States, under a new president's leadership, handle this abomination? Just as a later generation of policymakers cogitated year after year what to do about Syria after its people were thrown into the fires of hell in 2011, I was facing years of cables, memoranda, emails, intelligence reports, Washington and United Nations briefings, European journeys, and, above all, meetings in the White House Situation Room to deliberate what to do about the ravaging of Bosnia and Croatia. The experience resembled a roller-coaster ride that dipped and rose on the backs of hundreds of thousands of victims—killed, wounded, raped, ethnically cleansed, fleeing sniper bullets, cast out as refugees—of a conflict that seemed both resolvable and utterly intractable, depending on the day and whether political risk managers woke up with a clear mind or constipated thinking.

I begin this story where my memories are most vivid: the Situation Room, or what its veterans call the "Sit Room." Scarcely a day transpires without some mention in the media about this cavernous policy center in the White House. *The New York Times* reported on just one random day in April 2017 that "[President Donald] Trump removed Mr. Bannon, his chief strategist, from the National Security Council's cabinet-level 'principals committee'.... The shift was orchestrated by Lt. Gen. H. R. McMaster,

Mr. Trump's national security adviser, who insisted on purging a political adviser from the Situation Room where decisions about war and peace are made."[1] CNN's "The Situation Room" with Wolf Blitzer and many Hollywood movies and television series have popularized the window-less and now high-tech sanctum of foreign policymaking tucked under the West Wing offices of America's most elite power brokers. President Barack Obama invoked the room in his publicly declared love poem to wife Michelle for Valentine's Day 2016: "Somebody call the Situation Room because things are about to get hot."[2] Visitors to the Ronald Reagan and George W. Bush Presidential Libraries see displays of the Sit Room as it existed during those presidencies and that are now populated by gaggles of suddenly elevated students engaged in simulated crises they must re-solve or the world we know will end. No other nation but the United States has so prominently identified where critical issues of foreign and military affairs are deliberated by their leaders, despite the secrecy that envelops the Sit Room.

During the first term of President Bill Clinton, namely 1993 through 1996, I frequented the Sit Room as Madeleine Albright's senior adviser and counsel representing the interests of her and the U.S. Mission to the United Nations (USUN), which she led as America's "permanent repre-sentative" before her ascent to Secretary of State during Clinton's second term in 1997. I held a slot on the National Security Council (NSC) Deputies Committee, and Albright sat on the Principals Committee, the pinnacle of foreign policy decision-making under the president. I typically would attend as Albright's "plus-one" in the Principals meetings (when Deputies were invited to join their bosses) but had a chair at the Sit Room table be-hind my nameplate for the more frequent Deputies meetings.

The Deputies Committee, always led by Deputy National Security Adviser Sandy Berger during those years, was populated by the second highest official in each of the agencies represented by cabinet officers in the Principals Committee. These "Deputies" included the Deputy Secretaries of the State and Defense Departments, the Deputy Attorney General, the Deputy Chairman of the Joint Chiefs of Staff, and the Deputy Director of the Central Intelligence Agency. I had a sui generis identity as Albright's senior adviser and counsel whom she designated for the meetings while the officially designated USUN official on the Deputies Committee, USUN's Ambassador for Special Political Affairs Karl "Rick" Inderfurth, rarely could break from his daily duties on the Security Council in New York to attend the White House meetings. But when Inderfurth, a highly talented former journalist for ABC News, joined the Deputies either in person or by secure video transmission from New York, I usually sat in the room as his "plus-one."

The Balkans conflict of the early 1990s was the major foreign policy test, albeit one among many, during Bill Clinton's first term as president. America's policy gyrations on essentially the Bosnian component of the conflict bred intense criticism, deep skepticism, turbulent moments of hope and despair among officials, enormous carnage and human suffering, and a maddeningly complex peace settlement erected upon a field of shattered proposals. Yet, in December 1995, peace was finally achieved, and the Clinton administration took the lion's share of credit for it. But the journey there was rocky with mistakes and setbacks. While hindsight infuses history with wisdom, living the moment—as we will in the Sit Room—also teaches how history unfolds and decisions fraught with risk are made in real time.

This is the story of a three-year conversation that took place largely at one table in one room under the more publicly fabled rooms and offices of the White House as events relentlessly cascaded toward atrocities, land grabs, and political standoffs in the Balkans. There are essentially three acts—one each for 1993, 1994, and the three-scene year of 1995. Each act revealed how repeated failed ventures—as tens of thousands lost their lives and millions were forcibly displaced by ethnic cleansing—preceded the ending of the war with the Dayton peace negotiations in late 1995. Muddling through became the dominant operating principle as the magic bullet to end the imbroglio and prevail with a just settlement, particularly for the Bosnian Muslims, or "Bosniaks," evaded every discussion.

This book aims to demonstrate how options were advanced or abandoned at critical moments and the difference those decisions made in diplomacy and on the ground, particularly in Bosnia. Sit Room veterans kept digging the ditch deeper and deeper; as one of them, I enjoy no immunity from criticism. The often lone advocate of military projection and tough sanctions against the Serbs—my boss, Madeleine Albright—proved to be the most prescient voice at the table. Defense Secretary William Perry was the wise man. Richard Holbrooke, the State Department official who drove the warring parties to a deal at Dayton in 1995, was a force to be reckoned with wherever he set foot. National Security Adviser Tony Lake both frustrated and energized his companions in the Sit Room with dogged mind games. Others, including David Gergen as Clinton's seasoned public affairs adviser, were oracles of moral values.

The Sit Room is an essential but imperfect vessel of policymaking where the human costs tied to critical decisions are never far outside the hermetically sealed door. For three years all eyes turned toward Bill Clinton's Washington for a solution to the Balkans conflict, even though it had started out as "Europe's problem," and European nations had committed their troops to the U.N. peacekeeping mission there. Plans and proposals lay mangled on the Sit Room table day after day, week after week, month after month, and year after year. Why did so many people have to die or be ethnically cleansed from their towns waiting for the Americans to decide to act, yes, really act, to liberate them from their misery? This narrative tries to pin down the answer to that question.

I attended almost every Deputies meeting and a great number of Principals' conclaves during the first four-year term of the Clinton administration. I arrived in the Sit Room a few months into 1993 after waiting for the higher security clearance required for work there and while I toiled at other responsibilities as Albright's adviser in a world full of crises. The Deputies Committee met more frequently than the Principals Committee and made most foreign policy decisions, leaving those that could not be resolved by the Deputies, representing their agencies' frequently competing views, for the Principals to decide. If there remained gridlock among the Principals, the president typically would make a final decision despite the discord below him, which could include remanding it to us for further deliberation.

The Principals during Clinton's first term were led by the National Security Adviser Anthony ("Tony") Lake and included Secretary of State Warren Christopher; Defense Secretary Les Aspin and, following his resignation in 1994, William Perry; the Chairman of the Joint Chiefs of Staff and Army General Colin Powell and, following his retirement in late 1993, Army General John Shalikashvili ("Shali"); the Director of Central Intelligence James Woolsey, Jr., and, upon his retirement in early 1995, John Deutch; the vice president's national security adviser, Leon Fuerth; Albright; occasionally Attorney General Janet Reno and Secretary of the Treasury Lloyd Bentsen and, upon his retirement in late 1994, Robert Rubin; and Berger.

Lake and Berger acted mostly as honest brokers among coequal decision makers at the Sit Room table during Principals and Deputies meetings, at least in theory. In reality, the Pentagon (represented by both the Defense Department and the Joint Chiefs of Staff) typically brought the clout of vast sums of appropriated money and resources to the Sit Room and the unique perspective of military veterans who reminded us that they offered hard-earned experience. The Director of Central Intelligence or his deputy often hugged the military point of view after delivering the opening intelligence briefing. I usually could team up with Strobe Talbott, the Deputy Secretary of State, in the Deputies meetings and at least present a double dose of diplomatic reasoning and, indeed, our own experience to the issue at hand. However, there were times when I presented a third point of view—distinct from Foggy Bottom and the Pentagon—in light of what was occurring at the United Nations in New York or out in the field with U.N. peacekeeping operations or just Albright's bold take on a foreign policy issue.

The Sit Room was, until significantly renovated in 2006 and 2007, a fairly small windowless and wood-paneled room in the lower reaches of the White House that, during the 1990s, was relatively Spartan in design compared to its current multimedia, multiscreen character and multiple conference rooms of varying size. The room during the 1990s boasted two video-linked screens shielded behind wooden pantry doors. There were none of the high-tech visual aids one typically sees portrayed on the old television shows "24" or "West Wing" or see in contemporary cinema or in photographs of the same room today. This story takes place before the expanding and high-tech renovation that occurred during President George W. Bush's second term. In my day there, the Sit Room usually squeezed 10 chairs around a heavy wooden conference table. No pictures hung on the wood-paneled walls. We watched one of the TV monitors when Albright or Inderfurth was beamed in from New York over secure lines. One door led to a hallway and out to staircases that took one to the walk-in floor of the West Wing. The other door led to the communications nerve center of the White House. An aide sometimes would walk through that door bringing the latest cable or news or note from NSC staff to whoever was chairing the meeting. The president or vice president would enter from the other door, the one near the staircase, and all would rise out of respect and wait for him to sit in the leader's seat (with Lake or Berger shifting quickly to another seat at the table).

The White House had no Situation Room until 1961, when it was first created by President John F. Kennedy after the Bay of Pigs fiasco. The space used to be President Harry Truman's bowling alley. Kennedy made ample use of the Sit Room during the Cuban missile crisis of 1962 to read cable traffic. President Lyndon Johnson spent considerable time strategizing the Vietnam War in the room. President Richard

Nixon's national security adviser, Henry Kissinger, likened it to a dungeon. Neither Nixon nor President Gerald Ford made many personal visits to the Sit Room. But President George W. Bush's national security team hunkered down in it on September 11, 2001, to manage the initial hours after the terrorist attacks of that day, and he frequented the room. President Barack Obama was known to visit the Sit Room often for Principals meetings.

The renovations completely transformed the room so it now bears little resemblance to what it looked like during the Clinton administration and the years of policymaking covered by this story. We gazed at television monitors that boasted cathode ray tubes for monitors; we used faxes for communication; we relied on computers and telephones in the White House communications center next door with technology rooted in the 1980s. Cell phones as we know them today did not exist, and we could not check our email even in the corridor leading to the Sit Room. Indeed, email was still in its infancy. So when we sat at the Sit Room table, the only time one's head dipped down was to glance at a hard copy document or scribble a note with a real pen.

Surprisingly, for someone as claustrophobic as me, I found the Sit Room to be an inviting arena for decision-making. Surely today, with the much-expanded and renovated complex of three conference rooms and high-tech control center, officials have spacious quarters in which to remake the world. But in my time I found that working within a small and relatively tech-free environment can be liberating for the mind, encouraging discourse rather than recourse to electronic feeds.

At Deputies meetings, I would sit at the table with the other Deputies of the national security agencies. When I attended as Albright's "plus-one" at Principals Committee meetings, I sat against the wall behind Albright. This had the advantage of being close enough to pass notes or whisper occasionally in her ear, both of which I did only sparingly as she certainly did not need constant advice and it would look strange to handicap my Principal's stature at the table in that manner. But the disadvantage is that I could not read her facial expressions, which had character and would have signaled certain views of hers to me during the discussion. For some Principals' meetings, Albright would beam in on secure video from USUN in New York, and I would occupy a seat either at the Sit Room table or against the wall, depending on whether any seat was available at the table or I felt uncomfortable that day stepping up to the Principals' chairs without first being invited by Lake. But when I had the honor to sit among the Principals at the table, I felt the burden of policymaking ever more acutely and endeavored to maintain eye contact with whoever was speaking.

I always felt I was entering the most important room in Washington, indeed sometimes the world, when I walked through the Sit Room door. There the role of America among the peoples of the world would be deliberated that day and decisions made by either the Deputies or the Principals or pitched for ultimate resolution to the president of the United States. We all worked from detailed briefing papers and came prepared, usually, to discuss both the larger issues at stake and the details of risks and policy implementation that are essential to prevailing at the policy table, or at least making a credible argument for one's agency.

I would prepare memoranda for Albright prior to her Principals meetings and brief her on where other agencies, including State, stood on the issue of the day. That way she could enter the room with eyes wide open as to what would be advanced by each of her colleagues. It also gave me a chance, within the small world of USUN, to advise her of how I thought policy should be formulated in the Sit Room, whether for a Deputies or a Principals meeting. That extraordinary opportunity, and access, constituted some of the most challenging and proudest moments of my professional life. When I sat as the Deputy in Deputies Committee meetings, I had boundaries within which I spoke to reflect Albright's views and the interests of USUN while keeping a sharp eye on how Albright fit within the State Department's overall view of the situation. But I could speak independently of State at the table and sometimes did.

For four years (1993–1996), I entered the Sit Room typically several or more times a week and, as I calculated by early 1997, probably occupied the Sit Room more than any other official during the first term of the Clinton administration other than Berger, who chaired the Deputies meetings and joined almost all Principals meetings. Leon Fuerth, Vice President Al Gore's national security adviser, also was a near-constant voice for Gore in the room. Since USUN's brief covered all foreign policy and national security issues (as they intersected with the United Nations either directly or indirectly), I was on deck daily for Sit Room discussions throughout most of those four years. The State Department always would be represented too, but that individual could change, depending on the subject being discussed and the travel or other commitments that would prevent the Deputy Secretary of State from attending Deputies meetings.

In visiting the White House so often each week, I enjoyed the ten-minute trek along E Street and then New York Avenue to the residence's south entrance, as that would be the fresh air I needed and time to think before entering the Sit Room and its stagnant air. While we could place our cup of coffee or water on the table, I sometimes would sit there wondering when the next cup would be knocked and spill over all the classified papers on the table. I also enjoyed the walk back to State, for once again I inhaled nature's air, maybe absorbed some sunshine, and had time to mentally digest what I had just experienced before reporting back to Albright.

A cascade of other issues occupied the Deputies within the Sit Room during my four years at the table, including North Korea (and near war in 1994), Somalia, Haiti, Russia, China, arms control, intelligence matters, Rwanda and central Africa, and the Middle East. Deputies and Principals were jerked from one issue to the next, and on many days Bosnia simply was not the highest priority, or it competed greatly with others. So it would be misleading to view discussions about one topic as necessarily reflecting the full reality of the day, as we might shift quickly from one crisis to the next. A meeting on Bosnia might be followed immediately by a meeting on a conflagration elsewhere in the world. Policymakers can easily slip into a "What's next?" psyche about the flow of the day's discussions and decisions, without taking the time to reflect very deeply on what they have just deliberated.

In writing this book, I drew primarily upon relevant declassified documents of the Clinton administration that are available, particularly since late 2013, at the Clinton Presidential Library in Little Rock, Arkansas,[3] my declassified files, and my personal notebooks. As I did not write down notes while I was speaking in the Sit Room, this account avoids trying to reconstruct from memory much of what I personally said and focuses instead on the interventions of others. The opinions and characterizations in this book are those of the author and do not necessarily represent the U.S. government.

Throughout the years covered in this narrative, my colleagues in the Sit Room and I were daily consumers of the journalistic reports from the Balkans. Such outstanding and courageous reporting clearly informed us in real time as we formulated policy. There is a particular focus in this story, however, on other sources of information from diplomatic and intelligence channels that also informed our thinking.

The Sit Room is not only the most powerful room in Washington; it often bears that title for the world. For precious moments almost every day, the Sit Room is a theater in which war and peace compete. The dialogue in that room defines the essence of this book. What follows about the Sit Room and Bosnia can shine a light on how other conflicts of subsequent years may have played out in that chamber, with the United States acting quickly and decisively enough to turn the tide of history or stumbling into pathways of inaction or misunderstandings about erupting events in foreign lands.

Those entering the Sit Room face this reality: that people in peril will survive with hope or slide deeper into despair, depending on what officials decide over the next few hours in that historic room to uphold the integrity of America's place in the world.

Setting the Stage

TAKE WHAT YOU know about the American Civil War of the early 1860s—the unimaginable violence, racial oppression, and secessionist fervor—and imagine what could transpire across the Atlantic Ocean in Eastern Europe 130 years later where these three phenomena (ethnic and religious replacing racial) erupted into a war between and within nations and among peoples that also lasted four years. So much unified the citizens of the United States only to see the entire edifice of American society begin to collapse when Fort Sumner was bombarded on April 12–13, 1861. Fast forward to 1991: People who had been living and working together, attending schools and universities as fellow students, intermarrying, serving as comrades in the Yugoslav Army throughout the Cold War, and creating music and theater and dinner together, were suddenly torn asunder into three ethnic groups defined by their religious and political affiliations: the Bosnian Muslims (Bosniaks), the Croatian Roman Catholics, and the Serbian Orthodox Christians.

Two newly formed countries following the breakup of Yugoslavia in 1991 bore the brunt of the war: Bosnia and Herzegovina and its northern neighbor, Croatia, while Serbia-Montenegro fueled the conflict. Like the end of colonialism after World War II and the liberation of long submerged nations, the Soviet empire was dissembling into newly formed countries across Europe and Asia. Self-determination, in its many guises, was on the march again.[1] So Yugoslavia's break-up was not that surprising. But Western Europe's old guard and the United States, always the distracted superpower, were not expecting the violence that rapidly swept over Croatia in 1991 and over Bosnia starting in 1992.

The triggering of wars are complex unravelings of societies. But one can point to a single speech by rising Serbian leader Slobodan Milošević on June 28, 1989, in the Muslim-dominated Serbian province of Kosovo at Gazimestam, a Serbian memorial commemorating the Battle of Kosovo of 1389. There the Serb Army fought the invading Ottoman Army to a standstill but with such catastrophic losses that the Ottoman Empire, with far more forces to draw upon, ultimately seized control of the Serbian region. At Gazimestam, Milošević lit the fires of ethnic hatred and Serb superiority by stoking the will to fight for a unified Serb country.[2] What was political opportunism for Milošević became socially devastating for the people of much of Yugoslavia. The first brutal violence was unleashed by the Yugoslav Army against the Croatian cities of Vukovar in the east and Dubrovnik, a treasured UNESCO world heritage site on the Mediterranean Sea. Most of Vukovar was bombed into rubble and an estimated 1,131 civilians killed there. About 1,800 Croatian troops battled 36,000 Serb forces. Atrocities swept through the city as the Serbs destroyed it.

The iconic Croatian seaside city of Dubrovnik and its old town buildings of architectural splendor and historical significance suffered heavy damage from Serb shellings. More than 80 civilians were killed and 11,000 buildings damaged during the many days of artillery strikes in late 1991, including 13 civilians killed on December 2–3, 1991, when the fiercest bombardments hit the Old Town. The Serbs eventually seized control of large regions of Croatian territory along the northern border of Bosnia and inserted puppet governments ruled by local Serbs.

Bosnia's plunge for independence on March 3, 1992, outraged the leaders of Serbia and Croatia and their brethren on Bosnian soil, who were seeking their respective union with either mother Croatia or mother Serbia. A ferocious war ensued in Bosnia. The ethnic cleansing of more than two million people, mostly Bosniaks and, in smaller numbers, Bosnian Croats, had occurred by mid-1992 with little if no regard for the constraints of international law. In fact, "ethnic cleansing" came of age during the Balkans war. The term means the forcible displacement of a population (typically sharing common ethnic or religious origins) from its native territory and often using tactics that constitute war crimes, crimes against humanity, or even genocide. In the prosecution of ethnic cleansing, which is a colloquial term, tribunals examine the crime of persecution. Detention camps proliferated in Bosnia as bastions of torture, rape, and murder. A large number of atrocities in the Balkans war had occurred during 1991 and 1992, and the crimes that continued across Bosnia in later years (culminating in the genocide at Srebrenica) were hideous extensions of the brutality.[3]

The administration of the forty-first president of the United States, George H.W. Bush ("Bush 41"), still basking in its defeat of Saddam Hussein and liberation of Kuwait, responded meekly to the carnage in the hard-to-fathom Balkans. European powers agreed to send troops for the newly created U.N. peacekeeping protection force (UNPROFOR) to be stationed in both Bosnia and Croatia, but that hardly stopped the Bosnian Serb assault that ethnically cleansed huge swaths of Bosnia for the Serbian cause. By January 20, 1993, when the Clinton administration took over the reins of power in Washington, at least 45,300 people (mostly civilians) had been killed,[4] almost three million Bosniaks and Croats had been "cleansed" from their homes and towns in Bosnia and Croatia,[5] and Bosnian Serb forces controlled 70 percent of Bosnia's territory, compared to 10 percent held by the Bosniaks and 20 percent occupied by the Bosnian Croats.[6] In Croatia, about 30 percent of the territory was controlled by Croatian Serb militia.[7]

Ahead were three years of jousting between war and peace in the Balkans, although most of this story will center on the Bosnian part of the conflict where atrocities proliferated as American policymakers grappled with its nearly unyielding challenges in the Sit Room.

Ethnic Cleansing Maps 1991–1995

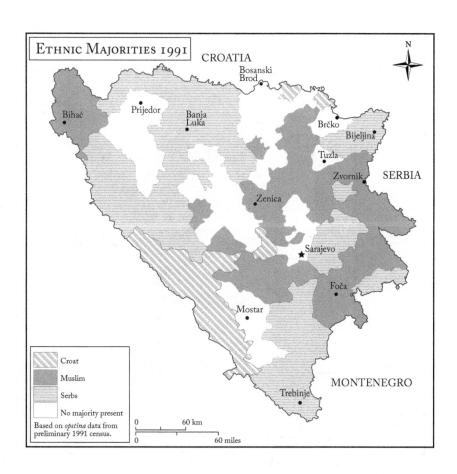

ETHNIC MAJORITIES 1991

CROATIA

Bosanski Brod

Bihać

Prijedor

Banja Luka

Brčko

Bijeljina

Tuzla

Zvornik

SERBIA

Zenica

Sarajevo

Foča

Mostar

MONTENEGRO

Trebinje

Croat

Muslim

Serbs

No majority present

Based on *opstina* data from preliminary 1991 census.

0   60 km

0   60 miles

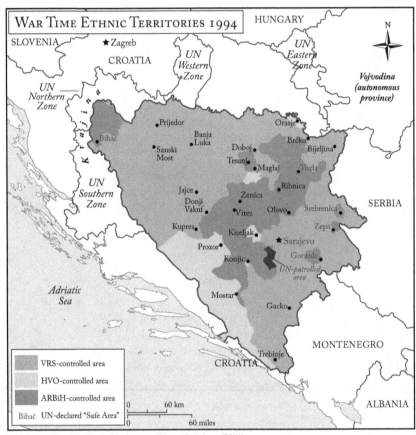

WAR TIME ETHNIC TERRITORIES 1994

SLOVENIA

HUNGARY

★ Zagreb

CROATIA

UN
Western
Zone

UN
Eastern
Zone

N

UN
Northern
Zone

Vojvodina
(autonomous
province)

Krajina

Prijedor

Orasje

Bihać

Banja
Luka

Sanski
Most

Doboj

Brčko

Bijeljina

Tesanj

Maglaj

Tuzla

SERBIA

UN
Southern
Zone

Jajce

Zenica

Ribnica

Donji
Vakuf

Vitez

Olovo

Srebrenica

Kupres

Kiseljak

Zepa

Prozor

★ Sarajevo

Adriatic
Sea

Konjic

Gorazde

UN-patrolled
area

Mostar

Gacko

MONTENEGRO

Trebinje

CROATIA

VRS-controlled area

HVO-controlled area

ARBiH-controlled area

Bihać UN-declared "Safe Area"

0 — 60 km

0 — 60 miles

ALBANIA

VRS-Army of Republika Srpska (also known as Bosnian Serb Army (BSA))
HVO-Croatian Defence Council
ARBiH-Army of the Republic of Bosnia and Herzegovina

Shattered Plans 1993

*The world has let a terrible thing happen in Bosnia, but
I always have been very reluctant to use American ground
forces and I am sure Bill Clinton will be unless we have
absolute objectives.*

AL GORE

This policy legitimizes ethnic cleansing.

MADELEINE ALBRIGHT

THE YEAR 1993, which this chapter covers, never got close to a peaceful
settlement of the Balkans conflict despite United Nations, European, and
American attempts to achieve one. There were several shattered peace initiatives, continued atrocities committed by all sides but mostly by the Bosnian
Serbs, a territorial division among warring parties that continued to reward
ethnic cleansing gains, and a U.N. Security Council declaration of "safe
areas" in Bosnia that became magnets for displaced Bosniaks. The capital
Sarajevo endured a second year of siege under sniper and artillery shelling
by the surrounding Bosnian Serb Army. Indeed, the siege of Sarajevo had
begun in April 1992 immediately after the declaration of independence of
Bosnia-Herzegovina. By the end of 1993, a military stalemate persisted in
Bosnia as a diplomatic challenge, second to none in the world, limped along.

At the beginning of the year, during the final days of the George H.W.
Bush ("Bush 41") administration and following 20 months of unrestrained
warfare and atrocities across first Croatia and then Bosnia, the intelligence
arm of the U.S. State Department confirmed in a classified memorandum
that what was occurring in Bosnia, in particular, was as close to genocide
as informed minds could determine:

Over the past year [1992] Bosnian Serbs have engaged in a range of
deliberate actions contributing to the attempted genocide of Bosnian

The Sit Room: In the Theater of War and Peace. David Scheffer.
© Oxford University Press 2019. Published 2019 by Oxford University Press.

Muslims. Although the word "genocide" has not been used in Intelligence Community reporting, INR [Bureau of Intelligence and Research] believes there is substantial evidence indicating that Bosnian Serb efforts to eliminate Bosnian Muslim communities have been widespread, systematically planned, and ruthlessly implemented. Although we lack clear proof of genocidal intentions among Bosnian Serb and Serbian leaders, the results of well-organized genocidal activities are evident throughout Bosnia.

Atrocities against civilians have been committed by all three warring factions (Bosnian Muslims, Bosnian Croats, and Bosnian Serbs). An extensive review of embassy cables and intelligence reports, however, strongly suggests that the magnitude and egregiousness of atrocities committed by Serbs in Bosnia amount to a program of attempted genocide. Although we do not have clear evidence of genocidal intent among Bosnian Serb and Serbian leaders, local Bosnian Serbs and militias have been actively engaged in a range of atrocities contributing to genocide. Our evidence suggests that the pattern and duration of genocidal activities varies within Bosnia, depending largely on the ruthlessness of local militia commanders.[1]

This provocative finding, one that can shape how policymakers prioritize the challenges of the day, was placed on the seventh floor desk of Under Secretary of State for Political Affairs Arnold Kanter a bare nine days before Bill Clinton was sworn in as the forty-second president of the United States. Drafted by a highly talented intelligence officer, Bill Wood, in the Intelligence and Research Bureau, five of his colleagues in INR cleared it. No other bureau was engaged. Kanter was the memo's only addressee, and it remains speculative whether any other official in the State Department at the time read the memorandum. The INR assessment of genocide in Bosnia, however deftly qualified the wording, left no impression on the incoming team of advisers, including myself, because none of us, to the best of my knowledge, saw it.

The genocide finding was nowhere to be found in Presidential Review Directive/NSC-1 (PRD-1) of January 22, two days into the Clinton presidency and signed by his new national security adviser, Anthony Lake. The significance of Bosnia to the Clinton team was set from the beginning when it became Clinton's first presidential review directive. PRD-1, classified "Secret" and thus unknown publicly, contained a list of five options and 26 questions, none of which addressed atrocities per se aside from asking about options for "stepping up efforts to establish a war crimes tribunal and to identify and bring criminals to justice . . ."

Some of PRD-1's questions would dominate Sit Room discussions for years:

- What actions would be required, up to and including the use of force, to ensure that neither Serbs nor others interfere with delivery of humanitarian relief supplies?
- Would it be possible to selectively lift the arms embargo so the GOB [Government of Bosnia-Hercegovina] could defend what it now holds but not launch significant counterattacks, and if so how? What training would Bosnia need to use any additional arms effectively? Who might be willing to provide equipment, money, or training?
- What would be required militarily and politically to halt further Serbian aggression in Bosnia-Hercegovina, including defending Sarajevo and other territory still held by the government?
- What would be required to establish and defend safe havens?
- What would be require[d] to roll back Serbian conquests in Bosnia-Hercegovina?[2]

The options were ambitiously stated:

- Concentrating on ensuring delivery of humanitarian relief supplies in Bosnia-Hercegovina;
- Stopping further Serbian aggression;
- Rolling back Serbian conquests to date;
- Taking punitive against Serbia for the effect it might have on others;
- Attempting to strengthen the Vance/Owen negotiating track;
- Building a strategy around reaffirmation of the Bush Administration's Christmas demarche, including a more detailed statement to the Serbs of what it means and of the instruments we are prepared to use to enforce it.[3]

Bush 41 had written a letter to Serbian President Slobodan Milošević a few weeks earlier on December 25, 1992, which read in part, "In the event of conflict in Kosovo caused by Serbian action, the United States will be prepared to employ military force against the Serbians in Kosovo and in Serbia proper."[4] This became known as the "Christmas warning." Muslim-dominant Kosovo, a southern province of Serbia, had been on a knife edge for years and even more so in late 1992 as Serbia's involvement with the Bosnian and Croatian conflicts suggested similar tactics in rebellious Kosovo. Bush 41 sought at a very late hour in his presidency to deter further aggressive conduct in the former Yugoslavia. (That particular war—between Serbia and Kosovo—nonetheless erupted on Clinton's watch in March 1999, long after this story's ending.)

The Principals

Clinton's cabinet of national security leaders—the Principals Committee—gathered in the Sit Room for the first time on January 28, 1993, and dealt exclusively with the plight of Bosnia. The cast of characters brought impressive credentials of their former lives to the table, but now they were bound to each other to make sense of the Bosnian mess and demonstrate, right off the starting block, that the Clinton team had a good grasp of America's foreign policy challenges. It was too early in the Clinton administration for me to start attending such meetings, as I was still undergoing security clearance procedures as one of Madeleine Albright's first hires, but a detailed record of the January 28 gathering was declassified.

First, though, picture the Principals, most of whom were sitting at the Sit Room table as powerbrokers for the first time. The veteran among them, in more ways than one, was U.S. Army General Colin Powell. He had been President Ronald Reagan's national security adviser and thus used to running such meetings. He was still serving as Chairman of the Joint Chiefs of Staff when Clinton assumed office. His four-year term that began under Bush 41, and thus his presence at the Sit Room table, would run until September 1993. Powell was the top military officer who ran the Gulf War in 1991 and achieved hero status in the result. His presence, at least when I saw him in the Sit Room that year, was intimidating if only because of his bulky self and stellar record of service. Born of Jamaican parents, he had grown up in the south Bronx as an African American who excelled in college and then the military. He had a fierce look on his face that completely changed with the occasional smile, and his sonorous voice landed explosively around the table. There were no dud remarks and no humor (at least as I recall) when he spoke. Powell's heavily decorated army uniform (with the four stars gleaming on each shoulder) contrasted mightily with the boring civilian garb around the table. His would be the cautious voice, typically trying to limit American engagement in Bosnia unless we complied with his missive, the Powell Doctrine. Under that edict drawn up with memories of the Vietnam War still fresh, Powell argued that the United States should only commit its armed forces to a conflict or mission when it could do so with overwhelming numbers of typically ground forces to achieve victory, with a clearly attainable objective, after nonmilitary options had been exhausted, with an exit strategy, and with the full backing of the American public.[5] It was a tough set of requirements to meet, particularly when faced with the imbroglio of Bosnia and Croatia.

Lake, fresh from his academic perch at Mt. Holyoke College and the Clinton campaign where he served as a top foreign policy adviser, steered the Sit Room meetings with a sly, knowing, and quizzical attitude, prodding the Principals to put their chips on the table. He had cut his chops on Vietnam as a foreign service officer, resigning in 1970 while working with Henry Kissinger because of the Nixon administration's secret bombing campaign over Cambodia. Lake served as the Director of Policy Planning at the State Department during the Jimmy Carter administration. Now he had ascended to one of the most powerful positions in the U.S. government. Lake's receding hairline and eyeglasses vested him with the wizened older philosopher look that seemed fitting alongside the ascent of a relatively young Bill Clinton (only 47) to the presidency and the weighty decisions ahead. His appearance reminded me ever so slightly of McGeorge Bundy, the NSC adviser to John F. Kennedy and Lyndon B. Johnson three decades earlier. Lake steered each meeting with his crackly voice toward outcomes that did not necessarily mean a decision was reached in each meeting; rather, I saw him taking serious note of the discussion among discordant Principals, and then he would shape his own recommendation to the president.

The newly minted Secretary of State was Warren Christopher, a Los Angeles super lawyer who had served in President Jimmy Carter's State Department and successfully negotiated the Iran hostage deal in 1980, although Ronald Reagan reaped the reward of the Americans' release on his inauguration day. Christopher's government service spanned decades, moving seamlessly in and out of private practice. Here he was again for his last hurrah, a grueling four years in which he played a critical role in bringing peace to Bosnia and stabilizing the country thereafter. Christopher spoke with a slightly high-pitched voice, eyes always darting around the table. I sometimes amused myself sitting behind Albright in the Principals meeting wondering when Christopher, often seated across from her, would jerk his eyes around and rest on mine. Was he internally asking, "Who is that guy?" Hopefully not after a while, but the darting eyes always piqued my interest. He had a frail short physique, as if a strong wind might blow him over. But he could speak quite tough at the Sit Room table, and no one dared underestimate his grasp of facts or the intelligence behind his views.

Clinton's first Secretary of Defense was Les Aspin, a longtime congressman from Wisconsin who had chaired the House Armed Services Committee since 1985. I remembered him well from my own days on Capitol Hill as a staffer on the House Foreign Affairs Committee. His demeanor and technocratic style of thinking had not changed just because he had entered the executive branch. Aspin was an intellectual who roamed around the Pentagon's budget with a hawk eye. He outsmarted and outmaneuvered many colleagues and opponents over the years. He was also rather sloppy, and critical papers bulged from his briefcase and scattered on the table. Aspin acted like a disorganized professor at times, seeking out data on random sheets of paper while uttering half sentences, his mind racing far ahead of his voice. He would slouch in his chair, legs crossed, chin on hand, formulating whatever thought he next barked. Aspin was fun to have in the Sit Room because he made you feel like the people's intellectual—a Studs Terkel—was present watching out for them.

The new Director of Central Intelligence was R. James Woolsey, Jr.

I had collaborated with him in 1992 on a report about U.N. peacekeeping for the U.N. Association of the U.S.A. He was sharp-witted, skeptical of most points of view, and a Washington lawyer wedded to the details of the task at hand. He had served in the Carter administration and as an arms control negotiator under Presidents Reagan and Bush 41. At the Central Intelligence Agency he had the whole post–Cold War world to master, with Russia replacing the Soviet Union. He was known as a neoconservative, and I thought he would be a strong voice for action in Bosnia. That happened occasionally, including during the second Principals meeting in early February 1993. He would open the Principals meetings with an intelligence briefing and then weigh in with typically skeptical and even caustic comments thereafter. Woolsey sometimes threw rhetorical grenades, perhaps reflecting what a CIA Director should do in policy meetings. But there are times when innovative policymaking is desperately needed and deserving of support. Nonetheless, he was a personable guy who could share a good laugh.

The vice president's national security adviser, Leon Fuerth, was Gore's avatar. Fuerth had long worked on Gore's staff on Capitol Hill, both when Gore was a congressman and later a senator. He started his career as a foreign service officer, including a posting in Zagreb, Yugoslavia (later, the capital of Croatia). Fuerth also had a stint with the U.S. Air Force and was highly regarded for his incisive knowledge and thinking about arms control.

His boss, Al Gore, clearly trusted him. When he spoke at either the Principals or Deputies table (as he held the seat for both), I knew I was listening to thoughts endorsed by the vice president. Fuerth became "Mr. Sanctions" during the Bosnian slog and was looked to, particularly by Albright who held the sanctions card in the Security Council, for information and advice on how and when to impose economic sanctions on Serbia and how and when to lift them. He spoke softly and in complete paragraphs, and intellectually, which bonded him with President Barack Obama's style. There would be the occasional wisecrack that triggered laughs or commiseration among those at the Sit Room table. One would ignore Fuerth at one's peril. I found him to be a gentleman who projected the gritty character of knowing what had to be done.

Dr. Madeleine Albright, a cabinet officer representing the U.S. Mission to the United Nations (USUN), joined Principals meetings either in person or by secure video link to New York. Her biography is well known—post–World War II immigrant from then Czechoslovakia, Ph.D. from Columbia University, professor at Georgetown University, mother of three daughters, National Security Council staffer during the

Carter administration, foreign affairs adviser in Democratic campaigns, Washington denizen. Her book, *Madame Ambassador,* is a must-read for anyone interested in this period of history and in how a highly talented woman maneuvered in what was still a world mostly powered by men in the 1990s.[6] As I have written before, she was the most powerful woman in the world during the 1990s. Albright was also my immediate boss for the entire eight years of the Clinton administration, including when I was Ambassador at Large for War Crimes Issues from 1997 to 2001, and she afforded me enormous access and opportunities to help shape policy. Working for Albright, I learned quickly to lean forward on issues. So I reflect upon those years with a naturally human bias for her. But do not let that stop you from reading on. Other than my assessment about Albright's overall contribution to the making of American policy on the Balkans during those years, I write what I saw and heard her do in the Sit Room and elsewhere and about my own work with her.

The final member of the Principals Committee meetings on a regular basis, indeed at every gathering, was Deputy National Security Adviser Sandy Berger, who also chaired the Deputies Committee meetings. Berger, a Harvard Law graduate, first met Bill Clinton during the George McGovern presidential campaign of 1972, and they remained fast friends thereafter. He worked in the Carter administration and then spent the Reagan and Bush 41 years as an international lawyer with a Washington law firm. Berger, who encouraged Clinton to run for the presidency, was senior foreign policy adviser during the 1992 campaign. I recall hearing his name often as I labored with the foreign policy team, wrote memoranda for Clinton, and did surrogate speaking for the candidate in the media. There never was any doubt of Clinton's reliance on Berger, who remained at the National Security Council, first as deputy and then, in the second term, as national security adviser succeeding Tony Lake.

In Principals' meetings, Berger sat opposite Lake at the other end of the conference table. He would listen intently and intervene only when a critical point others had missed needed to be made. Lake was the master of the Principals meetings and Berger respected that fact. In the Deputies meetings, he stuck to the agenda and gave everyone a fair shot at speaking and presenting views. Berger's classic method was to write notes on the manila folder in which the classified memoranda and other documents had arrived under his arm into the Sit Room. He used neither a legal pad nor a notebook—all of his notes were scribbled onto those manila folders. I suspect it will be a historian's challenge some day to decipher it all. Berger, who had a fatherly broad face, almost always slouched in his chair but then would jerk upright when he wanted to move on with the discussion. He often looked as if he needed some good exercise and an hour of sunlight. Berger expressed himself in staccato remarks and yet could be relied upon to articulate policy decisions accurately and thoroughly once reached. He always invited my views and written contributions. I deeply respected him and regretted the trouble he encountered a decade later with the handling of classified documents at the National Archives.[7] He passed away in late 2015.

The Inheritance

As the Principals sat down at the Sit Room conference table (and there was only one in those days) on January 28, 1993, they knew that a peace plan, developed by former U.S. Secretary of State Cyrus Vance and Lord David Owen of Britain, had been rolled out for inspection a couple of weeks earlier in the final days of the Bush 41 administration. The "Vance-Owen peace plan" was based on loosely unified autonomous cantons and drew internal boundaries in Bosnia largely determined by ethnicity as shaped, in significant part, by the ethnic cleansing assaults orchestrated by the Bosnian Serbs in 1992. Its viability was scarcely confirmed at the time as the warring parties expressed widely differing views about it. The Principals also knew that on January 14, NATO had helpfully offered its command and control structure for enforcing a no-fly zone over Bosnia that had been authorized by the U.N. Security Council a few months earlier, but lacking any enforcement mechanism.

Colin Powell and Frank G. Wisner, the Under Secretary of State for International Security Affairs who was still in his post from the prior administration, summed up the policy inherited from the Bush 41 administration as being "to deliver humanitarian assistance (using air power if necessary), support United Nations and European Commission mediation (but not necessarily the Vance-Owen proposals), refuse to accept borders changed by force or to legitimize ethnic cleansing, condemn war crimes, seek No-Fly zone enforcement, and arm the Bosnian Muslims (which [America's] Allies refused to do)."[8] Sandy Berger "noted that President Clinton during the campaign called for: enforcing No-Fly, being more aggressive about delivering relief assistance, and considering lifting the arms ban on Bosnia."[9] Though more proactive in tone, Clinton's campaign views were not that distant from the U.S. policy at the close of the Bush 41 administration.

Tony Lake laid out a conceptual framework, with three categories of ideas, for how the new administration could advance its policy toward Bosnia beyond where Bush 41 had left it at the end of his term:

- **Category 1: Actions doable soon without upsetting key partners (the UK, France, and Russia).** Ideas include: increasing humanitarian donations and considering airdrops of supplies, demanding access to all detention camps, and immediate release of all female prisoners.
- **Category 2: Initiatives probably doable with Allied cooperation but with difficulty and cost.** Suggestions include: increasing use of Ploce port and repairing the rail line to Sarajevo, tightening sanctions (especially on oil and financial transfers) and compensating Serbia's neighbors (especially Macedonia), seizing Serbian ships that violate sanctions, broadcasting into Serbia (using RFE [Radio Free Europe] or DoD [Department of Defense] assets), developing military-to-military ties, raising the profile on war crimes, cutting Serbian telecommunications links, and putting more monitors into Kosovo (plus Macedonia and Albania).
- **Category 3: Actions involving the threat or application of strong military force.** Possibilities include: enforcing No-Fly (by hitting air targets or airfields), lifting the arms embargo in Bosnia (at least for light weapons), "unleashing" UNPROFOR, protecting relief convoys with airpower. . . . sequestering all heavy weapons, demilitarizing Sarajevo (thereafter inserting 20,000 US/UK troops to protect it)."[10]

Powell closed the discussion with the third, most extreme, and darkest contingency plan for the use of military force in the former Yugoslavia:

The plan would attack counter-military [sic], -industrial, and -regime targets in Bosnia and Serbia-Montenegro. The first round of targets would include Banja Luka and Zaluzani airports, naval facilities in Montenegro, artillery around Sarajevo, facilities associated with Bosnian Serb headquarters at Pale, and some military or industrial facilities in Northern Serbia. Several Italian airbases and two carriers would be required. Follow-on attacks could hit tactical targets. Friendly losses would be low, but civilian casualties would be high;

large refugees flows would result. The public outcry would be great, key Allies might not participate, and "the Russians would go nuts," according to General Powell.[11]

If Powell's intention was to shock the Principals into an exceedingly cautious view of military action, he succeeded with at least some of them. This would fit a pattern with Powell. He opposed use of American military action in Bosnia and had made that view very clear, as late as September 1992 with Michael Gordon of *The New York Times*.[12]

The peace talks over the Vance-Owen peace plan mediated by the United Nations and the European Community broke down in Geneva. This would not be the last time the Geneva talks in their various guises over the years would collapse. But it was an inauspicious start for the new Clinton team as it deliberated its own initial steps. The stage was set for something, anything, to happen in Washington.

On February 3, the Principals met for the second time on Bosnia and made some headway in narrowing the new administration's policy options. Lake rejected the Vance-Owen map carving up the ethnic borders and declared consensus to press all parties toward a settlement, albeit with an ambiguous objective. "Lake suggested we work with the Bosnian Muslims to redraw the V-O map, sell it to the Europeans, and then impose it."[13] Military options were quickly sidelined. Powell pressed his advantage in the meeting:

> General Powell advised that airpower "solutions" won't work, and his preference (if a military option is called for) is to go in fast and heavy, intimidate the opposition, and hopefully scale back rapidly. His estimate of the force needed to enforce a V-O-type solution would be a "division package" of 20,000 troops for openers, triple that if rotations are needed over a long haul, UN Chapter Seven [Rules of Engagement], and $1 billion marginal costs over the first six months. General Powell also warned that Congressman [John] Murtha [Chairman of the House Appropriations Defense Subcommittee] has begun calling to ask the price tag.[14]

Opening Bid

The Principals gathered in the Sit Room on February 5. There exists a declassified transcript of that particular meeting, which is unusual, as I am aware of no other such complete verbatim transcripts. I quote from it liberally here to give you an opening flavor for how the Sit Room discussion, at least in the earliest days of the Clinton administration, progressed word for word. But I also set forth this long extract because the discussion was a critical one for the opening bid of the Clinton administration on its Bosnia policy.

Lake sought confirmation from the Principals that pursuit of the end game for Bosnian peace would place great pressure on the United States to help implement a settlement, including with military forces deployed in that wartorn country. Lake's introduction prompted the new American ambassador to the United Nations, Madeleine Albright, to set a different stage:

ALBRIGHT: Before we do that, I want to raise a more basic question. I am troubled by the conclusion we have reached. We are treating this area as of peripheral interest. History suggests it is more central. This policy legitimizes ethnic cleansing. It signals to the Central and east Europeans and to Russia that we will do nothing about it. The pieces in the draft PDD are "pretty pallid." I understand that deciding to use American forces in Bosnia would be crossing the Rubicon. But we should think about whether sweeping the problem under the rug creates more problems. The draft PDD is contrary to what Governor Clinton said and not commensurate with the importance of the issue.

WOOLSEY: I agree with Madeleine.

LAKE: (to Madeleine): You mean we should use force to enforce a settlement, not impose one?

ALBRIGHT: If we say we would never impose a settlement we are blessing ethnic cleansing.

. . .

CHRISTOPHER: We should be more aggressive in describing our negative position about the current Vance/Owen plan and the only way we would get people to agree is to be prepared to enforce a settlement. But we should not throw out Vance/Owen at this point and do it ourselves. The whole [European Community] and important figures on the Hill as well as the Russians support Vance/Owen. We cannot create a whole different structure. If an agreement can be reached, we should commit the U.S. to a greater degree of enforcement.

POWELL: I agree the draft [Presidential Decision Directive] is too pallid. It reads more like a press statement than a decision document. But what would Madeleine suggest we do?

ALBRIGHT: NATO action.

SEVERAL: I thought we had agreed that we would help enforce a settlement. . . .

. . .

POWELL: I thought we agreed that we would be willing to use force to enforce a settlement, but leave our willingness to do so "just behind the screen."

BERGER: What is the end toward which Madeleine would apply force? To get an agreement or enforce it?

POWELL: The military will do anything that is decided, but we need to know what "it" is that we are being asked to do.

. . .

BERGER: What does the use of force mean? Air power, or air and ground?

POWELL: Both. We can use air power but ultimately must go in and separate the parties.

LAKE: And the West Europeans won't do it alone.

. . .

LAKE: Let me clarify what we seem to be saying. Do we want to add to the President's package that we should say now that if all the parties voluntarily come to an agreement the US will say at the start that we are prepared to use force, including ground forces if necessary, as part of a NATO effort to help implement an agreement. An agreement that the parties had signed would include enforcement provisions.

BERGER: For now we should say only "including the use of force." [Aspin and others indicate agreement with Berger.]

LAKE: If asked whether that means ground forces, say we don't rule it out.

. . .

LAKE: Are you also proposing an option of lifting the siege of Sarajevo?

POWELL: The French have tossed that out recently. You can take out some artillery. That will make a difference even if no guarantee ending the siege. When the F-16s go home at night the shelling can begin again. Maybe we would luck out and get the same reaction we did by declaring the no fly zone and getting pretty good compliance without enforcement. But to really end the siege would take a full infantry division with air support.

BERGER: What would be the psychological impact on the Serbs of intermittent bombing, of planes taking out batteries on an intermittent basis?

POWELL: I think it would have a deterrent impact. They would have to decide whether to take on the U.S. If they decided to continue the shelling, knowing that we from time to time would get a target would reduce the shelling but not end it.

BERGER: The American people would see a big difference between using force when the parties have asked us to enforce an agreement, and preemptive use of force.

POWELL: Also, the relief effort would stop if we used force before a settlement.

WOOLSEY: The way the siege was supposed to be ended before was an agreement to put the heavy weapons in cantonments, but within range of Sarajevo. We should require that they move out of range.

FUERTH: We should insist that the guns be silenced or we will try to silence them, then that they be moved beyond range as part of a settlement.

WOOLSEY: Keep in mind the need for NATO agreement if we are to use our planes.

POWELL: If we decided to join the humanitarian effort on the ground, there would be great expectations that the US would force its way through. Field Marshall Dan Rather [anchor of the CBS Evening News] would criticize us if we did.

. . .

ALBRIGHT: What about war crimes?

CHRISTOPHER: That will be part of our diplomatic strategy. Part of Madeleine's job is to move it at the UN.

BERGER: Is there a tension or inconsistency between pressing on war crimes and trying to negotiate?

LAKE: We could focus on the grass roots offenders first rather than their leaders who give the commands.

. . .

VICE PRESIDENT [GORE]: I disagree [about committing U.S. ground forces]. The world has let a terrible thing happen in Bosnia, but I always have been very reluctant to use American ground forces and I am sure Bill Clinton will be unless we have absolute objectives. There is a tension between the word "agree" and "enforce." In that creative tension we might find the parameters of our role. If there truly is an agreement, the requirements of enforcement are minimal. The current Vance/Owen plan would need to be not only enforced but imposed. Then we would have the worst of both worlds. Vance/Owen has a terrible map, and would require lots of American blood and treasure. We do not need to bring to the table a willingness to commit forces. We bring the willingness of the world's leading power to help get a true agreement. We have a great opportunity to position ourselves as the principal spokesman and advocate of a Muslim dominated coalition. In a creative way, we would identify ourselves with the core of the Muslim world. [Israeli Prime Minister Yitzhak] Rabin has spoken out against what is happening in Bosnia. The pressure will build because they are all looking for a way out and looking for an excuse.

. . .

CHRISTOPHER: We should make an all out effort to persuade and convince the parties rather than impose a settlement. On the other hand, we are not talking about an agreement among three Church groups in California. This is the Balkans. It is not realistic to think that we can do without enforcement, even of a good agreement. To give an air of reality to our position, we have to say that the US will assist in carrying out the enforcement, in conjunction with the UN and NATO.

VICE PRESIDENT GORE: But the American people will not want to send our boys there.

POWELL: The risk of casualties would be relatively low if there is an agreement even by Balkan standards. None of the parties would stand up to a Western force that included the U.S. There would be some snipers or ambushes, but not major resistance.

At this point the President joined the meeting, and Colin Powell described the issue and repeated the last point to him.

POWELL: The nature of a Bosnian agreement will require ground forces. We can punish from the air but not enforce from the air. If there is a reasonably good agreement, even by Balkan standards, the casualties would be acceptable. None of the parties would take on a US/NATO force. There would be snipers, road blocks, ambushes, and the like but it would not be a big deal. It will be expensive. We might luck out and be able to flood the country with troops for a time and then get out.

THE PRESIDENT TO POWELL: What's your advice?

POWELL: We can perform this mission. But it would be expensive and could be open ended with no promise of getting out. But if we start down the road of diplomatic engagement, we must be willing to help enforce a settlement.

CHRISTOPHER: I agree. Vance/Owen as it stands would take a great number of troops to enforce. The alternative is a diplomatic strategy but unless we commit troops it won't get you where you want to go. So we are recommending a middle position, in which we would keep vague just what we will do but commit to some use of American forces.

ASPIN: I agree.

THE PRESIDENT (TO POWELL): Can we get out of Somalia first?

POWELL: We could get out of Somalia now if the UN would agree to take it over.

CHRISTOPHER: We won't have an agreement in the near term.

THE PRESIDENT: About six months?

CHRISTOPHER: That's about right.

. . .

BERGER: . . . . We could say this is a European problem and they should take responsibility for enforcing a settlement.

THE PRESIDENT (INTERRUPTING): We can't do that without giving up our whole position in the world.

LAKE: We will prepare a strategy for implementing this policy.[15]

The Principals, including President Bill Clinton and Vice President Al Gore, had spoken. Albright presented her blunt perspective about the reality of ethnic cleansing. Woolsey agreed. Christopher, while criticizing the Vance-Owen peace plan, laid the groundwork for Washington's embrace of it out of necessity. Powell offered sound military advice and a pragmatic view that if a peace settlement could be achieved, "flooding" troops into Bosnia would be manageable, albeit expensive and perhaps open-ended. He also spoke to the criticism we might encounter if we used American forces to push through humanitarian relief.

Gore doubtless piqued interest in the Sit Room with his resistance to using any American ground forces in Bosnia. His view threaded the needle of what was said during the presidential campaign only a few months earlier—that the United States would engage but, now we learned, not with ground troops. Yet it exposed Clinton and Gore to an obvious reflection: What was all that tough talk about during the campaign? With Clinton presumably agreeing with him by asking how long it would take to get out of Somalia first, and thus before acting in Bosnia, and being told about six months, he painted a grim picture for Albright's approach to press hard quickly with military options, including through action by NATO. Albright made clear she favored force with ground troops if necessary, to compel the Bosnian Serbs to the negotiating table and also to enforce a settlement. She took the lead in arguing the point later in the spring of 1993, albeit focusing only on air strikes. No one, other than Albright, seemed to factor in the continued cost to civilian victims in Bosnia while weighing the risks and costs of American engagement.

Legal Premise

Earlier that day, Albright asked me why the U.N. peacekeeping force in Bosnia, UNPROFOR, could not use the existing U.N. Charter Chapter VII enforcement authority under Security Council Resolution 770 of August 1992,[16] to ram through humanitarian aid to Bosniaks desperately in need of it on the ground. That resolution was the first such *enforcement* action (meaning U.N. member states had to comply with it) by the Security

Council in Bosnia, but it was agreed to long after fighting had enveloped the country starting in March 1992. Chapter VII resolutions often authorize the ultimate weapon to enforce Council decisions, namely, the use of military force. Resolution 770 did not do so explicitly, but then neither did other use of force resolutions. There was the usual insistence that the warring parties stop their fighting (a fantasy), and the Council urged full access for the International Committee of the Red Cross (ICRC) to camps, prisons, and detention centers that were sprouting up in the wake of the ethnic cleansing campaign and the war. Albright focused on the second clause of the resolution: "<u>Calls upon</u> States to take nationally or through regional agencies or arrangements all measures necessary to facilitate in coordination with the United Nations the delivery by relevant United Nations humanitarian organizations and others of humanitarian assistance to Sarajevo and wherever needed in other parts of Bosnia and Herzegovina."[17]

The option to use existing legal authorities in Security Council resolutions would bedevil our work on Bosnia for years. There were a total of about 90 Security Council resolutions on the Balkans, a large number of them adopted under the Chapter VII enforcement authority, from 1992 to December 1995.[18] Yet these authorities typically were not tapped because UNPROFOR was seen, particularly by Russia and the Europeans, as a neutral presence to facilitate the delivery of humanitarian aid, rather than as a more robust instrument for not only humanitarian assistance but also to challenge and deter aggressive actions and prevent or stop atrocities from occurring. The national governments deploying soldiers to UNFROFOR, including the United Kingdom and France, sought to minimize the potential use of force in order to shield their soldiers from the risks of combat. This was a constant struggle throughout the three years, one that was resolved in the end by acting outside of UNPROFOR constraints with NATO air power, the Dayton Accords, and then introduction of combat troops under NATO command to enforce the peace.

Christopher's Gambit

On February 10, two days after Vance and Owen briefed the Security Council about their peace plan, Christopher delivered a major speech setting forth the Clinton administration's policy, preceded by the February 5 meeting in the Sit Room. The Vance-Owen peace plan became the centerpiece of the new strategy, despite the criticism and near-rejection of it in earlier Principals meetings. The difference would be "active" engagement by Washington in the Vance-Owen negotiations, although the United Nations and the European Community would continue to lead them.

To launch our diplomacy, Clinton appointed a new man, career diplomat Reginald Bartholomew, as U.S. Special Envoy for the former Yugoslavia. Bartholomew was smart and dedicated, but he was not the best source of innovative thinking about Bosnia and rarely emphasized the fate of the war's victims during our policy discussions. With him on deck to shepherd the multilateral talks, the United States would seek a negotiated settlement to end the conflict, one not imposed but rather voluntarily reached by the warring parties. Actions would be taken to tighten the enforcement of economic sanctions against Serbia and thus "raise the economic and political price for aggression." Clinton would take steps to ramp up humanitarian assistance and to strengthen a no-fly zone over Bosnia. He also would seek creation of a war crimes tribunal at the United Nations. Finally, Christopher confirmed the U.S. commitment to "help implement and enforce an agreement that is acceptable to all parties . . ."[19] That would mean American ground troops if a peace agreement were reached.

Cast aside in Christopher's statement were any use of NATO air power to impose a settlement, as Albright had sought; any explicit rejection (rather an embrace) of the Vance-Owen peace plan or even of its gerrymandered map, which Lake had trashed at the February 3 Principals meeting; and any lifting of the arms embargo on Bosnia to help Bosniaks defend themselves against the heavily armed Bosnian Serb forces aided by Belgrade's army, the "JNA." Clinton had sought such a lift during the campaign, and Congress found it to be irresistible as a battering ram against him for years to come. The seeming renewal of hope for action under the Clinton policy conflicted with the caution and deference to Europeans written all over the Christopher statement. When he answered a reporter's obvious question about the absence of air strikes or lifting of the arms embargo, Christopher bluntly concluded "that they would not be constructive steps to the resolution of this problem . . ." Nor would the United States arrive at further talks about the Vance-Owen peace plan with a map, leaving that to the parties to sort out. "We're going to be in the role of sponsors, using our good offices. We have no prescribed solution," Christopher said at his press conference. "The solution is mainly up to the parties. But we think with the full weight of diplomacy and in the background of U.S. power that we can be helpful to the parties in coming to an agreement."[20] Since the Bosnian Serbs already had sorted it out on the ground with a massive ethnic cleansing campaign, capturing by February 1993 almost 70 percent of Bosnia's territory, the prospect of negotiations achieving any measure of fairness if left only to the warring parties grew dimmer. But hope is eternal and perhaps our diplomatic intervention could make a difference.

In the backwater of Christopher's February 10 statement rested "further actions to promote greater delivery of [humanitarian] aid." One week later the Principals met in the Sit Room to consider one such action: airdrops of humanitarian aid in eastern Bosnia, where ethnic cleansing by the Bosnian Serbs had isolated pockets of Bosniaks enduring the winter cold. The Principals first heard from U.S. Air Force Colonel Mike Koerner, the former air adviser to the UNPROFOR/Sarajevo commander, Phillipe Morillon, and future commander of a fighter wing in New Mexico and, ultimately, a Southwest Airlines pilot. The CIA's note taker recorded:

> Koerner stated firmly and repeatedly that the Muslims, Croats, and Serbs are equally guilty of attacks and atrocities, and that agreements they sign are equally unreliable. He described Muslim Mortar attacks on Sarajevo airport that wounded several French Legionaires. Focusing on eastern Bosnia, he explained that sources of reliable information there are few and far between.[21]

Koerner failed to distinguish the magnitude of atrocities by the three warring parties, as journalists were recording every day and as later demonstrated with decades of evidence gathering by the Yugoslav Tribunal, by repeatedly equating their respective conduct. He may have seriously distorted some of the Principals' thinking at the time.

Powell took up the main topic, though, and described the airdrop plan, which the Principals adopted unanimously:

> General Powell briefed in detail on the proposed [humanitarian aid] airdrops on Gorazde and Zepa, and possibly Srebrenica and Cerska. The initial drops would be at 10,000 feet to reduce the risks of AAA [anti-aircraft attacks] and missile attack; if not fired upon, they would reduce the flight altitude for greater efficiency. There would be no fighter escorts (so as not to compromise the humanitarian character of the mission), and SAR [search and rescue] support could be based at Split or (preferably) afloat on the aircraft carrier Roosevelt when it arrives in a couple of weeks. MC-130 aircraft might be used for night drops if security conditions require. Overall, this effort is expected to entail 4–5 sorties/day and be relatively inexpensive.[22]

Lake tasked Albright to promote enforcement of the no-fly zone at the United Nations. Security Council Resolution 781 of October 1992[23] had established a no-fly zone that banned military flights in the airspace of Bosnia, excluding UNPROFOR and humanitarian assistance flights. Shortly thereafter Resolution 786[24] authorized deployment of military observers to airfields in Bosnia, Croatia, and Serbia to monitor compliance. But actually enforcing the no-fly zone had proven elusive, with numerous violations by Serbian and Bosnian Serb aircraft.[25] Albright's goal was to put muscle behind the ban on military flights, namely, Security Council authorization for NATO air power to take down any prohibited aircraft in the no-fly zone.

Another tasking for Albright—to build at the United Nations some structure of accountability for the commission of atrocity crimes throughout Croatia and Bosnia—was met on February 22 when she joined with the French ambassador to shepherd to passage Resolution 808 that set in motion preparatory work to create the operational structure of a war crimes tribunal.[26] A few months later, the tribunal became a reality with adoption of Resolution 827, which established the constitutional framework of the International Criminal Tribunal for the former Yugoslavia (Yugoslav Tribunal).[27] Some observers viewed this initiative as an excuse to avoid military action, but that was a misperception. The Yugoslav Tribunal was a sideshow, of growing importance over the years, but nonetheless had little to do with most of the decision-making over political and military issues in the Sit Room.

The Deputies convened on February 26 by secure video teleconference system (or "SVTS," aired from video transmission rooms in the various agencies when gathering everyone in the Sit Room proved inconvenient) to focus on the planned airdrops of humanitarian assistance over beleaguered Bosniak communities.

Admiral David Jeremiah [Vice Chairman of the Joint Chiefs of Staff] predicted the airdrops will begin this weekend. We plan to leaflet Cerska, Zepa, and Gorazde Saturday night, and to drop humanitarian assistance (90% food, 10% medicine) on one of the three towns 24 hours later. We will add Serb or Croat locales if reliably reported to be in need. Bosnians acceptable to all three sides will help inspect cargos at Rhein-Main [U.S. Airbase in Germany], and a general at EUCOM [European Command, NATO] will brief the press after each mission. . . . The Deputies would welcome German and

Russian aircraft, and will allow Turkey and Pakistan to contribute goods delivered to Rhein-Main.[28]

U.S. special envoy Bartholomew then painted a grim picture in the effort to push forward the Vance-Owen peace plan in subsequent weeks:

> Bartholomew outlined three strategic goals: (1) provide for a survivable Bosnian state (which the [CIA Balkan] Task Force believes is impossible beyond a transitional period); (2) avoid openly victimizing the Muslims—they are the clear losers, but we should help them with the map, governmental arrangements, provisions for people returning to their homes, etc.; and (3) broaden the process to include additional confidence-building measures or interim steps conducive to a settlement, such as a comprehensive ceasefire in Sarajevo.[29]

The Vance-Owen map locked in much of Bosnian Serb ethnic cleansing gains, so for most of the Deputies to embrace a strategy that sought to persuade Bosniak approval of it demonstrated how entrenched the status quo was in the State Department, extending Bush 41–think deep into Clinton policymaking. Bartholomew's view about the Muslims as "clear losers" and his patronizing suggestion that "we should help them with the map" re-enforced the regressive character of the policy that Christopher had launched on February 10. The CIA's Interagency Balkan Task Force (BTF) had already concluded, remarkably, that there would be no Bosnian state following a transitional period that presumably implemented the Vance-Owen peace plan. Berger insisted "that the US not stake out any positions of our own" regarding the map.[30] Gore, slated to meet with Bosnian President Alija Izetbegović, a Bosniak, later that week, was going to tell him "that the cavalry is not coming" and that the United States would work with him "to get a better deal, albeit not the Muslim's own deal."[31] For the Bosniaks, the outcome of the Vance-Owen peace plan was in free fall. Albright and I took note of how precipitous that fall was becoming in the thinking of our colleagues.

Only One Dispatch

The cable traffic during the early months of the Clinton administration educated new political appointees—those who troubled to read the dispatches—of the obscene inhumanity of what had been occurring only months, weeks, or days earlier in the darkest corners of the Bosnian landscape. The summary of one such cable, sent on March 3 and 24 hours before the next Deputies meeting, offered a brief glimpse:

1. (U) THIS IS ONE OF A SERIES OF REPORTS OF SPECIFIC AND GROSS HUMAN RIGHTS ABUSES IN BOSNIA AND HERCEGOVINA (B-H). IT IS BASED ON AN INTERVIEW BY AN FSO [U.S. FOREIGN SERVICE OFFICER] WITH A 55-YEAR-OLD BOSNIAN MUSLIM MALE, WHO IS IDENTIFIED HEREIN AS V.G. V.G. WAS A PERSON OF SOME PROMINENCE IN THE FORMER YUGOSLAVIA. HE WAS IMPRISONED FOR 45 DAYS AT THE LUKA CAMP NEAR BRCKO, NORTHEASTERN B-H, DURING JUNE AND JULY 1992.

2. (U) AN EYEWITNESS WHOM THE INTERVIEWING FSO JUDGED HIGHLY CREDIBLE, V.G. CLAIMED TO HAVE SEEN HUNDREDS OF CIVILIANS BEATEN AND LEFT TO DIE OR EXECUTED BY GUN SHOT AT THE LUKA CAMP. HE SAID HE WAS SHOWN LARGE PILES OF HUMAN TORSOS WITH MOST APPENDAGES MISSING. HE REPORTED ON THE CASTRATION OF SOME PRISONERS AND THE DROWNING OF OTHERS. HE SAW GROUPS OF TEENAGE GIRLS BROUGHT IN REGULARLY ON WEDNESDAYS AND SATURDAYS FOR WHAT HE WAS CERTAIN WERE RAPE SESSIONS—ATTENDED BY A "NURSE" WHOSE JOB IT WAS TO "PREPARE" THE GIRLS. HE WITNESSED YOUNG MALE CROATIAN AND MUSLIM PRISONERS, SEPARATED INTO ROWS BASED ON ETHNICITY, FORCED TO COMMIT CROSS-ETHNIC SODOMY ON A NEARLY DAILY BASIS. AND HE DISCUSSED WHAT HE HAD SEEN OF EFFORTS TO CONCEAL MASS GRAVES.[32]

The content of V.G.'s witnessing "efforts to conceal mass graves" paints a harrowing picture of Bosnian Serbian butchery:

... V.G. DESCRIBED THE DISPOSAL OF CORPSES FROM LUKA PRISON. IN THE FIRST WEEK OF JUNE [1992], THE BODIES OF MOST OF THE 2,000 WHICH HE ESTIMATES WERE KILLED WERE THROWN DOWN A WELL AND EMERGED LATER FLOATING DOWN THE SAVA RIVER, SURFACING AT RESOLVO POLIE AND EVEN AS FAR AWAY AS BELGRADE.

V.G. SAID THAT, AS LUKE GUARDS BECAME AWARE OF THE SURFACING CORPSES, THEY TOOK TO CUTTING OPEN THE BODIES AND PACKING THEM WITH SAND TO KEEP THEM SUBMERGED. THIS EFFORT DID NOT ALWAYS SUCCEED. THE THIRD APPROACH WAS TO CHOP UP CORPSES AND BURN THE BODIES. BODY PARTS WERE ALSO LEFT TO DECOMPOSE "LIKE MANURE." V.G. STRONGLY URGED THE INTERNATIONAL COMMUNITY TO SECURE ACCESS TO THE LUKA HARBOR AND SEND UNDERWATER DIVERS DOWN TO TRY TO IDENTIFY THE NUMBERS OF CORPSES DISPOSED OF THERE IN JUNE AND JULY, AND TO MAKE SURFACE EXCAVATION OF SITES WHERE QUANTITIES OF HUMAN BONES CAN BE FOUND.[33]

Cables of this character flooded into my State Department office for years.

How to Respond

When the Deputies met by secure videoconference on March 4, they learned that the recently convened "peace" talks in New York had just collapsed with President Izetbegović and Bosnian Serb leader Radovan Karadžić (long before he was indicted and convicted by the Yugoslav Tribunal) leaving town. Berger asked the Deputies how the United States should respond if the Bosnian Serbs continue their offensive in eastern Bosnia. Three options emerged: tighten economic sanctions, use U.S. air power, and/or commit American ground forces. The Deputies opted to limit discussions with the allies to "beefing up the sanctions" and to confine talk about military action solely to Washington circles to avoid any leaks from the allies. The dire humanitarian situation for Bosniak refu-

gees who were crowded into Tuzla begged for an airlift of food and supplies. But grey-haired and pugnacious Lieutenant General Brian McCaffrey, a decorated war veteran representing the Joint Chiefs of Staff at the Deputies meeting, said in his distinctive growly voice that "an airlift into Tuzla would be feasible, but it would require a 'full-fledged military operation' and we should 'assume ground combat' to secure the area and set up a distribution system on the ground. He favored more escorted convoys instead." Under Secretary of State Frank Wisner reported that at his confirmation hearing that same day for a new post at the Defense Department, he received one clear message from the senators: "avoid the slippery slope to US military involvement."[34]

The next day, March 5, the U.S. Air Force, with army support, began the airlift and airdrop of humanitarian aid over eastern Bosnia, and, later that month, German and French aircraft joined the effort. "Operation Provide Promise" ultimately engaged aircraft from 21 countries and flew many thousands of sorties, risking the lives of their crews, over Bosnia and Sarajevo, in particular, until January 9, 1996. Thus the operation was longer in duration than any other humanitarian airlift or airdrop in history. The statistics are impressive and saved or helped sustain many lives: a total of 159,622 tons of food, medicine, and other supplies. The coalition aircraft also evacuated over 1,300 casualties for treatment in medical facilities. Among all of the setbacks in Bosnia over those years, I always thought we at least got this one right and that the service personnel who participated in Operation Provide Promise deserve much more than a handshake. They were lifesavers and should be very proud of what they accomplished.[35]

On March 8, the European Community foreign ministers agreed to implement stronger sanctions in the event Belgrade failed to press the Bosnian Serbs to accept the Vance-Owen peace plan. The next day the Deputies convened again by videoconference, at the request of Bartholomew, who was engaged in New York negotiations with the major leaders in the conflict. Nothing much was decided, but Bartholomew's observations revealed the resiliency of the Vance-Owen peace plan:

- Izetbegović is closer to signing on to V-O [Vance-Owen] but has some problems with his hardliners.
- Karadžić is increasingly isolated and will probably not accept V-O unless Milošević pushes him hard and provides some political cover.
- Vance and Owen plan has become marginally more understanding of Muslim position.
- He [Bartholomew] should go to area to get on-the-ground feel of situation, lean on Serbs, and encourage Muslims to sign.[36]

The Deputies had little choice but to ride the only horse available at the time, namely, the Vance-Owen peace plan, and trust in Bartholomew's honest efforts to bring all of the parties together to agree on a peaceful outcome for Bosnia. But some of us held our noses over the obvious stink of the plan's terms.

Multilateralist Strategy

The new UNPROFOR commander in Bosnia, Lieutenant-General Lars-Eric Wahlgren of Sweden, traveled to Srebrenica on March 11 to investigate reports of the increasingly desperate situation there of Bosniaks in need of humanitarian relief as Bosnian Serb forces encircled the east Bosnian town. On March 12 Albright testified before a House of Representatives subcommittee, chaired by Congressman David Obey, a liberal Democrat from Wisconsin. She reflected the Principals' opening gambit of caution about Bosnia and emphasized multilateral actions:

> [W]e will not act unilaterally when a multilateral presence is clearly needed and available. The multilateral force brought together to enforce an agreement must be strong enough to succeed in its mission. . . . The task of building coalitions among nations can be maddeningly frustrating and even stymie missions that, if left to unilateral means, might quickly achieve a worthy humanitarian objective, but jeopardize a long-term resolution of the conflict. We will neither walk away from this conflict nor rush in blindly or unilaterally to stop the aggression and atrocities. Our policy is multilateral in character and execution, unrelenting, and morally sound. It is unquestionably in our long-term interests to have the United Nations and our European allies fully engaged in any military endeavor within the former Yugoslavia.[37]

Albright described enforcement action only in the wake of a peace agreement, and not as a predicate as she had futilely argued at the February 5 Principals meeting. "The better the agreement the lesser the enforcement," she testified. Obey complained that "Milošević is a con artist trying to use time to strengthen his position. How do we view his intentions?" Albright replied, "He certainly conned the last administration. [French President Francois] Mitterand is now engaged. It is hard to assess Milošević's intentions. We need to bring the full force of the international community down on him. The Vance-Owen map reduces Serb areas. We have to be very watchful." Albright was being somewhat coy here as the Vance-Owen map indeed reduced some Serb areas, but it massively rewarded Bosnian Serb ethnic cleansing during 1992.

Later that day Albright sat down with journalist Carla Ann Robbins of *The Wall Street Journal* for an interview during which I took notes:

ALBRIGHT: We were left with a terrible mess. The West has not understood Yugoslavia, which was given a pass by the West. It was the first to break from the monolithic Communist empire. But [Yugoslav President Josep Broz] Tito was authoritarian.

We paid little attention to Yugoslavia after Tito died [in 1980]. A series of things disrupted the internal economy and were superimposed on serious ethnic problems. As northern republics did better, I felt they carried the southern ones. No one paid attention to this. We got conned by Milošević, and [former Secretary of State Lawrence] Eagleburger admits this. [Former National Security Adviser Brent] Scowcroft and Eagleburger were the experts on Yugoslavia, our prime experts. When they did not want to be understood in meetings, they spoke Serbo-Croatian with each other. We were all outraged by what we were reading. It was an unacceptable form of dealing with territorial change.

Clinton is an internationalist. The United States is actively engaged in international relations. There are strategic interests and a moral component. We cannot forget who we are.

Bosnia and Somalia on the ground are dreadful situations. The brutality of it got to me. Christopher declared in his February 10 statement that we have got a humanitarian responsibility. And we have strategic interests. The violence is spreading out of control. New minority issues are important for the United States and the international community, but they are not necessarily dealt with by force.

The decisions are made by Bill Clinton. He's the driving engine of this government. We have not ruled out anything at the moment. The first goal is to achieve a peace settlement. We have not committed or ruled that out. We're putting the full force of diplomacy behind this. It is not just a European problem. Realizing that is a big step for us.

Albright was sticking to the administration line in this interview, pressing diplomatic over military options. But her final remarks about the "big step for us" reflected her strongly held view that the United States had to step up to the plate to directly address the Bosnian conflict and its atrocities.

For the next week diplomats representing the warring parties met at United Nations Headquarters in New York City to discuss the Vance-Owen peace plan. At the beginning of their talks, the U.N. Security Council issued a unanimous presidential statement (nonbinding on the parties but demonstrating a unified Council point of view) demanding that the Bosnian Serbs explain why their aircraft violated the months-old no-fly zone and calling for an investigation.[38] The Bosnian Serbs essentially ignored the request.

CIA Thinkfest

The Central Intelligence Agency's Interagency Balkan Task Force issued a raft of analytical papers on March 23 about the hot-button issues defining the internal debates over the direction of Clinton's Bosnia policy.[39] The Pentagon also had just circulated an Issue Paper on *Lifting the Siege of Sarajevo*. Together, these papers presented policymakers with a dire perspective for action in Bosnia unless a peace agreement first was successfully negotiated and primed for implementation. The Pentagon's contribution to lifting the siege of Sarajevo was actually a plan for implementing a peace agreement with the warring parties having consented to demilitarize Sarajevo. The CIA doubted its feasibility.[40]

If there were no peace to implement pursuant to an agreement, then dire scenarios unfolded on the CIA's pages, written, it seemed, by Cold War analysts wandering in a maze of post-Communist realities where every option leads to an undesirable outcome:

> The central Serb goals in Bosnia have been and remain the destruction of Bosnia as a viable independent state and the incorporation of Serb-claimed regions into a greater Serbia. The current Bosnian Serb offensive in eastern Bosnia . . . appears aimed at eliminating the few remaining Muslim enclaves in the region. Barring the introduction of an external force strong enough to compel them to desist, the Serbs are unlikely to stop until they have achieved that goal. If the Vance-Owen talks have had an influence on Serb actions, it more likely is in persuading them to accelerate the pace of their efforts to achieve their goals before a settlement is reached. . . .
>
> The Serbs almost certainly believe it is critical to destroy Sarajevo as a symbol of a multi-ethnic state. . . .
>
> [T]here is little doubt that Serb "agreement" to a version of the Vance-Owen peace plan will not imply compliance with either the letter or spirit of an accord. The Serbs are not likely to withdraw from any territory they occupy barring the arrival of an international force able and willing to compel them to do so. . . .

The Serbs almost certainly do not believe that the international community will be willing to make the long-term commitment of large forces that would be necessary to hold Bosnia together. . . .

Given the Serbs' determination to settle the "Serbian question"—and their belief that the international community lacks the ability and will to make a long-term commitment to Bosnia—altering Serb calculations will not be easy.[41]

Threats [of air strikes] will neither intimidate the Bosnian Serbs nor persuade Belgrade to stop aiding them. Attacks [by air] on Serbia would be opposed by Russia and other countries, expand the violence, and probably wreck the Vance-Owen process. . . . Western airstrikes against targets in Bosnia and Serbia probably would make both Belgrade and the Bosnian Serbs even more defiant and re-sistant to making any political concessions to the West. . . . Such an action would spell the end of humanitarian relief efforts in Bosnia and possibly lead to a quickening of the pace of "ethnic cleansing" in Serb-held areas. They would also likely encourage the Bosnian Government to believe that Western intervention to roll back Serb gains was forthcoming and lead them to quit the Vance-Owen talks.[42]

Delivering light weapons to the Bosnian Muslims and launching multinational airstrikes against Serb positions would not have any lasting effect on the Bosnian Government's military situation, but would probably lead to the breakdown of the Vance-Owen talks and the shutdown of UN humanitarian relief mission.[43]

Lifting the arms embargo completely would increase the Bosnian Government forces' fighting capabilities in some areas and deflect Islamic criticism that the UN embargo is unfair, but would not enable the Bosnians to regain lost territories without long-term foreign assistance. They would likely encourage Muslim hardliners to back away from the Vance-Owen talks.[44]

Expanding the UN's humanitarian relief efforts through more assertive means would marginally improve the situation of some besieged Bosnian Muslims, but would likely lead to UN casualties and could endanger the overall relief efforts.[45]

Pressuring the Bosnian Serbs

The Principals pondered the fate of Srebrenica, which was becoming a humanitarian sinkhole, on March 25. But there fell onto the Sit Room table that morning a new reality when Bosnian President Izetbegović and the Bosnian Croat representative at the New York talks rather surprisingly signed the Vance-Owen peace plan, leaving the Bosnian Serbs as the out-liers. Washington welcomed Izetbegović's signature in particular, as he had to swallow hard to embrace the Vance-Owen map of Bosnian Serb territorial gains and the constitutional shake-up envisaged for his country. Now the task was to get the Bosnian Serbs to sign the document.

Ivo Daalder, who was a National Security Council staffer in the run-up to Dayton and later U.S. ambassador to NATO under President Barack Obama, wrote in his insightful historical account, *Getting to Dayton*: "Two options quickly emerged. One was to increase military pressure against the Bosnian Serbs—by lifting the arms embargo, by using U.S. and NATO air strikes, or by a combination of both. The other was to try to get a cease-fire in place and to offer some form of protection for Muslim enclaves, like Srebrenica, that were under Bosnian Serb assault."[46] But, as Daalder further noted, "Neither option was without its problems."[47] Using military force against the Bosnian Serbs ran into roadblocks with our European allies and might actually boomerang on the battlefield without a large infusion of American troops, and that card was not going to be played. Alternatively, obtaining a ceasefire would be viewed as throwing the Bosniaks under the bus and implicitly endorsing the ethnic cleansing of the country. The United States would have ceded the high moral ground to the murderous Bosnian Serb leaders and their patrons in Belgrade.

Some progress was made at the U.N. Security Council, where Albright was working toward formal authorization to enforce the no-fly zone over Bosnia. On March 30, the Security Council demanded full respect for international humanitarian law in the protected areas of Bosnia.[48] The Council adopted Resolution 816 under Chapter VII mandatory en-forcement authority the next day. For months there had been "blatant violations," largely by the Bosnian Serbs, of the Council's ban on mili-tary flights in Bosnian airspace, and they were not abating. The Security Council authorized, for all intents and purposes, NATO "to take, under the authority of the Security Council and subject to close coordination with the Secretary-General and UNPROFOR, all necessary measures in the air-space of the Republic of Bosnia and Herzegovina, in the event of further violations to ensure compliance with the ban on flights" of all fixed-wing and rotary-wing aircraft in Bosnian airspace, excluding flights authorized by UNPROFOR.[49] On April 12, NATO began flying its combat aircraft to enforce the no-fly zone over Bosnia.

The Clinton administration had substantially increased humanitarian assistance with the airlift operation by early April, which gave hope to Bosniaks trapped behind Bosnian Serb lines. Washington was engaging in the United Nations and European Community negotiations with Bartholomew's active participation, enforcing the no-fly zone with U.S. air power under NATO command and expressing its willingness to help enforce a peace agreement, if only one could be arrived at by the warring parties. At a minimum, the administration was determined to contain the conflict within the borders of Bosnia and Croatia and preserve Bosnia and Herzegovina as a sovereign state.

Early Options

So fortified, and yet perfectly aware that war, mass rapes, and ethnic cleansing raged onward in Bosnia, the Principals convened in the Sit Room on April 9. They thrashed about for two and one-half hours. The first topic was one that would dominate discussions until the fall of 1995: the apparent American commitment to rescue UNPROFOR troops from danger, including during any possible wholesale withdrawal of U.N. peacekeepers from Bosnia. Asked about any such American commitment by Tony Lake, General Powell "indicated that he thought there was no agreement with UNPROFOR *per se* but that there was a tentative understanding which grew from the period of the Canadian deployment [to UNPROFOR] that we would provide such assistance on a circumstantial basis when requested by the Canadians. He also believed that there was a similar agreement that was reached bilaterally with the Spanish, the UK, and French for their forces in Bosnia." When asked at the conclusion of the meeting how many American soldiers would have to be committed should Vance-Owen "come to pass," thus requiring enforcement of the agreement on the ground with or without UNPROFOR participation, Powell put the number at "approximately 30,000 out of the 70,000 to 75,000 troops that are likely to be committed."[50]

The Principals moved on to strengthening the U.N. Security Council–imposed sanctions on Serbia, which were designed to pressure Serbian President Slobodan Milošević to cease any support for the Bosnian Serbs and leverage him to influence key Bosnian Serb leaders to embrace the Vance-Owen peace plan and enter into a peace settlement. As a permanent member of the Security Council, Russia had the essential vote to unleash upon its client state, Serbia, tougher economic sanctions. "Albright indicated that [Russian Permanent Representative to the United Nations Yuli] Vorontsov told [Security Council ambassadors] that the Russians were hoping for a delayed vote and if the vote were forced now, the Russians would not abstain but would, in fact, veto such a resolution."[51]

Russian President Boris Yeltsin faced a critical April 25 referendum vote of confidence in himself and his economic and social policies in Russia as well as whether to call early elections. He thus sought to maintain a pro-Serbian image with the Russian electorate. A letter from Yeltsin to Clinton arrived during the meeting, arguing for a delay in any new sanctions. Lake nudged the Principals toward such a delay in the Security Council vote on new sanctions until after the Russian referendum. Christopher wanted a written commitment from the Russians about moving forward with sanctions right after the referendum vote. Albright "argued all kinds of downside concerns that would result from this, however, she grudgingly agreed to go along with the delay."[52]

The most contentious issue inevitably arose: What are the American options in Bosnia? Lake initially put three on the table: (1) continue to pursue the Vance-Owen track (sputtering along but without any prospect of closure with all of the parties); (2) cut a deal with the roughly existing geographic divisions in Bosnia (concede ethnic cleansing to the Serbs and call it a day); and (3) pursue a "fight-it-out option" lifting the arms embargo against the Muslims so that they could continue to press the Serbs (try to even the playing field but do not necessarily commit U.S. air power to defense of the Bosniaks and figure out whether it would be a multilateral lift with Security Council approval or a U.S. unilateral lift in defiance of the Council's arms embargo).

Admiral William Studeman, the Deputy Director of the CIA, recorded in his memorandum of the meeting, "The ensuing discussion proved that all of these issues are fairly intractable. A fourth option was ultimately introduced by Tony Lake which was argued as a unique option, although it may not be. This option had to do with the United States coming in with air power to support Muslim activities while not in lifting the arms embargo."[53] Lake knew this was Albright's option, and he tasked her to draft the pro and con memo on the fourth option while assigning other options for similar memoranda to Defense, State, and Vice President Gore's key adviser, Leon Fuerth. The tasking was a critical break point in policy discussions, as it gave each of the major players in Washington a chance to put his or her best case forward for the option each likely would favor. Studeman wrote, "No decisions were taken on the future direction of Yugoslavia policy should Vance-Owen fail, and it was my general perception that the individuals in the room found themselves quite far apart from each other. None held high hopes for Vance-Owen; DoD/JCS [Defense Department and Joint Chiefs of Staff] seemed most interested in variations on the 'cut-a-deal' option while others were in a more 'fighting' spirit."[54]

Albright's Bid for Air Power

Albright returned to her State Department office after the Principals meeting and tasked me to begin working on the memo that Lake had assigned to her to make the case for use of air power in Bosnia, including its downsides. She said, "We can level the playing field with air  power. The Serbs have to be pressured into submission. We won't achieve rollback of the Serbs but at least we will get them to accept the Vance-Owen lines and Bosnian Muslims will not be punished." I began by focusing on the legal case for using NATO air power. The argument centered on existing Security Council authorizations and what could be squeezed from them to punch out the Bosnian Serb aggressors and ensure delivery of humanitarian aid.

Albright delivered her memorandum to Lake on April 14. It became one of her most significant documents in eight years of service in the Clinton administration, as it set the stage for what would ultimately become the military key to the Dayton talks in 1995. It also presaged the creation of the United Nations "safe areas," which would include Srebrenica. She melded the humanitarian objectives behind UNPROFOR's deployment, particularly into besieged Bosniak enclaves, with a bold proposal to unleash American—perhaps NATO—air power against the Serbs. Jamie Rubin, who had just joined her staff in New York as the USUN spokesman, became a key advocate of her tough message on air strikes, and joined in the drafting. I focused on the humanitarian aims and legal authorities. The two-and-one-half page "SECRET" memorandum is recited in its entirety below.

April 14, 1993
MEMORANDUM FOR THE NATIONAL SECURITY ADVISER
FROM AMBASSADOR MADELEINE K. ALBRIGHT
SUBJECT: OPTIONS FOR BOSNIA:

1. ISSUE FOR DECISION

Whether to use American air power to supplement an enhanced UNPROFOR presence in Bosnia and Serbia.

2. BACKGROUND

We have never tested the proposition that American military intervention might intimidate the Bosnian Serb militia and their patrons in Belgrade. That premise should be tested. Air power supporting an UNPROFOR presence in key Muslim enclaves ought to create a doubt in Serbian minds that they can pursue their objectives unchecked, a doubt that certainly does not exist today. If this is true, then we would be in a better position to bring pressure to bear on the Serbs to cease their aggressive behavior and sign the peace accords.

A military package which includes air strikes and internationalization of the enclaves could collaterally facilitate the delivery of humanitarian assistance to besieged civilian populations and aid in the defense of civilians under military attack, one of our highest priorities.

3. U.S. OPTIONS

On February 10, the Secretary outlined a six point program for dealing with Bosnia. Since that time our options have been narrowed while the situation gets worse. Our objective was to level the playing field for the Bosnian Muslims, but while we have made significant progress on the six points, the tide of battle now calls into question the very survival of Bosnia.

Lifting the arms embargo, almost our only remaining publicly announced option, is our greatest threat, but it also has the greatest potential cost and may be the hardest to accomplish. Once we lift the arms embargo, we lose control of what would certainly be a flow of Muslim weapons, not only into Bosnia, but also into the surrounding area. The consequences of more arms could have significant ramifications for neighboring countries.

4. OBJECTIVES

The limited objectives of air power—unilateral or multilateral—should include:

1) To get the Serbs to sign the agreement.
2) To demonstrate the commitment and will of the U.S. to prevent "ethnic cleansing" and erase its effects.
3) To help defend remaining Bosnian Muslim enclaves.

4) To provide retaliation in the event that Bosnia Serb military actions prevent humanitarian land convoys.

5) To help protect UNPROFOR from Serb retaliation.

Two significantly more controversial objectives would be:

6) To strike at Serbian military assets that are being used in an aggressive manner in Bosnia or from Serbia.

7) To strike at Bosnian Serb strategic targets (i.e. power nodes, communications and infrastructure in cities like Banja Luka) to demonstrate a real cost for continued aggression.

5. AUTHORITY

Recognizing that legal authority alone will not provide a receptive political environment, a strong case can be made that sufficient authority already exists under Article 51 of the Charter and the Chapter VII provisions of UNSC resolution 770 to employ air power for at least objectives (1) through (5) and perhaps (6) and (7), without obtaining new and explicit Security Council approval.

Having said this, we have to recognize that public denial of our authority by the Secretary-General or by the United Kingdom and France, would severely undercut our case that we have international support or authority for our actions. We may be able to get the support of our allies and possibly the UN Secretary-General, but only if we are willing to commit adequate U.S. military assets to do the job.

6. CONSEQUENCES

Air strikes could result in shutting down the land operations by humanitarian agencies and the United Nations and change the nature and role of UNPROFOR. But neither institution has the current capability to do much except to extend the demise of Bosnia-Herzegovina. Today the reality is that humanitarian operations are increasingly being blocked on the ground by Bosnian Serb action.

Further delay in applying a genuine military component to the Bosnian situation risks humanitarian catastrophe for Bosnian Muslims and the total collapse of most of Bosnia to Serb control. Failure to act will embolden the Serbs to overwhelm remaining pockets of Bosnian Muslims, target Bosnian Croatian-controlled regions, consolidate control over areas of Croatia still held by Serbs (like Krajina), and threaten Kosovo and Macedonia.

7. SUPPORTING INITIATIVE

If we are prepared to use air power, I would recommend a further initiative which would supplement and enhance the effectiveness of our control of the skies.

We should create United Nations Protected Enclaves. The creation of United Nations protected enclaves (defended by U.S./ NATO/Russian forces under an UNPROFOR label) and supported by U.S. air power will be the only way to add the necessary ground component capable of saving these towns and regions from Serb intervention and assault. This would be similar to the security zone created in Northern Iraq in 1991. [U.S.] Embassy Belgrade has strongly recommended that Srebrenica be declared a UN-protected area.[55]

Albright's memorandum was a bold cut-and-thrust maneuver around the far more cautious and conventional thinking that dominated the State and Defense Department positions in the Sit Room. Her proposal boiled down to bombing the Serbs into submission, both at the peace table and in stopping the atrocities against the Bosniaks and Croatians. We aimed to walk through the back door of humanitarian aid to meet the larger war and peace issue. The justification for this military action rested, in our view, on the inherent right of self-defense that the Bosniaks sought our help to act upon, as recognized in Article 51 of the U.N. Charter.[56] From the American perspective, we would be acting in "collective self-defense," as permitted under Article 51, to assist the Bosniaks.

But more explicitly, we believed that U.N. Security Council Resolution 770[57] could be interpreted reasonably to permit use of air power to end the fighting and support humanitarian objectives. As earlier noted, the resolution employed the mandatory enforcement powers under Chapter VII of the U.N. Charter to authorize "States to take nationally or through regional agencies or arrangements all measures necessary to facilitate in coordination with the United Nations the delivery by relevant United Nations humanitarian organizations and others of humanitarian assistance to Sarajevo and wherever needed in other parts of Bosnia and Herzegovina."[58]

There were other Security Council resolutions that were useful to the cause. The most prominent was Resolution 771,[59] which strongly condemned ethnic cleansing and decided, once again under Chapter VII enforcement authority, "that all parties and others concerned in the former Yugoslavia, and all military forces in Bosnia and Herzegovina, shall comply with the provisions of the present resolution, failing which the Council will need to take further measures under the Charter."[60] The most important compliance issue was to cease ethnic cleansing and other violations of international humanitarian law. Pressing the Council to endorse the unleashing of air power flowed naturally from Resolution 771. The enforcement of the ban on air flights over Bosnia that Resolution 816[61] authorized also lent itself to some interpretative juggling for purposes of unleashing air power, in part to deter any Serbian intent to violate the no-fly zone. Since we knew that our allies and U.N. Secretary-General Boutros Boutros-Ghali likely would oppose proactive interpretations to use established authorities for unconventional military action, we were prepared to take the heat in the hope that other Washington officials also demonstrated the will to act.

Albright could count in her corner the support of Gore but only for air strikes and not deployment of American ground troops. She was prepared to act unilaterally on air strikes, but we were uncertain whether Gore would go so far as to act alone without NATO consent and participation on air strikes. Lake and Christopher favored lifting the arms embargo against the Bosniaks and limited air strikes to defend them as they achieved sufficient armaments. The Pentagon's Aspin would only go so far as to commit to defending the Bosniak enclaves. Democratic Senator Joe Biden of Delaware came out slugging hard during a visit to Bosnia to launch air strikes against Serb artillery positions.[62] A group of key State Department diplomats and intelligence officers signed an internal dissent letter in April, quickly leaked, complaining about American inaction in the face of atrocities.[63]

On April 16, Clinton stated during a press conference, "At this point, I would not rule out any option [for Bosnia] except the option I have never ruled in, which was the question of American ground troops. . . . I think the time has come for the United States and Europe to look very honestly at where we are and what our options are and what the consequences of various courses of action will be. And I think we have to consider things which at least previously have been unacceptable."[64] Over the next two days the Principals met and circled around two options for the president's decision. The first option proposed lift and strike—lifting the arms embargo against the Bosniaks in particular and striking to defend them in the face of fresh Serbian assaults. The second option proposed reaching a ceasefire among the warring parties and ensuring the protection of the Bosniak enclaves.[65]

Working with Venezuela's ambassador to the United Nations, Diego Arias, Albright joined his lead to press forward in the Security Council on April 16 with Resolution 819, which declared Srebrenica a "safe area," and called for the end of Belgrade arming the Bosnian Serb paramilitaries.[66]

The next day Albright pushed through Resolution 820 denouncing the Bosnian Serb refusal to sign the Vance-Owen peace plan and tightening sanctions on Serbia-Montenegro.[67] And thus the edicts of the major powers rested for a week before the next turn of the Balkan wheel.

On April 28, the Security Council rejected Serbia-Montenegro's attempt to join the United Nations as the Federal Republic of Yugoslavia, or successor to the post–World War II Socialist Republic of Yugoslavia, now dismembered, when the Council adopted Resolution 821.[68] That admission would not be accomplished until the year 2000 when the "Federal Republic of Yugoslavia" joined the United Nations.[69] This disruption on Belgrade's radar screen did not, however, derail the Vance-Owen talks among leaders of the warring parties and other leaders of the former Yugoslavia that resumed the next day, April 29, in Athens. In short order, Radovan Karadžić, the Bosnian Serb leader, signed the Vance-Owen peace plan. But he did so on the condition that his act be ratified by the Bosnian Serb Assembly in Pale, the Bosnian Serb "capital," a highly problematic vote since the Vance-Owen peace plan required some clawback, albeit minor, on ethnic cleansing gains made in 1992 and early 1993 by the Bosnian Serb militia. So, in fact, Vance-Owen had not yet been approved by the Bosnian Serbs.

May Day Decision

The critical meeting on the making of America's Bosnia policy, a decision that would hold for at least several weeks, occurred at the White House over a five-hour slog on May 1. This was a "foreign policy team" meeting (Clinton, Gore, and top NSC and cabinet foreign policy advisers including Christopher, Albright, Aspin, Powell, Lake, and Berger), and thus I was not there to sit behind Albright in a conventional Sit Room Principals meeting. But Ivo Daalder recounted the decision made that day:

> All options (except U.S. ground troops) were once again debated. In the end, Clinton opted for lift and strike, the option that by then had the support of all his senior advisers with the exception of Aspin, who continued to favor a cease-fire and protection of Muslim enclaves. Even Powell supported lift and strike, believing that once armed and trained, Muslim forces on the ground would improve the effectiveness of air power. The president and his foreign policy team opted for lift and strike notwithstanding indications from the Europeans suggesting that they would resist any proposal to lift the

arms embargo. They surmised that with the public outrage accompanying the assault on Srebrenica and the refusal by the Bosnian Serbs to accept Vance-Owen before the UN-mandated deadline of April 26, attitudes among the allies might change enough to permit a more aggressive policy. But everyone knew it would be a hard sell. The president assigned Christopher the unenviable task of talking to the allies, telling him, "You've been a great lawyer and advocate all these years—now you've really got your work cut out for you."[70]

Sitting in the State Department, I watched the cable traffic and news reports flow in as Christopher journeyed to London, Paris, Moscow, Brussels, Bonn, and Rome to sell the lift-and-strike policy to very skeptical allies and the Russians, all of whom had skin in the game. This was particularly true of the nations contributing troops to UNPROFOR, where their soldiers' lives were at risk and no leader could accept increasing that risk. Karadžić had thrown a zinger into the effort when he conditionally signed the Vance-Owen peace plan, thus giving Christopher's European counterparts the perfect excuse to back off in what seemed to them a real chance for a negotiated peace settlement.

Christopher also confronted exactly what Albright endured in New York at the United Nations until the late summer of 1995. Years later she spoke of the allies' condescending attitude: "Whenever I suggested we have the issue of lifting the arms embargo—or whatever suggestions I made—either the British or the French ambassador would say to me, 'You can't say anything; you have no troops on the ground.' Every time. So I finally said to David Hannay, the British representative, 'As a point of personal privilege, I would like to ask you not to say this to me every single day.' It didn't matter what the issue [about Bosnia] was. I heard this comment. But it was a sign of the contradiction that existed [in our Bosnia policy]."[71]

As Daalder observed, "Christopher's self-described 'conciliatory approach'—consisting of talking points that, at least in Whitehall, started with the phrase, 'I am here in a listening mode'—differed so completely from the prevailing norm that the allies could not believe that the administration was serious. Indeed, London and Paris were as distraught over the fact that the Clinton administration was not really willing to take the promised lead of the West's Bosnia policy as they were over Washington's decision to propose a course of action they had explicitly and repeatedly rejected."[72]

Meanwhile, back in Washington, Clinton seemed to waiver on his own policy while Christopher stumbled through Europe. He likely feared for his relationship with Yeltsin and whether lift and strike would even work. If it failed, it would be on his shoulders. Aspin was quoted as saying to Lake and Peter Tarnoff, the Under Secretary of State for Political Affairs, "Guys, he's going south on this policy. His heart isn't in it. . . . We have a serious problem here. We're out there pushing a policy that the President's not comfortable with."[73]

Christopher wrote in his memoir of the time that "although the lift and strike remained formally on the table, attention turned to how we could keep the conflict from spreading and deal with the humanitarian problems it had created."[74] So, as Daalder concluded, "[i]n what would become a pattern in the administration's approach to Bosnia in these early years the failure of a U.S. policy initiative was soon followed by Washington adopting the approach favored by the Europeans. In this case, the new policy consisted of defending six Muslim enclaves that the UN on May 6 had declared 'safe areas.'"[75] But Clinton refused to deploy American troops into what he described as "a shooting gallery."[76]

During an appearance on NBC's "Meet the Press" on May 2, Gore downplayed the significance of Karadžić's signature to the Vance-Owen peace plan, saying there would have to be concrete changes on the ground, such as cessation of artillery shelling. Gore confirmed that the United States would participate in international enforcement of Vance-Owen if it were approved but that the exact nature of the American role had not been determined. He described the U.S. goal as ending ethnic cleansing and preventing the change of international borders by military force. The border between Bosnia and Serbia-Montenegro was an international boundary that must not be violated, he said, and stressed that Washington had an interest in preserving that boundary and in preventing the spread of the war. The Serbs had to comply with the ceasefire, end the shelling and siege of Sarajevo, and lift obstruction to humanitarian aid deliveries.[77] These were welcome words from Gore that helped Albright in New York. I only hoped Clinton would echo them, soon.

In early May the Bosnian Serb Assembly trashed the Vance-Owen peace plan with a vote of 151 to 2 against it (and 12 abstentions), so there was no surprise there. A couple of weeks later a referendum among Bosnian Serbs supported the assembly's rejection of Vance-Owen, so the people backed their leaders to the hilt. As if to retaliate against Pale's arrogant rejection of international efforts to end the conflict, the Security Council

adopted Resolution 824 on May 6, which established under Chapter VII
enforcement authority six "safe areas" in Bosnia, including Sarajevo,
Tuzla, Žepa, Gorazde, Bihać, and, amplifying Resolution 819 of April 19,
Srebrenica. The Council ordered that the safe areas "should be free from
armed attacks and from any other hostile act" and "the withdrawal of all
Bosnian Serb military or paramilitary units from these towns to a distance
wherefrom they cease to constitute a menace to their security and that of
their inhabitants . . ." A relatively small number of UNPROFOR military
observers were tasked with monitoring the safe areas.[78]

Albright spoke before the Security Council following the adoption of
Resolution 824:

> Let us be honest. The current resolution is a palliative. The only
> solution is for the Bosnian Serbs to agree to peace, to live in tol-
> erance of their neighbors, and to give up for judgment those who
> have plunged their country into war and fouled the good name of
> the Serbian people. Let me remind the Bosnian Serb leadership that
> my government has in recent days made it clear that we are con-
> sulting with our allies about new, stronger, and tougher measures.
> Their implementation, or lack thereof, of this and all other relevant
> Council resolutions in the next days will determine whether we and
> the rest of the international community decide that the use of force
> is inevitable.[79]

Albright's uncompromising words held too much promise, but they demonstrated her own strong views about what should be the consequence of
Bosnian Serb equivocation or noncompliance.

NATO quickly authorized contingency planning for a peacekeeping
force of a revamped character in Bosnia and calculated the need for 60,000
troops. On May 7, the Security Council issued a statement reaffirming the
Vance-Owen peace plan as the basis for a peaceful solution in Bosnia.[80]
Three days later the European Community foreign ministers, meeting in
Brussels, summarized their position on Bosnia: The Vance-Owen peace
plan is the dominant political goal. The European Community will provide monitoring personnel to hold Milošević to his promise to stop aiding
the Bosnian Serbs. The United States and Russia should provide troops to
protect the newly declared safe areas. No options were excluded, but any
action must be under U.N. auspices. The Europeans expressed concern
about the future of Croatia and the continuing violence in Bosnia.[81]

Playing Tough

On May 22, key governments met in Washington to adopt a "Joint Action Plan" that recalibrated a tougher stand with the Bosnian Serbs in particular. The United States, France, the United Kingdom, Russia, and Spain agreed to continue humanitarian aid, rigorously enforce sanctions and the no-fly zone, unleash close air support (including U.S. aircraft) to protect UNPROFOR if it is attacked and requests help, place monitors on Bosnia's border with Serbia, move quickly to set up a war crimes tribunal, use the Vance-Owen process as a foundation for a political settlement, cooperate to prevent a spillover of the conflict elsewhere in the region, and keep open the possibility of tougher measures.[82] But "lift and strike" or "lift or strike" had disappeared from the collective calculus. "The focus had shifted from intervention to containment."[83]

Three days later, on May 25, the Security Council made good on one component of the Joint Action Plan: to create an operational war crimes tribunal. Security Council Resolution 827 launched the enterprise and from that point onward the International Criminal Tribunal for the former Yugoslavia (ICTY or Yugoslav Tribunal) not only existed, but it ultimately became a dominant actor in the aftermath of the Yugoslav wars by bringing 160 men and one woman (Bosnian Serb leader Biljana Plavšić) to justice for atrocity crimes over at least two decades of investigations, indictments, trials, and appeals. But in 1993 the Yugoslav Tribunal was only a newborn concept that would take years to fully launch. Its most important work, and accomplishments, occurred long after the Dayton Accords were signed in Paris in December 1995.

The Deputies met in the Sit Room on May 26 and 27 to follow up on the Joint Action Plan. The thorniest, and most time-consuming, issue at the meetings was how to define the limits of the U.S. commitment to provide air support to UNPROFOR, including its implications.

> . . . There was considerable concern that the commitment could turn out to be open-ended, either because the commitment to support UNPROFOR forces under attack would become transmuted into a commitment to support the "safe havens," or because aggressive UNPROFOR moves to extend the safe havens could involve us in a confrontation not of our making.
>
> There was a consensus that we must make clear both privately and publicly that our commitment is limited to the UNPROFOR

forces themselves (and does not, for example, extend to organizations like UNHCR or inhabitants of the "safe havens"), and that it represents a continuation of past commitments (the Bush Christmas declaration) rather than a new commitment. There also was a consensus that we must be involved in defining the rules of engagement for UNPROFOR to avoid giving a blank check to UNPROFOR or national components. On a related question—the position to be taken on the French draft UN resolution on safe havens—the decisions [*sic*] was that we could support the language of the resolution.[84]

The Pentagon reeled back the air support commitment by narrowing it considerably and limiting the types of UNPROFOR actions that would give rise to the risk of needing air strikes to protect the U.N. peacekeepers.

U.N. Security Council Digs In

The Deputies eased the way toward approval of a French-led resolution before the Security Council, namely, Resolution 836 of June 4.[85] It was one of the more ambitious Council resolutions in the entire four-year conflict. In a preambular provision, the Council set forth its principles for a "lasting solution to the conflict." They consisted of the "immediate and complete cessation of hostilities; withdrawal from territories seized by the use of force and 'ethnic cleansing'; reversal of the consequences of 'ethnic cleansing' and recognition of the right of all refugees to return to their homes; and respect for sovereignty, territorial integrity and political independence of the Republic of Bosnia and Herzegovina . . ."

There followed U.N. Charter Chapter VII enforcement provisions to "ensure full respect for the safe areas," including deployment of UNPROFOR troops into the safe areas "to deter attacks against the safe areas, to monitor the cease-fire, to promote the withdrawal of military or paramilitary units other than those of the Government of the Republic of Bosnia and Herzegovina and to occupy some key points on the ground, in addition to participating in the delivery of humanitarian relief to the population . . ."[86]

Resolution 836 authorized UNPROFOR to act in self-defense and to "take the necessary measures, including the use of force, in reply to bombardments against the safe areas by any of the parties or to armed incursion into them or in the event of any deliberate obstruction in or around those areas to the freedom of movement of UNPROFOR or of protected humanitarian convoys. . . . [and decided that] Member States, acting nationally or through regional organizations or arrangements, may take, under the authority of the Security Council and subject to close coordination with the Secretary-General and UNPROFOR, all necessary measures, through the use of air power, in and around the safe areas in the Republic of Bosnia and Herzegovina, to support UNPROFOR in the performance of its mandate [to defend the safe areas] . . ."[87]

The official Clinton administration position in June 1993 reflected a fresh appreciation for where the dominant responsibility for the atrocities and warfare lay, even though the response to it remained strictly within the narrow parameters set in the Joint Action Plan that conformed with the restrained views of France and the United Kingdom, in particular. On June 23, the State Department informed the Serbian Crown Prince of Yugoslavia, Alexander II Karađorđević, in response to his letter of May 6, "Our assessment, however, is that the burden of responsibility for this pointless tragedy lies overwhelmingly with the Bosnian Serbs. While we condemn the recent Bosnian Croat and Bosnian Government forces' actions in central Bosnia, these events, odious as they are, pale in comparison to the atrocities and ethnic cleansing that have been the hallmark of the Bosnian Serbs' campaign of aggression for more than a year." The letter continued, "The imposition of economic sanctions by the UN Security Council against Serbia and Montenegro. . . . was necessary . . . in order to bring pressure on Serbia and the Bosnian Serbs to halt the brutal aggression and bloodshed in Bosnia. We continue to support the imposition of these sanctions and believe that they should be lifted only if the necessary conditions set out in Security Council Resolution 820, including the withdrawal of Bosnian Serb troops from territories occupied by force, are met."[88]

This response to the Serbian royal family, comfortably ensconced in London, had no discernible impact and doubtless remained unknown to key members of Congress, who were reaching the boiling point of frustration with the Clinton administration and continued warfare in Bosnia. But during June 1993 important developments were unfolding in Europe, New York, and Washington. The Security Council reiterated, in Resolution 838, its demand that Serbia cease supplying the Bosnian Serb paramilitaries.[89] On the same day, June 10, in Athens, the North Atlantic Council (NAC), the governing ministerial body of NATO, agreed to protect UNPROFOR with NATO firepower if it were attacked.[90] The United States also announced its willingness to send a small contingent of troops to Macedonia to join a U.N. peacekeeping initiative there and deter any Serbian aggression against that country.[91]

Several days later, Bosnia's Alija Izetbegović, Croatia's Franjo Tudjman, and Serbia's Slobodan Milošević met in Geneva to discuss reworking the Vance-Owen peace plan for the ethnic partition of Bosnia. But on June 18, Izetbegović walked out of the Geneva talks vehemently disagreeing with the partition plan that Milošević tabled. To make matters worse, on June 20, Bosnian Serbs, by a 98 percent margin approved a popular referendum calling for the unification by Republika Srpska, the self-proclaimed autonomous Bosnian Serb territory in Bosnia, with mother Serbia. Then a joint Serb-Croat proposal for a confederal settlement was tabled in Geneva on June 28, only fueling the flames of separatism and conspiratorial designs to carve up Bosnia and ultimately attach large ethnic chunks of it to either Croatia or Serbia. To top it off, the next day the Security Council rejected a draft resolution seeking to exempt Bosnia from the Council-mandated arms embargo of 1991. I pondered, as mid-year approached, whether the Bosniaks were totally screwed.

Another Turning Point

The month of July 1993 became another turning point in American policy on Bosnia. The humanitarian situation was going from bad to worse, particularly in besieged Sarajevo as the Bosnian Serbs shelled it constantly and kept up sniper warfare against civilians. The tactics of war and the associated atrocities of horrendous character had been reported by the intelligence agencies, in State Department cables, in civil society reports, and by journalists from the day President Bill Clinton swore his oath of office on January 20, 1993. Albright relentlessly emphasized the carnage. And yet I found throughout my service in the Clinton administration, and I wager this held true for George W. Bush and Barack Obama and certainly for Donald Trump, that until the president actually witnesses the horror on television and understands its importance for his (or her) legacy, all of those government and civil society reports and printed media articles mean almost nothing in terms of making an impression that shifts policy into high gear. Unless the war and its atrocity crimes are literally shoved in front of the president's face with the knowledge that the rest of the world is witnessing the same hideous images, policymaking drags along without the push it needs from the top.

Clinton saw on CNN, while attending the Group of Seven meeting in Tokyo in early July, the awful realities besetting the people of Sarajevo in particular.[92] Such gut-wrenching imagery, which replicated 26 months of violence in Bosnia and Croatia that had been presented almost daily to the White House in intelligence reports and policy briefings, compelled him to revisit his policy on Bosnia. "Clinton explicitly told Lake that he wanted him to look at all options—including the use of American ground forces. Lake believed that the president was committed this time, and he asked Aspin to order up a full panoply of military options to address the situation in Sarajevo and other enclaves under siege by Bosnian Serb forces."[93] There then proceeded much activity at the State and Defense Departments, the National Security Council, and in the Sit Room at Principals-only meetings to deliver a more assertive policy to Clinton.

Only Albright supported the introduction of American ground troops alongside air power into Bosnia, while other Principals endorsed the lesser, but still powerful, option of unleashing only air strikes. The objectives would be to end the siege of Sarajevo by the Bosnian Serbs and loosen their grip on other "safe" areas and compel them to negotiate a peace settlement.

The Dual Key

Lake and Bartholomew flew to Europe to persuade the British and French governments of the more robust American posture, because we strongly preferred gaining their support than the alternative of going it alone. In contrast to Christopher's failed mission of a few months earlier, Lake and Bartholomew intended to assert an American intention to act, with or without the Europeans but preferably with them. Their talks in Europe were followed by more discussions in Washington with the British and French and then arduous deliberations by the North Atlantic Council in Brussels. That gatehouse of ministers who can authorize a NATO action announced their agreement to a policy change on August 2: Preparations would begin for air strikes to end the "strangulation of Sarajevo and other areas" if it continues, against those responsible, including the Bosnian Serbs. But then came the kicker, which would bedevil the White House and ultimately NATO itself for two very long years: Any air strikes would require the full buy-in by and coordination with the United Nations.

Thus was born the notorious "dual-key" arrangement, whereby nothing could transpire to enforce the newly articulated policy without the dual agreement of both the relevant U.N. body or authority, such as the U.N. Secretary-General or UNPROFOR commander, and the relevant NATO commander. The British and the French, both with thousands of troops deployed in UNPROFOR, held great influence with the U.N. side of the dual key and thus had essentially neutered Clinton's initiative. It was just another way for our allies to shove the United States aside because, as Albright experienced so often, they knew we were not risking our own troops and believed Washington was not entitled to dictate anything about air strikes on the very territory where European soldiers were operating as peacekeepers.

Dead End

While the Clinton initiative was well under way, Albright traveled to Capitol Hill for a frank exchange with lawmakers in late July. The heightened internal discussions within the administration were largely unknown on the Hill. She heard that the Clinton administration must no longer take a pass on Bosnia and that its credibility was at stake. Christopher's defeatist statement on Bosnia the day before had inspired reporting about a "dead end"[94] and left some astounded, as they believed Milošević had achieved thug status among world leaders. They did not know whether Bosnia was lighting up any screens in the White House. In the meantime, American inaction in Bosnia left respect for the United Nations at an all-time low, and the credibility deficit would cripple the institution for at least a generation. And to top it off, one of the last remaining Communist dictators, Milošević, would get everything that he wanted.

Albright replied that at the Security Council, the French and British reminded us that they have troops on the ground. If we were to lift the arms embargo, their troops would be attacked. These allies had told us that when the United States deployed troops on the ground, they would listen to Washington about lifting the embargo. Would the American people tolerate sending their own troops to be peacekeepers and possibly enter combat in Bosnia? If the answer was "no," then we would never convince our allies to lift the embargo. The impasse had created major divisions in the United Nations, which was indeed losing credibility.

She was hammered about the administration's strategy, including whether to lift and strike unilaterally or multilaterally. Albright admitted grappling with these questions. What are the priorities? What is or is not destabilizing? She hinted at the internal debates occurring at that time. Albright was advised that the administration must articulate more forcefully what the United States had done and not done in Bosnia. On the good news ledger, there had been humanitarian assistance and containment. But the United Nations needed to be strengthened, not weakened. We had two choices: (1) the United States acted unilaterally; (2) the United States acted multilaterally. Washington must be prepared to act unilaterally when vital interests were at stake, recognizing that we had two vetoes to manage: the veto in the Security Council and the veto in the Pentagon.

The next day Albright visited columnists and reporters of *The New York Times* in their Washington offices on I Street NW. They were curious about the safe areas, how they came about, and why it was taking so long to defend them. Albright told them that the six safe areas were created out of pressure from the nonaligned countries, represented forcefully by Venezuela on the Security Council, and that it "came up the night we were voting sanctions. Srebrenica was under assault. The French also really pushed the safe areas. We did not believe them to be the final answer, only an interim answer. The French saw the safe areas as a way to save a Bosnian state, but it's not a perfect solution."

I scribbled my private thoughts at the time: *The point we needed to make about the safe areas is that they are a perfect example of how far we need to go on peacekeeping, that it has taken more than two months to organize the defense of the safe areas. We need a system whereby when the Security Council adopts a resolution, we can implement that resolution quickly. Safe areas are a good example of a prolonged effort by the U.N. Secretary-General and NATO to organize the concept, get forces lined up, and set the rules of engagement.*

Reporter Elaine Sciolino noted opinion polls showing that Americans would accept U.S. participation in UNPROFOR, but there was big opposition to unilateral troop deployments. "The Blue Helmets cannot be some new species of sitting duck," she lamented. Veteran war reporter David Binder believed the White House saw "Yugoslavia as a hot potato for the last 24 months. Under Clinton, there's tough rhetoric, then you back off. There is no consistent U.S. role. Are you going to reach some kind of consistency?"

Albright shot back, "You are wrong. We have been consistent." She stressed the airdrops of humanitarian aid and the American lead on creating a war crimes tribunal and enforcing the no-fly zone. She conceded that we had not persuaded other permanent members of the Security Council and the "non-non-aligned" (those countries outside the nonaligned and major power blocs at the United Nations) to lift the arms embargo. R.W. Apple Jr., one of *The Times'* most famous journalists of the preceding 40 years, concluded the interview with Albright unmoved by her defense: "I do not find the U.S. position very consistent." If only he knew of the internal battles to achieve consistency, I thought. But each in their own way, Albright and he were correct.

Backsliding

The Deputies next convened on July 26 with Bartholomew attending. The cast at Deputies Committee meetings in the Sit Room could vary, depending on the issue at hand and whether the Principal wanted the Deputy of the agency at the table or another high-level official who might be the most knowledgeable and operationally proficient for the matter. Also, over the four years of Clinton's first term, the Deputies in each agency periodically changed, and that would bring new faces to the table. Special envoys like Bartholomew occasionally were invited in by Berger to brief the Deputies and participate in the decision-making. As individual Deputies enter this story, I will introduce them.

Bartholomew delivered his own assessment: "[Bosnian President Alija] Izetbegović will accept partition [under Vance-Owen] because he has no other choice. He'll keep this confidential for now for domestic political reasons. At Geneva he will vent and then he'll enter the negotiations actively. The Bosniaks will accept the pact under duress and not of their own free will. Some small U.S. military help would be of great assistance."

But Bartholomew's appeal to inject some American military might into the mix fell flat. A proposal to install a U.S. chief of staff in UNPROFOR headquarters in Zagreb was shot down quickly, with the Pentagon considering it "a dumb idea," particularly in light of UNPROFOR's weak appearance recently as the safe areas remained at great risk. There was a distinct view among the Deputies that injecting American leadership into UNPROFOR would only tarnish the American military's reputation as the peacekeeping force struggled to survive in the face of Bosnian Serb aggression and intransigence.

Berger dumped a bucket of pragmatic issues on the Sit Room table, while in Principals-only meetings Lake worked to change the dynamic and energize the overall Bosnia policy. The Deputies agreed that there was "no pressing need to open Tuzla airport, although the humanitarian situation there was likely to worsen and the issue to emerge again." Opening the Tuzla airport would require a military commitment the Deputies were racing away from that day. There were 1,200 Bosnian Serb soldiers outside Tuzla, and the airport was within range of their artillery. Bartholomew predicted, "The Tuzla mess is going to get worse." Berger said we would revisit the issue and tasked a further study. Sanctions against Croatia were approved "as a way of forcing it to cooperate with the Muslims and cease collaboration with the Serbs in central Bosnia . . ."[95]

The Bosniaks, led by Izetbegović, rejected outright a so-called "union" peace plan on July 30 that was a combination of Vance-Owen and Serbian plans for a tripartite confederation. These types of plans, fueled by Belgrade, exhibited obvious intent to sequester the Bosniaks into their own corner of Bosnia and create confederal units that could easily break off to either Serbia or Croatia.

Adding to the weaker-than-expected August 2 announcement of the dual-key arrangement for use of air power, there was some further backsliding on the use of American military clout in Bosnia a few days later. Two National Intelligence Officers, one covering Europe and the other Russia and Eurasia, delivered a memorandum to CIA Director Woolsey on August 5 that may have responded to Senator Bob Dole's op-ed in the August 1 edition of *The Washington Post*, in which he called for unilateral air strikes.[96] They wrote without acknowledging what had just occurred in Brussels with the adoption of the dual-key formulation, which left the use of air power in the hands of both the United Nations and NATO.[97] There was no consent to unilateral use of American air power. The CIA analysts aimed their arrows directly at Dole and probably Albright, who had argued in July for unilateral air strikes:

1. Action Recommended: That you advise your NSC colleagues of our view that any US unilateral military action in Bosnia will break the international coalition.

2. We understand that the US may be considering air strikes in Bosnia without further international consultations. Based on our reading of diplomatic reporting and public allied statements, we believe such actions would precipitate the following:

Key NATO allies (including Britain, France, and Canada) would:

- Consider unilateral actions as jeopardizing their troops and possibly begin withdrawing them.
- Break with us in the UN Security Council.

Other NATO allies would judge this a major breach of alliance procedures. Russia would:

- Join or initiate a condemnation in the UN.
- Possibly unilaterally lift the embargo against Serbia.
- See its domestic political balance shift toward Yel'tsin's opponents as they blame Yel'tsin's alleged subservience to the US for the US action.

The UN Secretary General would condemn the US and help orchestrate an attempt to bring the US back into an international consensus.

3. In short any unilateral US action without further consultations with NATO and with the UN would have very negative short-term and long-term consequences for our traditional and developing alliance.[98]

While this darkest of assessments about any U.S. unilateral initiative on the military front reflected the common view of most Principals and Deputies, for the following two years the July initiative in the Sit Room, as modified with NATO's consensus in Brussels on August 2, at least endorsed a *multilateral* air-strike option, albeit heavily constrained by the dual-key mechanism. The North Atlantic Council approved the operational plans for the air-strike option on August 9 and agreed that the U.N. Secretary-General would have to authorize the very first air strike, inferring that authority for later air strikes could be delegated to other U.N. officials.

Anthony Lewis, a Pulitzer Prize–winning columnist of long standing with *The New York Times*, called me the same day with acidic comments. He had just published his op-ed entitled, "Tragedy and Farce," in which he sharply criticized Clinton, European allies, and the United Nations, and called for unilateral military attacks if others failed to join us.[99] In his conversation with me, Lewis accused the U.N. peacekeeping force of being the "handmaidens of genocide, sitting by while genocide rages." UNPROFOR was doing nothing about the fundamental problem, he said. Even in humanitarian functions, UNPROFOR was reduced to a "pathetic" level of performance. Lewis rejected the fear that military action against Bosnian Serb forces was inadvisable because it would result in attacks on U.N. forces. What was occurring in Bosnia was aggression "as naked as Hitler's against Poland." This was not a situation, he argued, that was appropriate for traditional peacekeeping forces. "The correct and only answer," Lewis said, "would be an Article 51 or Chapter VII response [under the U.N. Charter] that attacks the aggressor. Bombs should fall on Milošević." He had a sympathetic ear on my end of the phone line, but Lewis' views and remedies had no takers on the seventh floor of the State Department or at the Pentagon or the White House.

Humanitarian Plight

The next day the deteriorating humanitarian situation in Bosnia came to a head in Washington. Albright pleaded with Christopher, Lake, and Aspin that the United States respond immediately to the dire health crisis in Sarajevo and, where feasible, in other safe areas in Bosnia. There were clear weaknesses in U.N. procedures for medical evacuation from Sarajevo, and more emergency flights were needed. The many pockets of human misery in Bosnia needed medical airlift capabilities, field hospitals, and pharmaceutical supplies. Could not the Defense Department arrange more medevac flights for Sarajevo? Why not deploy MASH units to the safe areas? Albright's appeal followed our efforts during the summer of 1993 to address the humanitarian and medical emergency in Bosnia. The Deputies Committee had refused to approve our proposal in July to use U.S. assets to help open the Tuzla airport for humanitarian airlifts. Our frustration over deciding but not deciding led to repeated appeals by Albright and me in the Deputies Committee and interagency meetings for American engagement on the humanitarian front, itself a direct consequence of the atrocity crimes being waged against civilians.

Albright's entreaty fell on deaf ears, or at least that was my impression as I saw nothing concrete come of it that summer. Two weeks later the medical situation inside Bosnia remained chaotic and frustrating, but we learned more about what was needed. The ICRC told us that none of the proposals of assistance met the real needs of water, electricity, and fuel. If these needs were addressed, they could greatly lessen evacuation requests. In fact, the ICRC asked us not to send medical personnel, field hospitals, or other staples of relief. The Pentagon's capabilities for emergency med-evac flights would be welcome, but the European evacuation flights into and out of Sarajevo were basically meeting the need, we were told. The real problem was on the ground and identifying emergency cases. The U.N. High Commissioner for Refugees (UNHCR) was not coordinating well with the International Organization for Migration and a "no can do" indi-vidual at UNHCR appeared to be the bottleneck. My task was to seek his removal from Sarajevo, which became another bureaucratic slog.

Washington was being deprived of much useful information because there essentially were no U.S. personnel stationed in Bosnia to report on humanitarian needs and that meant support would be very limited. We desperately needed more information, and the nongovernmental or-ganizations deployed in Bosnia, for all of their good intentions, were not sharing enough of it with us. We struggled to coordinate an overall net-work of information that government agencies could rely upon.

Siege of Sarajevo and the Map

Meanwhile, Izetbegović boycotted the Geneva talks to protest the Serbs' continuing siege of Sarajevo, although by August 8 Bosnian Serb General Ratko Mladić, who many years later would be convicted of atrocity crimes by the Yugoslav Tribunal,[100] reached a partial agreement with the United Nations on a phased withdrawal from the mountains around Sarajevo.[101] On August 16, leaders of the warring parties again met in Geneva and agreed "in principle" to turn Sarajevo into a demilitarized, U.N.-administered city for an interim period after a settlement was reached.[102] Two days later the United Nations publicly announced that NATO was prepared to launch air strikes to support UNPROFOR in Bosnia if the Secretary-General so requested.[103]

The warring parties received a new version of settlement terms, in-cluding a revised map partitioning Bosnia, on August 20 from Lord David Owen and Thorvald Stoltenberg, a Norwegian diplomat who had suc-ceeded Cyrus Vance to press forward with the only peace plan in play. But it was not getting any easier. The map awarded the Bosnian Serbs 52 percent of the nation's territory, while the Croats would take 18 per-cent and the Bosniaks 30 percent. Any viewing of the map would lead

Bosniak officials to declare defeat after two years of Serb and Croat territorial seizures. The Owen-Stoltenberg map validated ethnic cleansing in the name of peace and capitulation, and yet those percentages were dented only slightly a month later when the next peace plan was rolled out. It thus was not surprising that on August 27, following the advice of Izetbegović that the new plan was unacceptable, the Bosnian Government Assembly rejected it and claimed more territory back from the Bosnian Serbs in particular. The Bosnian Serb Assembly, however, accepted the plan but demanded that the Croats be given more territory under it. The Bosnian Croat Assembly declared a Bosnian Croat republic in the wake of the Owen-Stoltenberg plan.

Lake's Misbegotten Memo

During the August vacation break in both Principals and Deputies meetings, Lake wrote a memorandum, dated August 25 and entitled, "Bosnian End-Game Strategy," to Clinton. Lake strategized how to handle Izetbegović and the Owen-Stoltenberg plan and map. He wrote that "[o]ur reporting suggests that Izetbegović wants an agreement." That proved wrong a few days later, at least in terms of how Izetbegović and the Bosnian Government Assembly viewed the deal on the table. Lake was confident enough of a different, more positive, outcome that he set forth contingency planning for implementation of a peace agreement based on the Owen-Stoltenberg plan and including the commitment of American troops. He also put down a marker for reconstruction assistance and a phased lifting of sanctions.[104] The optimistic tenor of the memorandum may have cheered Clinton. But Lake was way off the mark, and nothing came of it.

In late August the Bosnian Serbs and Bosnian Croats accepted the new Owen-Stoltenberg plan with its "union" of three ethnic republics awarding them with the territories seized in ethnic cleansing campaigns. It only took two days of further talks in Geneva for Izetbegović to walk out over the territorial carve-up in the Owen-Stoltenberg map.

Assertive Multilateralism Takes a Beating

Frustration boiled over, in a larger context, at a September 3 strategy meeting in the Sit Room that Gore attended. Albright was there, and I joined as her "plus-one." Lake complained that "we're getting the hell

beat out of us." We were failing to explain our purposes, and he complained to Albright about the muddle over "multilateralism." Albright had
been advancing a strong case for "assertive multilateralism" at the United
Nations, before Congress in hearings, and in her speeches.

Months earlier, I had suggested the term "assertive multilateralism"
to her during a planning session in her elegant Waldorf-Astoria suite
in New York, which was the official residence of every U.S. permanent
representative to the United Nations (although no longer once Chinese
investors bought the Waldorf-Astoria Hotel in 2014). In my view, the
term "assertive multilateralism" precisely described what the United
States should be doing to achieve the most effective foreign policy: assert America's considerable power and influence in multilateral forums
like the United Nations and NATO and among our allies so as to share
the burden of foreign crises that would be far costlier and riskier to
address on our own. Republicans on Capitol Hill scoffed at what they
mislabeled her "aggressive multilateralism," and that criticism was
clearly beginning to bite in the White House. Lake kept up the attack,
complaining that Boutros-Ghali appeared to the public as if he was running our policy, and that we were on the defensive on Capitol Hill. He
advised Albright to think counterintuitively and not always trumpet
multilateralism.

Rather than attack Albright, Lake should have demonstrated more
spine to project the value of assertive multilateralism to advance American
goals, because that was the only realistic way to proceed. Lake's unfair dig
at Albright seemed desperate in an inescapably multilateral world.

Everyone was urged to pump out speeches to turn the tide of the
public's perception of Clinton as being detached from foreign policymaking. David Gergen, a highly respected and cerebral journalist who
had worked for Presidents Richard Nixon, Gerald R. Ford, and Ronald
Reagan, was brought into the White House to help with Clinton's image

and build public support for him. A tall, balding
man who looked like a Midwest Main Street banker
coveting a set of trophies from his high school bas-
ketball days, he towered over the table even while
seated and said that Clinton needed to be perceived
by the public as being more involved in the Israeli-
Palestinian situation. George Stephanopoulos,
Clinton's youthful political adviser and former
Rhodes Scholar and Capitol Hill staffer, wanted the

public to see the president engaged in more substantive work on foreign affairs generally. For example, he should be photographed chairing the Principals Committee meetings in the Sit Room.

Aspin interjected that maybe Clinton could show how domestic and foreign policy are interconnected. But Lake (who clearly was an agitated man that day) said he had no interest in sacrificing foreign policy on the altar of domestic priorities. "We got off track with all the domestic focus," he complained. It must have been, I thought, all that "It's the economy, stupid" rhetoric that had guided the campaign and the first year of the Clinton presidency. Gergen interjected, reminding everyone of another foreign policy challenge weighing heavily on the administration: "If we lose NAFTA [the pending free trade treaty with Canada and Mexico], that will be a terrible blow to our foreign policy."

That gave Berger an opening to narrow the problem, claiming, "Bosnia is polluting the water. We need to articulate our policy on Bosnia." Albright proposed, "We need a strong speech on Bosnia so as to put it in context without slipping into propaganda." Undaunted by Lake's acerbic remarks earlier in the meeting, she added, "We need to make the case that the way to avoid fighting two regular wars simultaneously is through multilateralism, that the United Nations can act as an early warning system."

The discussion rambled but hit a range of foreign policy issues. Gore, seated next to Lake, weighed in supporting Albright on both multilateralism and Bosnia. Berger suggested a theme of "reinventing the UN," just as Gore had taken up the mantle of "reinventing the federal government" for the Clinton administration. Stephanopoulos commented on various opportunities in the world that were appealing targets for the president. He said Clinton was best at articulating optimistic scenarios. Stephanopoulos saw the future as, "Foreign policy can make your lives better." The meeting ended inconclusively as one where many ideas lay on the table, and Lake had the job of patching them together into something coherent for the Principals to run with. Gore eased his way out of the Sit Room while the rest of us—or perhaps it was only me—were befuddled.

Such strategizing and prolific speechifying that month made little difference in changing the anti-multilateralism crusade overtaking Washington just prior to the killing of 18 Marines in Mogadishu, Somalia, on October 3, which dug an even deeper ditch for our efforts at the United Nations and to generate the political will in Washington and across the country to intervene in the Bosnian conflagration.

Invincible Plan

On September 13, the stuttering peace talks resumed in Geneva. Two days later the NAC authorized planning to commence on implementation of the on-again, off-again peace plan in Bosnia. Hopes were high that renewed talks would produce the golden egg. By September 20 there appeared to be some progress as the three Balkan presidents—Milošević, Tudjman, and Izetbegović—met with Owen and Stoltenberg aboard the British *HMS Invincible* in the Adriatic Sea. At least the European Community knew where it stood after the so-called "Invincible Plan" emerged: 49 percent of Bosnia would be controlled by the Serbs, 33 percent would fall under Muslim control, and the Croats would take 17.5 percent. The Muslims would gain access to the Adriatic and the Sava River at designated points. There also would be a three-kilometer corridor connecting the Muslim enclaves in eastern Bosnia. Sarajevo would remain a unified city but administered by the United Nations for two years, and Mostar would fall under European Community administration for two years.

The Invincible Plan proved less than invincible in coming weeks. Although the Bosnian Assembly accepted the plan on September 29, it did so on the condition that territory seized by force be returned to the Bosnian government, thus disrupting the percentage carve-outs for the map. Both the Bosnian Croat and Serb Assemblies voted to withdraw any territorial concessions made to the Bosniaks. Further negotiations stalled.

The "Black Hawk down" debacle in Mogadishu, Somalia, on October 3 and 4 swamped all of our circuits that month and dominated Sit Room meetings.[105] This would happen often over the years, as other crises took hold and we put Bosnia on cruise control for days or, occasionally, weeks at a time. In mid-October, Albright learned that Boutros-Ghali was willing to approve air strikes in Bosnia provided a Security Council resolution authorized them. At bottom, however, the Europeans with peacekeeping troops in UNPROFOR continued to prevent serious consideration of such a resolution. There were no U.S. troops on the ground and that greatly diminished U.S. leverage and influence.

Humanitarian Redux

Nonetheless, the humanitarian situation in Bosnia began to look dire again as winter loomed. I explored numerous avenues of support over these weeks and prepared for the next Deputies Committee meeting on

Bosnia, which occurred on October 28. The Deputies considered how to activate some useful response to the humanitarian crisis in Bosnia. We learned that the winter could be worse than the year before. The delivery of aid was imperiled. There would be no access to secondary roads once the snow fell. Cooperation by the Bosnian Serbs and Croats would be essential to reach distant villages. No one was begging yet, but that would come. The airdrops, particularly of medical supplies, would be even more vital. About 40 percent of the Bosniak population would need food deliveries over the winter.

Albright wanted several initiatives underway, quickly: to authorize an American MASH unit in Zagreb to care for a limited number of seriously war-wounded Bosnian children, to open the Tuzla airport, to support NATO air cover under some circumstances, to consider forcing open the Tuzla-Brcko and Split-Sarajevo roads, to shift international negotiating efforts toward humanitarian access, and to respond immediately to the supply needs of the all-important Tešanj Hospital in central Bosnia. But several Deputies worried about achieving any access on the ground to accomplish many of these aims. Berger tasked the Pentagon to explore the MASH issue and close air support for humanitarian convoys, but rejected using U.S. military helicopters to deliver aid.

Some in the Sit Room wondered whether sufficient fuel would be available in Sarajevo, as petrol has the multiplier effect needed to keep the heat on, food cooked, and vehicles running. Fuerth strongly opposed relaxing sanctions on Serbia-Montenegro in exchange for Serb guarantees that the Bosnians would receive humanitarian aid, and Albright did not want to lift sanctions without much greater Serbian cooperation with the Yugoslav Tribunal. Berger tasked Peter Tarnoff, the Under Secretary of State for Political Affairs attending the meeting, to reorient the Owen-Stoltenberg talks toward humanitarian priorities for the winter. Ending the war now took second place to averting a humanitarian catastrophe.

Two weeks later, on November 16, at the second Deputies meeting on humanitarian aid for Bosnia, the Pentagon assessed the need for increasing the pace and tonnage of airdrops of humanitarian aid. While the U.S. military was prepared to "participate" with UNPROFOR at the Tuzla airport, they still would not do so with U.S. personnel or equipment, which only showed the often disconnected nature of such decisions. Though they had consumed one month of studying the matter since the last Deputies meeting, the Joint Chiefs of Staff and the State Department were tasked once again to work, this time together, to come up with criteria for a MASH unit in Zagreb to help war-wounded Bosnian children. I won-dered what was so complex about that equation that it required setting up time-delaying criteria while children perished or slipped into permanent disabilities.

For months Albright and I, along with the U.S. ambassador to Croatia, Peter Galbraith (son of famed Harvard economist and Kennedy admin-istration ambassador, John Kenneth Galbraith) and Laura Bowman on Albright's staff, had pushed for a seemingly simple initiative: to set up the MASH unit. The need for it was clear; it would be a high visibility means of bringing American medical help to the fore in the conflict; the MASH unit would be well received; and we would be tapping an underused resource—our armed forces medical personnel. The cynics in Washington, however, argued the difficulties in providing impartial treatment. How would the MASH unit distinguish juvenile combatants from civilian children, as the former would detract from the primary mission to help civilians? I re-acted, who cares? A wounded juvenile is a *child* and needs medical treat-ment. The cynics also wondered where the patients would go after their MASH care, but those were solvable logistical issues well within the reach of officials at Foggy Bottom, at the Pentagon, and in Zagreb.

Self-Defense

I also argued at the meeting that any criticism of the Bosniaks must not be seen to impinge on their right of self-defense and that any Serb sanc-tions relief—always being proposed by someone at State, the Pentagon, the NSC, or our European allies as the mythical magic bullet for Serb cooperation—must be tied to prior Serb performance in turning over in-dicted war criminals. Indeed, one week later the foreign ministers of the newly named European Union (casting off the "European Community" signage) supported a Franco-German proposal "to offer gradual suspen-sion of the sanctions against Serbia-Montenegro if the Bosnian Serbs make territorial concessions to the Muslims, a peace plan is implemented, and Belgrade cooperates with a 'modus vivendi' in the Krajina. Final lifting of all sanctions would depend upon a global settlement."[106]

The European Union proposal was presented to Izetbegović, Karadžić, Tudjman, and Milošević in Geneva on November 29 but met with another round of turbulent negotiations that pointed to nowhere. Indeed, one day later the Bosniaks delineated a map claiming only one-third of Bosnian territory that Karadžić immediately called "overexaggerated." Then the

Bosnian Serbs proposed dividing Sarajevo into "twin cities" in which the Bosniaks would retain control of the city center and the Bosnian Serbs would control the southern and western suburbs. Imagine the peaceful co-existence that would have ensued. The bizarre idea was a nonstarter with the Bosniaks. The Geneva talks reached another dead end on December 2 with the notion of suspension of sanctions burping up again a few weeks later, but again to no effect. The fine hotels and restaurants of Geneva were profiting handsomely from the indecision of the warring parties.

By early December 1993, the situation had deteriorated in Sarajevo, with intensified Bosnian Serb shelling that also was directed against Mostar to the west, with rising deaths and casualties. Of what purpose, I pondered in advice to Albright at the time, is the NATO commitment of the prior summer to use air power to stop the shelling of Sarajevo if it is not activated under these conditions? She understood perfectly, but silence from other Principals, Boutros-Ghali, and key NATO allies was deafening as we comfortably celebrated the winter holidays far from the misery in Bosnia.

2

Ethnic Cleansing Wins 1994

*[The Bosniaks] are always looking to the United States to
save them. But they are disappointed in you.*

KLAUS KINKEL

So peace is now our worst-case contingency?

LEON FUERTH

DURING THE MEANDERING year of 1994, tactics of jockeying and
strategizing in the Sit Room over America's role in the Balkans were
plagued with procrastination, fear of the unknown, and a futile search
for alternatives to bold action. The situation among European allies was
no more promising as the year began. The British and French hinted
that they would abandon the U.N. Protection Force (UNPROFOR) soon.
They had little interest in air strikes to spur progress on any front. The
European Union refused to strengthen the sanctions against Serbia. The
warring parties had stopped negotiating seriously. Two days of talks in
Vienna on January 4 and 5 between the new Bosnian Prime Minister
Haris Silajdžić and Croatian Foreign Minister Mate Granić had failed to
reach agreement on territorial issues. Later in January, British General
Michael Rose assumed command of UNPROFOR in Bosnia. His prede-
cessor, Belgian General Francis Briquemont, requested to be relieved of
his command in protest over what he believed was an unwillingness to
enforce U.N. resolutions and insufficient resources for UNPROFOR to
carry out its mission.[1]

A weariness had set in, and if, by good fortune, the victimized civilians of Bosnia and Croatia got through the winter without humanitarian
catastrophe, the prospect of the war resuming at full throttle in the spring
was déjà vu all over again. Few wanted to endure that, and yet spring was
coming.

The Sit Room: In the Theater of War and Peace. David Scheffer.
© Oxford University Press 2019. Published 2019 by Oxford University Press.

European Journey

During an early January 1994 side visit to Bosnia and Croatia as part of a much broader European journey with the new Chairman of the Joint Chiefs of Staff, General John Shalikashvili, Madeleine Albright and I confirmed a long-festering fear that the humanitarian situation was hurtling toward gridlock and collapse. The situation had worsened since the summer. One-half of all humanitarian shipments could not reach their destinations. The three parties—the Serbs, Croats, and even Bosniaks at times—obstructed the delivery of humanitarian aid and ignored basic principles for such assistance. Humanitarian workers were directly targeted. Nicholas Morris of the U.N. High Commissioner for Refugees told us, "We assume sacks of flour will be fired on. But we stop if they fire on the windshield or the cab." Both the Bosnian Croats and Bosnian Serbs viewed such aid as undermining their strategic interests. The food shortage was man-made, with each side arguing that foreign assistance was keeping the enemy well provisioned to fight another day. Some of the aid workers told us that not only had their aid shipments become hostage to the fighting, they saw themselves struggling to help civilians at risk with more determination than the leaders of the ethnic groups being attacked. Albright, always aiming to solve the problem, pondered once again whether the use of NATO air power could open up the humanitarian channels. Yet, predictably, top U.N. aid officials told us that if air power were used, there would be significant loss of life and it would prevent any shipments of aid. But that was a presumption and not a fact.

One official of the International Committee of the Red Cross (ICRC) conceded to us that the protection of civilians in Bosnia was an abject failure. Ethnic cleansing had prevailed. Despite ICRC visits to almost 20,000 detainees behind the front lines, their officials could not transfer all the information they knew to the Yugoslav Tribunal because that would

have violated the organization's long-standing practice of confidentiality and probably prevented the organization from continuing its work in Bosnia, Croatia, and elsewhere.

When Albright and I visited the Special Representative of the Secretary-General for the Former Yugoslavia, Yasushi Akashi, at his top-floor red brick headquarters in Zagreb on January 5, 1994, the conversation quickly soured.

Akashi, a senior Japanese diplomat, was a cunning man who had earned favorable reviews for his management of the U.N. peacekeeping force in Cambodia (UNTAC) prior to his assignment in the Balkans. Behind his wire-rim glasses and sharp eyes, however, was a very calculating and cautious representative of U.N. Secretariat interests.

Albright pressed Akashi to use NATO air power and expressed her concern over the delay entailed in waiting for the requisite approval from his boss, U.N. Secretary-General Boutros Boutros-Ghali, under the "dual-key" approach. Akashi urged patience and argued against relying on solely military decisions. He knew that field officers with UNPROFOR were frustrated with humiliations they and their soldiers were absorbing, but he was not so troubled. "We would like to exercise more restraint, even under fire," he said. He claimed that he should decide the first use of close air support as that could shorten the time required to get an approval from the Secretary-General to perhaps two hours.

Albright responded that "no good deed goes unpunished." The frustration level all around was high. She noted that the U.N. Security Council was dealing less and less with military options because no one knew quite what to do, even though "[EU negotiator Thorvald] Stoltenberg always sounds optimistic." She said, "In the Security Council, there's a different mood." French General Jean Cot, who wielded field command over the 27,000 peacekeepers of UNPROFOR in Croatia and Bosnia, had criticized the Council. Despite Cot's more assertive view about the use of force, Albright told Akashi that did not help matters, as there could not be a public break between UNPROFOR and the Security Council. Everyone was concerned about the time delay on close air support, and they presumed that Boutros-Ghali would defer to other U.N. officials, like Akashi, to delay even further. His initial approval would need to be followed up quickly by the military in the field. "We must act rapidly in these situations," Albright said, "as it is a sign of the operational effectiveness of the United Nations." Meanwhile, Albright told Akashi, it remained important for UNPROFOR to help achieve the objectives of the Yugoslav Tribunal.

Looking at Akashi, I saw his eyes glaze over on both points. He just muttered, "If NATO air support is left to the military, that would be wrong. Actually using air power must be a political decision. If left to the generals, we would be at war by now." Sitting in the middle of a raging war, I could only view Akashi's comment as absurd. Albright was frustrated but politely responded, "Ultimately this could be the example of how an international organization deals with a regional organization like NATO."

The dysfunctional relationship had proven itself that afternoon in Akashi's office.

Hours later Albright and I met with General Cot. He said the warring parties were nowhere near signing onto the Owen-Stoltenberg peace plan. He was proud that there was a December 23 ceasefire but doubted it could be extended much longer. "Today," Cot said, "the Bosnian Muslims have picked up their energy and waged battle against the Croatians. In a way, the Serbs are the interested spectators. But the Serbs won't wait long to start their own initiative. These battles are hampering delivery of aid. They are fighting for Bosnia. That really is not our problem. UNPROFOR's mandate is humanitarian aid."

Albright's gripe with Cot over his publicly criticizing Security Council resolutions led to a tense exchange. "These resolutions have to have meaning," she advised Cot. He responded, "I express myself as a military man, put simply. So perhaps it is not surprising that I am not understood in New York. When the resolution on the Vance plan was voted, there were no means to implement it. Sometimes what the Council adopts is a swindle, suggesting that more men will arrive than actually do. I have to get soldiers company by company to respond to atrocities. As a battalion commander, I can do that. But as a general, that's impossible! There's a big gap between the mission here and the means to accomplish it."

Albright responded frankly to Cot's cynicism:

We are living through a neuralgic period on peacekeeping. This has been a year of learning at the United Nations. We have strength- ened [U.N. Under Secretary General] Kofi Annan's [Department of Peacekeeping] shop, created a competent [U.N. Headquarters] oper- ations center, and drawn on the experiences of UNTAC [Cambodia], UNSCOM [Iraq], and El Salvador. So I'm troubled when we go public with these problems. When I started at the United Nations one year ago, the United Nations was at a high point. Ten months later, the U.N. is under attack. Maybe it's all my fault. But I would hope our commanders would make those statements within the bosom of the family. The atrocities would be much worse if UNPROFOR were not here to witness them. The atrocities here are the disasters, not the United Nations.

A dead silence descended on Cot's bare office, and he looked embar- rassed. Albright continued, "We're very grateful to UNPROFOR. So, first

UNPROFOR must assess the humanitarian situation. Second, it must support the Yugoslav Tribunal. We also are witnesses and I can spread the reality about these atrocities." Within days the French government recalled Cot to Paris as apparent punishment for his public remarks that he should be able to call NATO air strikes without waiting for U.N. approval.[2] Ironically, it was precisely that kind of authority that Albright insisted upon for British General Rupert Smith when he commanded UNPROFOR in Bosnia during the summer of 1995 and maneuvered to exercise such power to launch air strikes and bring the parties to the negotiating table at Dayton.

The next day, Albright and her staff, along with the U.S. ambassador to Croatia, Peter Galbraith, met with the top Serb authorities in Croatia as well as the Serb leaders in conquered, and destroyed, Vukovar at the far eastern edge of Croatia on the banks of the Danube River. I felt we were walking straight into the enemy's camp. Albright remained mostly silent in these meetings and allowed Galbraith to carry the conversation. The Serbs had so much to say to Albright, including delusional retreats into historical events, which in their view justified the atrocity crimes consuming the region, that we were mostly in a listening mode inside the dingy conference rooms where we gathered. Milan Babić, the so-called president of the so-called Republic of Serbian Krajina, a Serb carve-out of seized Croatian territory, described Muslim refugees in the Serb-controlled areas of Croatia as "arriving like snails with all their belongings on their backs. They arrive and then attack the minority Serbs. Some of our mayors want the Croats to return because at least they are stable as opposed to the Muslims."

In Vukovar, one Serb leader sought our sympathy:

We're a small and poor people and have not been able to get out the truth to the world. The [famous sixteenth-century Stari Most] bridge in Mostar was destroyed by the Muslims but the United States says the Serbs destroyed the bridge. The Serbs cause whatever is bad. Whatever is good, it's a Croat deed. Not true! I'd lie if everything said by Serbs was good. But look, we fought for our homes. We did not go to Vietnam or Argentina [the Falklands War]. We just defended our homes. We've been living here for 700 years.

The Croatians started this war. They began to kill and set on fire whatever belonged to Serbs. Once started, it is very hard to stop it.

In fact, there was no mystery that it was Bosnian Croat shelling that brought down Stari Most Bridge on November 9, 1993.[3]

After Galbraith delivered a strong and remarkably balanced assessment of the situation and how there must be an accommodation between Serbs and Croats, one of the Serb leaders turned even more defensive: "There has been an injustice committed against our people because others are not well informed. You are not aware of historical facts in this part of the world. The [Serb] Chetniks killed my grandfather. My mother spent four years in a [Nazi] German concentration camp. Nuremberg closed that case. This is not the first war to break out, you know. What about Vietnam, Cambodia, and Argentina? Where was your objectivity after what happened there? History repeats itself many times. In Bosnia, the warring parties are the Croats and Muslims. Serbs are not the warring party." Babić responded to a hypothetical from Galbraith about letting Croats return to Serb-seized territory within Croatia with the view that Croatians would recognize a Serbian state and become citizens of that new nation. "If they are not war criminals, they can live among us," he proclaimed. He invited us to take a walk around Vukovar to understand his claim of its Serbian character.

So Albright, Galbraith, Jim O'Brien, I and other staffers toured Vukovar by car and on foot. A devastated urban landscape confronted us. Serbian shelling of Vukovar in 1991 had cleansed it of Christian Croatians, and the local Serbs clearly resented our presence. We walked about the open-air market while Albright, whose public notoriety was well known by then, endured taunts from the Serbian vendors. During our drive through Vukovar, a stone was thrown at the staff van, shattering the glass of the window next to O'Brien and me. A CNN cameraman in the press bus behind us jumped out immediately and broadcast the incident internationally.

Our derided group drove by the hospital building where 255 non-Serb civilian patients and prisoners of war who were being treated had been dragged out and then mass-executed and buried at a place called Ovčara outside of Vukovar on November 20, 1991. We were driven out to Ovčara later the same day as Ukrainian peacekeepers guarded the site. In one corner of Ovčara was a muddy patch of soil shaded by some trees—an inglorious resting site for victims whose bones and tattered clothes would be excavated as forensic evidence for the successful prosecution of Mile

Mrkšic and Veselin Šljivančanin of the Yugoslav People's Army (Serbia) before the Yugoslav Tribunal.[4]

As dusk fell, our rickety Soviet-era U.N. helicopter flew west from Vukovar over the war-ravaged countryside of Croatia. I looked out at a landscape of villages and farmhouses whose red-tiled roofs were haphazardly cratered from the shelling of a still-threatening war. There were few cars or tractors visible.

Back in Zagreb, Albright told Croatian President Franjo Tudjman that the last city she saw appearing as devastated as Vukovar was Mogadishu in 1993, and yet, she exclaimed, Vukovar was in the heart of Europe! She told him such atrocities had to be punished and pressed him on the merit of the Yugoslav Tribunal and cooperation with it. Albright stressed the importance, for the peace process, of expunging a sense of collective guilt for such crimes. We would not realize until later, as more information came forth, including archival records unearthed in the *Blaskic* appeals case before the Yugoslav Tribunal,[5] how deeply implicated Tudjman himself was in orchestrating atrocity crimes in Bosnia. The Yugoslav Tribunal prosecutor probably would have indicted him had he lived,[6] but Tudjman died of cancer in December 1999. Albright, knowing what had been decided in the Sit Room earlier, concluded by telling Tudjman, "There are those who talk of sanctions against Croatia. I hope it will not be necessary."

During our visit to the region we visited U.S. Admiral Jeremy Boorda, Commander in Chief, Allied Forces Southern Europe, who exercised additional duties directly tied to the Bosnian war. He shared his own biting criticism of Security Council resolutions and anaemic troop commitments. Boorda claimed that despite his bluster, French General Cot would not approve any air strikes whatever authority might be vested in him. In many instances, Cot could have used Security Council Resolution 836 authority to call in bombers, but he refused to do so. The cruel irony, Boorda said, was that by providing humanitarian assistance, the "allies" were perpetuating the war. He conceded, however, that most of the airdropped assistance got to the people in need and if it stopped, people would starve.

Boorda, a short, handsome fellow built like a boxer, was a highly prescient commander. With Albright and me listening intently, he argued for a theater approach to civilian protection rather than reliance on enclaves.

In his view, NATO was the answer, not UNPROFOR. Anticipating the Dayton Peace Accords almost two years distant, he said the next step had to differ from UNPROFOR and that we must anticipate the worst-case scenario, which in fact turned out to be Srebrenica in July 1995. He believed that the United States should be writing the peace plan, a prediction that bore truth during the summer and fall of 1995. Sadly, Boorda had too much foresight to persuade rigid bureaucracies at home and in the United Nations. He lived to see peace arrive in Bosnia, but on May 16, 1996, he took his own life at his home in Washington, D.C., following questions raised about two Vietnam War combat decorations he had worn on his uniform and despite plausible explanations for them.[7] I mourned the death of one of the most impressive military minds I encountered while in government service.

Albright's travels took her to Bonn, Germany, shortly after the meeting with Boorda. The city was still the capital of Germany as plans proceeded to christen the rebuilt and far more impressive Berlin years later as Germany's government nucleus. Bonn had the postwar occupied look I had grown accustomed to seeing elsewhere in Germany, with American-constructed barracks peppering the city. The long day, starting in Zagreb, was growing late, and the overcast skies of Bonn were gloomy but oddly appropriate for a weary group of American diplomats.

During our early evening meeting with German Foreign Minister  Klaus Kinkel, a youthful, impeccably dressed, slim, and ramrod-seated man, he told us that a crossroads had been reached in the former Yugoslavia. This comment arose from the stalled Owen-Stoltenberg talks. The Germans, he said, aligned themselves with the American attitude, namely, not to weaken the Bosniaks in reaching a solution. But "we seem to be at a point where it is all collapsing. The weakest link in the chain is the Muslims," he said. "They want combat if they can get weapons. I saw [Alija] Izetbegović last week and he is not willing to sign or even seek an agreement anymore. He says, 'Let us wait and overcome the winter.' They are always looking to the United States to save them. But they are disappointed in you!"

Kinkel continued, "I told [Tony] Lake and [Warren] Christopher that the United States must not push the Muslims into a solution that leaves them with an unacceptable situation. But at the same time you need to press them to arrive at a solution, which we need as quickly as possible." He believed there was waning interest in Bosnia among the French and British, and they could soon withdraw from UNPROFOR. (On January 21, British Defense Minister Malcolm Rifkind confirmed that his government had been considering withdrawal from UNPROFOR but not unilaterally.[8]) Their general attitude, Kinkel said, was, "[j]ust let them kill each other." He concluded, "We'd like to see the hand of the United States in this." He did not say what the solution should be, but Kinkel appeared to view the toughest challenge as being Izetbegović and what the Bosniaks would settle for in terms of the final map. I left the meeting pondering what the German foreign minister had intended to convey to us—retreat, intervention, more engagement, none of the above?

Albright did not slow down on the war crimes front. On January 17, while we were in The Hague on the last stop of our European tour, she announced the handover of hundreds of refugee testimonies to the Yugoslav Tribunal. This would only be lead evidence as tribunal investigators would need to re-interview refugees of interest to them for prosecutorial purposes, but more was better than less and there was no time wasting to jump-start the tribunal.

The next day Bosnian Serb and Bosniak negotiators meeting in European Union–sponsored talks in Geneva failed to reach any settlement (to no one's surprise), with each side accusing the other of intransigence. Radovan Karadžić said he would make no more concessions prior to future talks. The Bosniaks pronounced the terms of the Geneva talks as utterly unacceptable. In the ever-changing leadership of the top UNPROFOR command for Bosnia and Croatia, on January 26 French Army General Bertrand de Lapresle was named to replace General Cot. On February 3, the Security Council requested that Croatia, within two weeks, withdraw all of its forces from Bosnia or face possible economic sanctions.[9]

Albright's long European journey, which also included the many newly independent East European states wishing to join NATO through a preparatory procedure called "Partnership for Peace," impressed her in contrast with the spoiler thrashing about in the Balkans. While we heard enthused leaders of other former Communist governments yearning to build upon the strengths of their virgin democratic aspirations and join the Western world of constitutional and capitalist democracies shielded by NATO's military might, the Bosnian conflagration bluntly contradicted and threatened those hopes.

Albright sent a trip memorandum to President Bill Clinton upon our return from Europe that was uncompromising in its view that the war and atrocities had to be ended under U.S. leadership. The future of NATO, of its expansion into Eastern Europe, of the United Nations, and of American leadership in the world was at stake, she argued.[10] Ivo Daalder, who worked on Lake's staff at the NSC, described the turn of the wheel that January: "Tony Lake had separately come to the same conclusions and began an internal NSC review to determine what could be done. At a meeting with the president and his principal foreign policy advisers in late January 1994, a consensus emerged that a more aggressive U.S. approach to the negotiations was necessary, including putting air power in the service of diplomacy. Christopher was asked to translate ideas into a coherent strategy. His paper reflecting input from Lake, Albright, and the new secretary of defense, William Perry, reached Clinton on February 4."[11]

The Christopher memorandum called for U.S. leadership in trying to find a diplomatic solution by both threatening the Serbs with air strikes if Pale refused to negotiate seriously and strengthening the Bosnian negotiating position by forging an alliance between the Bosniaks and Bosnian Croats. In a private cover letter to the president, Christopher pleaded for a new approach: "I am acutely uncomfortable with the passive position we are now in, and believe that now is the time to undertake a new initiative. . . . It is increasingly clear there will likely be no solution to the conflict if the United States does not take the lead in a new diplomatic effort."[12] Albright's trip memorandum doubtless influenced Christopher's newfound boldness.

Sarajevo Ultimatum

Despite the constant ebb and flow of violence that accompanied ethnic cleansing and should have shocked policymakers into more urgent action on any given day of 1992 or 1993, it was the day after Christopher's paper and letter reached the Oval Office that a particularly gruesome attack in Sarajevo reverberated globally and in Washington. On February 5, 1994, a mortar attack on the Markale marketplace in Sarajevo killed more than 60 vendors and shoppers and wounded about 200 other civilians.[13] On a Saturday, the Principals Committee convened within hours after the bombing. Potential air strikes topped the agenda, but new Defense Secretary William Perry strongly objected. Lake put off making any decision and instructed Christopher and Albright to consult with key allies in Europe.

Les Aspin had resigned as Defense Secretary on February 3, 1994, the political price he paid for failing to approve deployment of armored vehicles and gunships to U.S. forces in Mogadishu prior to the debacle there on October 3, 1993. His successor, Dr. William Perry from Stanford University, had been Aspin's Deputy Secretary of Defense and someone I had gotten to know well at the Sit Room table during the past year. He was a renowned engineer and weapons expert and conveyed the wise man aura at the Sit Room table, expressing himself with professorial ease and perfect diction at all times. Perry's deep voice and chiseled face commanded respect. He reminded me of my own father, also a professor with similar physical features who was unflinching in serious discussions. Time and again through to the end of the Bosnian war and the Dayton talks, Perry's presence in the Sit Room was a calming stabilizer injecting logic and often a pathway to agreement among the Principals. Even though Perry and Albright would disagree sometimes, for example on the utility of air strikes, I never heard anyone speak ill of him as a fellow policymaker.

For several months, the opportunity to change the course of history inspired initiatives to negotiate a ceasefire and seek to lift the Serbian siege of Sarajevo, which would be enforced with the threat of NATO air strikes. An American-led negotiation created the joint Muslim-Croat "Federation" in March 1994. A new cabal called the Contact Group, with representatives from the United States, Russia, Britain, France, and Germany, launched into talks in April to create, once again, a map of Bosnia that divided the territory between the Federation (uniting Bosnian Croat and Bosniak ethnicities and territory) and the Bosnian Serbs at 51 and 49 percent, respectively, thus preserving much of the Serbian ethnic cleansing campaign but offering a deal to them to stop the fighting.

The months immediately following the February 5 mortar attack on the Markale marketplace in Sarajevo thus generated a new momentum that seemed to hold promise in the wake of the sheer horror of that particular bombing, the source of which seemed logically to be the Bosnian Serbs laying siege to Sarajevo. Clinton tasked Albright to establish culpability with a U.N. investigation. Radovan Karadžić and other Bosnian Serb leaders were claiming, with hideously concocted excuses, that Bosnian government forces were responsible for the carnage by placing dug-in landmines in the market triggered by a Muslim mortar shell, all for the purpose of unleashing

NATO air strikes.[14] A subsequent trial before the Yugoslav Tribunal found that the bombing was sourced to Bosnian Serb-controlled territory.[15]

The mortar attack inspired a belated but logical response in Washington and European capitals, namely, to rid Sarajevo of the threat of artillery bombardment by creating a demilitarized zone of significant width around the capital city, so that the Bosnian Serbs, who almost completely surrounded Sarajevo, were pushed back far enough to deprive them of the logistical capacity to shell the city either with mortars or other short-range artillery. The French devised a plan that, reaching out from the center of Sarajevo, would impose a 30-kilometer zone free of heavy weapons. But the French also insisted on thousands of combat-ready troops to ensure compliance. Clinton and the Principals were not going to provide those troops. So an alternative "exclusion zone" was devised, which would be a 20-kilometer-wide zone from the center of Sarajevo and require either the withdrawal of heavy weapons or placing such weapons under U.N. control. The alternative would be air strikes to enforce the plan. The mortar attack on February 5 also inspired a final prong of the plan: Any attacks on civilians inside the 20-kilometer exclusion zone would trigger air strikes against the aggressor in retaliation. In reality, that target likely would be the Bosnian Serb forces manning the siege of Sarajevo.[16]

On February 7, European Union foreign ministers called for the use of "all means necessary including the use of airpower" to lift the siege of Sarajevo and begin implementing the Invincible Peace Plan. Two days later the North Atlantic Council approved the plan with issuance of its "Sarajevo ultimatum" and a deadline of February 21 for its conditions, including weapons removal from the new exclusion zone around Sarajevo, to be met. Quickly, on February 10, a ceasefire negotiated by U.N. officials and the Bosnian Serbs and Bosniaks took hold for Sarajevo. But further talks between the warring parties in Geneva recessed inconclusively shortly thereafter.

In Washington, the Deputies met on February 9 to discuss primarily sanctions enforcement against Serbia, but the Sarajevo ultimatum launched the discussion. Frank Wisner, from his Under Secretary perch at the Defense Department, opened fire first. I respected Wisner for the crispness of his views, command of facts, and ability to articulate how the State Department and Pentagon could collaborate rather than lock horns over foreign policy. His shiny bald head, wire-rim glasses, strong but cultured voice, and short, stocky body made an impression at the Sit Room table. His father's reputation as a famous intelligence official of World War II and Cold War fame preceded him. The son, Frank, exhibited considerable worldly experience and lobbed the occasional historical perspective into discussions.

Wisner expressed concern about the Sarajevo ultimatum overshadowing the political track, which the Pentagon was still counting on to achieve peace without resort to U.S. military might. Sandy Berger responded, "We're not talking about bombing the Serbs into a settlement. But NATO's willingness to use force should encourage a settlement." Wisner sought a different emphasis. "The political side is major. Bombing is minor. That should be the right order. A political strategy with military elements is the better approach," he said. Admiral David Jeremiah, Vice Chairman of the Joint Chiefs of Staff and thus their Deputy, echoed Wisner and complained that "the military side is too noisy!" His was a sophisticated military voice at the table, but hardly forward-leaning. While most of us in the Sit Room were relieved, indeed grateful, that NATO had finally stepped up to the plate that day and delivered an ultimatum that could make a real difference on the ground following the bloody mortar attack on Markale, Wisner and his pals at the Pentagon were nervous about threatening force to underpin diplomacy. What else is new? I asked myself.

We turned our attention quickly, however, to sanctions against Serbia, almost as if it could be the counterpunch that fortified the Sarajevo ultimatum as long as no one went soft on enforcing them. The Russians kept trying to reverse gears on sanctions in the Security Council, and our challenge was to hold firm on Resolution 820 of April 1993, which was the flagship sanctions resolution.[17] Allocating federal budget funds to staff up monitoring and other enforcement measures for the sanctions remained a major challenge, leading one Deputy to quip, "We have problems budgeting sanctions enforcement, but seem to have lots of money to fly fighter aircraft all over Bosnia [to enforce the no-fly zone]."

The Deputies examined how to sequence the ending of sanctions against the Serbs with tough conditionality. This was Leon Fuerth's turf within the Principals and Deputies meetings, so he explained the ways to move forward. Fuerth included leveraging sanctions to compel Serb cooperation on atrocity crimes investigations and arrests by the Yugoslav Tribunal, a point Albright was insistent on pressing in these meetings. We considered telling the Europeans that Washington was determined to push sanctions to the final stage and, if necessary, to hit Serbia's banking system and radically clamp down on Serbian business entities abroad. Berger concluded with the view that sanctions-tightening should be sequenced with the diplomatic strategy.

Step one would be to extract from the Europeans full enforcement of the sanctions. That would not prove easy as there were constant suggestions from across the Atlantic that liberalizing the sanctions regime would incentivize Slobodan Milošević to bend in our direction. Indeed, at a February 15 meeting, Charles Redman, a career diplomat who had succeeded Reginald Bartholomew as the new U.S. envoy for the Balkans, thought a peace settlement might be possible but asked if anything could be done to ease the sanctions, to build in clear humanitarian exceptions. Fuerth held firm, though, and argued that to liberalize the sanctions regime only plunged us into "grey areas. It is better to enforce the sanctions resolution with clear authority." In any event, Security Council Resolution 820 expressed the Council's "readiness, after all three Bosnian parties have accepted the peace plan and on the basis of verified evidence, provided by the Secretary-General, that the Bosnian Serb party is cooperating in good faith in effective implementation of the plan, to review all the measures in the present resolution and its other relevant resolutions with a view to gradually lifting them . . ."[18]

Step two would be to force a reasonable bottom line on the Serbs and impress upon them that "the current road only gets steeper." Much would hang on how Resolution 820 would be interpreted so as to avoid having to adopt any new resolution in the Security Council, a step certain to be resisted and probably vetoed by the Russians.

Croatia also was on our minds, as the Deputies had been planning sanctions of some character against Zagreb to curtail its assistance to the Bosnian Croats often fighting the Bosniaks. The prospect of some type of financial sanctions appeared most realistic, and we agreed to approach the European Union to probe the possibilities there.[19] Then, as so often would be the case during the spring of 1994, the Deputies turned their complete attention to the gathering war clouds over North Korea, and the Balkans were left far behind.

Albright appeared on NBC's "Meet the Press" in mid-February and described the "parallel strategy" of "negotiate and strike." "What we are basically doing," she said, "is marrying together the threat of the use of force and the use of force with the diplomatic track."[20] On February 17, the United Kingdom, France, Spain, and Sweden agreed to redeploy more of their UNPROFOR forces to Sarajevo in response to UNPROFOR Commander Michael Rose's appeal to beef up the city's defenses.

The Principals convened in the Sit Room on February 18 to assess the overall situation in Bosnia nine days after the Sarajevo ultimatum. They learned that only 68 of 700 Bosnian Serb heavy weapons facing Sarajevo had been turned into U.N. canton areas. Four hundred Russian troops redeployed from U.N.-protected areas in Croatia to Sarajevo to facilitate Bosnian Serb compliance with the withdrawal of heavy weapons from the 20-kilometer exclusion zone around the city raised some eyebrows about their precise role. Admiral Boorda was working on the logistical challenges of removing the Serb artillery. He also had to finalize target lists to employ in the event of Bosnian Serb noncompliance and determine quickly what, under the dual-key arrangement, UNPROFOR would refuse to approve for air strikes. General Rose appeared determined to make the exclusion zone work without calling in air strikes.

The relatively new Chairman of the Joint Chiefs of Staff, bespectacled and heavily decorated U.S. Army General John Shalikashvili (or "Shali" as colleagues called him) began to convey himself more emphatically in the Sit Room about Bosnia strategy. It is a reality of government service at the highest levels that often one enters a meeting, as in the Sit Room, without really knowing the rich heritage that infuses the personalities at the table. They are simply who they are at that moment— Chairman of the Joint Chiefs of Staff, Secretary of Defense, Attorney General—and the discussion of the day ensues. All I knew about Shali was that he was foreign born (Republic of Georgia) and had masterfully commanded Operation Provide Comfort in northern Iraq following the Gulf War of 1990–1991. Only later would I learn that he was of noble Georgian blood, that he had survived as a refugee child in Warsaw during most of World War II, that his father had first fought against the Germans and then been compelled to fight against the Soviet Army before being transferred to the western front and captured in Normandy after D-Day, and that Shali's family lived in Pappenheim, Germany, for eight years before they moved to Peoria, Illinois. There he learned English (watching a lot of American movies), became a U.S. citizen, and, after graduating from a small college, entered the U.S. Army. Shali fought bravely in Vietnam and scaled the command ladder one hard-earned rung at a time. His Polish accent distinguished him at the Sit Room table, but also gave him an aura of invincibility. When he spoke, he projected the voice of experience and intimate knowledge of how the U.S. Army in particular works.

Shali described to the Principals how the target lists were being drawn up and that if they are contested, it would go up the chain of command to Boutros-Ghali for the United Nations and to Manfred Woerner, NATO's Secretary-General, in order to turn the dual key. The "strike" strategy centered on proportionality, namely, to hit some but not necessarily all of the artillery that had not been removed from the exclusion zone and to minimize any collateral damage. If UNPROFOR balked and refused to turn the key for strikes, Shali wanted to know how we would respond. Albright acknowledged that the United Nations was uncertain whether the redeployed Russian soldiers in fact would help with the weapons removal. The U.N. attitude on air strikes could be summed up: If we have our people (UNPROFOR) on the ground, don't hit us. But she and the French ambassador to the United Nations were "holding Boutros-Ghali's feet to the fire" to approve air strikes if the need arose.

Shali aptly noted that not only Russian peacekeepers were guarding the Bosnian Serb artillery around Sarajevo by that stage. Other UNPROFOR troops were involved in the exercise. There was a Sunday 7 p.m. deadline for the complete weapons pullback. Another Principal noted that French President François Mitterrand had just said that troop contributor capitals, and not their commanders on the ground, should make decisions on whether to participate in air strikes. Shali dryly clarified, "There's a standard NATO procedure" for the air strikes, regardless of Mitterand's views.

LAKE: Will we have go to the United Nations and say you [the United Nations] must go ahead [with the air strikes]?
ALBRIGHT: Boutros-Ghali will rely on Akashi for advice.
SHALIKASHVILI: Once you push Akashi, he gets very tough.
ALBRIGHT: The President should call Boutros-Ghali. [Lake nods in agreement.] I have told Boutros-Ghali that the credibility of the United Nations is at stake.
LAKE: Tell him that the credibility of the U.S./U.N. relationship is at stake.
TARNOFF: Christopher should cable NATO members to keep discipline among them.

There ensued a long discussion about how to include and yet control the Russians on both the UNPROFOR and diplomatic fronts. Lake noted that the Russians did not want to defer to the Sarajevo ultimatum issued by NATO's North Atlantic Council, which was unsurprising as Russia was not under NATO's umbrella. Russian Foreign Minister Andrei Kozyrev would be invited to Washington to smooth the waters.

Our public relations strategy would be unequivocal: The NATO decision stood, and we welcomed apparent progress so far. It was not a Russian initiative, a point we needed to drive home because of those 400 Russian peacekeepers wandering around the outskirts of Sarajevo. It was a NATO decision, and we stood behind the Sarajevo ultimatum. As for any NATO allies who might waver, Christopher emphasized Clinton's earlier point while visiting Brussels: If you don't mean it, don't vote on it. The Principals would blitz the Sunday talk shows: Albright and Shali on CNN's "Late Edition," Christopher on ABC's "Brinkley Show," and Perry (beamed in from Aviano Air Base in Italy) on NBC's "Meet the Press."

David Gergen, with his characteristic common sense reading of the larger picture, advised, "The President has to demonstrate American steadiness—on North Korea, on Japan trade, and on Bosnia." He suggested the Principals look at how American leadership in fact prompted the Russians to come round in Bosnia. There should be a common set of talking points—three or four of them—and everyone should pound away at them. "The President wants two main points in his statement: First, that we spell out our interests. Second, that no one try to define what could be defeat because that is not going to happen." But an astute Perry asked, and closed the meeting, with a question that left some smirking: "So what *are* our interests?"

The Sarajevo ultimatum worked, at least for a while. On February 20, U.N. and NATO officials determined that the Bosnian Serbs had complied with the ultimatum and thus created a heavy weapons–free exclusion zone of 20 kilometers diameter around the center of Sarajevo. The ceasefire was holding there as well. Several key events transpired rapidly: Two days later the Bosniak and Bosnian Croat forces signed a nationwide ceasefire agreement.[21] On February 28, NATO made history with its first combat action when U.S. fighter planes shot down four Bosnian Serb aircraft that had violated the no-fly zone established by the United Nations almost one year earlier and enforced by NATO aircraft.

The Federation

On the first of March a framework agreement to establish a Croat-Muslim Federation in Bosnia was signed in Washington. This had been a high priority for the Clinton administration for months, and the Sarajevo ultimatum presented the opportunity to bring it to closure. Its aim was to compel the end of fighting between the Bosnian Croats and Bosniaks and agree on shared political control of a wide swath of Bosnia under their dominion, including what would be achieved in the ethnic territorial division of the Bosnian nation during negotiations with the Bosnian Serbs in a peace agreement. It was expected that the Federation would give the Bosniaks in particular a stronger hand in such future talks. On March 18, after days of intense negotiations in Vienna and then Washington, the formal deal was signed by Izetbegović, Tudjman, and the president of the so-called Croatian Republic of Herzeg-Bosnia,

 Krešimir Zubak, and became known as the Washington Agreement.[22]

Bringing the Bosnian government to the signing table in Washington was not without its difficulties. Bosnian Foreign Minister Haris Silajdžić met with Albright in Washington on February 25 for a "frank" exchange of views as the Bosniak-Croat talks shifted into high gear:

ALBRIGHT: The United States wants to work with you to create a viable state. I'm always blamed with the expectation that the United States is the cavalry coming, but then it is does not come. The simple reality is that it is not coming! It is very important for you to be realistic and flexible. . . .

SILAJDŽIĆ: We expected democracies to understand the mistake of the arms embargo. We expected more from the United States. The arms embargo hurts the U.S. as well as us. We expect to be able to buy guns and shoot our enemies. If the arms embargo continues, all of this will be irrelevant. The Serbs are attacking cities again today.

ALBRIGHT: The international community has let you down. If we lift unilaterally, then collective agreements on embargoes as a tool will be gone. We can be of assistance at the negotiating table. The diplomatic initiative will accomplish more than shooting your way through. I know it's hard for you to accept this. But help us to help you. The Croat-Muslim entity is a good approach.

SILAJDŽIĆ: We know we must be reasonable, but that has limits. The bottom line is the territorial integrity of Bosnia-Herzegovina. . . . I am confused by Vice President Gore's comparison of Libya and Iraq with Bosnia.

ALBRIGHT: On the contrary, what Gore meant is that if we unilaterally lift the arms embargo, then we would lose support for sanctions against those rogue states. The Vice President did not mean to compare the two situations.

At the time Albright was at the forefront of efforts at the United Nations to impose tough sanctions regimes against both Libya under Momar Gadafi and Iraq under Saddam Hussein. She knew better than anyone else in the Clinton administration what would happen to those efforts to compel both regimes to comply with Security Council enforcement resolutions on disarmament if the United States unilaterally lifted the U.N.-mandated arms embargo of Bosnia. The credibility of our arguments to hold firm against Libya and Iraq, particularly with Russia and China and even with the Europeans, would be severely undercut.

A "Semi-Roll" in Bosnia

On March 8, the Principals reviewed the situation unfolding in Bosnia following two weeks of Serb compliance with the Sarajevo ultimatum. Lake and Albright were absent, so Berger chaired the meeting while Rick Inderfurth occupied Albright's chair and I sat behind him. Perry claimed we were on a "semi-roll" in Bosnia. The Bosnia-Croat ceasefire was holding, there was NATO resolve, and General Rose was demonstrating considerable vigor on the ground. Perry believed the United States should do what it could to stoke the momentum. The British were considering more troops for UNPROFOR. Shalikashvili agreed with Perry on the need for more troops in Bosnia in order to consolidate gains, as long as they were not American troops. But the reality was that the United States was poised to provide troops for the Macedonia peacekeeping operation (UNPREDEP), which aimed to deter any Serb incursions south into Macedonia. If there were to be a permanent peace settlement, then American troops would have to go in to enforce that settlement. By staying out of Bosnia now, he said, we were increasing our chances for congressional support later on for the large deployment that a peace settlement would demand.

Berger placed three caveats on the U.S. commitment to man UNPREDEP. First, Congress would have to be on board with the deployment. Second, we would not do it ourselves; other countries must join us. Third, an American commander must lead the peacekeeping force. In the short term a price would have to be paid on Capitol Hill given the Greek lobby there, always upset over anything done with "FYROM," or the Former Yugoslav Republic of Macedonia, over which Greece claims historical sovereignty. (I use the common reference to "Macedonia," as did the Deputies and Principals, hereafter while accepting that the formal name of the country has been the Former Yugoslav Republic of Macedonia and in 2018 the Republic of Northern Macedonia.) But Strobe Talbott countered, "A smart Republican would have to think hard about opposing this. We have to get people used to the idea that U.S. forces are in the region. Of course there is the possibility that some on the Hill will be irrational about it."

Perry believed the Macedonian deployment would "propel the peace process forward. It is worth the risk of a Congressional debate . . . and should get the British on board with more troops for UNPROFOR. We should not shrink from a Bosnia debate on the Hill right now." Talbott agreed and added that we should not deprive General Rose of what he needed to get a fragile peace. Inderfurth interjected, "If the United States stood still, we would be open to charges of undermining the peace." Fuerth said that Senator Robert Dole, a fierce pro-intervention hawk on Bosnia, "long ago argued for troop deployments in Bosnia. We are doing what he wanted." By that he meant we would deploy to Macedonia and at least show American army boots on the soil of the former Yugoslavia, for starters.

The Principals talked about filling up UNPROFOR ranks with troops from Eastern Europe and those governments seeking to join NATO through the Partnership for Peace program that Albright and Shalikashvili had toured Europe to promote several months earlier. They haggled over how the Pentagon could get reimbursed by the United Nations for airlifting peacekeepers into Bosnia. The Principals debated how to maintain friendly relations with Greece and Turkey over Balkans issues. As recorded by Norman Schindler of the CIA's Interagency Balkan Task Force (BTF):

> The meeting ended with a discussion of US relations with Greece and Turkey and how decisions on Macedonia and Bosnia would impact on both. There was a consensus to emphasize the need to examine all issues together—more US troops to Macedonia, providing KC-135 tankers for Turkey, denying the Turks an opportunity to play in Bosnia—and how this would impact on our relations with Greece and the upcoming Turkish elections. . . . In setting policy priorities, no participant challenged the assertion that priority should be given to managing the crisis in the former Yugoslavia—including

Macedonia—and that resultant problems with the Greeks would just have to be managed.[23]

One week later the Security Council, in Resolution 908,[24] extended UNPROFOR's mandate for six months, authorized 3,700 additional personnel, and approved "all necessary measures" to extend close air support for UNPROFOR troops in Croatia. The Council also approved the reopening of Tuzla's airport in eastern Bosnia for humanitarian assistance flights. On the same day, March 31, Albright and Shalikashvili visited Sarajevo and pledged reconstruction aid and ground troops, provided there was a peace settlement.

The Next Battleground: Goražde

The south Bosnian city of Goražde, one of the United Nations' safe areas, became the next battleground in Bosnia as the Bosnian Serbs shifted their attention away from Sarajevo, protected by the NATO ultimatum of February 9, to other Bosniak communities within Serb-controlled territory. Serb artillery attacks on civilians in Goražde intensified during the first week of April 1994. The Security Council approved a statement on April 6 condemning the Bosnian Serb attacks on Goražde and associated ethnic cleansing operations.[25]

The Principals, without their Deputies, convened in the Sit Room on April 8 to focus on the plight of Goražde and the prospect of air strikes against Bosnian Serb targets. The outcome of that meeting was reflected in how NATO responded on April 10 when two U.S. F-16s launched the first-ever NATO air strike against a ground target (in this case, a Bosnian Serb artillery command facility near Goražde). The next day a second air strike was launched as the Bosnian Serb attacks continued. Albright called the NATO air strike a "picture perfect" operation and that it "should be seen as a signal for the other safe havens."[26] But in retaliation for the air strikes, Bosnian Serb forces detained U.N. and humanitarian aid personnel. They also threatened to shoot down U.S. aircraft.[27]

The Principals, joined by Clinton, met on April 10 to assess the situation. Clinton left early to speak to the press about the first air strike.[28] The two-and-one-half-hour meeting ended with discussion about evacuating Americans from the rapidly unfolding genocide in Rwanda. But most of the meeting focused on Bosnia. The dual key arrangement worked, surprisingly, and General Rose stated "that airpower 'would be turned on again' if Serb attacks continued . . ."[29] The Principals "were divided on whether to seek a Sarajevo-type exclusion zone around the city, or a more limited demand for a Serb withdrawal from recent gains combined with a threat to attack any forces firing on Goražde." No decision on either option was reached in the hope that planned talks between UNPROFOR and the Bosnian Serbs would offer some guidance, but those talks never took place.

Rose's superior, overall UNPROFOR Commander, French General Bertrand de Lapresle, "was less inclined than Rose to approve additional air-strikes against Serb forces. Indeed, de Lapresle seemed to be staking out a position that could lead the Serbs to conclude that they can get away with anything as long as UN personnel are not targeted." The French appeared to be getting cold feet on risky military operations for domestic political reasons. And the Russians were upset with the NATO air attack. Russian Deputy Foreign Minister Vitaly Churkin told U.S. envoy Charles Redman when they met in Belgrade "that the Serb offensive was due in part to Muslim provocations, and suggested that there should also be some Bosnian withdrawals if the Serbs are ordered to retreat from their recent gains."[30]

I joined some of my colleagues who were regulars in Deputies meetings at the time, including Under Secretary of State for Political Affairs Peter Tarnoff, Wisner from Defense, and General Mike Sheehan, who was Director of Operations, J-3, in the Joint Chiefs of Staff, for a Capitol Hill briefing on April 13 about the dire situation in Goražde. The task was complicated by the typical diversity of views among members of Congress. We executive branch officials had to explain why NATO had struck for the first time against a ground target in Bosnia, namely, Bosnian Serb forces attacking Goražde. This had been done without prior consultation with Congress, and tough questions arose about where the authorization for such strikes derived from in the first place. Wisner answered the collective query smartly, emphasizing the urgency of the situation and explaining that it unfolded in dire conditions over a period of less than two hours before the strikes were launched from NATO aircraft.

Wisner summarized the legal case, which I had previously recited in Deputies meetings: U.N. Security Resolution 816 authorized enforcement of the no-fly zone over Bosnia in late March 1993. On April 12, 1993, NATO implemented that no-fly zone. In early June 1993, Security Council Resolution 836 authorized close air support (CAS) and defense of the safe areas. On June 10, NAC met in Athens and supported CAS for UNPROFOR. On June 18, the administration briefed Congress of its intention to provide CAS. In early July 1993, General Shalikashvili enhanced the mission of Deny Flight to provide CAS for UNPROFOR troops. Thus there was "accumulated authority" for the United States to operate under NATO Command and with U.N. Security Council authorization over the skies of Bosnia.

While Sarajevo had been the focus of NATO air support actions, particularly during February 1994, the security of Goražde, held by Bosniak forces, was under severe risk by April 1994. The small number of U.N. monitors deployed there were under direct attack by the Bosnian Serbs. NATO aircraft struck and temporarily stopped the assault. General Rose repeatedly delayed further close air support while negotiations with the Bosnian Serbs in the theater of operations continued. NATO aircraft made supersonic passes, which stopped the Serb shelling at times, only for it to be continued. When NATO bombs finally fell, only one out of four hit their targets. For 24 hours prior to the Hill briefing, no Bosnian Serb shelling had occurred. It appeared that for the moment, the Serb offensive had been halted.

During mid-April the news from Goražde only worsened. The Serbs were executing a pincer movement against the city. There were fears that the safe area was about to fall. We learned that General Rose had sought close air support for UNPROFOR troops in Goražde but that Akashi had denied the request, thus effectively withdrawing CAS from the area. One British peacekeeper had died from Serb gunfire. Indeed, Bosnian Serb militias were taking up positions around Goražde that had been formerly held by Bosniak forces. By April 18, only 12 U.N. monitors remained in Goražde, the Serbs held ICRC workers under house arrest, and 25,000 desperate refugees crowded into the city center. The only thing holding back the Bosnian Serbs was the threat of intensive urban warfare. Rose firmly believed that air strikes, and not just CAS, would be required to save Goražde. One U.N. official told us in Washington, "The town is blowing to bits."

Albright's reaction to this news was firm: There should be no discussion of easing sanctions on Belgrade. We had to respond to the humanitarian situation in Goražde. She supported various air-strike options. Akashi managed to achieve useful agreements with the Bosnian Serbs in following days. But the stakes were mounting. At the Holocaust Museum in Washington, Albright delivered a speech stating, "What we have witnessed in the former Yugoslavia goes beyond war to the brutalization of law and civilization itself."[31]

In rapid order, events unfolded. On April 16, a British fighter aircraft enforcing the no-fly zone over Bosnia was shot down near Goražde as Bosnian Serb fighting intensified. The next day Akashi negotiated a cease-fire for Goražde with Karadžić, who agreed to release detained U.N. personnel and withdraw Bosnian Serb forces from the enclave, although lacking any deadline to do so. Karadžić also rejected any immediate deployment of UNPROFOR troops to Goražde, which he could do as he held the key to them traversing the lines of Bosnian Serb forces surrounding the city.

It was not until May 31, 1994, however, that the Principals met again in the Sit Room to discuss the situation in Bosnia. During the interim, from mid-April until late May, the security of Goražde had been strengthened with decisive actions by NATO and the Security Council. On April 22, NATO threatened air strikes against Bosnian Serb forces unless they halted their attacks on Goražde and withdrew by three kilometers. They also had to pull back their heavy artillery beyond the 20-mile exclusion zone surrounding the city or risk air strikes. NATO then expanded the threat of air strikes in the event of Bosnian Serb violations of any of the exclusion zones around U.N. safe areas in Bosnia. The Security Council seconded NATO's demands for a Bosnian Serb pull-back, calling for a ceasefire and insisting that detained U.N. personnel be released immediately.[32] Akashi negotiated a ceasefire for Goražde with Milošević and the Bosnian Serbs. On April 23, he secured an agreement with the Bosnian Serbs that they would end hostilities in Goražde, withdraw heavy weapons from the 20-kilometer exclusion zone, and guarantee freedom of movement for U.N. and relief personnel. Several days later Akashi concluded an agreement that allowed a British convoy access to Goražde while allowing Bosnian Serb tanks to patrol the exclusion zone under UNPROFOR supervision. On April 26, the Contact Group met for the first time in Sarajevo to try to resume negotiations among the warring parties. They failed.

Contact Group Terms

The Contact Group countries (Britain, Germany, France, Russia, and the United States) reconvened on May 13 in Geneva and agreed to terms for resuming negotiations with the Bosnian Serbs. The Bosnian Serbs would have to agree to a four-month ceasefire; the Contact Group would insist that the Croat-Muslim Federation get 51 percent of Bosnia's territory and that sanctions against Serbia would continue and be eased only if Belgrade cooperated with the search for peace. But a few days later, on May 17, the

French, weary of no tangible progress in the peace negotiations, unilaterally announced their plan to withdraw 2,500 of the 6,900 French soldiers in UNPROFOR over the following six months.

At the Sit Room meeting on May 31, U.S. envoy Charles Redman told the Principals that the Russians were prepared to accept the Contact Group map. But the Bosniaks were not convinced and started with a 58 percent territorial bid, insisting that they needed to "go back to where we live." There were still an estimated 130 to 150 Bosnian Serb troops lurking within the Goražde exclusion zone, and until they vacated that area, the Bosniaks would boycott the Contact Group talks. Christopher reported that Russian Foreign Minister Andrei Kosyrev had told him that morning that he would try to get the Bosnian Serb soldiers moved out. Albright thought a Security Council presidential statement (a nonbinding but consensual statement by the Council powers) on getting the Bosnian Serbs to withdraw from Goražde's exclusion zone would be possible and recommended a push in the Security Council. In her view, it would take a lot of tugging on Washington's part to achieve the 51/49 territorial split with both parties (a view that bore truth at Dayton more than a year later). She, however, was no fan of allocating so much territory to the Bosnian Serbs. She asked, "Why are the Serbs being rewarded [for their ethnic cleansing]?" Lake countered that he thought the 51/49 division of territory was "a very legitimate position for us to take."

"Is the Status Quo So Bad?"

Another lengthy Principals meeting ensued on June 14, 1994. The Bosnian government was insisting on 58 percent of the territory in a peace deal. Its prime minister, Haris Silajdžić, remained deeply concerned that the Contact Group was embracing only 51 percent of territory for the Federation. Christopher urged for the Contact Group to wind up the terms and map-making exercise as soon as possible that week and then schedule a ministerial meeting in June. In his view, our best chance was a map marginally acceptable to Sarajevo. A multilateral lift of the arms embargo remained a very difficult proposition for our allies; London explicitly wanted to maintain the status quo. The French spoke of a period of air strikes at the end of which the arms embargo could be lifted. Christopher wanted to hold the threat of congressional override, namely, to lift the arms embargo unilaterally, in the background. "It has a certain 'go to hell' appeal to it," he noted.

Shalikashvili confirmed that the North Korean nuclear crisis, then bearing down on us, had a real impact on the Bosnian crisis. A Bosnian peace settlement would require taking American troops out of Germany, and then "only to implement a peace agreement." He said it would be "tough to do two regional crises [North Korea and Bosnia] at once," and that some logistics units "might get tied up." Fuerth sardonically mused, "So peace is now our worst-case contingency?"

Christopher rescued Shali from Fuerth's moment of truth. "A multilateral lift of the arms embargo would reach the best result," he said. "But there is real resistance. Things aren't so bad in Bosnia today. The Europeans are telling us not to lift the arms embargo, as doing so would unleash a 'real war.' UNPROFOR would exit Bosnia and more U.N. troops would be killed in the process. So we are back to where we were a year ago. The Russians would have a tough time swallowing NATO air strikes and we need Moscow to pressure the Serbs." Lake countered that NATO strikes would be strictly an effort to bomb the Serbs into settling for peace. Lifting the arms embargo would create a new reality on the ground, one that meant having to fight a war. "The Serbs have put themselves beyond the pale," he said. The embargo would have to be lifted for the Croatians also. And if the Bosnian Serbs started overrunning the Bosniaks, the United States would have to intervene.

Albright disagreed with Lake. "We've done well in the last few months with limited U.S. exposure," she said. Albright was deeply concerned about lifting the arms embargo too soon. Russia's U.N. ambassador, Yuli Vorontsov, was complaining about the risk of igniting a Croat-Serb war. Albright argued for continuing down the path with the potential of air strikes and opting for a strike and lift (rather than lift and strike) policy, with only the potential of lift being considered. Lake countered, "What kind of strikes?" Albright described strikes to force implementation of a peace agreement. "I would bomb them hard, to force a settlement. Ultimately the arms embargo would be lifted."

Shali intervened to explain that the *threat* of strikes works, while strikes themselves actually do not, in his view, achieve the objective. The United States could not strike unilaterally, as all would have to be coordinated through NATO. Many of our NATO allies who were also UNPROFOR troop contributors would object to any unilateral strike option. If UNPROFOR departed, there would be no one on the ground to spot for the unilateral U.S. air strikes. Albright was not suggesting end-running NATO on air strikes, but such was the give and take in the Sit Room. She quickly explained that the air-strike option was much preferable to first lifting the arms embargo, which would stock the Bosnian Serbs with new guns faster than it would the Bosniaks.

Perry backed up Albright, as he was "very disturbed about lifting the arms embargo." He asked how one could possibly bring Britain, France, and Russia on board for a lift. Other alternatives had to be explored first. For example, what about sealing off the Serb-Bosnia border? Fuerth, the Deputies' sanctions expert, said it could be done but only with Milošević's cooperation and verification by a border-monitoring force. Redman said that if a border closing were pursued, it would have to be combined with "something that is a tough fallback [namely, a huge concession on monitoring to Milošević]." Lake said with a grimace, "This would leave too much power in Milošević's hand." Christopher agreed, saying, "It puts us in league with Milošević." Lake added, "Milošević started this conflict years ago, and now we would be in bed with him. I'm underwhelmed."

Tarnoff, as Christopher's "plus-one," spoke from the wall of the Sit Room and steered the discussion back to NATO authorities. He argued for enforcing existing authorities for NATO air strikes. Shali pondered how to execute a reasonable strike at a safe distance from UNPROFOR troops. We would have to strike where there was no fighting, namely, high-value targets still harmful to the Bosnian Serbs. We would have to find some target that UNPROFOR could agree on with us. And the dual-key problem would need to be overcome to achieve any realistic effectiveness. Redman suggested redeploying UNPROFOR troops to reduce their vulnerability. But we still would have to prepare for the worst case under any strike option.

Then the discussion opened up in a surprising way. Christopher proposed using air power to pressure the Bosnian Serbs rather than for strictly self-defense purposes. Redman saw a "new reality" leading to the lift option. We would tell the Bosnian Serbs that the pressure would continue to mount. At some point NATO would be on the Bosniaks' side. But Shali asked, "Is the status quo so bad?" Lake likened the idea to enforcing existing rules so, yes, the status quo worked. Redman countered that neither side was content to sit where they were in Bosnia. We had to offer reasonable chunks of territory in the negotiations. "The status quo may not look as stable as we want," he warned. Lake lamented, "We're stumped." "As we always have been," Perry murmured.

The Principals pondered how we would persuade the Bosniaks to agree to a peace settlement and how to pressure Russia to bring the Bosnian Serbs to the negotiating table. Redman believed the Bosniaks would remember their losses in eastern Bosnia and be unlikely to support a peace deal unless there were serious consequences for violating it. The remedies would include air strikes, lifting of the arms embargo, and closing the border with Serbia. But we needed to determine the purpose of any lifting of the arms embargo and establish how it should be tied to conditions for a peace settlement. Tarnoff wanted the Contact Group countries to work together on applying military pressure and overcoming U.N. impediments to effective action. Christopher said he preferred lifting the arms embargo because "the Serbs are stubborn," but we would have to achieve support for a lift from our allies—no easy task.

Shali returned to the fact that neither side had agreed to the Contact Group map. Lifting the arms embargo would be explosive if there were no prospect for peace; we would risk spreading the conflict to Macedonia, Kosovo, and Albania. Lake replied that if there were no Contact Group map, there would be no ministerial meeting of Contact Group countries and the warring parties to schedule. Shali advised that in light of the North Korean crisis and the need to keep sufficient U.S. forces deployed in South Korea, he questioned how capable the United States could be in implementing a peace agreement in Bosnia, which would require a massive military intervention. "There ain't enough stuff to do it," he bluntly counseled. "We have to think through how muscular we want to be." Lake replied, "Well then, we may argue for lifting the arms embargo." Another voice at the table uttered, "Let's just muddle through."

On June 8 another Band-Aid was applied when the Bosniaks and Bosnian Serbs signed a renewable month-long ceasefire agreement at talks mediated by Akashi and which would take effect on June 10. Two weeks later the Bosnian Parliament elected a cabinet of eleven Muslims and six Croats, who would run both of the ethnic governments of the Federation until broader elections in the fall of 1994. Also around that time the Contact Group met in Paris to deliberate more on the territorial map and incentives to the warring parties. At the end of the month, the Security Council issued a presidential statement expressing its concern with another breakdown in ceasefire talks.[33]

In the Ditch Again

By July the Bosnian Serbs rejected the entire peace effort through the Contact Group, and all slid back into war, atrocities, and hopelessness. The Bosnian Serb forces fired on a U.N.-approved flight leaving the Sarajevo airport in

late July, hitting the plane and wounding its Ukrainian peacekeeper pas-
sengers. Prospects for a workable policy to salvage peace in Bosnia once
again turned utterly bleak. The Clinton administration, long unwilling to
commit to war in Bosnia, continued to navigate this no-win situation with
its European allies, at the United Nations, and in the halls of Congress.

The Principals convened in the Sit Room on July 27 at what was clearly
another crossroads in America's fitful policy on Bosnia. We were in the
ditch again, and no one could find the ladder to liberate weary policymakers from the intractable issues of the Balkans. There were moments
when the persistent power of the U.N. Security Council to determine future steps in Bosnia was lost in the Washington fog of endless strategizing.
The Principals had to bear in mind that the Council controlled the future
of UNPROFOR. Without American troops deployed within the ranks of
UNPROFOR, Washington's influence in guiding actions on the ground
in Bosnia remained minimal. That was the bogeyman Albright had long
before identified to anyone listening.

At this critical Principals meeting, and at the Deputies' and Principals'
gatherings that followed in 1994, the Rubik's Cube that characterized Bosnia remained unsolved. The CIA briefing memorandum predicted: "The meeting is likely to be a frustrating experience. None of the
options is without problems. It will be very difficult to win Contact Group
agreement for truly robust options—options that will really punish the
Serbs and appear to the outside world as decisive action. Indeed, the
Administration senses a public relations disaster in the making as it tries
to stave off Congressional pressure for stronger action."[34]

But into the breach marched the Principals. Albright argued that the
Security Council was frustrated, to put it kindly, with U.N. Secretary-
General Boutros-Ghali. Now would be the time, she said, to obtain Council
approval for close air support for UNPROFOR in its humanitarian mission
without the need for the much-maligned dual-key arrangement requiring
Boutros-Ghali's engagement. Tony Lake conceded what had seemingly become self-evident, namely, that UNPROFOR had to be removed in coming
months in tandem with a multilateral lift of the arms embargo that had
been depriving the Bosniaks of weapons to defend themselves. He and
others in Washington had been evasive about what would happen during
the interim period of a UNPROFOR withdrawal and the point when there
could be a sufficiently armed Bosniak Army to defend Federation territory,
particularly if a unilateral lift of the arms embargo sponsored only by the
United States were achieved.

Shali, speaking softly in his Polish accent but bedecked with sufficient military honors to impress all, predicted that the likely consequence of UNPROFOR's withdrawal would be a halt to humanitarian aid. Once that happened, the world would look to the United States and its full military might to save the civilians of Bosnia. Think about that, he seemed to taunt us.

Lake then flipped several questions onto the Sit Room table: What do we mean by a multilateral lift of the arms embargo? Does it mean we wash our hands of Bosnia? Or would a lift of the arms embargo be part of a commitment to challenge the Bosnian Serbs? What would happen to the eastern enclaves, like Srebrenica? Does this become a real war scenario for the United States and for NATO, in contrast to the flawed humanitarian mission of UNPROFOR? Should we plan for a unilateral lift if the multilateral lift idea once again fails to attract sufficient support in Europe? Should the exclusion zones (which prohibited placement of heavy weapons in designated territories around safe areas) be enforced and extended?

Christopher and Albright pressed for enforcement of the existing exclusion zones and planning for more such zones in Bosnia. They prevailed on that point at the meeting as a matter of planning, although implementing the idea in coming months was another fiasco. Strict enforcement of the exclusion zones ran counter to UNPROFOR's sense of mission and security, not to mention the training of its soldiers, and that was the gridlock that perhaps could be overcome in New York. But how? Could we engage UNPROFOR and its contributor nations if we advocated strict enforcement of the exclusion zones and yet we had no dog in the fight with American soldiers, while our European allies were deployed on the ground at great risk?

Lake cautioned that any multilateral lift of the arms embargo would be a last resort option given Europe's opposition to it. Initially, our negotiators would press hard on Milošević to influence the Bosnian Serbs to stand down. (Milošević manipulated that influence for his own gain exclusively.) We would work with the United Nations on implementing NATO's agreed position on close air support for humanitarian convoys. (U.N. commanders likely would never call on NATO's support.) We would lay down a marker with our allies: If these measures did not work, such failure should lead to a multilateral lift of the arms embargo. (Our allies, however, had no intention of lifting the arms embargo.) If UNPROFOR did not respond to threats to civilians and to its peacekeepers, the Security

Council must order them to do so. (Albright knew achieving that vote was next to impossible.) Another Principals meeting ended with nothing realistic accomplished.

A cable from the U.S. Mission to NATO in Brussels on July 23 cast a reality check on the entire exercise:

GAINING A NAC DECISION TO EXTEND EXCLUSION ZONES AND TO MOVE TO STRICT ENFORCEMENT—ESPECIALLY THE LATTER—WOULD BE MORE DIFFICULT THAN EARLIER NATO DECISIONS ON BOSNIA. SO FAR, NATO'S ENGAGEMENT IN PLANNING HAS HELPED REINFORCE THE EFFORTS OF THE CONTACT GROUP, BUT THIS DEVICE CANNOT IN TIME SUBSTITUE FOR DEALING WITH DIFFERENCES IN THE ALLIANCE ON SPECIFIC STEPS. A POSTIVE NAC DECISION WOULD PROBABLY REQUIRE A REQUEST FROM THE UN, CERTAINLY THE FIRM SUPPORT OF CONTACT GROUP MINISTERS THAT IS REFLECTED IN KEY DELEGATIONS HERE, AND—AT LEAST FOR STRICT ENFORCEMENT— MORE SUPPORT FROM UNPROFOR THAN TIGHTENING OF SANCTIONS AND SHOULD BE PROGRESSIVE—BEGINNING WITH EXTENSION OF EXCLUSION ZONES (1 TO 4) BEFORE MOVING TO STRICT ENFORCEMENT. A SEPERATE [*SIC*] NAC DECISION COULD BE NECESSARY BEFORE MOVING FROM EXTENSION TO ENFORCEMENT. U.S. LEVERAGE ON THE ALLIES COMES LESS FROM CONCERNS THAT THE WAR COULD CONTINUE THAN FROM WORRIES THAT NATO (AND U.S. LEADERSHIP) MIGHT OTHERWISE BE AFFECTED. A U.S. THREAT TO LIFT THE ARMS EMBARGO UNILATERALLY MUST BE CREDIBLE TO BE EFFECTIVE, AND THAT COULD IMPLY WILLINGNESS TO USE AIR POWER. U.S. LEVERAGE OVERALL COULD BE HELPED BY GREATER PRECISION ABOUT OUR MILITARY CONTRIBUTION [NAMELY, TROOPS] TO A PEACE SETTLEMENT.[35]

Bosnian Serb soldiers cut off the main route into Sarajevo to all civilian and commercial traffic on July 27, further strangling the capital city. The next day the Bosnian Serb Assembly rejected the Contact Group peace plan, and, in response, the Contact Group governments tightened sanctions on Serbia.

Several days later, on August 2, the Principals met over the worsening situation in the exclusion zones around Sarajevo and Goražde. Reuters had reported that morning:

> Serbs are flouting U.N. weapons-exclusion zones in Bosnia with brazen regularity, moving tanks and big guns in and out of the areas both to frustrate targetting [*sic*] by NATO jets and to engage Moslem [*sic*] forces.
>
> The presence of heavy weapons within a 20-km (12-mile) radius around U.N. "safe areas" of Sarajevo and Goražde ringed by hostile Serbs should in theory provoke NATO air strikes under a U.N. Security resolution.
>
> But U.N. peacekeepers appear to have decided to tolerate the violations as long as the Serbs do not shoot at civilians and the military balance is not disturbed.
>
> U.N. officers defend their hesitancy to call in NATO air strikes by saying there is no point inviting retaliation against U.N. soldiers for the sake of an anti-aircraft gun.[36]

With such news before the Principals, Perry argued for stricter enforcement against the Bosnian Serb forces, while Christopher and Redman countered that current authorities did not permit stricter enforcement actions. We would have to figure out how to talk to UNPROFOR and its troop contributors to tee up tough enforcement measures, namely, air strikes. The Defense Department and Joint Chiefs of Staff were tasked to draw up a paper on strict enforcement of Sarajevo and Goražde exclusion zones, either with or without UNPROFOR troops present.

Another Principals-only meeting convened on August 10. There was much discussion of the sanctions being employed against Serbia. Tying relaxation of sanctions to cooperation on war crimes issues had long ago failed to attract support from our allies, and it suffered at this meeting. The BTF concluded in the aftermath:

> Only the US seems to favour retaining linkage between cooperation on war crimes and the relaxation of sanctions. The Principals agreed to revise the US position and to insist only that there must be some progress on war crimes before Belgrade can receive funds from international financial institutions and similar benefits. While all deplored the war crimes, the Principals generally felt that linkage

with sanctions could impede a settlement, which was the more important goal. In addition, the tribunal will be issuing indictments this fall which could be interpreted as making progress on war crimes. However, the US will still seek some boilerplate language involving complying with Security Council resolutions which would implicitly mention war crimes.[37]

Albright's fellow Principals had succumbed to the intoxicating presumption that lifting pressure on atrocity crimes accountability and rewarding the Serbs with an easing on sanctions would result in better behavior by Belgrade. As they were excluded, no Deputies witnessed such folly that day.

Other issues included the difficulties in enforcing ceasefire violations in Sarajevo and Goražde with air power and plans for a withdrawal of UNPROFOR. "The military planners believe they can provide close air support in case the units are attacked and air cover while they withdraw." The Principals then agreed that the administration should "speak with one voice on Bosnia. For that reason, officials were advised to seek guidance before handling press queries."[38] I wonder in retrospect at whom this was scolding was aimed. Nonetheless, in my experience trying to find that one voice among the cacophony of proposals, plans, humanitarian catastrophes, and international players sometimes eluded the highest officials.

Will the Arms Embargo Ever Be Lifted?

The Principals straggled back into the Sit Room, now with their Deputies, on August 17. Frustration filled the diplomatic arena as the conflict and humanitarian crisis had only worsened on the ground, and the grand strategy remained adrift. They explored how to enforce sanctions against Serbia, which was arming the Bosnian Serbs, including monitors at the border crossings with Serbia in order to shut down arms trafficking to the Bosnian Serbs. But the toughest issues were the all-too-familiar ones, starting with lifting the arms embargo. Christopher explained the rationale for the lift strategy as one not designed to secure the Contact Group map of Bosnia that validated ethnic cleansing; rather, it would be intended to enable the Bosniaks to defend themselves. Caution signs immediately swept the faces in the room. Then he pulled out his ace of spades. That meant we were seeking a Bosniak military victory over the Bosnian Serbs, for that goal would require a long war, which we were not prepared to contemplate. The question arose, "What are the limits of our support?" The answer: The United States was not prepared to send in military advisers or combat soldiers, but we were prepared to ship in arms and equipment, although some doubted the likelihood of even that gesture of support.

Chastened but not defeated, Lake sought alternative options and, following a pregnant silence in the room, continued: We indeed would support a multilateral lift of the arms embargo, and if that occurred (by some miracle), we would be prepared to provide arms, alone if necessary, to the Bosniaks.

Adding to Sit Room theatrics, Lake's view suddenly turned darker. If a lift of the arms embargo were to be achieved, he believed the Bosnian Serbs would quickly snap up the "safe area" eastern enclaves (Srebrenica, Goražde, and Žepa, in particular) and head straight for Sarajevo, and there would be nothing we could do about that. This was the first hint I heard in the Sit Room that Srebrenica was expendable. It swept over me so quickly I did not fully digest its import, but I should have.

Indeed, our own analysts were advising that air power alone could not save Sarajevo. We would have to be prepared (while conceding the loss of the eastern enclaves) to open up land routes to Sarajevo, an action that would require at least a division of U.S. troops (about 20,000 soldiers). This would be joined with an offensive air campaign to inflict punitive damage on the Bosnian Serbs, including a direct hit on Pale, their nominal capital.

UNPROFOR's Fate

Lake's scenario raised the inevitable issue of UNPROFOR's fate. The national security adviser, recognizing that UNPROFOR was not a combat force, proposed that Washington urge U.N. peacekeepers to stay in position, especially in Sarajevo, to the greatest extent possible. Walter Slocombe, an Under Secretary from the Defense Department sitting in as Perry's deputy, countered that the UNPROFOR contributor nations

all said they would leave if there were a lift on the arms embargo, and, to rub it in, they insisted that the United States help them withdraw! That contrarian outcome—in order to retreat, *invade* Bosnia—would haunt this "UNPROFOR withdraws" proposal to its dying days following the Srebrenica genocide, when military action became much more plausible and UNPROFOR only a sideshow.

Perry interjected that to the extent UNPROFOR troops were present, we would have to coordinate air power with them. Christopher cautioned that we urge UNPROFOR to stay only if they did not inhibit the use of air power and did not get in the way of U.S. actions. This was a surreal suggestion at the time as the European troop-donating nations to UNPROFOR viewed any uninhibited use of air power as a direct threat to the safety of their peacekeepers on the ground.

In his dress whites, Admiral William Owens, the Vice Chairman of the Joint Chiefs of Staff and a highly respected nuclear submariner and intelligent interlocutor at the table, noted that the dilemma cut both ways: We needed UNPROFOR for spotting Bosnian Serb targets, but if the peacekeepers left, they would free up the terrain to actually hit the targets. The ever-restrained British General Rose, commanding UNPROFOR in the field, was warning that air power alone would not save Sarajevo and that two or three divisions would be needed to defend the city. Lake discounted sending in such forces to defend Sarajevo. Skeptical of Rose's assessment, the Principals ordered a study of how air strikes could save Sarajevo. But Lake declared, eleven months prior to the fall of Srebrenica and the genocide of Muslim men and boys, that the administration needed to inform the Bosnian government of the stark reality—*that the eastern enclaves would fall, and would be permitted to fall.* I do not know whether that message was ever explicitly delivered to Sarajevo, but it wedged itself into my mind that day.

Perry returned to the dilemma posed by a continuing UNPROFOR presence on the ground: Air strikes would be less robust because of their presence. If UNPROFOR were to leave, the tactical monitors for targeting would have to be indigenous Bosniaks. Lake speculated about redefining UNPROFOR's mission only to guard the safe areas and Croat-Muslim Federation region, thus largely abandoning their central mandate to facilitate humanitarian aid to civilians, so many of whom were trapped on Serbian-controlled territory. This was madness, I thought, as Lake had no answer to the fate of those destitute survivors of the Serbian ethnic cleansing who would be left out in the cold, literally, as fall turned to winter. We were to endorse a hunkering-down strategy fraught with huge uncertainties other than certain humanitarian catastrophe.

Christopher then warned that his colleagues were engaging in mission creep, the bogeyman of all showstoppers in the Sit Room. Mention "mission creep," and all must freeze in midsentence and pay homage to originalism in Pentagon planning drills. Christopher said that many in Congress thought they were voting for a lift of the arms embargo *and* the departure of UNPROFOR, not lift and replace UNPROFOR with American soldiers. Changing the game plan would require a tremendous educational effort on Capitol Hill. Christopher reminded everyone that when he futilely sought European support for the lift-and-strike option in the spring of 1993, the intent was to launch temporary strikes and not a sustained campaign of strikes to support the long-term defense of the Bosniaks.

Strike and Pray

David Gergen, who had arrived at the White House to help Clinton jack up his public opinion ratings, wondered how we had agreed to let the eastern enclaves fall and not even proffer an argument of self-defense for them. Lake focused on Sarajevo in response, arguing that the capital city could fall if the air-strike option failed to concentrate on *that* city's defense. I sat behind Albright wondering, and writing this down at the time, "Gergen's right—we're not really letting them defend themselves [in the eastern enclaves]. 'Strike and pray' = strike to save Sarajevo, pray for the fate of the eastern enclaves." George Stephanopoulos, a key Clinton aide at that time, said the alternative was American troops on the ground. Lake countered, "Or don't lift [the arms embargo]" and muddle through. Christopher reminded everyone that President Clinton had favored a multilateral lift option for the express purpose of *not* using American ground troops.

Lake returned to his theme of the day: Despite what was discussed only a few weeks earlier in that room, the United States was no longer wedded to defending all exclusion zones and the eastern enclaves. The Bosnian government had to understand this fundamental point. There would be no air support for the eastern enclaves, not even tactical air support. Albright was stunned and exclaimed, "But then we don't have a map [of Bosniak safe areas] anymore!" The special U.S. envoy, Charles Redman, had been invited into this Principals meeting, and he conceded the point, saying it was unrealistic to stay tied to the defense of a map. For those defending their sovereign territory and their homes from ethnic cleansing, Redman's comment was obscene.

Gergen pressed his original point further. If the arms embargo were to be lifted, two weeks later Goražde would fall and thousands would be slaughtered and refugees would stream out of that city. Perry agreed, bluntly predicting that lifting the arms embargo would be "a goddamn catastrophe." Albright observed that Congress had not focused on the stark reality that the United States would lose in any vote in the Security Council on a multilateral lift. Once that fact was recognized, administration officials would have to explain to Congress that a *unilateral* lift would compel U.S. military commitments on the ground and in the air over Bosnia. Albright argued for muddling through and seeking to lift the arms embargo only as a last resort. We first had to play out all options with Milošević, she concluded.

Admiral Owens returned to the central question: If UNPROFOR stayed and the arms embargo was lifted unilaterally or multilaterally, precisely how would that be managed? Perry quickly answered, "Lifting the embargo means the United States enters the war on the side of the Bosnian Government and we would have to start taking action against Serbia." Perry came around to Albright's view—that muddling through would be preferable to what would be required of the United States with any other option. Gergen also agreed, noting that the more we thought through the options, the more we might want to sustain the status quo, *if only to save the eastern enclaves.* But Lake challenged them, arguing that muddling through might be the worst possible option. "I wouldn't want to sell insurance to anyone in Goražde right now," he said. Albright suggested we strategically bomb the Serbs. Lake insisted we arm the Bosniaks. Albright persisted: "If the Bosnian Serbs are increasingly isolated, why not bomb them strategically and coerce them into submission? Let's do it through NATO." (One year later, after the Srebrenica genocide and another Sarajevo marketplace shelling, that is precisely what happened.) Lake resurrected Redman's point that we were no longer wedded to the map, a point that prompted Redman's boss, Warren Christopher, to lean back and quip, "Well, the map is useful historical evidence." Gergen had the last word: "Let's make sure the next report has a scenario of consequences for the eastern enclaves."[39]

It did not take long for the Pentagon to follow up with an assessment that the eastern enclaves could not be saved, and analysts were not even sure about Sarajevo's ultimate fate. We knew that the Bosniaks still sought the lift of the arms embargo but only if the lift was *not* accompanied by a withdrawal of UNPROFOR, despite the fact that the European troop contributors were telling us that UNPROFOR's departure would be the certain result of lifting the arms embargo. Nor did the Bosniaks want the lift if it would lead to the Serbs' conquest of the eastern enclaves—precisely what Washington assumed would happen in the event of a lift! The contradictions kept piling up on the Sit Room table.

Holbrooke Engages

The Principals reconvened on September 13. The tone at the meeting was far more emphatic than in the past. That may have been because Richard Holbrooke, who had just been sworn in that day as the Assistant Secretary of State for European and Canadian Affairs following his stint as U.S. ambassador to Germany, was present. I came to know Holbrooke well during these years and often acted as intermediary between Albright and him, which led to occasional episodes of personality management. The dynamic between the two was challenging because Albright outranked Holbrooke, both as a cabinet officer and as a member of the Principals Committee. I think that must have grated Holbrooke at times. If Albright was busy on another matter, he did not want to wait in order to be put through to her. Sometimes he would instruct me to walk into her office and slip her a note while she was on the phone or meeting with someone else, announcing, "Holbrooke is on hold for you." She would wrap up at her own pace and connect with him on the phone. Albright was the ultimate master of phone diplomacy, and she handled Holbrooke with efficiency and grace while seated calmly at her desk (while I imagined Holbrooke pacing back and forth from wherever he was calling).

Holbrooke was a tall, dark-haired, bespectacled, intellectually sparkling, and imposing man. He also demonstrated a certain informality at times—feet propped up on desks and tables, cutting his nails in front of you, praising and then chiding you in front of your colleagues—that only accentuated his distinction from others. Holbrooke was a diplomat of extraordinary skill and energy who made an enormous difference throughout his career and, in particular, America's policy on Bosnia. He was a bulldog who bulldozed his way toward solutions.

Rather than create or perpetuate the problem, which many in public service do to lazily bolster their power and influence, Holbrooke always tried to solve the problem. In that respect, Albright and Holbrooke shared a common denominator, and they often succeeded, in their different ways, to reach the end posts. As with Albright, I admired that trait in Holbrooke and knew that when he engaged, he focused on the end game of conquering whatever policy puzzle stymied others. His inability to focus long on his counterpart's eyes during a conversation and his impatience with conventional or unimaginative thinking could be condescending, but his brilliance and limitless diplomatic drive made up for the "living with Holbrooke" phenomenon. When he collapsed in a State Department elevator and died shortly thereafter in December 2013 at the age of 69 while trying to navigate the Afghanistan and Pakistan labyrinth for the Obama administration, America lost a diplomat for the ages.

In the Situation Room that September day in 1994 Holbrooke flatly predicted, as the consequence of the lack of a plausible transatlantic policy, that Srebrenica and Žepa "are gone." Lake added, "We all assume the eastern enclaves are gone." Those words rang in my ears for months thereafter and bore truth ten months later as Srebrenica and then Žepa fell. Shalikashvili, seemingly oblivious to Lake's comment, calmly reiterated that he had no idea how NATO would exercise air power if UNPROFOR left, because there would be no ground controllers to spot the targets.

The only way UNPROFOR could leave would be to inject a sizable buffer force to protect them upon their withdrawal, and everyone was looking to the United States to provide those forces. Prior planning had been predicated on a multilateral lift of the arms embargo that would strengthen Bosniak defenses. If that did not occur, the Pentagon's plans would have to be rewritten to contemplate a long-term commitment. Shali said he had always understood that the United States and NATO would use their *air power*, not combat troops, to aid a withdrawing UNPROFOR. Holbrooke countered that the British and French would oppose using air power to punish the Serbs during any withdrawal of UNPROFOR. He said for starters the Muslim women of Srebrenica would prevent a UNPROFOR withdrawal, so forget about using close air support to defend Srebrenica if the British and French held to their views. Holbrooke nonetheless warned of an imminent withdrawal by the French and British peacekeepers under worsening conditions. Shali and Perry insisted on the need to slow down the talk of a UNPROFOR withdrawal.

Clinton had committed to visiting the United Nations on October 15 to seek a multilateral lift of the U.N.-imposed arms embargo. But the Principals balked. As Lake put it, "Even with Albright's genius, chances are slim to get this adopted. We must keep planning an alternative." Perry concluded that the alternative to enforcement of the exclusion zones would be lifting the arms embargo. But Holbrooke warned that the major beneficiary of lifting the arms embargo would be the Bosnian Serbs and that the lift would erase the split between Milošević and Karadžić. Only in the last few days, he said, was Izetbegović understanding the true consequences of a lift of the arms embargo. Albright reminded her colleagues that she was isolated on the lift option in the Security Council.

Lake's memorandum to Clinton the next day explained the pressure tactics that would be waged against the Bosnian Serbs to accept the Contact Group plan:

> Principals agreed we should press forward with our current strategy aimed at maximizing pressure on the Bosnian Serbs to accept the Contact Group proposal. In addition to encouraging Milošević's steps to isolate the Bosnian Serbs with limited sanctions relief, we will make an all-out effort to implement the disincentives agreed earlier by the Contact Group, in particular to carry out air strikes in response to violations of the exclusion zones. This will require pressuring Boutros-Ghali and reluctant allies (especially the UK) to override the objections of the UNPROFOR commanders to any use of air power.
>
> Principals continue to see major risks in lifting the embargo, even if done multilaterally. [Clinton scribbled "again" with his inverted check mark next to this sentence.] They recognized that there may be factors arguing for delay when the October 15 deadline . . . rolls around: Allies and the Russians may argue that more time is needed for other Contact Group measures to play out, and thus oppose a lift resolution in the Security Council in November; and the Bosnians themselves may prefer to wait till spring if there is no way to persuade UNPROFOR to remain after lift. Indeed, the JCS military planners have concluded that the rearmament program and air campaign that must accompany lift could be more effectively pursued if we delayed [lift] for 4–6 months.
>
> Nevertheless, Principals agreed that we had to uphold our commitment to the Congress to act on multilateral lift after October 15, and that the prospect of lift provides important leverage vis-à-vis the Serbs and our Contact Group partners.[40]

On the ground in Sarajevo, events spiraled downward. On September 15, the Bosnian Serbs diverted power from one of the two power lines energizing the city to the Bosnian Serb hub of Pale south of Sarajevo. Both electricity and the water it powers were crippled. Three days later, General Rose threatened the Bosnian Serbs with air strikes after fire fights with Bosniak forces inspired the Bosnian Serbs to lob artillery shells into Sarajevo. Then, on September 22, NATO fighter jets struck a Bosnian Serb tank rolling through the Sarajevo exclusion zone after it attacked a French armored personnel carrier assigned to UNPROFOR.

Alarmed with these and other developments, the Security Council adopted three resolutions on Bosnia that were well intentioned but reminded me of a mouse trapped on a circular treadmill. In Resolution 941, the Council demanded the cessation of violations of international humanitarian law and the ethnic cleansing of Banja Luka, Bijeljina, and other areas, and sought unimpeded access for U.N. and ICRC personnel.[41] The Council adopted Resolution 942 to condemn Bosnian Serbs for refusing to accept the Contact Group plan and resolved to reinforce previous enforcement measures as long as they rejected it.[42] In Resolution 943, as a reward to Milošević for agreeing to close the Serbian border with Bosnia for trade (other than humanitarian food, medicines, and clothing), the Council suspended its sports ban on Serbia and Montenegro.[43] None of these resolutions had much effect for either peace or war in Bosnia.

On September 26, Sweden joined the United Kingdom, France, Russia, Denmark, and Canada in publicly announcing a withdrawal of their respective troops from Bosnia if the U.N. arms embargo were to be lifted. The writing was so firmly on the wall regarding an actual lifting of the arms embargo—that UNPROFOR would abandon the entire war zone— the idea of continued debate over the utility of the lift option became surreal in policy circles. Clinton's plans to seek a multilateral lift after October 15 collapsed, and he never made good on his U.N. venture.

Frustrated, the U.S. Senate passed the Nunn-Mitchell amendment, which required that if the Security Council failed to achieve a multilateral lift of the arms embargo by November 15, no congressionally appropriated funds could be used by the U.S. Navy or otherwise to enforce the existing arms embargo against Bosnia.[44] However, Clinton preempted it on November 10 by announcing that his administration no longer would enforce the arms embargo against the Bosniaks.[45] Albright had spent late October lobbying Security Council members to exempt the Bosniaks from the arms embargo, but the United Kingdom, France, and Russia had refused. Clinton's decision would complicate our diplomacy at the United Nations and with the Contact Group. But his political instincts proved right, as the no-enforcement guidance was sufficient to douse congressional angst for a while.

Meanwhile, the Yugoslav Tribunal finally swung into action on November 7 with its first indictment, which was against Dragan Nikolic, a Bosnian Serb commander of the Sušica detention camp in eastern Bosnia where torture of Bosniak and other non-Serb prisoners was the order of the day under his command. On November 8, a judicial hearing was held in Germany to begin the process of transferring another Bosnian Serb, Duško Tadić, to The Hague, where he ultimately stood trial for crimes against humanity and war crimes. The prosecution of Tadić, who was indicted on February 13, 1995, would prove to be the first trial of the Yugoslav Tribunal, as Nikolic was not captured until April 20, 2000.[46]

Wait and See

Another Principals meeting convened on November 18 to focus on Bosnian Serb attacks and the deteriorating humanitarian situation around the Bihać enclave in northwestern Bosnia. They only agreed to contingency plans in the event the situation worsened with more Serb attacks on civilians or UNPROFOR or the "strangulation" of Bihać. The Balkans Task Force reported, "The Principals also developed a menu of options for more robust action, including establishment of an exclusion zone, use of close air support, airstrikes against radars that 'paint' NATO aircraft over Croatia, hot pursuit of aircraft over Krajina Serb Territory, and striking Udbina airfield [held by the Serbs south of Zagreb]."[47] Nothing requiring action over the skies or on land in Bihać was authorized. A "wait and see" mindset dominated Sit Room deliberations. Bihać's plight was plagued with diplomatic, humanitarian, and military complexities. Albright spoke of the need for more U.S. leadership, that the crisis could not just be dealt with in New York and at NATO. Clinton, Christopher, and Perry would have to weigh in with NATO allies.

Lake agreed with the need to engage Clinton, ultimately with letters from him to Contact Group leaders. Jim Woolsey's successor as the new CIA Director, John Deutch, reeled at the "ghastly consequence" of the Nunn-Mitchell amendment, which would cut off U.S. funding for enforcing the sanctions regime against Serbia if there was no multilateral lift approved by the Security Council. He said, "Any serious person will conclude that multilateral or unilateral lift will involve war." Albright recommended putting the multilateral lift resolution into "blue" at the Security Council, which meant she need not put it to a vote but could reserve the right to call it up with 24 hours' notice. Lake replied, "Go blue!"

NATO aircraft bombed Udbina airfield in Serb-held Croatia territory on November 21, but limited the strikes only to the runway, rendering it temporarily inoperable. The Serbs quickly detained UNPROFOR personnel in retaliation. Clinton appealed to French President François Mitterrand to launch air strikes on local Serb forces around Bihać, but Mitterrand refused, given that French troops manned UNPROFOR there. By November 25, Christopher, Perry, and Lake concurred, a few days prior to the next Principals meeting, that the policy of using air strikes to pressure the Croatian or Bosnian Serbs was dead.

Shattered Proposals

The Principals met on November 28 to survey the field of shattered proposals otherwise known as Bosnia. Albright joined by secure videoconference from New York while I sat at the table in the Sit Room. The familiar terrain of the multilateral lift proposal, unleashing NATO air strikes, and assisting with a withdrawal of UNPROFOR dominated the long discussion. The fate of Bihać hung in the balance as Bosnian Serb forces closed in. Lake summed up the initial musings over the futility of doing anything in the absence of a ceasefire with the Bosnian Serbs by saying the United States could not promise much. In particular, he saw no way to launch strategic bombing to force a Bosnian Serb withdrawal without NATO unity on the policy. The viability of any close air support depended on whether NATO first took out the Bosnian Serbs' anti-aircraft weapons.

Once again, it was David Gergen who made the obvious moral point: "Don't we have an obligation to the people of Bihać? There are U.S. Marines offshore to rescue our own, but not even UNPROFOR's soldiers. Does that make sense?" Christopher reiterated that we had a long-standing commitment to help UNPROFOR, and we could not walk that back now. Lake and Shali clarified, yes, but not with U.S. ground forces! Albright and Lake entered a verbal duel, with Albright trying to maintain the safe areas as demilitarized areas and Lake telling her to stop trumpeting the safe areas—the United Nations failed to protect them. Albright countered, "We have to do something up here [in New York]!" She meant the United States had to step forward with a proposal to ensure the security of the safe areas. Lake poured cold water through the video waves: "What are you prepared to do about it?" She responded sharply, "Tony, don't destroy the United Nations in the process." Lake speculated, I surmised more out of frustration than logic, about allowing the Bosnian Serbs to form some sort of confederation with Serbia. Albright sparred about the fate of Sarajevo and the eastern safe areas. It would have gotten more contentious but for

Perry's intervention, which pointed to an answer, at least for the Principals on that particular day.

Perry said in his professorial tone:

> We need a revitalizing approach to this problem. Our policy has been to contain this war, provide humanitarian aid, limit the violence, enforce the no-fly zone, and ensure that NATO will protect the exclusion zones. We have accomplished little more than limit some of the violence. We have very little leverage to affect Serbian behavior. We are unable to use air strikes as leverage. We are unlikely to force a peace plan, particularly the Contact Group plan. We have two near-term decisions. First, no peace plan works with the unilateral lift and we need to confront the Republicans on the Hill with that reality. Second, we need to repair the damage to NATO. That means assisting UNPROFOR troops if they get into trouble and that any air strikes we launch will be robust, not token in character. They must be credible strikes. This adds up to a muddling through strategy, but there is no alternative.

Despite Perry's common-sense words, the alternative dictating a complete UNPROFOR withdrawal from Bosnia returned to the Sit Room table. Shali attested that it would take eight brigades or two and one-half divisions (about 50,000 soldiers) to safely extricate UNPROFOR from Bosnia with or without Serbian permission. The United States would have to join its NATO allies in achieving any such safe withdrawal with at least two brigades (over 10,000 troops) of U.S. Army soldiers to begin with and attack helicopters. Shali likely understated what Washington eventually would have to commit to the larger extraction force, particularly if other NATO allies did not step forward. It was one of his rare optimistic projections.

"This is no drop-in crisis situation," he cautioned. "It's a planned escort out, permissive or non-permissive. It would take two to three months to get UNPROFOR out of Bosnia." Gergen noted, "Well, those advocating unilateral lift of the arms embargo will have to be prepared to pull the trigger on two brigades of American soldiers." Lake asked the Joint Chiefs of Staff for a paper for Clinton so that he could make a decision on the UNPROFOR withdrawal plan. "[T]he President would be asked to endorse a US offer to put ground forces at NATO's disposal to extricate UNPROFOR personnel in case of emergency."[48] He noted sardonically that if all hell broke loose after American troops covered the withdrawal of

UNPROFOR contingents, they would have saved the British peacekeepers only to bury the Bosniaks. Perry insisted that if NATO proceeded with escorting a UNPROFOR withdrawal, the United States had to lead the effort, including with its own troops. He believed the administration should make an unequivocal, strong statement that we would fight any unilateral lift of the arms embargo. Fuerth wanted to know if Clinton was prepared to veto any bill forcing a unilateral lift, including in a defense bill. Lake was silent.

The end result of the Principals meeting was summarized by the BTF the next day:

> Principals agreed that, in the short-term, US policy should focus on achieving a cease-fire in the Bihać area and Bosnia as a whole. At the same time, the Serbs should be pressured to ensure adequate humanitarian deliveries for the winter months. Principals expressed a desire to continue pursuit of a political settlement and a willingness to offer some concessions to the Bosnian Serbs in an effort to bring them along. These concessions would include a willingness to consider territorial swaps using the Contact Group map as a basis for discussions and—ultimately, but not now—an offer that the Bosnian Serbs could confederate with Serbia.[49]

The latter point reflected Lake's speculation as a "concession" for the Bosnian Serbs, which was not what actually transpired in the Sit Room that day. I heard not a single other voice join in Lake's speculative leap, and thus there was no Principals' conclusion as such. A Serb confederation would have ripped Bosnia and Herzegovina apart as a nation state. It was a remarkably misleading moment in the making of American foreign policy. There seemed to be no means to reverse ethnic cleansing or save the besieged towns and cities across Bosnia. At least the Pentagon would do what it was very good at doing: plan a major operation that no one wanted to see take place. I left the Sit Room that day knowing that we had kicked the can far down the road as winter set in.

With cold winds enveloping Sarajevo, U.N. Secretary-General Boutros-Ghali visited the city for the first and only time during the war on November 30. Albright had called him before the trip to encourage him also to visit Bihać and demand a ceasefire, but he did not heed that advice. Instead, he plunged into Sarajevo only to be met by a loud public protest in the streets. The people of that embattled city had waited a long time for the

United Nations to save them from the Bosnian Serb siege and its resulting humanitarian crisis, but to no avail. Nor had Boutros-Ghali shown much political will to turn the dual key on air strikes against the Bosnian Serbs. Even Karadžić failed to show up for his scheduled meeting with Boutros-Ghali, demonstrating a profound lack of respect for the U.N. leader.

The UNPROFOR withdrawal paper that Perry was tasked to prepare for Clinton, and which would have clearly briefed him about providing assurances to NATO that the United States would commit ground forces for an extraction of the peacekeepers from Bosnia, was abandoned. The CIA reported: "Perry, however, apparently got cold feet on committing US ground troops following a meeting he had with nine key Congressional leaders. As a result, the recommendation was never made to the President and Principals will consider the issue again today [December 2, 1994]."[50]

That consideration, absent any Perry memorandum, indeed took place at a Principals-only meeting on December 2, which "amounted to a brain-storming session on future policy options and the implications of com-mitting US ground forces to help extricate UNPROFOR from Bosnia. President Clinton subsequently decided to provide the allies with a com-mitment, in principle, to provide ground forces 'subject to US approval of the plan and further consultations with Congress.'"[51] Shortly thereafter, administration officials briefed Congress on the president's commitment. "Other aspects of US policy include firm opposition to unilateral lifting of the arms embargo, support for a continued UNPROFOR presence in Bosnia and efforts to achieve a negotiated settlement, and a commitment to multilateral lift if the Serbs refuse to accept a cease-fire and negoti-ations."[52] The desire for sustained UNPROFOR deployment in Bosnia re-flected what the CIA reported was the National Security Council's concern "that political realities would make it difficult for NATO forces to simply stand by and do nothing while on the ground in Bosnia if the Serbs—in response to the UNPROFOR withdrawal and prospect that the arms embargo would be lifted—are in the process of 'strangling' Sarajevo and overrunning the eastern enclaves." America would be in the war then and taking sides. Indeed, "several of the Principals believe that multilateral lift is almost as bad as unilateral lift, and the issue could once again [in the Principals meeting] arise whether the US should abandon multilateral lift now."[53]

In the aftermath of a Principals-only meeting on December 12, Lake wrote a memorandum to Clinton describing how the administra-tion would deal with Congress in coming weeks to garner support for

Clinton's decision "in principle to commit U.S. ground forces to assist in UNPROFOR withdrawal . . ." Lake described how America's allies wanted UNPROFOR to remain in Bosnia, particularly if its withdrawal resulted in a lift of the arms embargo. So U.S. policy ironically would turn toward "increasing UNPROFOR's effectiveness: redeploying or reconfiguring UNPROFOR so that it can better defend itself against Serb attacks; opening a humanitarian corridor from the coast to Sarajevo; and (once again) disabling Serb heavy weapons at collection sites around Sarajevo as a basis for withdrawing UNPROFOR personnel from these vulnerable sites. We will continue to take the position that if, despite our best efforts, UNPROFOR withdrawal cannot be avoided, then our strategy should be to lift the arms embargo multilaterally."[54]

Clinton was facing a Republican-controlled Congress in the wake of the disastrous November 1994 national elections that decimated his Democratic ranks in Congress. The Republicans had been beating the drums for unilateral lift. So the Principals decided to "step up our consultations on Bosnia with the incoming Congressional leadership," with the aim "to build support for our diplomatic approach and to highlight the dangers of unilateral lift—in terms of damaging NATO and making the U.S. solely responsible for the conflict."[55]

In from the Cold

The isolation of the Deputies from Bosnia decision-making for several weeks—ill-conceived punishment for alleged leaking by somebody to the press—finally ended on December 19. Depriving the Principals and the White House of the Deputies' expertise and experience makes little sense and can lead to unnecessary mistakes. Rick Inderfurth sat as Albright's deputy for this meeting as by then I had started a short Christmas break. The Deputies agreed to meet at least once weekly on Bosnia matters. The Defense Department was primed to present options to make UNPROFOR more effective and keep it in Bosnia. But there had been no NATO approval yet to strengthen UNPROFOR beyond some additional equipment. NATO had reached no consensus "in favor of expanding UNPROFOR's mission, or on measures to establish land and air bridges to Sarajevo."[56]

The meeting was unexpectedly dominated by former President Jimmy Carter's ad hoc diplomacy in the region. He called Berger during the Deputies meeting "to report that he had worked out a 'statement of intent' to be signed by Bosnian Serb 'President' Karadžić and Army Commander

Mladić that would endorse negotiations to commence on December 27 and end by January 15, 1995, on a cessation of hostilities to last at least five months. The cessation of hostilities would be used to negotiate a comprehensive settlement using the Contact Group plan 'as the basis for negotiations of all points.' "[57] The Deputies considered the Carter formulation as better than nothing, particularly its bid for a ceasefire, as the negotiations component, we all knew, was a futile gesture.

On December 29, the Bosnian Serb Assembly endorsed the Carter-inspired ceasefire and agreed to negotiations based on the existing Contact Group plan. This was not all that difficult for the Bosnian Serbs to embrace as it was winter and the warring sides typically lay low during the early months of the year. And talking about the Contact Group plan was just that—talking. Two days later, on December 31, Bosniak and Serb officials signed separate texts agreeing to a four-month ceasefire starting on January 1, 1995.

The year ended with an ad hoc American initiative that lured the Bosnian Serbs into an agreement putting off to another day what would really become of Bosnia. "Once the Administration," as Ivo Daalder wrote years later, "decided that NATO was more important than Bosnia and that effective military pressure would no longer be available to influence the course of events there, it was logical to adopt a more flexible negotiating stance—including one that would be seen by many as rewarding the aggressor."[58] Perhaps, but the decisive year of war, atrocities, and peace negotiations was set to begin.

3

To Stay or Not to Stay
January–June 1995

Milošević knows he's not the master of the universe anymore.

BOB FRASURE

To attempt to walk some middle ground between war and withdrawal is a delusion.

JOHN MENZIES

THE STALEMATE IN the war, sealed with former President Jimmy Carter's intervention of late December 1994, lasted well into the next year. But policy meetings continued, indeed at a far more frequent pace for the Deputies. Little did we know at the time that we had entered a tumultuous year that would bring both horror and peace to Bosnia. But the Deputies were under no illusion that heavy diplomatic lifting would be required to prevent an outbreak of hostilities when the Carter ceasefire expired on May 1, as well as manage relations with Slobodan Milošević and the sanctions regime against Serbia, keep Congress briefed and cooperative, meet humanitarian needs through the winter, and steer all parties toward the still illusive permanent peace agreement. And then, of course, there was the Pentagon, NATO, and U.N. planning required to inject tens of thousands of American soldiers and other NATO troops and heavy equipment into Bosnia *if* the decision were finally reached to withdraw UNPROFOR lock, stock, and barrel.

The four-month cessation of hostilities agreement among the warring parties, negotiated by Carter, took effect in early January 1995. The Deputies convened on January 6 in the Sit Room to deliberate various tasks on the Bosnian agenda. The cast and their "plus-ones" in the room would hold fairly firm throughout the year. Sandy Berger chaired as the Deputy National Security Adviser. Aside from the number two officials

The Sit Room: In the Theater of War and Peace. David Scheffer.
© Oxford University Press 2019. Published 2019 by Oxford University Press.

in each of the agencies, who frequently appeared at their assigned seats at the table, key individuals focusing on Bosnia often appeared either in the alternative or as their "plus-ones." Leon Fuerth, the constant participant in Principals and Deputies meetings, and Richard Saunders represented Vice President Al Gore. Peter Tarnoff, the highbrow Under Secretary of State for Political Affairs, and Robert Frasure, a pragmatic career foreign service officer and superb negotiator and tactician on Bosnia, sat for the State Department. Walter Slocombe, Under Secretary of Defense for Policy, was a rather gruff and cautious but brilliant Rhodes scholar and Washington lawyer who weighed in throughout 1995 in the Defense Department's seat, joined by Joseph Kruzel, an incisive and dry-humored Deputy Assistant Secretary of Defense for European and NATO Policy.

Nancy Soderberg, former Ted Kennedy aide and chief of staff for the National Security Council (NSC), often joined from her White House office only a few steps away. Analysts Douglas MacEachin and Norman Schindler reported in from the CIA. Lieutenant General Wesley Clark, a key military participant throughout the year and at Dayton (who would become Supreme Allied Commander of NATO during Bill Clinton's second term), and Brigadier General John Walsh typically represented the Joint Chiefs of Staff (JCS). I continued to represent Madeleine Albright and the U.S. Mission to the United Nations, joined by my colleague, James O'Brien, a lawyer at the State Department who added incisive legal and strategic thinking to Albright's team. Alexander Vershbow, Brigadier General Donald Kerrick, and Bill Danvers—each on secondment from their respective agencies (Vershbow from State and Kerrick and Danvers from the Pentagon)—and Ivo Daalder and Susan Rice often joined the group as National Security Council staffers. Later in the year, Frasure and Kruzel lost their lives on Mount Igman near Sarajevo while on a diplomatic mission with General Clark and Richard Holbrooke.

We agreed to extend the sanctions relief on Serbia for only another 100 days given Serbian President Slobodan Milošević's cooperation with international efforts to pressure the Bosnian Serbs, but such relief would be terminated if Serbian performance deteriorated. The Deputies planned immediate briefings on Capitol Hill regarding the sanctions relief extension and overall Bosnia policy. We discussed how to restart the Contact

Group negotiations, albeit without any workable suggestions. Finally, we wanted to generate a list of surrogates outside of the administration who could speak favorably about Clinton's Bosnia policy.

One week later, the Deputies met for almost two hours to examine several tough issues, including the increasingly precarious situation in Croatia. Admiral William Owens, the Deputy Chairman of the Joint Chiefs of Staff, joined General Clark. Richard Holbrooke, holding forth as Assistant Secretary of State for European and Canadian Affairs, sat with Frasure representing the State Department. The paradoxical plight of UNPROFOR initially seized the Deputies' attention. The new strategy, formulated in late 1994 by the Principals, was to strengthen UNPROFOR's presence in Bosnia so as to avoid injecting a NATO shield to protect the peacekeeping force's withdrawal that would trap American forces in an almost certain widening war. But to embolden UNPROFOR and keep it deployed for at least another year would cost considerable funds, and Congress insisted on reducing the aggregate U.N. peacekeeping bill for the United States.

Not only would the Clinton administration's new push to keep UNPROFOR in the Balkans contradict congressional desires to lift the arms embargo, which everyone claimed would require UNPROFOR's withdrawal (and ultimately reduce Washington's peacekeeping bill at the United Nations), the administration had the gall to request even more peacekeeping funds from Congress to sustain a beefed-up UNPROFOR in Bosnia! UN Secretary-General Boutros Boutros-Ghali appealed for 6,500 more troops for UNPROFOR, which would cost the United States about $60 million of additional funds—money not yet budgeted for fiscal year 1996. "Our credit card has been cancelled," Berger moaned. No one knew where the fresh troops would be recruited, although Defense Secretary William Perry shamelessly asked India to rescue UNPROFOR with its troops.

The Deputies recognized the tension between strengthening and expanding UNPROFOR and controlling the costs of not only that peacekeeping force but others as well. They agreed to address the problem at the next meeting but also keep up diplomatic efforts to bolster UNPROFOR.

Holbrooke pivoted to the Contact Group, which had met the day before in Paris, and his favorite topic: diplomacy. Bosnian President Alija Izetbegović privately reaffirmed the Contact Group plan as a "starting point" for the negotiations with the Bosnian Serbs. There were good prospects that Contact Group officials would visit Pale by the weekend to engage with Bosnian Serb President Radovan Karadžić and General Ratko

Mladić. The diplomats in the Contact Group were still haggling among themselves over whether the Contact Group peace plan must be accepted by the parties for negotiations to commence or whether the talks would be held "on the basis of" the plan. The "acceptance" option was essential for the Bosniaks, and they insisted that the Bosnian Serbs embrace the Contact Group plan first before serious talks begin. Holbrooke and the Germans held firm on "acceptance" in the Paris discussions, while the British wavered. Carter had given up the "acceptance" condition in his letter to Pale, and that did not sit well in Sarajevo or with Holbrooke. Saying, "We cannot abandon this," Holbrooke stressed the 51/49 split of Bosnian territory, and no less for the Bosniaks, must be locked in. If Karadžić really intended to negotiate, Holbrooke said, then he "can work his way out of his semantic box and add the word, 'accept.'"

Berger agreed to hold to "acceptance" as a starting point for the strategy with the Bosnian Serbs. Holbrooke wondered whether Karadžić would feel he had to start giving up land if he agreed to the 51/49 territorial division for the talks. If he did not negotiate, then the split could not be forced upon him. "War would resume in nine to eleven weeks," Holbrooke predicted.

Slocombe proposed that the Deputies backstop the Contact Group negotiations by meeting daily during the talks. If they failed within four months, then we would deal with that failure. We needed to look hard at what the United States was prepared to do substantively and what inducements we would pitch for the negotiations. Berger asked for papers on resuming the Contact Group negotiations and what would happen if they broke down. Land swaps would be required for the 51/49 formula; the Bosniaks would have to accept that the fate of the eastern enclaves would be negotiable; constitutional issues and political arrangements would prove more important than land swaps, but the United States should not take Sarajevo's position on such matters for the time being. "The issue," Berger said, "is how activist we want to be, and how far forward to lean in the talks." Holbrooke added that we needed to know our posture toward the parties, what our role would be in the negotiations, what the issues were, and our attitude on constitutional arrangements and land swaps. He did not believe the Bosniaks actually needed a lifting of the arms embargo, but they needed the prospect of it to trigger support on Capitol Hill and elsewhere.

Berger raised the complex of Croatia issues, which centered on the future, if any, of UNPROFOR on Croatian territory. Croatian President Franjo Tudjman had just informed U.N. Secretary-General Boutros Boutros-Ghali that day of his intention to terminate UNPROFOR's mandate in Croatia when it expired on March 31. Holbrooke quickly jumped in, arguing that we did not want Tudjman to force the withdrawal of UNPROFOR. I knew he meant that such a departure of UNPROFOR would set up a Croatian offensive against Serb forces occupying the so-called Republic of Serbian Krajina and trigger real warfare. Tudjman intended to deliver a prominent speech the following day calling for UNPROFOR's termination. To prevent it, we would have to offer him something.

Holbrooke turned to me and recommended that Albright talk to Kofi Annan, U.N. Under Secretary-General for Peacekeeping Operations, right after our meeting. The U.S. ambassador to Croatia, Peter Galbraith, who happened to be in Washington and attending the Deputies meeting, asked, "Why?" He claimed that the Croatians were frustrated: Serbia had not recognized the government. The economic agreement was not being implemented. There was no political integration in the Serb-held regions. For Tudjman, pulling out UNPROFOR was an essential precondition to launching an armed attack on the Serbs. [Tony] Lake shortly thereafter reported to Clinton that Galbraith believed that "Tudjman has consciously opted for retaking the Krajina by force."[1] I worked for Albright, not Galbraith, and told her it would be a good idea to call Annan.

Galbraith recommended one of two courses at the Deputies meeting: The first one would be "hardball." Our commitment to use sanctions leverage on Belgrade would be contingent on Tudjman pursuing a peaceful course of action in Croatia. We would leverage sanctions relief on Serbian recognition of the Croatian government. The alternative course of action would be to extract from Zagreb what was essential, including a new diplomatic initiative to meet their needs. Galbraith posited that UNPROFOR headquarters remain in Zagreb, that the peacekeepers police the ceasefire in Croatia with a two-kilometer separation zone, that economic confidence-building measures be implemented, that humanitarian convoys to Bihać and Banja Luka be safely undertaken, and that a liaison office in Knin, Croatia, be maintained to facilitate negotiations. Galbraith did not believe all 10,000 UNPROFOR peacekeepers were still needed in the Serb sectors of Croatia. "The ethnic cleansing is done, so UNPROFOR just sits there," he said.

Diplomatically, Galbraith said that Tudjman craved "attention." The United States needed to send a high-level delegation to Europe to discuss the needs of Croatia. The Deputies decided to press for political reintegration of the U.N. Protected Areas (UNPA) in Croatia based on the revised "Zagreb-4 plan," which was a plan principally authored by Galbraith to achieve a peace settlement in Croatia. They agreed not to "threaten to withdraw the President's commitment to link Serbian sanctions relief to progress toward a Krajina settlement, or threaten other punitive steps, at this time."[2] They decided upon a full court diplomatic press with the Croatians to turn the tide in favor of continued UNPROFOR deployment in the U.N. Protected Areas and avoid a fresh war on Croatian territory.[3]

But Holbrooke voiced a raw idea: Why not clean out UNPROFOR from the UNPA (where the Serbs resided) and redeploy them to government-controlled land? That would permit Croatia to wage war against the Serbs and push them out of Serbia since U.N. peacekeepers would be redeployed elsewhere.

Admiral Owens stressed that the safety of UNPROFOR troops remain paramount: either they were withdrawn from Croatia or radically redeployed. Berger agreed that it would be a "profound mistake" to put the UNPROFOR troops at risk; he instructed that work be done on redeploying them if that became the final decision. Clinton had no interest in lifting sanctions on Serbia while Krajina remained unresolved. Tudjman needed to be told not to deliver any UNPROFOR withdrawal speech. But if he went ahead with it, Tudjman must not close the door to semi-withdrawals or redeployments of UNPROFOR.

In Lake's memorandum to Clinton describing the Deputies meeting, he wrote in the final paragraph: "We will continue to press the Croatians to reverse course, and we will need to consider rolling back aspects of our bilateral relationship to signal our opposition to Tudjman's high-risk gambit. Tudjman needs to know that his brinksmanship will not be cost-free and that this integration into the West is in jeopardy. This said, we need to be careful not to drive Tudjman into an unholy alliance with Milošević to carve up Bosnia. Thus we will proceed with ongoing plans to accelerate diplomatic efforts aimed at a settlement that reintegrates the Krajina while providing substantial autonomy for the Serbs." Clinton scribbled a note on the Lake memorandum: "I think we have to be *very* careful with last paragraph—let's discuss Monday."[4] The idea that our policy would be aimed at "providing substantial autonomy for the Serbs," thus to some extent validating their ethnic cleansing of parts of Croatia, had not been presented to the Deputies and would have triggered

Albright's keen interest, if not objection. Perhaps Clinton was signaling his concern about that particular point and also any outcome that would carve up Bosnia.

The Lake memorandum also contained an assessment by the intelligence community that proved wrong. Lake wrote, "Our Ambassador [to Croatia Peter Galbraith] believes Tudjman has consciously opted for retaking the Krajina by force. The intelligence community, however, believes the chances of success are low—particularly if Milošević's forces intervene in support of the Krajina Serbs, as they are likely to do."[5] In fact, Tudjman unleashed Croatian Army forces into the Krajina six months later, in early August 1995; "Operation Storm," though controversial in its execution and leading to prosecutions before the Yugoslav Tribunal, proved successful in routing the Serbs and retaking Croatian territory. Milošević did not deploy any Serb forces to save his own people in Krajina or elsewhere in Croatia as they fled east to Serbia for refuge.

Croatia on Our Minds

Despite our efforts to the contrary, Tudjman announced his denial of any extension for UNPROFOR in Croatia when its deployment expired on March 31, 1995. On January 25, the Deputies convened on Bosnia and Croatia issues. Joseph S. Nye, Jr., the Assistant Secretary of Defense for International Security Affairs and my professor at Harvard decades earlier, represented the Defense Department. Gordon Adams, a budget whiz from the White House Office of Management and Budget, made a rare appearance. The lagging prospect for resuming Contact Group talks with the warring parties attracted little more than a request to keep all of the Deputies informed of daily developments in that sphere. The more significant focus of the meeting proved to be managing UNPROFOR's future in both Croatia and Bosnia.

Berger set out the three primary objectives of American policy that day:

First, expand UNPROFOR troop support in Bosnia. Second, press for redefinition of UNPROFOR's mandate in Croatia. Third, the United Nations should take a hard look at how UNPROFOR peacekeepers were deployed in the Balkans. I stressed Albright's need to consult with the U.N. Secretariat to manage this agenda, for without their active cooperation we would be dead in the water. Lieutenant General Wesley Clark suggested she persuade her U.N. colleagues that "[t]his is about our resolve to strengthen UNPROFOR, not fold our hands."

Berger proposed redeployments of UNPROFOR troops from Croatia to Bosnia to achieve a ramp-up of 6,500 additional peacekeepers there. That would save U.S. appropriators some money, but the State Department still would need to seek a supplemental appropriation to cover more personnel and equipment for UNPROFOR. U.S. policy backed UNPROFOR staying in Croatia, but Nye added the caveat, "with a scaled-down mandate." After both Tarnoff and Frasure reviewed precisely how UNPROFOR could be scaled down in Croatia and built up in Bosnia, they would advise Albright on lines of advocacy in New York. Clark was tasked to develop talking points for the Hill on why we were supporting a buildup of UNPROFOR in Bosnia, even if the additional 6,500 peacekeepers were not drawn from UNPROFOR's 14,000 soldiers in Croatia. Tarnoff had the job of developing options for how to finance the gambit. Berger emphasized that the ball was in State's court to reconfigure UNPROFOR and launch a new diplomatic initiative to prevent a UNPROFOR withdrawal from Croatia, not to mention Bosnia.

I reported that the United Nations believed the threat assessment for UNPROFOR withdrawal from Croatia was the same as for withdrawal from Bosnia. With Tudjman's deadline of March 31 for the termination of UNPROFOR's mandate in Croatia now seemingly set in stone, we would have to decide if we could commit to a withdrawal with NATO troops protecting UNPROFOR's flank. The Bosnia scenario repeated itself for Croatia, leading policymakers to press for UNPROFOR remaining in the two-nation theater so as to avoid the necessity of a NATO (and largely U.S.) extraction force of tens of thousands of soldiers to protect UNPROFOR's withdrawal. Berger mollified the grim-faced Deputies with the observation, "It's doubtful you would need a large NATO force for withdrawal from Croatia, compared to Bosnia, particularly if we secured Tudjman's request for or consent to the NATO deployment." Clark agreed to undertake a fresh threat assessment for UNPROFOR withdrawal, but he doubted there would be much to distinguish the threat posed in either country.

Berger said the entire strategy would be a hard sell on Capitol Hill, where Congress would see U.S. soldiers entering Croatia simply to enable Tudjman to go to war once UNPROFOR departed. Fuerth argued that we persuade Tudjman to accept a scaled-back UNPROFOR presence to monitor ceasefire lines in Croatia. Of course, if Tudjman were determined to push the Serbs out of Croatia, Fuerth's proposal would fall on deaf ears.

We knew in the Sit Room that obtaining Croatian support for maintaining UNPROFOR in the country had become very slim. This did not mean we necessarily envisaged a heated-up war to drive out the Serbs as an imminent probability, but the prospect of such a campaign by Tudjman generated a resigned sense of support, however shallow, for a continued UNPROFOR presence.

Bosnian Prime Minister Haris Silajdžić, a Bosniak, was in town, and Nye wanted to steer him in the right direction. He suggested letting Congress work on Silajdžić a bit and deflate his expectations about what Congress would support and fund. The objective should be for Silajdžić to gain a more realistic sense of the perils of a unilateral lift of the arms embargo and balance that with private assurances that the United States stood behind the Bosniaks in the Contact Group negotiations.[6]

The Deputies meeting on February 2 included Holbrooke, Deputy Secretary of Defense John Deutch, Gordon Adams of the White Office of Management and Budget, and, representing the Joint Chiefs of Staff, Lieutenant General Daniel Christman. Adams's presence emphasized how the administration's Balkans policy had become a major budgetary challenge with Congress. Susan Rice, who covered U.N. peacekeeping issues on the NSC staff, and in the Obama administration would become the U.S. Permanent Representative to the United Nations and then national security adviser, joined her colleagues Vershbow and Kerrick. The meeting centered on two issues. The first was whether Serbia would be pressed to diplomatically recognize only Croatia or also Bosnia. Recognizing Croatia would lessen the possibility of a direct military conflict between Serbia and Croatia over the fate of the U.N. Protected Areas and such Serb-dominated regions as Krajina.

Holbrooke believed that Milošević and Tudjman should be given full rein to mutually recognize each other's government. If they tied the knot, then we could take up the next task of persuading Milošević and Izetbegović to recognize each other. Tarnoff quipped, "There goes Bosnia." Holbrooke: "I don't agree." Another voice in the room believed that if there were only a Tudjman and Milošević recognition exercise, without the support of the Muslim Croat Federation, then that act would "kill Bosnia," as it would leave the Bosniaks isolated and Bosnia wide open for territorial grabs by Serbia and Croatia. Holbrooke responded, "Then we need to petition Tudjman not to make any deal that carves up Bosnia." Fuerth said any such dual recognition, lacking Bosnia, would cripple sanctions enforcement against Serbia.

Holbrooke broadened the discussion, saying, "We don't want Milošević to intervene if there's war with Krajina. If he intervenes in Krajina, it will be a whopping war that will spread to Albania and Macedonia." He continued, "The value of bilateral recognition of Croatia and Serbia is the best shot we have to keep Serbia out of the Krajina war. So don't insist on Milošević recognizing Bosnia as well." But Tarnoff disagreed: "Don't concede that. We have to hang very tough on triple recognition." Croatia, Serbia, and Bosnia had to be pressed to recognize each other, actions that would blunt military answers to their mutual problems. Berger sought a strategy on triple recognition. Tarnoff suggested that as part of a Serbia-Croatia mutual recognition, the military would have to commit to sealing the border between Serb-led Krajina and Serbia. Berger instructed that Secretary of State Warren Christopher write to the Contact Group ministers to enlist their support in pursuing triple recognition, which, he surmised, could lead to a suspension of sanctions against Serbia. However, the Serbs assumed they would get an autonomous Krajina and had not expected a sealed border. So it would not be easy.

Berger wanted to know where matters would stand by April. He posited three requirements and a question: First, the United States must decide that it would participate if necessary were UNPROFOR to withdraw from Croatia. The Principals also would have to weigh in. Second, NATO planning for protecting any withdrawal must be well advanced. Third, we would need to deploy 800 communications personnel soon to various locations in Croatia and a decision to that effect must be made. Finally, would Tudjman agree to a reconfiguration of UNPROFOR on Croatian soil and thus sustain the peacekeepers' presence there?

Slocombe posited that Tudjman would not change his decision to terminate the UNPROFOR mandate. If the United Nations asked to use UNPROFOR in Croatia in order to support UNPROFOR's operations in Bosnia, Tudjman probably would consent. So far, Tudjman had only agreed to some U.N. observers remaining in Croatia. When presented with five elements of a scaled-back mandate for UNPROFOR, Tudjman had equivocated. Slocombe said Tudjman set the end of July as the target window for full withdrawal of UNPROFOR from Croatia. (Tudjman probably had in mind Operation Storm, which would commence in August 1995 to recover Serb-controlled territory in Croatia.)

John Deutch, who had been the Pentagon's Deputy in the Sit Room since March 1994, weighed in. Deutch was a tall chemist and professor from the Massachusetts Institute of Technology, who had a dry wit and

disarming personality. Like Les Aspin, he was a bit sloppy with papers bulging out of his briefcase but knew the programs and budget of the Department of Defense with remarkable clarity. I always found him pleasant to converse with and knew he was close to Clinton.

Deutch argued that the United States, in response to a major NATO tasking, would have to participate with its troops in getting UNPROFOR out of Croatia or Bosnia. The planning would have to start immediately. These determined efforts would be tough to explain on Capitol Hill. Berger stressed finding out what the United Nations was planning for a UNPROFOR withdrawal, as U.N. officials had not determined exactly what type of NATO assistance would be required in Croatia. Berger wondered whether the United Nations was going to seek a quick reaction combat force in a nonpermissive environment or ground forces for a more conventional escort operation undertaken with the consent of all parties. Deutch noted, "We have to assume war and plan for it." Wesley Clark believed that NATO would have to agree to commence discussions with Croatian officials about prepositioning NATO troops in the country. Fuerth asked what would happen if war broke out in Croatia and we were pulling UNPROFOR out of Bosnia. No one chose to answer that question. Berger said the Deputies must present a plan to the Principals with a strategy for a UNPROFOR withdrawal mandate and how NATO would plan for it, including the American role.

The Deputies turned to the second major issue: how to augment UNPROFOR in Bosnia while UNPROFOR left Croatia. Deutch asked why UNPROFOR's strength in Bosnia had to be bolstered. Holbrooke answered, "We have to support augmentation if we are to prevent UNPROFOR withdrawal [from Bosnia], because they need strengthening." Slocombe added, "But it's also to change the way UNPROFOR does business, to toughen up its method of operation. We are not, however, changing its mandate." Clark jumped in by saying the intent was to have enough forces to create a more robust presence. The British and French sought to increase UNPROFOR forces for the sole purpose of protecting UNPROFOR's withdrawal from Bosnia.

Berger was visibly agitated and instructed Clark to explore what all of this really meant. What did the United Nations want and why? I nodded to Clark, signaling I would help him by contacting Albright to get the U.S.

Mission to the United Nations (USUN) on top of the issue. Clark would need to report back on U.N. intentions, objectives, rationale, and operational impact.[7] Berger then looked around the table and instructed Fuerth to configure a new sanctions relief package to entice Milošević to recognize both Croatia and Bosnia. He instructed Tarnoff to prepare a diplomatic strategy for triple recognition and include options for recognizing Slovenia and Macedonia as well, thus further isolating Karadžić.

What should Washington's response be if Milošević recognized only Croatia? Tarnoff and Clark would seek ways to keep UNPROFOR deployed in theater, determine how to handle Tudjman prior to the March 31 expiration date for UNPROFOR in Croatia, work out a refined mandate for and minimize risks to UNPROFOR, and draft decision points for UNPROFOR's complete or partial withdrawal from Croatia. Clark had the additional tasking of further military planning for UNPROFOR's withdrawal from *both* Croatia and Bosnia. The most immediate task would be to prepare a recommendation to the Principals on U.S. participation, in principle, in any NATO operation that would support UNPROFOR withdrawal from Croatia, including immediate contingency planning.[8] The Joint Chiefs of Staff proposed deploying U.S. troops only "if events on the ground require it (as opposed to deployment from the outset to assist the entire withdrawal)."[9]

By early February, the Principals and the Deputies essentially had given up on achieving a negotiated settlement between the Bosnian Serbs and the Muslim Croat Federation. Carter's ceasefire deal was not inspiring any real movement toward a permanent peace. The Contact Group was bust, having achieved almost nothing as the presumptive conductor of the whole process. So a different tact emerged in Washington. The CIA's Interagency Balkan Task Force (BTF) was skeptical following the February 2 Deputies meeting, where we had focused on a "triple recognition" initiative with Milošević as a means to miraculously smother war aims with newly erected official diplomatic relations among the warring parties. Contact Group members agreed to try this initiative and to offer Milošević significant sanctions relief if he played ball.

But the BTF balked: "We believe it unlikely that Milošević will extend meaningful recognition to Croatia, and there have not even been any hints that he would recognize Bosnia. At the same time, Milošević will not want to appear obstinate to the international community and—as was the case in his agreement to close the inter-Serbian border—may seek to manipulate the recognition issue to his advantage." The BTF, however, repeated its flawed projection of Milošević's willingness to assist the Krajina Serbs: "Recognition would do nothing to resolve the Krajina issue, and Zagreb's ultimate failure to achieve an agreement with the Krajina Serbs on autonomy could be used by Belgrade as an excuse to intervene if fighting breaks out."[10]

The BTF contested the assessments of some, perhaps a majority, of the Deputies in recent meetings. The intelligence team disagreed, correctly, with the "likelihood that renewed fighting in Croatia inevitably would spill over into Kosovo and Macedonia." That did not happen in August 1995 in the aftermath of Operation Storm. But they misjudged the "likelihood that fighting will begin in Croatia before the cease-fire collapses in Bosnia." In fact, the war erupted again in Bosnia once the Carter cease-fire lapsed on March 31. The Srebrenica genocide occurred weeks before Operation Storm commenced in Croatia in early August. Finally, the BTF shot down the view that "Macedonia is a 'tinderbox' and deployment of additional NATO troops is necessary to ensure stability." They wrote, "We agree that Macedonia has problems, but they are economic and ethnic— not the sort that NATO troops can help with. . . . [D]eployment of additional NATO troops—a pet project of Secretary Perry—would not help anything and could actually create problems by raising concerns among Serb ultranationalists in Serbia at a time when Milošević is trying to appear more forthcoming on recognition issues."[11]

Mutual Recognition

The Principals met alone in the Sit Room on February 7. I did not record any debriefing from Albright about the meeting, which was normal as the discussion was supposed to remain secret at the time even from the Deputies. But the NSC "Summary of Conclusions" reported that the Principals agreed on the mutual recognition strategy as "a positive step toward resolving the Balkans conflict, although not a panacea." They clearly were pinning their hopes on a highly problematic strategy that would not impress the Bosnian Serbs or Tudjman, both of whom had clear military objectives underway for 1995. The French were proposing an international conference to achieve triple recognition, and the Principals tasked Christopher to shape the conference agenda and make clear conditions for American support and participation.

The Principals authorized discussions with Contact Group partners to ease sanctions on Belgrade in exchange for implementation of mutual recognition. They decided to keep pressing "Croatia to retain at least a reduced UNPROFOR presence" but to plan for UNPROFOR withdrawal as had been requested by Tudjman. That meant prepositioning communications personnel and equipment in Croatia to guide NATO's assistance for the withdrawal. They agreed for this Phase I task for both Croatia and Bosnia, as UNPROFOR could withdraw from either or there could be the challenge of implementing a peace agreement that would require NATO deployments. The United States "would inform NATO Military Authorities of the forces the U.S. would provide to an UNPROFOR withdrawal operation from Bosnia, while reaffirming that their actual deployment would be contingent on a final review of the plans and consultations with Congress."[12]

One further decision on Croatia emerged from the Principals meeting. "They agreed to recommend to the President that he authorize U.S. participation in a NATO operation to support UNPROFOR withdrawal from Croatia should it become necessary." This would parallel Clinton's earlier decision, in principle, "to commit U.S. ground forces to a NATO operation supporting UNPROFOR withdrawal from Bosnia." Nonetheless, the Principals also "discussed efforts at the United Nations to strengthen UNPROFOR in Bosnia." Keeping UNPROFOR in Bosnia remained their first priority. But they "discussed a longer-term strategy in the event diplomacy fails to achieve a negotiated settlement and UNPROFOR withdraws from Bosnia and Croatia." They were interested in trying to contain any such renewed fighting, "with special emphasis on strengthening forces in Macedonia to deter expansion of the war."[13] The focus on Macedonia proved less important than the Principals thought at the time, and it caused them to misdirect their attention. Strengthening the safe areas in Bosnia, like Srebrenica and Žepa, would have been a more useful exercise.

Six days later the Principals sat alone again in the Sit Room and dug deeply into the bogeyman of mutual recognition. They saw it as the only option left standing to prevent more war. The Bosnian Serb Assembly again had rejected the Contact Group peace plan. It also decided to prohibit unauthorized contacts between Bosnian Serb individuals or groups with the Contact Group in order to block those who might favor the plan. The BTF had "no indications that Milošević is serious about recognizing Croatia," and continued "to be concerned about the implications of suspending sanctions. . . . [W]e think it will be difficult to get the front-line states to reimpose sanctions, contributors to the monitoring regime will be reluctant to keep their monitors deployed along Serbia's borders with its neighbors, and the suspension would provide an irreversible benefit to the Serbian economy in terms of money and goods." To add a new uncertainty, the BTF was trying to determine the veracity of a potential Serbian violation of the sanctions regime following helicopter flights across the "inter-Serbian border" to the Srebrenica region.[14] The "inter-Serbian border" terminology, I thought at the time, was an odd way to describe the border between the nation of Bosnia and Herzegovina and the nation of Serbia.

Despite Albright's reticence over playing the sanctions card too loosely, the Principals plunged headfirst into sanctions relief for Milošević, agreeing to "a total suspension of sanctions on [Serbia] in return for mutual recognition," albeit subject to a host of conditions:

— that Milošević's recognition of Croatia, Bosnia, Macedonia, and Slovenia in their internationally recognized borders be genuine and unequivocal;
— that sanctions be suspended for 2-month periods, with a positive vote by the UN Security Council required to renew each time;
— that the sanctions enforcement regime against [Serbia] remain in place, so that sanctions can be reimposed on short notice;
— that the "outer wall" of sanctions be kept in place, in other words, measures going beyond U.N. Security Council resolutions: no assistance from the International Financial Institutions or the European Union; no granting of a U.N. seat to [Serbia]; and no readmission to the Organization of Security and Cooperation in Europe (the United States would not recognize [Serbia] at this time);
— that there be a significant toughening up of the monitoring regime on the Bosnia/Serbia and Croatia/Serbia borders, including several hundred more monitors plus equipment such as radars to help deal with the helicopter problem;
— that there be continued firm adherence by Milošević to the Contact Group plan for Bosnia;
— that Milošević endorse the principles in the Zagreb-4 peace plan for Croatia, namely the reintegration of the occupied areas under Croatian sovereignty, with autonomy for historically Serb-majority areas;
— that nothing be done to in any way affect the commitment to the International Criminal Tribunal for the former Yugoslavia;
— that before the United States pursues Milošević's recognition of Croatia, we insist that Tudjman agree to extend UNPROFOR's mandate in return for recognition;

- that the sanctions relief not go into effect until after the "inter-Serbian border" is more tightly closed and the Europeans have deployed the additional monitors required; and
- that we secure Tudjman's agreement to terminate economic relations with the Krajina Serbs, since this could undermine the effects of Milošević's cut-off of support to the Krajina and permit the Bosnian Serbs to receive support through the back door.[15]

Among these many conditions, only a few were left standing as ongoing ventures after the mutual recognition initiative collapsed soon thereafter. These were the sanctions enforcement regime, the "outer wall" of sanctions, and the commitment to the Yugoslav Tribunal, all of which Albright had pressed hard to sustain. Anticipating the possibility (indeed high probability) of failure, the Principals "directed our Contact Group representative to put down a marker that, if this initiative fails and the war resumes, our partners will reciprocate our flexibility by supporting the kinds of coercive measures against the Bosnian Serbs that they agreed to previously but never implemented. We would not, however, make their commitment to such measures a quid pro quo."[16] Those measures likely centered on more air strikes, enforced exclusion zones, and unchallenged humanitarian access.

The unraveling of the grand plan for mutual recognition became evident later in February. Milošević reacted negatively to what had morphed into the revised Contact Group proposal guided by the Principals' conditions from February 13. The BTF reported, "Milošević refused even to receive the Contact Group probably because he was offered only suspension rather than complete lifting of sanctions. Reportedly the French and British are furious, and the Russians will try to convince Milošević to meet with the Contact Group. . . . While Milošević could be posturing in an effort to get even more, the chances of war erupting in Croatia are growing."[17]

The Principals met in the Sit Room on February 21 for a depressing review of the situation. There were unconfirmed reports of violations of the no-fly zone by helicopters and fixed-wing aircraft that NATO had the responsibility to enforce under U.N. Security Council mandate. It was embarrassing for NATO to have these reports tossed around when the evidence of such violations was lacking. The Principals requested that NATO correct the public record but also provide detailed documentation of recent activity and remind everyone of NATO procedures to enforce the no-fly zone.[18]

With intransigence particularly evident in Belgrade, the Principals took any sweetening of the sanctions relief off the table. But they decided not to add Serbian cooperation with the Yugoslav Tribunal "as an additional condition for sanctions relief in the context of mutual recognition." This was a setback for standing firm on tribunal compliance. The Principals "agreed, however, that further relief from the 'outer wall' of sanctions would still be subject to many additional conditions including cooperation with the War Crimes Tribunal." That became important in subsequent months and years of hard bargaining with Milošević, as the outer wall was the final hurdle to fully returning to the international community.

Anticipating a failure in achieving a negotiated settlement, the Principals tasked the Deputies to "undertake a review of potential scenarios to frame policy choices likely to be faced in the next 2–3 months." Curiously, Milošević had requested a one-time meeting with New Mexico Congressman Bill Richardson, who would become the next American ambassador to the United Nations and then Secretary of Energy during

Clinton's second term. Richardson, who became New Mexico's governor in 2003, had established a reputation for ad hoc diplomatic encounters with dictators and "strong men" holding Americans hostage or otherwise being very difficult adversaries. But the Principals opposed the request, "as Milošević already has direct high-level access to the U.S. Government."[19] That access included Robert Frasure, the State Department's point man with Milošević, and Holbrooke, Frasure's boss. So Richardson did not get the chance to spin his magic with Milošević.

The Deputies convened in the Sit Room on February 22 for a lengthy discussion about the flagging mutual recognition initiative (dubbed "Plan B") and military planning for UNPROFOR's future. Frasure reported that Russia's foreign minister, Andrei Kozyrev, had no luck persuading Milošević to meet with the Contact Group. The British, French, and Germans were flying into Belgrade anyway the next day to knock on Milošević's door. Berger, backed by the Deputies, said Milošević should understand that the sanctions relief deal would not be on the table forever. The European team needed to plant the seed of uncertainty in his mind.

Frasure reported that the diplomacy on Plan B, mutual recognition, was going nowhere. Milošević was not prepared to settle on the terms, as he "had been deceptively positive about Plan B because he wanted to have discussions with the US."[20] If we offered to permanently lift sanctions, then maybe Milošević would come around. But, Frasure argued, we should not offer this because "[w]e have to assume war will break out in Croatia and then Bosnia." He suggested "old-fashioned Western consultations with a mixture of containment, UNPROFOR withdrawal, and diplomatic disengagement threatened." But the Deputies should not offer Milošević any more carrots. "We don't want to get caught in Milošević spin," he said. Frasure said the Russians still were unenthusiastic about Plan B, and emphasized again that Milošević might "go to the negotiating table if sanctions were lifted in advance."[21] The mood at the Sit Room table dipped considerably. "Deputies agreed that prospects for success were low for achieving mutual recognition in exchange for sanctions relief."[22]

What Are the Options?

The Principals had spoken at their February 21 meeting about a bottom-up review of Bosnia and what the options could be for the next four to five months. They tasked the Deputies to get it done. What would be the three or four most likely situations to evolve in coming months? What are U.S. objectives? Berger speculated those objectives would be minimizing the number of U.S. personnel on the ground, maintaining NATO cohesion on Bosnia, containing the war, and providing humanitarian relief. But Berger noted the paradox that if the goal was to minimize or prevent any deployment of American soldiers, that would contradict any commitment to assist with a UNPROFOR withdrawal, which would require large numbers of U.S. troops. I pressed a further objective of U.S. policy: to ensure accountability for the war crimes in Bosnia.

Fuerth pondered our basic strategic options, namely, whether to beef up UNPROFOR with more robust rules of engagement or to eject UNPROFOR and slide in a multilateral lift of the arms embargo afterward. Frasure, returning to the challenge of Croatia, called for a tough approach to Tudjman in order to keep UNPROFOR deployed there, with a redefined mandate. Another possibility, he said, could be a different organization, like the Organization for Security and Cooperation in Europe (OSCE), taking up monitoring duties if UNPROFOR withdrew. The Deputies "directed that a strategy be promptly developed [by State] that outlines how to deal with Tudjman in the run-up to the March 31 UNPROFOR mandate expiration and steps that can be taken to retain an international force of some type as a deterrent to renewed fighting."[23] We still hung onto the hope that Tudjman could be persuaded to retain UNPROFOR in some fashion on Croatian territory.

Berger "raised the need to explore strategic options, such as beefing up UNPROFOR with more robust engagement rules or withdrawing UNPROFOR and moving towards multilateral lift."[24] The Deputies would have to develop a systematic way to look at a range of options over 60 to 90 days, including how to manage Congress on lift options. And we would have to analyze the survivability of the Contact Group as a viable negotiating body with the warring parties.

Tarnoff warned that Croatia had to be dealt with quickly and could not wait for the bottom-up review. Frasure again stressed the need to reverse Tudjman on the fate of UNPROFOR. Slocombe questioned whether a UNPROFOR withdrawal from Croatia would have any impact on the fighting, as it had been so ineffective in Bosnia. What were the American interests and how should we prioritize them? That, of course, was the constant question before the Deputies throughout every discussion we had about any topic. But Slocombe was right to place it on the table again. Berger targeted the next week to produce what the Principals had requested. The assumption had to be that the Contact Group process had exhausted itself (although we awaited the next day's hoped-for encounter in Belgrade with Milošević).

UNPROFOR Paradox

The second part of the meeting about augmenting UNPROFOR presented the usual paradox of talking one moment about augmentation and the other moment of withdrawal. Both options remained very much alive. Lieutenant General Christman, sitting in the Joint Chiefs of Staff chair, reported relatively mundane details of what UNPROFOR had approved from NATO's initial offer of assistance to strengthen its capabilities in the field: transport helicopters, night-vision goggles, over-snow vehicles, heavy engineering and construction equipment, and 128 more personnel for U.N. monitoring duties. The Deputies approved the JCS list. But given the uncertainty of UNPROFOR's future, they "deferred decision on more robust options until the policy options review [was] completed."[25]

Attention focused on what would be needed for a UNPROFOR departure from Croatia occurring before the peacekeeping force left Bosnia— a reversal of fortune now that Tudjman appeared to have Krajina in his sights. General Wesley Clark spoke of an integrated plan, or "audible" plan "that would be flexible enough to allow either Bosnia only withdrawal, Croatia only, or both missions."[26] Deutch promised an operational plan by March 1 and a tactical plan by the end of March that anticipated either Croatia or Bosnia being the first to eject UNPROFOR. But then he dropped the proverbial bomb: The cost of the audible plan would be between $1.3 billion and $1.9 billion to execute, the lion's share of which the United States would have to shoulder. Congress surely would balk, I thought. We would have to seek a large supplemental appropriation to cover the UNPROFOR extraction bill, and that is never an easy task.

Berger reminded everyone that Clinton had not yet made a firm decision about American assistance for UNPROFOR's withdrawal from Croatia. It would be foolish to brief Congress until Clinton had at least decided on the plan in principle. Deutch suggested scheduling time with Clinton in order to consult directly with him. Frasure feared that if NATO entered Croatia to help UNPROFOR leave, Tudjman would next request that NATO stay to secure his borders![27] Clark noted the "absolute necessity" of prepositioning 130 NATO troops in Croatia soon to prepare for a UNPROFOR withdrawal, so that they were deployed at least two weeks before departure began. Once the decision was made, Clark would need 72 hours to deploy the troops.

But there was push-back from others at the table. "Tarnoff was concerned that prepositioning impacts negatively on efforts to get Tudjman to change his mind since he'll believe NATO now accepts the withdrawal as irrevocable. Kerrick suggested that State urge other Contact Group states to push delay of prepositioning in the [North Atlantic Council (NAC)]. On prepositioning Deutch remarked he is nervous because of the message it sends the allies, especially given that the President has not yet decided whether to promise US ground troops to withdraw from Croatia. He thought this decision needs to await an evaluation of our overall Croatia strategy."[28]

The next day I joined an inter-agency working group meeting on UNPROFOR, along with several colleagues from Deputies meetings. At that time UNPROFOR had a total of 38,000 troops in Bosnia and Croatia. We talked about deploying part of a main NATO force to cover the departure of UNPROFOR from Bosnia in early April. Indeed, Albright had recommended that morning that a contingent of NATO forces be deployed due to the risk of hostility once the ceasefire ended in Bosnia on March 31. The estimated 70,000 soldiers required for the NATO extraction force actually would include about 13,000 troops drawn from European soldiers already deployed in UNPROFOR. So that would leave about 57,000 troops needed to march into Bosnia, an imposing number to everyone. We were told that of the $1.3 billion to $1.9 billion cost of covering UNPROFOR's withdrawal, the United States would have to pay more than $1 billion of the total amount. The United States already was in arrears on its U.N. assessment for UNPROFOR to the tune of $280 million, of which $34 million was owed to NATO countries for their deployments. An additional $220 million would be charged to the U.S. Treasury soon to cover outstanding UNPROFOR costs. Add it all up and the bill for Washington was astronomical. Any supplemental bill likely could not be acted upon quickly enough to cover a rapid deployment. Clark warned that the United States could not delay prepositioning NATO troops just because we had not figured out how to pay for it. The risks were too great in the region.

I departed Washington in late February 1995 as deputy head of the U.S. delegation to the first round of U.N. talks in New York on establishing a permanent international criminal court. James O'Brien, a State Department lawyer and my trusted colleague in Albright's Washington office who joined me at many Deputies meetings, took the USUN chair on February 28 for a discussion that mostly teed up position papers for review at a March 2 meeting. The Deputies focused on trying to turn Tudjman around on UNPROFOR. "They requested that the State strategy paper be expanded to include a list of incentives and disincentives designed to obtain a positive decision from President Tudjman on retaining UNPROFOR or a similar force. . . . Deputies asked that the disincentives include specific areas of U.S. and European assistance that we might threaten to suspend if Tudjman refuses to retain UNPROFOR in the separation zone, as well as possible carrots to induce his cooperation."[29]

But while trying to forestall a UNPROFOR withdrawal from Croatia, for starters, the Deputies once again continued planning for "prepositioning NATO communications assets to support a NATO-led operation to withdraw UNPROFOR from Bosnia and/or Croatia." About 100 U.S. personnel would be required for the prepositioning contingent in Croatia.[30] They decided to present the Principals with two options on the most immediate priority of prepositioning NATO forces in the two countries. "Option One would authorize U.S. support for prepositioning now as a precautionary move without prejudice to possible future decisions regarding

UNPROFOR withdrawal, U.S. participation, and the funding for such actions. Option Two would defer a decision on prepositioning until the military operational plan is reviewed and Congressional authorization and funding have been obtained."[31] Both options left open any commitment to actual NATO, and thus American, deployment to cover UNPROFOR withdrawal from either country.

The next Deputies meeting, on March 2, which I was back in Washington to attend, included the three most powerful State Department players other than Secretary Christopher, namely, Strobe Talbott, Tarnoff, and Holbrooke. Holbrooke was flying off to meet with Tudjman in a few days, so the Deputies devised a strategy to persuade Tudjman to reverse his decision to terminate the UNPROFOR mandate at the end of March. "They agreed that retention of [UNPROFOR] interpositional forces along the confrontation line is vital to prevent renewed fighting between the Croatian and Krajina Serb forces. The price for retention of the interpositional force for Tudjman may be agreeing to demand for [NATO] forces along Croatia's border with Bosnia, but it is not clear we can support a border force and American participation would be very difficult. If Tudjman is willing to agree to the interpositional force, Deputies agreed that Ambassador Holbrooke should only offer to discuss a possible border force with Allies."[32]

The raw prospect of a UNPROFOR withdrawal from either Croatia or Bosnia still hung over the Deputies, and they agreed to present to the Principals for decision whether and how to preposition NATO communications assets to support a NATO-led operation to extract the peacekeepers.[33] The National Security Council had drafted a paper entitled, "Former Yugoslavia Policy Review," dated February 27, 1995, in which it identified four policy options, all of which the BTF deemed "undesirable":

- Continue our present policy of muddling through;
- Adopt a policy of neutrality and focus on active containment;
- Apply a policy of containment and undertake a long-term quarantine of Greater Serbia, as we did with the USSR; and
- Increase US commitment to the Bosnian Government; apply military pressure to compel Serb acceptance of a settlement.[34]

The next step would be for the Principals on the next day, March 3, to react to the Deputies' strategy and plot Holbrooke's forthcoming meeting with Tudjman. "They approved the overall approach set forth in the State

Department paper and draft talking points: on the one hand, a tough message insisting that Tudjman allow interpositional forces to remain in the separation zone between Croatian and Krajina Serb forces, and raising the prospect of punitive measures if Tudjman remains intransigent; on the other hand, an understanding of his difficult political environment and a willingness to work with him on a new mandate for a force to replace UNPROFOR."[35]

Tudjman's demand for peacekeeping forces or observers along Croatia's international border was a nonstarter for the Principals, who insisted there would be no U.S. troops contributed to any such force. They feared that any such deployment would commit U.S. forces to defending Croatia in the event Milošević (or even the Bosniaks) decided to attack. Coyly, the Principals authorized Holbrooke to address the issue if Tudjman agreed to retain the interpositional force in the separation zone. But he could do so only by saying he was ready to take up the proposal with U.S. allies and yet not leave any impression that NATO would embrace such a mission on Croatia's international borders.

Perhaps Tudjman would compromise on UNPROFOR if promised a visit to Washington to celebrate the one-year anniversary of the Bosniak-Croat Federation. The Deputies had recommended this, and the Principals agreed, provided Holbrooke would convey the Deputies' conditions "that the minimum requirement for such a visit would be a three-month extension of UNPROFOR's mandate and Tudjman's agreement to retain interpositional forces as part of any UNPROFOR successor force."[36]

Finally, the Principals took up the persistent issue of NATO pre-positioning of communications personnel at least in Croatia to prepare for a UNPROFOR withdrawal from either Bosnia or Croatia. They decided to recommend to Clinton that he support NATO's decision to deploy such personnel, but added a caveat that there be prior consultations with Congress. The Principals shortly thereafter decided to delay this recommendation for a week. They also "agreed that, in the Congressional consultations, we would characterize this as a limited, precautionary move that is being taken without prejudice to a possible future decision to deploy U.S. forces as part of a NATO-led withdrawal of UNPROFOR." The painful task of obtaining congressional approval of the necessary funding for a NATO intervention would condition any decision for Washington's support.

In Lake's memorandum to Clinton on March 6 reflecting the Principals' decisions, he described the tensions associated with "Step Two" of the prepositioning exercise. On the one hand, prepositioning was vital to follow if there were to be on actual NATO shield for a UNPROFOR withdrawal. It was a "put your money where your mouth is" moment in our Balkans policy. NATO's Step One, initiated in February 1995, had been to establish "an enhanced theater communications system," the setting up of which did not involve any U.S. forces. But Step Two required deployment of about 450 U.S. military personnel, including 320 to government-controlled areas of Croatia, among a total of nearly 1,800 NATO personnel. UNPROFOR could not start withdrawing with any sense of order until about eight weeks after the prepositioning occurred, so delaying a decision, according to General John Shalikashvili, would put Allied forces at risk.

Describing why support for Step Two would be necessary, Lake also conceded how awful the entire exercise could become. While it would signal U.S. leadership in NATO, Step Two

> could set in motion a series of events leading to UNPROFOR's withdrawal [the whole point of the prepositioning exercise!] and renewed fighting, with NATO and U.S. forces left on the ground to deal with the aftermath. . . . Emboldened by NATO and U.S. forces in Croatia, Tudjman could become even more intransigent on accepting an UNPROFOR successor force. This could move us closer to an actual commitment of ground forces for a large-scale operation to extract UNPROFOR, the exact dimensions of which will remain unknown until the plan is completed in about two weeks. . . . If they withdraw, renewed fighting is a certainty and the wider war we feared will have been facilitated by NATO's deployment into Croatia. While we anticipate a subsequent NAC decision will be taken to deploy the forces into Croatia, with each incremental step, it becomes more unlikely that our decision will be reversible. In fact, if NATO decides to conduct the operation, large-scale U.S. participation is inevitable.[37]

If that skepticism were not enough to muddy Clinton's thinking about next steps, Lake described the cynical attitude of some of America's allies in Europe about the whole prepositioning bid. France strongly objected and joined with other allies in believing the move would undermine efforts to change Tudjman's mind on UNPROFOR's future, signaling that NATO was preparing anyway for a UNPROFOR withdrawal. A wider war would ensue as the arms embargo might be lifted and air strikes would intensify. "Allies prefer to keep UNPROFOR in place and muddle through."[38]

Since actual deployment of the prepositioning personnel still would require a decision by NAC, Lake recommended approval so that "the U.S. not be seen as obstructing NATO military planning needed to reduce the risks to Allied forces." He recommended that Congress be consulted first before informing NATO of Clinton's decision.

Clinton approved Lake's recommendation to support Step Two subject to congressional consultations and a subsequent NAC and Principals' decision before there would be actual deployment of U.S. forces. But it is no wonder he wrote "discuss" next to his characteristic inverted check mark of approval. Clinton was struggling with a "damned if you and damned if you don't" dilemma, one that even White House Chief of Staff John Podesta pointed out with pros and cons in a cover memorandum to the president. Podesta wrote, "While recognizing the real risks, NSC Principals recommend approval of U.S. participation in Step Two. Leon [Fuerth] and George [Stephanopoulos] concur, though George is concerned that this might trigger a War Powers debate." Clinton scribbled, "Tony, I want to revisit when the VP returns fm trip—visit w/ Tudjman. BC."[39]

The day before the next Deputies meeting on March 9, the BTF reported that Holbrooke believed he had "won Tudjman's agreement to a continued international presence that would include forces in the separation zone and along Croatia's border with Bosnia and Serbia." The BTF also speculated that the Deputies would "consider how to respond to Milošević's counterproposal on recognition of Bosnia and Croatia, which would include complete lifting of sanctions against Serbia in exchange for endorsement of the Contact Group plan by all parties and continuing negotiations aimed at a Bosnian union comprised of the Croat-Muslim federation and an independent Serb entity, both whom could confederate with their neighbors." This would be a "diplomatic nonstarter," of course, as it would mean the Bosnian Serbs not only had ethnically cleansed sought-after territory in Bosnia, but would "confederate" that seized territory with Serbia, whatever that meant (although surely a Greater Serbian nation). They would have won the war outright. Milošević presumably was saying all of this with a straight face to Holbrooke.[40]

Albright sat in the Deputies seat on March 9. Tarnoff, Holbrooke, and Frasure represented State again, and Deutch and Slocombe sat for the Defense Department, while Admiral William Owens joined for the Joint Chiefs of Staff. I sensed that Albright wanted to influence the process so that Holbrooke, with his bulldozer personality, would not run away with it. Though they were friends and respected each other, they also were competitors in the shaping of the Balkans policy. There needed to be a cabinet-level counter-weight to Holbrooke in the Sit Room, and Albright served that role.

Holbrooke's agreement with Tudjman for a new international presence in Croatia seized the Deputies' attention. "In welcoming the agreement, Deputies noted the discrepancy between Tudjman's expectations of the force controlling Croatia's international borders and what Allies will likely support." More work was required to understand which principal allies would constitute "control" of the border as understood in the agreement. There had been extremely negative views in Washington and among allies until then about any NATO presence along Croatia's borders with Bosnia and Serbia. Nonetheless, planning would proceed with a meeting of Vice President Gore and Tudjman in Copenhagen on March 12 to finalize the agreement and prepare for a possible meeting among Clinton, Tudjman, and Izetbegović on March 16 to celebrate the one-year anniversary of the Federation. But any visit by Tudjman to Washington depended on the Holbrooke agreement being finalized and announced in advance.

The "Deputies agreed that Ambassador Albright should wait until after the agreement has been announced before circulating a draft UN Security Council resolution that would establish the mandate of the new UN force. They agreed, however, that she should preview the main elements to Contact Group counterparts."[41] Much rode, then, on the Holbrooke-Tudjman agreement being successfully concluded.

On March 12, Tudjman announced his endorsement of the agreement reached with Holbrooke earlier in the month. The agreement included a new mandate for a U.N. peacekeeping force, one that would be called the U.N. Force in Croatia (UNFIC). The BTF wrote, "In addition to probable difficulties in defining UNFIC's role in 'controlling' or 'monitoring' crossing points, some troops contributors will insist on a unified command for all of the former Yugoslavia, and it may be difficult to develop a force of sufficient size if Croatia insists that only Western troops be included. The withdrawal of significant numbers of UN troops as UNPROFOR transforms itself may be accompanied by increased skirmishing between the two sides."[42]

Another Policy Milestone

The March 17 Principals-only meeting was one of the most significant of the entire war. The preparation for it had been extensive, with production of policy reviews of considerable depth and importance for the future of American policy. On February 27, the National Security Council had circulated a "Former Yugoslavia Policy Review," and on March 16, the Principals received an "Update for Principals" paper from the NSC staff. On the same day, the BTF summarized the NSC paper as one noting "that earlier discussions revealed a consensus against taking more forceful measures to support the Bosnian Muslims or to punish the Bosnian Serbs and Serbians. [NSC's] Vershbow raises the concern, however, that the favored and more limited 'muddle through' containment policy might not work given the Muslim determination to fight and inevitable Congressional pressure to lift the arms embargo once the war escalates and the CNN factor sets in. The key area of contention remains whether the US should continue the present policy of supporting the Muslims (State position), or shift to a more neutral position and urge the Muslims to scale back their expectations for a political settlement (DoD position)."[43]

The NSC update paper, though noting that Tudjman's March 12 announcement had reduced chances of renewed war in Croatia, predicted that "an escalation of the war in Bosnia remains likely as the end of the cessation of hostilities approaches with no movement on the diplomatic track." Tudjman and Gore had "agreed to work on the mandate for a new UN peacekeeping force in Croatia."[44] The NSC paper offered a sober assessment of the current situation:

> The ceasefire is already showing signs of unraveling and both sides seem confident of success in a new round of fighting. Silajdžić has declared that the Bosnian Government will not extend the ceasefire beyond April 30 and that Western emphasis on containment amounts to an unacceptable attempt to freeze the status quo. Milošević's response to the offer of sanctions relief for mutual recognition has been utterly inadequate and Serbian enforcement of the border closure with Bosnia has fallen off markedly since the second 100-day period began in January. The Contact Group is on its last legs and advocates of a lifting of the arms embargo are beginning to stir in both houses of Congress.[45]

The broad strategic choices summarized by the NSC, and which agency supported which one, offered little hope for a satisfactory outcome for U.S. interests:

(1) Stick with the present policy: continue to support Bosnians rhetorically, continue diplomatic efforts with reduced expectations of success, focus on containment. (State favored this position.)

(2) Shift to a policy of neutrality regarding terms of settlement and active containment of the conflict; end or suspend Contact Group activities; acknowledge we cannot produce a better deal for the Bosnians. (DoD favored this position.)

(3) Containment of conflict and long-term quarantine of Greater Serbia, including reinforced sanctions on Belgrade for the long haul. (No Deputy favored this position.)

(4) Renewed push for military measures in support of Bosnians: withdraw UNPROFOR, multilateral lift and strike. (No Deputy favored this position.)[46]

Vershbow saw options 1 and 2 as making "prevention of a new war and containment, rather than achieving a political settlement, our priority goal. They also have the same flaw: they ignore the fact that the Bosnians would rather fight than settle for the status quo, and they will not readily cooperate with a containment strategy. If the war escalates and Bosnian suffering once again dominates the headlines and CNN, Hill pressures to lift the arms embargo could become hard to manage."[47] Then, in conclusion, Vershbow wrote, "In the final analysis, therefore, we may *not* be able to prevent the Bosnians from going on the offensive in the spring. The best case may be that the renewed fighting does not lead to any major Bosnian reverses and the current stalemate remains when winter returns. The worst case is that the Serbs respond by overrunning the eastern enclaves and strangling Sarajevo again. Although UNPROFOR countries may hunker down and not decide to withdraw even in the latter scenario, Congress may force the issue with unilateral lift."[48] By the summer, the worst case enveloped the eastern enclaves and changed the course of the war and diplomacy.

But the Principals could not foresee the future on March 17 when they met in the Sit Room, without their Deputies. Given their key roles, though, Holbrooke was absent; Christopher brought Frasure with him as the American point man for the Contact Group and negotiations with Milošević. Albright and all other Principals except one participated in this one-and-one-half-hour meeting. Douglas MacEuchin, Deputy Director of Intelligence, sat in for the CIA, as Woolsey had resigned on January 10. Alice Rivlin, head of the Office of Management and Budget, also attended, given the budgetary implications of what would be discussed.

The NSC summary began with a grim but realistic assessment:

Principals discussed overall U.S. strategy toward the former Yugoslavia and steps to prevent or contain renewed war in

Bosnia this spring. They agreed that, in view of our limited leverage and the importance of maintaining the cohesion of NATO we should maintain our current approach of diplomatic engagement, provision of humanitarian relief, keeping UNPROFOR in place, and measures to contain the conflict. Principals agreed that we should continue to support the Bosnian Government's goal of a political settlement consistent with the Contact Group proposal, but that we should seek to lower public expectations of immediate success; we should also avoid nurturing any illusions on the part of the Bosnian Government that we can deliver a settlement or that the U.S. or NATO will intervene militarily on their behalf.[49]

The Principals tasked Frasure to "explore the possibility of an agreement on constitutional arrangements for the future Bosnian union as a basis for securing Milošević's recognition of Bosnia." This was a forerunner of what ultimately transpired at Dayton later in the year. They authorized drawing up more sanctions to pressure the Bosnian and Krajina Serbs. The Principals were desperate to prevent a full resumption of hostilities once the Carter ceasefire ended on March 31 and supported efforts to persuade the Bosniaks to back off any offensive actions. "The Principals discussed ways to restore UN and NATO credibility in order to deter new Bosnian Serb military attacks on the eastern enclaves and other areas." NATO air power was discussed "to discourage Serb efforts to strangle Srebrenica and other safe areas."[50]

The Principals agreed to work toward completing negotiations by the end of March in New York for a U.N. Security Council mandate for a new U.N. peacekeeping mandate in Croatia. "They noted the continuing difficulties reported by Ambassador Albright with the Croatians on defining a realistic understanding of the mission of 'controlling' the international borders." They endorsed a scaled-back option of only 80 personnel (including 20 Americans) for the much-vaunted NATO prepositioning force for a UNPROFOR withdrawal from Croatia and/or Bosnia. This was a far cry fewer in numbers than had been on the table for months (1,800 total, with 450 being U.S. personnel). But skittish allies had prevailed with a smaller number. Then, reflecting the contradictory policy that was strangling Washington, "Principals agreed that, in informing Congress, we would characterize this [prepositioning] as a limited, precautionary move that is being taken even though we oppose UNPROFOR withdrawal."[51]

Meanwhile, contradicting the "limited" concept being briefed to Congress, the Principals proposed that the president agree to the larger prepositioning force, which would conduct its training in Germany. "The actual deployment of these additional U.S. personnel to Croatia would be subject to another Principals and NAC decision." So the merry-go-round of policy actions on the fate of UNPROFOR kept turning. The Principals agreed to brief Clinton, finally, on NATO's "OPLAN 40104," which would require a large U.S. military intervention to protect any UNPROFOR withdrawal from Bosnia or Croatia. It was increasingly becoming vital for Clinton to understand the dimensions of the NATO extraction plan and to recognize the incredible mountain to scale with Congress to obtain the authorization and funding for such a massive commitment of U.S. forces and equipment to the region.

Lake's action memorandum to Clinton on March 18 reflected the Principals' decisions. He advised Clinton that "the Tudjman decision reduces the threat to the U.S. forces who will deploy to Croatia. But the ever-increasing likelihood that large-scale fighting will resume in Bosnia this spring necessitates the continuation of prudent military steps to prepare for UNPROFOR withdrawal should it become unavoidable."[52] Lake did not think UNPROFOR withdrawal likely anymore for the Croatian theater, at least in the short term. But pressure from Capitol Hill, particularly from powerful Republican Senators Bob Dole and Jesse Helms, to rid the region of U.N. control or influence as UNPROFOR withdrew and NATO presumably took over, was palpable. Dole and Helms sent a letter to the White House with those demands and one more: that the allies commit to support multilateral lifting of the arms embargo post-withdrawal as the quid pro quo for U.S. participation. That was a likely game-stopper, as it invited all-out war again in Bosnia, which the Europeans would not seek to facilitate with infusions of new weaponry.

Lake notified Clinton of the need to brief him on OPLAN 40104, which was a vital but curious message, namely, to remind the president of the need to get a critical issue—a major commitment of U.S. military power—onto his schedule.[53] Would Clinton have to turn to John Podesta, his chief of staff, and instruct him, "Put this on my schedule, now!"? Several months later Albright and I drove across the Potomac River to the Pentagon and received a full briefing about OPLAN 40104, which was impressive for what it would require of U.S. forces and resources for a military operation of that size.

Clinton authorized U.S. support at NATO for the mini-deployment of the prepositioning force of up to 20 U.S. personnel, following notification of Congress, and agreed that a larger force of 450 Americans conduct training in Germany in the event the NAC and Principals agree to actually deploy them to Croatia and Bosnia.[54] These minimalist steps represented all that Clinton was asked to decide following the grand policy review.

On March 26, Karadžić ordered the mobilization of the entire Bosnian Serb population to counter a Bosniak offensive, then in its second week. The next day the Contact Group urged both Sarajevo and Pale to extend the ceasefire beyond May 1 and pledged to continue efforts to facilitate negotiations. But fighting on the ground seemed inevitable.

The Principals Pivot

The Principals met again on March 28 with three topics to discuss: Croatia and a new U.N. peacekeeping force, Bosnia and the prospect of renewed fighting, and sanctions policy toward Serbia.[55] Albright secured flexibility to navigate her way toward adoption of a Security Council resolution that would transition from UNPROFOR to a freshly mandated and reconstituted peacekeeping force for Croatia. She was up against the need for the United Nations to consult "with the parties during the first weeks of April to iron out the details of implementation."[56] So there would be no immediate turnover to a new world of peacekeeping on March 31 when UNPROFOR's mandate technically expired. The Principals decided to freeze out the obstructionist Krajina Serbs from U.N. meetings with the Contact Group, despite Russian desires to the contrary.

Rather than press forward with planning for a UNPROFOR withdrawal from Bosnia, the Principals pivoted in the opposite direction. They "agreed that we should continue our efforts to prevent or contain a reescalation of fighting in Bosnia as the end of the cessation of hostilities approaches [March 31]. Noting the Bosnian Government's request for a more robust UNPROFOR posture before agreeing to extend its mandate, Principals agreed that we should immediately approach the British and the French on measures to make UNPROFOR more robust."[57] Lake tasked such consultations with the French and British without delay. The Principals also directed that the Bosnian government be informed of such efforts to build a more robust UNPROFOR in Bosnia and thus secure Sarajevo's support for it.

The prospect of a more robust UNPROFOR in Bosnia led the Principals to decide to tighten only the "inner ring" of sanctions against the Bosnian and Krajina Serbs, who directly confronted UNPROFOR, while leaving the "outer ring" of sanctions against Serbia-Montenegro unchanged. Diplomatic efforts, they believed, needed to be focused on holding the European allies firm on the "inner ring" sanctions as part of strengthening UNPROFOR.[58] Once again, the Principals sought means to avoid a UNPROFOR withdrawal and insertion of its companion NATO extraction effort that would require tens of thousands of U.S. forces, and thus explored by every possible means to keep UNPROFOR in Bosnia.

The U.N. Security Council adopted three resolutions on March 31 that breathed some life support into UNPROFOR by renewing its mandate and dividing its peacekeepers into three separate commands, one each for Croatia, Bosnia, and Macedonia. The Croatian component would become the U.N. Confidence Restoration Operation, or UNCRO, while Macedonia's operation would become the U.N. Preventive Deployment Force, or UNPREDEP. Bosnia's component remained stuck with the tarnished name of UNPROFOR.

Milošević Rejects Mutual Recognition

On April 11, Milošević blew up the mutual recognition (Plan B) initiative of the United States and the Contact Group. One of the State Department's key participants at the meeting in Belgrade, foreign service officer Chris Hill, who would play an even larger role on Holbrooke's negotiating team later in the year, including at Dayton, and in subsequent years he would hold the American ambassadorships to Macedonia (FYROM), Poland, the Republic of Korea, and Iraq as well as become the Assistant Secretary of State for East Asian and Pacific Affairs, cabled to Washington that Milošević had flat-out rejected Plan B. He summarized:

MILOŠEVIĆ REPLIED TO THE CONTACT GROUP PROPOSAL ON RECOGNIZING BOSNIA ... WITH A CLEAR NO, AN ASSESSMENT SHARED BY ALL MEMBERS OF THE CONTACT GROUP AFTER AN APRIL 11 FIVE-HOUR MEETING/DINNER

WHICH STARTED AT 6:00 P.M. HE EXPLAINED THAT TO RECOGNIZE THE CURRENT STATE OF BOSNIA (AS OPPOSED TO THE FUTURE UNION OF BOSNIA) WOULD BE TANTAMOUNT TO RECOGNITION OF THE IZETBEGOVIĆ GOVERNMENT, A MOVE WHICH WOULD BE "COUNTERPRODUCTIVE" AS IT WOULD DRIVE THE BOSNIAN SERBS INTO A WAR FEVER FED BY A SENSE OF ABANDONMENT AND BETRAYAL.

MILOŠEVIĆ INSISTED THAT THE ONLY WAY TO CONVINCE THE BOSNIAN SERBS THAT THEY ARE ON THE WRONG TRACK IS TO OFFER BELGRADE "FULL SANCTIONS RELIEF IMMEDIATELY." MILOŠEVIĆ DID NOT SHARE THE SENSE OF URGENCY ABOUT THE SITUATION ON THE GROUND IN BOSNIA. ALL SIDES HE BELIEVES—INCLUDING IZETBEGOVIĆ—ARE INTERESTED IN EXTENDING THE CEASE-FIRE. THE ONLY GLIMMER OF HOPE FOR THE RECOGNITION PACKAGE WAS WHEN AFTER FIVE HOURS, MILOŠEVIĆ LOOKED DOWN AT THE TWO PAGE PROPOSAL LYING FACE DOWN ON THE TABLE IN FRONT OF HIM, AND SAID: "OKAY, I'LL READ IT." FOLLOWING THE MILOŠEVIĆ MEETING, THE CG [CONTACT GROUP] MET BRIEFLY AT THE FRENCH EMBASSY TO COMPARE NOTES AND TO CHASTISE THE RUSSIAN REP ZOTOV FOR HIS REFUSAL TO ENDORSE THE PROPOSAL IN FRONT OF MILOŠEVIĆ AND FOR HIS COMMENTS TO THE PRESS CALLING FOR FULL SANCTIONS RELIEF.[59]

The full text of Hill's cable offers insights into Milošević's arrogant rejectionism at this stage of the Balkans war. Everything in his mind centered on how progress would be made if Serbia received full relief from the sanctions. He chastised the Contact Group members for repeating issues he had discussed "endlessly" with all of them in the past. He claimed that Serbia had "nothing to do with the war" and voiced his disbelief at the Contact Group not seeing his side of things. "Maybe you want to keep the war on," he said. Milošević regarded the Contact Group's offer of a suspension of sanctions in return for recognizing Bosnia, in particular, as a "humiliation." The helicopter flights heard over Srebrenica were a figment of someone's imagination, he fumed: "They are probably Muslim or Turkish. Besides, they were heard going from Bosnia into Serbia. What would they be carrying? Wood and potatoes?"[60]

Hill wrote that Milošević insisted his willingness to recognize the "Bosnian Union" (of the Croat-Muslim Federation and a Bosnian Serb political entity) was a fair offer, which in reality meant he was leaving open the prospect of a Greater Serbia as the "Union" broke apart. "MILOŠEVIĆ INSISTED THAT BOSNIA TODAY IS NOT A STATE, 'IT'S A BATTLEFIELD.'" But Milošević left his harshest words for the Bosnian Serb leaders. Hill wrote, "HE WAS DERIVSIVE ABOUT THE BOSNIAN SERB LEADERSHIP, CALLING THEM ALL 'LIARS'. 'KOLJEVIC IS DRUNK EVERY DAY BY 10:00 AM.' AS FOR KARADŽIĆ, 'HE'S NOT A PSYCHIATRIST, HE'S A PATIENT!'. . . . THE BOSNIAN SERB LEADERS, MILOŠEVIĆ BELIEVES, ARE OBSESSED BY THE IDEA THAT IF THEY ACCEPT THE CONTACT GROUP PLAN WITH ITS MAP, THEY MAY BE STUCK WITH IT IF THEY ARE UNABLE TO WORK OUT THE SWAPS THAT THEY BELIEVE THAT THEY FEEL HAVE TO BE MADE, SUCH AS A 16 KM BRZCKO CORRIDOR."[61]

The final comment elaborated upon the Russian representative's obstinacy. Hill wrote, "AT THE END OF THE POST-MORTEM, THE GROUP PUT ZOTOV IN THE HOT SEAT FOR HIS COMMENTS TO THE BELGRADE PRESS EARLIER IN THE DAY TO THE EFFECT THAT MOSCOW SUPPORTS FULL SANCTIONS RELIEF. STEINER [GERMANY'S REPRESENTATIVE TO THE CONTACT GROUP], LOOKING INTENTLY OVER HIS WIRE RIMMED GLASSES, HELD UP THE CG PROPOSAL IN HIS HAND AND ASKED ZOTOV WHETHER HIS GOVERNMENT SUPPORTED IT. ZOTOV, VISIBLY PERSPIRING AND TUGGING AT HIS COLLAR, EXPLAINED THAT HE CONSIDERED IT NOT AS A CONTACT GROUP PROPOSAL, BUT RATHER AS SOMETHING 'WORKED OUT IN THE CONTACT GROUP.' ZOTOV PLEADED: 'IT WAS THE BEST I COULD DO.'"[62]

The Belgrade meeting was soon followed by another Principals-only meeting on April 14. The preparatory papers for this particular meeting provide insight into the state of planning and the perplexing policy choices facing the administration only two weeks before the end of the ceasefire. The BTF memorandum predicted that in light of the debilitating meeting with Milošević, "[t]he Contact Group will be put 'on the shelf' until some future point when negotiations hold out more promise for achieving a settlement." Senior policymakers did not appear "as concerned as they should be about developments in Croatia." The United Nations' plans for U.N. Confidence Restoration Operation in Croatia (UNCRO) to inspect traffic along the Bosnian and FRY borders "would be totally unacceptable to the Croatians." Strengthening UNPROFOR in Bosnia with effective implementation of its mandate "could be used as a carrot to urge the Bosnian Government to renew the cease-fire." But the allies would not want to change the UNPROFOR mandate.

As for Congress, the BTF recognized the immediate need to brief members about OPLAN 40104, but worried about additional issues of congressional interest such as extending sanctions relief to Serbia, the looming expiration of the ceasefire in Bosnia, and Senator Dole's likely introduction of a unilateral lift resolution. The BTF speculated that the Principals might establish an interagency briefing team to discourage support of a unilateral lift, if only to narrow the margin of victory for Dole and ease the way for a presidential veto.[63]

The Joint Chiefs of Staff tackled head-on in their information paper how to strengthen UNPROFOR in Bosnia, which was their highest priority to avoid following through on OPLAN 40104. Yasushi Akashi and UNPROFOR General Bernard Janvier claimed there was no need for anything more and that UNPROFOR's successes had not been recognized. The British were very reluctant to change anything with UNPROFOR, where they had thousands of troops deployed. "The British, French, and the UN will likely resist all efforts to move UNPROFOR beyond a current Chapter VI impartial posture," reported the JCS.[64] This meant keeping UNPROFOR strictly as a peacekeeping force and not empowering it to engage in combat under a U.N. Charter Chapter VII mandate.

But the JCS paper put forward six options to pursue under the existing Chapter VI mandate of impartial peacekeeping: secure the Sarajevo and Tuzla airports; establish a ground corridor to ensure free flow of aid to besieged Sarajevo; establish other ground corridors between Sarajevo and the eastern enclaves to ensure free flow of humanitarian aid to them; create ceasefire lines that have been politically negotiated; increase the number of, and consolidate UNPROFOR into, safe areas and exclusion zones and provide sufficient ground and air mobility assets and a "quick reaction force" to secure the safe areas; and finally, enhance the capabilities of UNPROFOR with heavy-lift helicopters, engineer battalions, and other assets.[65]

The JCS filed two information papers for the Principals meeting that reported on the status of OPLAN 40104 for UNPROFOR withdrawal from Bosnia and/or Croatia. The NAC had recently authorized deployment of "Minimum Step 2," which would place about 80 communicators into Croatia and Bosnia, 12 to 15 of whom would be American. While SACEUR

(Supreme Allied Commander for Europe, who was U.S. Army General George Joulwan) required further NAC approval for assembly, training and deployment of the Full Step 2 forces (1,526 communicators, of which 450 would be American), he "indicated, upon further reflection, he will not likely deploy Full Step 2 until the UN formally requests a NATO-led withdrawal of UNPROFOR."[66] SACEUR's caution spoke volumes of how unpopular actually following through on OPLAN 40104 was at NATO and in the Pentagon.

Adding to the go-slow approach was the fact that the French had finally agreed to deployment of Minimum Step 2, but so late that they caused a delay of three weeks at NATO to achieve that objective. To cap it off, the JCS concluded: "Unlikely further deployment of prepositioning will occur until there is a NATO decision to proceed with the withdrawal. The decision to withdraw is contingent upon a new UNSC resolution and Transfer of Authority of UNPROFOR to NATO."[67] Decisions dependent on other decisions also dependent on other decisions—an elaborately constructed decision tree that almost guaranteed inaction.

Dead End

The State Department's briefing paper for the Principals meeting on April 14 painted a grim picture of the situation, evidenced by its title, "Bosnia: Going for a Small War." Diplomatic efforts were at a dead end. Izetbegović's conditions for extending the ceasefire, namely, Milošević's recognition of Bosnia or Karadžić's acceptance of the Contact Group plan, would not be met. The unproductive Contact Group would be kept in "mothballs." The aim now would be to keep "the fighting to the lowest possible levels," and convincing Sarajevo to do so. Two incentives would be working for a robust UNPROFOR and introducing a U.N. resolution that blessed the Contact Group map (dividing Bosnia up as 51% Federation and 49% Bosnian Serb). A "robust UNPROFOR, which in essence means an UNPROFOR ready to enforce the exclusion zones, would help deflate pressure on the Hill for lifting the arms embargo." But the British and French would have to endorse the robust option. The idea behind the approved map would be the linkage of a Security Council resolution endorsing the Contact Group map "to continuation of the cease-fire or a private commitment to limit fighting." But State was skeptical: "However, whether this is enough to convince the Bosnians to delay action on a matter of supreme national interest is highly questionable."[68]

In a second State Department paper focusing on Croatia, the U.N. Secretariat's plans for UNCRO included an "implementable" plan that the

Security Council would be asked to approve "irrespective of whether the parties embrace it entirely." Albright had emphasized to U.N. representative Akashi and European Union envoy Thorvald Stoltenberg "that time is limited." The paper continued, "We must try to meet minimum Croatian expectations that Zagreb gets something out of all the recent fuss besides a name change [from UNPROFOR to UNCRO]. [The government's] anxiety that Tudjman will be seen at home as having sold out is real. This is reflected in Croatia's latest letter to Boutros Ghali, which is tough in putting demands on UNCRO that are not entirely reasonable. From our viewpoint, UN redeployment out of the UNPA's and onto their periphery, i.e. the separation zone and the international border, is important. What the border force actually does is less important, provided it at least puts more soldiers at checkpoints [than] UNPROFOR did."[69]

The U.N. Security Council futilely adopted a French-inspired resolution on April 19 containing the usual wish list to refrain from fighting, extend the ceasefire, and resume talks for a peaceful settlement. Two days later both Sarajevo and Pale refused to extend the ceasefire beyond May 1.

The Deputies convened in the Sit Room to discuss Bosnia after a long interlude on April 27. Tarnoff, Holbrooke, and Frasure represented State, while Slocombe and Joseph Kruzel sat for Defense. Wesley Clark covered for the Joint Chiefs of Staff. The requisite BTF paper painted an anemic picture of UNPROFOR:

> United Nations peacekeepers in Bosnia (UNPROFOR) continue routine operations in the face of increased harassment and the general breakdown of the Cessation of Hostilities (COH) agreement. UN forces continue to protest harassment and respond if fired on, but have not yet adopted a [sic] more assertive measures. The UN has put on hold plans for up to 6,500 additional peacekeepers. Efforts to upgrade UNPROFOR equipment and mobility continue—albeit at a leisurely pace. Major European contributors likely will support these efforts, but almost certainly would oppose strongly more aggressive UN tactics. . . . Serb forces continue to treat the peacekeepers with contempt and relations between the two parties are worsening. . . . Government forces may be obstructing UN observers in an effort to limit access to areas in which they plan offensive operations as well as venting their frustration at the peacekeepers' attempts to remain impartial.[70]

We had another round of operational challenges to tackle that day.

A Fresh Negotiating Gambit

Though Milošević had bluntly rejected the mutual recognition deal on April 11, the Deputies resurrected it with a newly formulated sanctions relief package in the hope it would entice him. Frasure proposed a fresh negotiating gambit with Milošević. The American interests were to obtain the strongest possible recognition of Bosnia by Serbia, achieve a new U.N. mandate for border control with a freestanding U.N. contingent of about 400 to 500 civilian monitors, frame a sanctions relief package that would be attractive to Milošević while still leaving us with leverage over him, achieve at least a two- or three-month extension of the cease-fire in Bosnia, and keep UNPROFOR in place. Implementing OPLAN 40104 with NATO's extraction of UNPROFOR "is a suicide note for the Administration." Bosnian Vice President Ejup Ganić told Frasure that if Bosnia were recognized by Belgrade and the "inter-Serbian" border were indeed closed, then Sarajevo would be amenable to a two- or three-month extension of the ceasefire. Joined by Tarnoff, Frasure believed that "Sarajevo would be satisfied with a vague recognition of Bosnia within its internationally accepted borders since they were really anxious to negotiate."[71]

As summarized by the NSC, the "Deputies agreed that any further suspension of sanctions will require genuine recognition by Milošević of Bosnia's internationally-recognized borders and a real sealing of the Bosnian Serbs' border. Deputies agreed that no lifting of any sanctions would be appropriate at this time and that suspension of certain sanctions for finite periods of time was the most we could accept. They authorized Ambassador Frasure to propose option 'a' from the OVP's sanctions relief chart (Tab A). Noting that other Contact Group partners would likely seek broader sanctions relief, Deputies agreed that Ambassador Frasure could inform Contact Group partners that he would need to seek Washington's approval to move even part of the way toward option 'b' from the [Office of Vice President] sanctions chart."[72]

Fuerth, the author of the sanctions relief chart, said, "This is a stay of execution if it succeeds." One long-term tactic would be a siege of Pale, the Bosnian Serb capital. Another challenge would be "closing the back door" of trade to Serbia across its border with Croatia. Berger proposed that the Deputies decide not to lift anything yet on the arms embargo, pursue further serious closure of the border between Serbia and Bosnian Serb territory, suspend financial transactions, press a cross-recognition formula that Sarajevo found acceptable, and send Frasure on to Belgrade for private talks with Milošević prior to the next Contact Group meeting. I cautioned that the mutual recognition formula must be acceptable to the United States as a matter of international law, and that meant no shortcuts. Holbrooke reported that Christopher had called Bosnian Prime Minister Silajdžić to request that the government extend the ceasefire while exercising its right to self-defense.

The Deputies then tackled the plight of Sarajevo. The Bosnian Serbs had violated the 1992 agreement regarding the unrestricted use of Sarajevo's airport. "Holbrooke mentioned that in retaliation for Bosnian offensives, the Bosnian Serbs had intensified pressure on the airport. He considered it outrageous that the US couldn't get its diplomats into Sarajevo; the Administration's opponents might have taken advantage of this had not the media been preoccupied with the news stories on the Oklahoma bombing."[73] (He was referring to the April 19, 1995, terrorist bombing of the Alfred P. Murrah Federal Building in Oklahoma City, killing 168 people.) The French, according to General Clark, might land at Sarajevo even without approval. "Scheffer mentioned a UN resolution confirming that UNPROFOR has the right to keep it [Sarajevo's airport] open, but Berger noted it only condemns the action and doesn't really do anything. Someone mentioned rumors Akashi would trade fuel deliveries to UNPROFOR in the eastern enclaves for changed airport procedures."[74] Mention the potent strength of a Security Council resolution, and what could be done if its authority were actually implemented, and someone, this time Berger, would swat it away with the cynical remark that it "doesn't really do anything." That became a self-fulfilling prophecy as the resolution's power lay untested.

I briefed other Deputies on prior Security Council actions concerning the Sarajevo airport. The Bosniaks proposed establishing a demilitarized zone around Sarajevo, which meant that Bosniak forces also would have to be willing to pull back just as would the Bosnian Serbs. The United Nations apparently wanted to try it. The Deputies tasked Tarnoff to explore the idea further with the Bosnian government.

The BTF memorandum of the Deputies meeting reported, "Slocombe assessed that after the Bosnians started this spring's offensives, the Serbs had demonstrated it holds all of the cards. The West would probably 'huff and puff' and eventually the airport will reopen under somewhat less favorable circumstances than before. Berger noted that at one time we would have been firmer, but there is no willingness by the British or French to assert themselves vigorously."[75]

Holbrooke Trashes OPLAN 40104

The discussion turned to the infamous OPLAN 40104 and a NATO-led withdrawal of UNPROFOR from Bosnia. Berger said it all required much more consideration. "We can't sustain support on the Hill the more UNPROFOR is rendered impotent," he complained. He pondered whether the mission statement for the NATO extraction force would be: First, NATO would remain neutral in all direct actions insofar as possible. Second, the NATO extraction force would protect and aid civilian humanitarian organizations to the maximum extent commiserate with the mission. Third, we had to avoid a humanitarian catastrophe upon NATO's withdrawal. Slocombe said this still left unanswered what we would do if there were a civilian catastrophe after UNPROFOR's pullout, while the NATO force was still deployed. Tarnoff noted the endless wrangling in Washington and in NATO circles over such questions. We had no choice, he said, but to address the civilian and humanitarian consequences of OPLAN 40104.

Holbrooke revolted at the idea of even discussing OPLAN 40104, saying the withdrawal of UNPROFOR cannot be allowed to happen. American efforts should be focused on keeping UNPROFOR in the field. "Holbrooke feared events in London and Paris were moving towards a dramatic outcome, but neither ally was willing to take the steps to make UNPROFOR effective."[76]

The Deputies "agreed to defer further discussion until the Principals receive the JCS briefing on OPLAN 40104 on April 28. At that time, the NSC would determine the process that would be used to finalize answers to the questions as a basis for review by Deputies and Principals."[77] Brigadier General Donald Kerrick predicted UNPROFOR would withdraw "if the fighting becomes intense or the US pushes unilateral lift. . . . Tarnoff predicted extensive wrangling within the government and alliance over these policy issues."[78] Bureaucratic machinations, domestic and international, won the day.

When only the Principals met on April 28, Ambassador Rick Inderfurth sat in for Albright. They kept hoping for flexibility from Milošević and agreed "to suspend some additional sanctions if Milošević unambiguously recognizes Bosnia within its internationally-recognized borders." But they erected a difficult condition that the Contact Group members, not Milošević, would have to satisfy as well if such sanctions relief were to be provided: They would have to commit "to tighten the closure of the

Serbian-Bosnian border and to take similar measures to seal Croatia's border with Bosnian Serb areas, the 'back door' through which significant circumvention has occurred."[79] So Serbia would see more goods flow into that country upon Milošević's recognition of Bosnia but only if the borders were sealed so that Bosnian Serbs were even more isolated from supplies that otherwise would arrive across the border with either Croatia or Serbia. The likelihood of such a confluence of actions taking place was practically nil.

The Principals believed the Bosnian Serb "strangulation" of Sarajevo, particularly their attempt to assert control over Sarajevo airport in defiance of U.N. authority, had to be countered. They asked that options for NATO action to reopen the airport be developed. This required taskings to update intelligence assessments at the airport, including Bosnian Serb intentions and goals, review of existing U.N. and NATO mandates "that would permit the use of military force to reopen Sarajevo Airport, end the strangulation of Sarajevo, and escort flights into Sarajevo," and various military and diplomatic options to open the airport and keep it operational.[80]

Finally, the Principals authorized continued U.S. support at NATO for OPLAN 40104 "as long as support did not entail actual commitment of U.S. forces to the operation." That would require "another Principals and Presidential decision and consultations with Congress."[81] Clearly, the political and military will to actually follow through on OPLAN 40104 rested on very thin ice. Indeed, the Principals had not yet really presented the full OPLAN 40104 and its endgame to Clinton for his approval. Many "sensitive political questions" had to be answered first. They also "directed that a post-UNPROFOR withdrawal strategy be developed to facilitate answering the unanswered policy questions relating to the actual operation."[82]

No one wanted to move from paper plans to the field, namely, deploy thousands of U.S. soldiers into a war theater for a NATO operation to evacuate UNPROFOR troops. But we had to keep up the appearance of planning something, although what it would entail in reality and in the aftermath was still highly problematic. It could turn into a messy extraction operation, followed, if many in Congress had their way, with a unilateral lift of the arms embargo and probably unilateral (U.S.) air strikes, all while NATO forces (significantly American) either remained deployed to respond to resumed hostilities and a humanitarian catastrophe or exited Bosnia as well, leaving behind a war that would only spell defeat for the United Nations, for NATO, for the Clinton administration, and most likely for the Bosniaks. The equivocation demonstrated, once again, by both the Deputies and the Principals settled like a fog over the Sit Room.

Lake tried to lift some of that fog in his memorandum to Clinton on May 2, 1995, reporting on the Principals meeting a few days earlier. He conceded that "the chances of securing genuine Serbian recognition of Bosnia are low, since Milošević continues to demand a lifting of all the sanctions (which the Contact Group has conditioned on recognition of all the former Yugoslav states). Nevertheless, if allies make good on sealing the border, it can—over time—increase the economic squeeze on the Bosnian Serbs and pressure them to accept the Contact Group plan. The Croatians, for their part, seem prepared to cooperate in closing the 'back door.' "[83] In fact, all of this was very wishful thinking, the kind that can result from overthinking a diplomatic and military challenge and human-itarian imperative.

On the fate of Sarajevo and its airport, Lake alerted Clinton to the pros-pect that if NATO action were required, he would have to get to British Prime Minister John Major and French President François Mitterand and overcome their objections. "Bill Perry noted the need to consider how to respond if the Serbs retaliate in other areas, such as by attacking the eastern enclaves. We will, of course, seek your approval before going down this road."[84]

Lake took the opportunity to concisely brief Clinton about OPLAN 4014, drawing upon Shali's description to the Principals. Lake wrote:

> The plan involves roughly 70,000 NATO troops, including 25,000 from the U.S. and will cost between $1.5 and $2 billion dollars (for the U.S., an additional $600 million beyond the cost of ongoing operations). Under the plan, in the first two weeks UK- and French-led units would secure the routes from the Adriatic to Sarajevo, opening the way for U.S. troops to push through to Tuzla and on to the eastern enclaves. The withdrawal of UNPROFOR troops would then unfold over the subsequent 2–3 months. Because of the length of the operation and the eight-week lead-time involved, the OPLAN also includes rapid response capabilities to extract indi-vidual UNPROFOR units in emergency situations.[85]

Despite the Principals agreement to proceed with planning, Lake cau-tioned Clinton about the many imponderables facing policymakers before he would be asked to approve the plan: "Is our post-withdrawal policy still to lift the arms embargo and, if so, how will that affect NATO's posture during the withdrawal? How to deal with Serb attacks on the eastern enclaves during and after the operation? Will NATO enforce the exclusion zones? How to deal with civilians seeking NATO protection or evacuation and with refugees? What is NATO's role in delivering humanitarian aid?" Lake wanted to pose these questions to members of Congress as well in order to demonstrate to them that the scale of the withdrawal operation and policy dilemmas "should help dampen support for unilateral lift and build support for our efforts to contain the fighting and keep UNPROFOR in place."[86] Despite all of the NATO chest-thumping, that was the bottom line: minimize fighting and keep UNPROFOR on the front line.

In a very familiar closing line by any subordinate, including the national security adviser, who wishes their briefing or advice to the boss to stand uncontested, Lake wrote, "If you have any problems with the OPLAN's approach we can discuss it further with you or provide you an early briefing on it."[87] He was graciously offering Clinton the opportunity to question or even object to OPLAN 40104, or just let it proceed in its crippled way, undisturbed. All Clinton scribbled on the memorandum's first page was a note to distinguish an American hostage issue in Bosnia, which Lake had noted at the end of his memorandum, "from other outstanding issues. Let's discuss. BC." Clinton neither objected to OPLAN 40104 nor embraced it. He was muddling through just like the rest of us.

Fighting consumed U.N. Sector West in Croatia once the four-month ceasefire ended. Croatian forces launched an offensive to retake the region and seized virtually all strategic points, prompting Tudjman to declare victory. But the Krajina Serbs fired rockets into downtown Zagreb and the nearby Pleso airport in retaliation. On May 3, the Serbian missile strike hit a children's hospital and the National Theater in Zagreb, killing one person and wounding 40 others. For such civilian targeting, Krajina Serb President Milan Martić years later would be convicted of war crimes by the Yugoslav Tribunal.[88] Akashi brokered a ceasefire between Croatia and the Krajina Serbs, so the intensive fighting ended for the time being.

Croatia Redux

The Deputies convened on May 4 as Croatia hung on to the tip of the ceasefire with the Krajina Serbs. Tudjman went on national television the day before saying that Croatia would respond to further attacks on Zagreb "most resolutely." We had a report of five new rocket attacks on the city, but there was no further confirmation of it. The BTF reported to the Deputy Director of Intelligence, "If reports of another attack on Zagreb are true, it will be difficult to prevent an escalation of hostilities." Cynically, the BTF described the NSC paper on the Croatian crisis as one containing a strategy that would "press all parties to halt military operations and exercise constraint (I know what you're thinking!)." The memorandum continued: "The NSC proposes that we consult with NATO and the UN about the possibility of threatening to use NATO airstrikes against Krajina Serb targets in the event of future attacks on Zagreb or bombing missions out of Udbina Airfield."[89] The BTF also described the discord among Contact Group members, with the Europeans favoring giving Belgrade significantly more sanctions relief than the United States in exchange for recognition of Bosnia. The Europeans were prepared to lessen international leverage on Serbia for their cooperation on other issues. Add to this the deteriorating humanitarian situation in Bihać threatening mass starvation and the United Nations' request to resume airdrops. Croatia was in bad shape that day.

Tarnoff, Holbrooke, and Frasure once again represented the State Department. We reaffirmed the mutual recognition strategy, or Plan B, in what was becoming a Hail Mary pass every time either the Principals or Deputies met that spring. Frasure was deployed to meet with Milošević and repeat the same proposal to him. Echoing the NSC paper, the Deputies "agreed that the U.S. should press President Tudjman and the Krajina Serbs to halt military operations and exercise restraint." They would press Croatia to take an "accommodating position that could include the demilitarization of the recaptured areas, the return of Serb civilians to their homes and the [re-stablishment] of UNCRO authority in Sector West and other areas of conflict." We agreed to support a Security Council resolution condemning incursions by all sides in Sectors South and East of Croatia and calling for the restoration of UNCRO authority in all areas. But, in response to Krajina Serb threats, the Deputies "agreed that we should be prepared to bypass the dual-key system if a NATO response were not approved by the UN."[90] All of these decisions reflected ideal briefing paper options, but would mean little in the theater of operations in coming days.

Fuerth lamented that the British and French were proceeding on entirely different assumptions, namely, to repair the Serbian economy. He asked whether the U.S. position should be to help Milošević resurrect his own economy. In his view, the British and the French wanted to be first in line to get the contracts, symptoms of their "fear and greed." If we were to release frozen Serbian assets under the sanctions regime, "they will disappear forever and the interests of other successor states of the former Yugoslavia would be screwed," Fuerth said.

Holbrooke concluded, "We have abandoned the Contact Group as a negotiating forum. It's now up to Frasure's meeting with Milošević on Saturday." There could be no lifting of sanctions until Pale accepted the Contact Group plan. Fuerth's list would become the operative one: what could be suspended without Pale coming on board.

The Deputies decided not to offer Britain and France anything more. The meeting with them the next day would only be for appearances. The real meeting would be Frasure's with Milošević. Tarnoff asked, "Why are we doing this? Who are we representing? The Bosniaks? Are we doing what the Bosnian Government thinks will strengthen its position? The Bosnian Government wants recognition of international boundaries and if they don't get a state or government all to themselves, that's o.k."

Holbrooke offered a sobering assessment of Croatia. "We don't have a strategy to prevent attacks. Tudjman served our purposes to close the 'back door' on the Bosnian Serbs. He won't withdraw from Sector West." Slocombe countered, "We need to press Tudjman very hard. He broke his word on offensive actions. There should be no NATO air strikes to save Tudjman." Berger qualified this by requesting a review of NATO and U.S. options to defend the American personnel already in Croatia. Fuerth said it was not in our interest to expand the war in Croatia, but Tudjman should not be boxed in either.

Hope and Despair

The Bosnian Serb forces shelled Sarajevo on May 7, thus launching their first major attack since the end of the ceasefire. Ten civilians were killed and 40 wounded. UN Secretary-General Boutros-Ghali, however, refused to turn his key to unleash NATO air strikes in response to the bloody attack. Essentially disarmed, we wondered back in Washington how to climb out of the defeatist trenches we had dug and endured for so long.

The next day the Deputies were back in the Sit Room with both hope and despair beckoning us inside. Albright, who wanted to report to the Deputies directly from the United Nations, joined by secure video (STVS) feed from New York while I sat at the table. Optimistic news arrived from the State Department's Tarnoff and Frasure in the form of a new and more liberal sanctions relief package if only Milošević would play ball. Tarnoff announced, "This is a big issue and the best opportunity we've had to put a package together. The French have been very clear in the last 48 hours that their participation in UNPROFOR will end by a date certain unless there's a cessation of hostilities and a peace process. So we have come to terms on a plausible package of sanctions relief with Milošević and it has the support of the Bosnian Government. Yes, it involves some compromises on our part."

Frasure doubled down: "We really are at a crossroads. The UN mandates are collapsing. NATO extraction is looming. Milošević is in a foul mood. He does not like being trumped by Tudjman. Milošević knows he's not the master of the universe anymore. He knows the United States is not prepared to lift sanctions until Pale accepts the peace plan, and that we are prepared to block progress in the Contact Group if necessary."

On Monday of that week, Milošević had shifted his views. Frasure continued, "He said that Karadžić is not credible. He is open to a public agreement between himself and the Contact Group, one that suspends sanctions with simultaneous recognition of Bosnia and Herzegovina and more effective monitoring of international borders. The rest of the sanctions would be peeled off once there's acceptance by Pale. Milošević has figured out that Pale will be *his* hostage." Frasure went on to explain that Serbia would get its seat back in the OSCE, which would take over border monitoring with beefed-up numbers and bid Lord Owen farewell. In addition, OSCE missions would return to the Serbian province of Kosovo. Washington had long sought to monitor the fragile situation there with its Muslim population.

Frasure turned blunt with the assembled Deputies:

We have a credible last ditch chance with this plan [to suspend certain sanctions against Belgrade]. But it requires a more forthcoming position from this room on sanctions suspension. We still need to do more with lifting financial sanctions down the road and we will go nowhere on any permanent lifting of sanctions until Pale accepts the plan. So you have a three-pronged plan to consider: First, Serbian recognition of Bosnia and Herzegovina. Second, installation of a credible border regime under OSCE monitoring. Third, sanctions suspension for Belgrade. If this is agreed upon by the Contact Group and Milošević, then Bosnia, which already has accepted these terms, will announce a unilateral suspension of hostilities and welcome OSCE take-over of the border monitoring mission.

Fuerth's aide, William Wise, emphasized what Pale would have to do to achieve lift of the sanctions regime: The Bosnian Serbs would need to clearly accept the agreed-upon peace plan and agree on new constitutional principles for the nation of Bosnia and Herzegovina. "If Mladić is willing to say yes, then we can deal with him," Wise said.

Albright was skeptical of the entire plan to suspend sanctions. "We have to leave ourselves some leverage," she cautioned. "Let's load up the suspension as heavily as possible with conditions of performance. It's our only protection." She pivoted to Croatia, warning that "the United Nations was claiming that the Croatians had made no withdrawals, and that frustration with the Croatians was increasing in the Security Council, several members of which have troops in Croatia."[91] Albright worried that "the Russians will find support for a strong resolution condemning Zagreb because anger against Croatia is rising in the Council. The U.N. is counting on us for channels to Tudjman." So the Deputies, fully aware of their weak hand, agreed to urge Tudjman "to exercise restraint."[92]

For weeks the situation in Sarajevo, particularly at its airport, had been deteriorating with Bosnian Serb forces preventing access to the airport with increasing frequency. Albright surmised that the only rationale left for keeping UNPROFOR in nominal control of the airport "is because it's too hard to give up." Negotiations over Sarajevo airport, she feared, "would go awry." She also noted dryly that incoming French President Jacques Chirac had told British Foreign Secretary Douglas Hurd several weeks earlier: "We don't really have a problem with a greater Serbia, do you?" Berger responded, "If the authority of UNPROFOR over Sarajevo and the airport collapses and we can't perform humanitarian missions, it will be increasingly impossible to justify UNPROFOR's existence. You can choose your Security Council resolution [among many] that offers plenty of authority to act! But instead, Sarajevo will collapse and Boutros-Ghali will be happy to see UNPROFOR depart."

The day before, on May 8, Akashi had turned down a request by local UNPROFOR officials in Sarajevo for close air support.[93] The State Department saw the dilemma as magnified by the prospects of OPLAN 40104. "The key to keeping UNPROFOR on the ground and to avoiding the deployment of U.S. ground troops in Bosnia is to take aggressive and decisive measures to keep Sarajevo Airport open for all traffic. The legal authority exists to do so and military options are being prepared." "Existing authority" would permit NATO air power to provide close air support in defense of UNPROFOR troops at the airport, air strikes because Sarajevo was "being strangled," and air strikes because the Sarajevo exclusion zone was being violated.[94]

Albright asked, "What do we do about Akashi?" We needed to sidestep Akashi's resistance to using NATO air power to protect UNPROFOR and the Sarajevo Airport or, more dramatically, dislodge Akashi from his leadership of UNPROFOR. She said that moving against Akashi would not be easy. "France might be with us, but the British won't be." The Pentagon's Walter Slocombe interjected, "The dual key is not a veto. It goes up NATO and U.N. chains of command. In order to bypass Akashi, we have to get both French and British support. If [UNPROFOR Bosnia Commander] General [Rupert] Smith approves but Akashi does not, then Smith could go directly to NATO." Albright countered, "But Walt it's both: The British and French [as troop contributors to UNPROFOR] as well as Akashi would have to agree [to turn the U.N. part of the dual key for use of NATO air power]. Both are the problem."

Indeed, Commander Smith, who was a British lieutenant general, requested air strikes on Bosnian Serb gunners on May 10 in retaliation for the May 7 shelling of Sarajevo, but he was overruled by Akashi, who apparently feared that such military action would upset the recently brokered ceasefire in Croatia. Frustrated U.N. officials in Sarajevo called for a review of their role in Bosnia.[95]

The Deputies were told during our May 9 meeting that there were no obvious military options left for Sarajevo. Slocombe speculated, "The British may drop a few bombs on a few targets. But if that does not work, what is the United States prepared to do?" Berger said with a sigh, "There is a fundamental disinclination to reassess our position." Slocombe responded, "Yes, as long as we can muddle along. But it's getting bad. There may not be any stomach in this city to fight." Berger quipped, "There certainly is no stomach after looking at the JCS plan." That plan set out options for military action to secure the Sarajevo airport, but then backed none of them. Albright viewed any fundamental reassessment as starting from the premise that "the situation is worse."

Then OPLAN 40104 reared its head. JCS Deputy Chairman Owen reminded everyone of the need to obtain a separate NAC order to actually deploy U.S. and other NATO forces to Bosnia. They would need training and preparation of troops. Clark estimated a 24,500 U.S. troop commitment. Vershbow cited the need to answer unanswered questions in OPLAN 40104 first. Slocombe responded, "Well then, we have to get serious about this [OPLAN 40104]." The policy question would need to be posed to the Principals the following week. They had to identify units for deployment into Bosnia, but the Pentagon had not even begun specialized training yet. "We had forces training for the Haiti intervention in 1994 for months," Slocombe noted. The BTF summarized this uncertainty of OPLAN 40104: "The Deputies held an inconclusive discussion of SACUER's request to issue an Action Request for the enabling and main force in OPLAN 40104 to be forwarded to NATO. While they agreed that the request went beyond existing Principals' authorization, there was considerable confusion about the meaning and implications of particular steps aimed at implementing OPLAN 40104. JCS was tasked to prepare a paper clarifying these issues for the Principals."[96]

The Pentagon's paper appeared on May 12 and revealed the limitations built into OPLAN 40104. There would be no "follow-on mission" following the withdrawal operation, and thus no mission creep. NATO forces would remain completely neutral and "not support Bosnian government or Croatian military forces." They would be authorized "to take necessary self-defense measures, including lethal force if required, to protect themselves and U.N. personnel from any faction, including civilians . . ." The withdrawal priority would "be to remove UN personnel . . . first, then UN forces' weapons, and then UN equipment." NATO would "assume command and control of all UNPROFOR units throughout [Croatia and Bosnia] to conduct emergency, partial, or total withdrawal operations." The dual key would be extinguished once NATO launched the withdrawal operation in all active areas but would be retained in areas where UNPROFOR was not actually being withdrawn. Then, in the ultimate expression of non-engagement, the Pentagon stated: "NATO forces will not attempt to defend Bosnian Muslim, Croat, or Serb civilian populations and will not undertake to evacuate civilians from the enclaves (or elsewhere). However, to the extent it can, without adversely impacting the withdrawal effort, NATO forces will be authorized to:

− Respond to attacks on civilian populations in area where NATO forces are operating.
− Support humanitarian assistance (aid delivery, refugee relocation, etc.) efforts of [the U.N. High Commissioner for Refugees (UNHCR)] and [nongovernmental organizations]."[97]

This left open the opportunity for Bosnian Serb forces to flood into enclaves and other areas where UNPROFOR had departed and NATO was no longer operating so that they could terrorize and otherwise attack and ethnically cleanse Bosniaks from such territory. And with such guidance NATO would be rendered impotent to respond as it scurried out of the country. The ramifications were mind-boggling.

On the same day, May 12, Frasure informed Christopher in a memorandum that the Contact Group had just reached full consensus during their meeting in Frankfurt for "a Bosnia recognition/border/sanctions suspension package that should be fielded with Milošević in Belgrade next week and with the Bosnians." They had agreed to a six-month suspension of designated sanctions requiring a positive Security Council renewal vote; no lifting of Phase One sanctions until Pale accepted the package; more flexibility on financial transactions but assets would remain frozen; Serbia and Macedonia would get seats in the OSCE, which would take over border monitoring; and the OSCE mission would return to Kosovo (as well as Sandzak and Vojvodina). Frasure was tasked to present all of this to Milošević the next week. However, he described the Contact Group's "great concern about the rapidly deteriorating situation inside Bosnia, especially in Sarajevo. (We always need to be aware of the possibility that we are playing diplomatic word games with ourselves while the war spins out of control.) All sides agree that something must be done about the airport, and air strikes might be necessary. It was agreed that we should warn both the Bosnians and Mladić (via Milošević) to pull back from the precipice." Frasure concluded, "We all recognize that this is all a long shot venture. But with the Frankfurt meeting, we seem to be off to a good start."[98] In reality, the war would spin out of control soon enough.

Just to remind us of what was at stake, John Menzies, a courageous and highly talented career American diplomat who became the U.S. ambassador to Bosnia and Herzegovina in 1996, phoned into the State Department Operations Center on May 16 to report the "heaviest fighting he's ever seen" and predicted it would resume at dusk. He noted that a 12-year-old girl had just been killed in the shelling. Menzies was on the front line of diplomacy during the siege of Sarajevo, going so far as to sleep on a cot in his office at the ramshackle U.S. embassy in a virtual 24/7 call to duty.

Only the Principals met on May 16 in the Situation Room. They were presented with essentially the same list of unresolved issues as the Deputies had discussed a week earlier. Beforehand, Albright discussed the forthcoming meeting. She had problems with Boutros-Ghali's recommended plan for UNPROFOR that morning during a closed-door Security Council meeting: redeployment and reduction in the number of troops and, where necessary, modifications to the UNPROFOR mandate due to the escalation of hostilities and threats to the peacekeepers. Albright believed that experience had shown that a weak response would not impress the Bosnian Serbs with UNPROFOR's presence. If a diminished mandate meant abandoning the eastern enclaves or the exclusion zone around Sarajevo, then the United States could not possibly support it. Ambassador Galbraith in Zagreb was on the warpath with Akashi, reporting that Akashi had not informed the Croatian government of Martic's threat to bomb the city. Galbraith believed that the will of the Security Council was not being honored by Akashi, "that he's in contempt of the Council and either should resign or U.S. will take UNSC action."[99]

The Principals were presented with a State Department paper entitled, "Bosnia: Formulating a Post-Unprofor Withdrawal Strategy." Ominously, the paper admitted, "OPLAN 40104 makes no provision for a NATO mission in Bosnia, such as support for humanitarian relief efforts, after UNPROFOR withdraws." The role of NATO might be enhanced and the arms embargo lifted if the withdrawal of UNPROFOR is contested by Bosnian Serb forces and could possibly lead to NATO taking sides with the Bosnian government, but such NATO action would require further approval in Brussels. "Without new UN resolutions, the authorization for NATO close air support and the protection of safe areas and exclusion zones may lapse with UNPROFOR's withdrawal."[100] The American role in the post-UNPROFOR landscape would be fraught with risk:

> UNPROFOR's withdrawal from Bosnia will increase pressure on the U.S. to become more involved in Bosnia, diplomatically and militarily. If withdrawal is precipitated by passage in the U.S. Congress of a unilateral lift bill, the U.S. will be under great pressure to help arm and train Bosnian troops. While Congress wants to lift the arms embargo, it might try to tie our hands in using military force, seriously complicating our ability to help. If the withdrawal is the result of British and/or French exhaustion, we will still be under great pressure to support the Bosnian Government by lifting the arms embargo.[101]

Finally, the State memorandum speculated that if there were a UNPROFOR withdrawal, the United States would have to decide on a lifting of the arms embargo, unilaterally if necessary or with a few allies if they dared to take the leap, using military force to create pathways for humanitarian relief to Sarajevo and the eastern enclaves, employing air power to retaliate against Serb violations with or without NATO approval, and training Bosniak forces in the event of a lifting of the arms embargo.[102]

A National Security Council discussion paper the next day, May 17, reiterated much of what had been pondered over at Deputies and Principals meetings for months. The fundamental U.S. policy objectives remained obtaining "a political settlement that satisfie[d] basic Bosnian government requirements and roll[ed] back some Serb aggression," ended or reduced the fighting, prevented the spread of the conflict to other parts of the region, maintained relief supplies and cohesion with allies, and avoided "American entanglement in fighting on the ground in the Balkans."[103] The paper endorsed the policy preference to keep UNPROFOR deployed on the ground and thus avoid actually implementing OPLAN 40104. Achieving that goal required muddling through with the status quo, "restabilization" of the existing UNPROFOR mission with more robust enforcement of the existing mandate, withdrawing UNPROFOR from untenable positions while pursuing more robust enforcement of remaining mandates, or retrenching and retreating by withdrawing UNPROFOR to fewer positions and pursuing an even less vigorous approach to mandate enforcement. The State Department believed the only "realistic choice may be to seek Allied support to 'retrench and reinvigorate'. Trade U.S. support for retrenchment for allied and UN pledge to pursue more robust enforcement of remaining mandate, including NATO airstrikes."[104]

The NSC paper poured another pitcher of cold water all over OPLAN 40104. Just planning for NATO coverage of a UNPROFOR withdrawal could precipitate such a withdrawal. The paper noted, "Key is not allowing the existence of a 'NATO withdrawal force' to prompt either UN troop contributors to seek early withdrawal or Bosnians to act to cause UNPROFOR withdrawal in the hopes that NATO will replace the UN. A clear 'firebreak' is required between completion of NATO preparation for OPLAN 40104 and initiation of OPLAN implementation."[105]

The U.N. Security Council sought to tamp down the Croatian situation with a resolution on May 17 demanding that the Croatian government and Krajina Serb forces withdraw from U.N. separation zones in Croatia and refrain from any further violations of those zones. The Council warned of unspecified actions if the two sides did not comply.[106]

Back to Milošević

Two days later the Principals met alone, without their Deputies, in the Sit Room for a two-hour strategy session on Bosnia. Holbrooke joined Christopher. OPLAN 40104 was deferred for another day. Rather, the focus remained on how to succeed in negotiations with Milošević and how to sustain UNPROFOR on the ground in Bosnia and Croatia. Frasure had met with Milošević the day before, May 18, in Belgrade to press him on the Contact Group agreement that would suspend some of the sanctions against Serbia in exchange for its diplomatic recognition of Bosnia and tightening of the "inter-Serbian" border to squeeze the Bosnian Serbs. Milošević had presented a counteroffer during the meeting that sought considerably more relief, to which the Principals crafted a response in the Sit Room. A summary of the Contact Group Agreement, Milošević's counteroffer, and the Principals' proposed response to it were presented at the meeting.[107]

The Principals agreed that a cable would be sent to Frasure with fresh negotiating instructions containing their own counterproposal to Milošević's views. On three sensitive issues, the Principals agreed to maintain their "existing position that Serbia/Montenegro could be treated as 'a' successor state but not 'the' successor state to Yugoslavia" and that "Serbia's admission to OSCE should be simultaneous with restoration of the long-duration missions to Kosovo, Sandjak and Vojvodina." They firmly rebutted Milošević on further significant flexibility to the Contact Group agreement on suspension of sanctions.

Always bearing in mind the need for accountability for the atrocities that had devastated Bosniaks and Croatians, Albright successfully achieved Principals' reaffirmation that "any lifting of the 'outer wall' of sanctions (access to [international financial institutions], full participation in international organizations) should be tied to cooperation with the War Crimes Tribunal [ICTY] and progress toward a broader regional settlement, including restoration of autonomy to Kosovo."[108] Following the next Principals meeting on May 23, where there was much discussion about the state of negotiations with Milošević, Albright sent Lake a memorandum reinforcing this condition for the "outer wall" of sanctions. She wrote, "I remain concerned that any change from our announced policy will expose the President to considerable criticism and erode our credibility in negotiations for peace settlement. On March 13, the President told Representative [Steny] Hoyer [Democrat from Maryland] that the Serbs should not expect to join the international community—exemplified by membership in international organizations, attendance at international conferences, and access to financing from the international financial institutions—until they affirmatively comply with requests of the International Tribunal." She continued, "The victims of atrocities deserve justice. Removing persons who would foment violence will reduce causes of future conflict. Finally, the Tribunal is one aspect of our Balkans policy that has received consistent public and congressional praise." She concluded, "After working to place the Tribunal and the law it supports on the combatants' agenda, we should not back away now."[109] Albright's defense of the "outer wall" and its leverage for cooperation with the Yugoslav Tribunal never wavered, and as a result, the outer wall remained standing until the last full day of President Clinton's presidency, January 19, 2001, when he lifted the sanctions except for continuing constraints against 81 Serbs, including Milošević, on transactions with the United States.[110]

At the May 19 meeting, the Principals sought to breathe new life into UNPROFOR as the best alternative to implementing OPLAN 10404. They believed that retaining UNPROFOR in Bosnia "was critical to U.S. interests" and that there should be an "enhancement" of UNPROFOR's ability to fulfill its existing mandate. This included "an enhanced air supply plan for the eastern enclaves on an urgent basis and that unhindered use of Sarajevo airport was imperative." The Joint Chiefs of Staff were instructed "to take this window of opportunity to press allies for as robust an enhancement of UNPROFOR as possible," and Albright was tasked to ensure that options presented for agreement at the United Nations reflect this robust agenda for UNPROFOR.

The Principals returned to the Sit Room solo-style on May 23 for 90 minutes of deliberation on Bosnia. The BTF pre-brief explained that since the last Principals meeting, Frasure had not made progress with Milošević on the Contact Group agreement on mutual recognition and that State was considering various outstanding issues, a prominent one being that "Milošević is reluctant to agree to recognition of Croatia, Slovenia, and Macedonia as a condition for lifting of sanctions." Meanwhile, Galbraith warned that "the risk of war in Croatia will go up if Tudjman does not get anything out of the Frasure-Milošević talks." As for OPLAN 40104, the pre-brief summarized the Pentagon's limited view of the mandate for the

NATO-led extraction of UNPROFOR: "The force would not evacuate civilians, would not defend the enclaves against Serb attack, and would take all necessary means to defend itself if attacked." But the political risks were evident: "The NSC representative to the Bosnia [inter-agency working group] has expressed concern that this limited mandate would not be politically do-able. He has painted a scenario in which Administration officials would need to, in effect, ask Congress to expend significant funds for a NATO operation in which 20,000 US ground troops would be deployed to Bosnia to assist the Serbs in overrunning the eastern enclaves."

The BTF's Norman Schindler concluded: "These concerns have led some in the Administration to wonder whether we should continue to support OPLAN 40104. In their view, if we do support it, we need to get serious about planning for implementation. If we do not support it, we need to develop alternatives, including one in which no NATO forces are used."[111] The Principals addressed these conflicting views the next day.

After discussing Frasure's back and forth with Milošević and unresolved tough issues, the "Principals noted the French and British pressure to 'cut a deal,' and conflicting reports as to whether the French were bluffing or serious about withdrawing their UNPROFOR troops if no agreement was forthcoming. They also noted the problem of uncoordinated Russian diplomatic approaches to Milošević. Principals agreed to let process simmer for now with Milošević, and to approach the French, British and Russians to stiffen resolve and restore Contact Group solidarity."[112] There was thus no evident progress on the negotiating track.

UNPROFOR and OPLAN 40104

The bulk of the Principals meeting was consumed by the prospect of a UNPROFOR withdrawal and OPLAN 40104. Considerable clarity emerged from the Sit Room that day about American intentions: "Principals agreed that U.S. policy following UNPROFOR withdrawal would be to seek multilateral lift of the arms embargo, limited support for arming and training the Bosnian forces, but no commitment to air strikes. Principals agreed that U.S. security assistance should be largely limited to the provision of financing for Bosnian arms purchases from other suppliers, and that training should be by a third party if possible; they ruled out training by the U.S. on Bosnian territory."

But as for OPLAN 40104, questions and not decisions guided the meeting. The Principals tasked subordinates to try to answer such questions as the possible use of NATO forces for civilian protection, assisting movement of refugees from the enclaves, the possible breakdown of humanitarian efforts while NATO was in theater, what to do about prisoners or released prisoners of war that fell into NATO hands, and how to determine to whom NATO would return disputed areas. The easiest mega-answer to all of these questions did not escape the Principals, who "agreed that the magnitude of the problems associated with both OPLAN 40104 implementation and post-withdrawal strategy made it imperative to keep UNPROFOR in place, and [so they] agreed to urgently approach the French to get them to reconsider their possible withdrawal from UNPROFOR."[113]

The Principals further worried that even a partial extraction of UNPROFOR, particularly from an eastern enclave, could provoke "an all-out withdrawal operation." They were exceptionally cautious about the "firebreak point" for U.S. engagement in OPLAN 40104. When would implementing the plan become "inevitable" and at what point would U.S. forces be required to travel to Europe for training under the plan? The earliest possible date for such deployment from American shores was judged to be the third week of June 1995. Further, the JCS understood that the Supreme Allied Commander for Europe would not request any deployment of the force in Europe unless and until there were a U.N. decision authorizing UNPROFOR withdrawal. So the Security Council would turn the final key for any NATO deployment under OPLAN 40104. The Principals sought more information from SACEUR about how the training of the withdrawal force would take place.

There were so many doubts, firebreaks, and alternatives being built into OPLAN 40104 that the Principals' preferred option, namely, to keep UNPROFOR in place with enhanced capabilities, dominated policy discussions. But the final days of May 1995 challenged much of the wishful thinking in the Sit Room.

A Delusion

UNPROFOR Bosnia Commander Rupert Smith demanded on May 24 that the Bosnian Serbs cease their attacks on Sarajevo. At about the same time Albright and Defense Secretary Perry met with Boutros-Ghali in New York to urge more aggressive use of air power following a month of Akashi's refusal to recommend turning the dual key.

As day follows night, Akashi informed the Under Secretary-General for Peacekeeping Operations, Kofi Annan, on May 26 that he had authorized additional air strikes against the Bosnian Serbs and, in particular, bunkers in their ammunition depots. The Bosnian Serbs had struck all of the safe areas other than Žepa the night before. And elsewhere there were reports of "over 70 dead and over 150 injured in Tuzla, mostly from an air-burst weapon that exploded over a crowded city street." Akashi claimed that the Bosnian Serbs had failed to heed his warnings to comply with the February 1994 agreement on heavy weapons and their failure to return four weapons taken from the weapons collection points, as well as "their continued firing of heavy weapons in and around Sarajevo in violation of that agreement and related Security Council resolutions." Akashi wrote that he might authorize more NATO air strikes, as "there is no indication that the Bosnian Serbs are inclined to respect any of these conditions." He also noted that the Bosniaks were in compliance with the heavy weapons' warning, but he wondered whether they would be in compliance by that day's deadline to remove all heavy weapons from the exclusion zone or turn them in at a weapons collection point.[114]

But for UNPROFOR Commander Smith, the NATO air strikes were neither here nor there. He no longer knew what the objective was in Bosnia. In a meeting with John Menzies, Smith pleaded for "a clear plan behind me as to where we're going." He wanted "a bigger aim than four weapons getting back into collection points." He asked, "Do we fight a war?" That would require crossing what he described as the "pain barrier." The only question that mattered to Smith was whether the allies could surmount the pain barrier and fight the war that had to be fought. Were they prepared for body bags, a long-term commitment that includes money and other resources, and a willingness to escalate? The Security Council, in his view, could cross that barrier but only with the risk that UNPROFOR, diplomatic missions, and others trapped in Sarajevo could become hostages. If the Council did not cross the "pain barrier," then he exclaimed, "Don't talk to me about air strikes, weapons collection points, exclusion zones, or safe areas." He would give up and take UNPROFOR with him. Smith believed he had failed with the UNPROFOR mandate and that "air power will not solve this problem." He worried about what would fill in behind an UNPROFOR withdrawal.[115]

Menzies offered his own assessment of the situation:

COMMENT: SMITH REAFFIRMED OUR VIEW THAT THE UNPROFOR MISSION IS DRAWING TO AN END, REGARDLESS

OF THE RESUMPTION OF ROBUST ACTION. UNPROFOR CANNOT GO BACK TO THE STATUS QUO ANTE, AND YET IF IT FAILS TO ESCALATE, AND MUST ACCEPT INSTEAD A NEGOTIATED, FACE-SAVING SOLUTION, IT WILL BE UNABLE TO ENFORCE ANY ELEMENT OF ITS MANDATE: THE SAFE AREAS, TEZ [exclusion zones], AND PREVIOUS REGIME WILL BE LOST COMPLETELY AND CANNOT BE REPLACED BY THIS UN MISSION. IF THE UN DETERMINES TO CONTINUE WITH AN ENFORCEMENT OPERATION, THE MISSION WILL END: UNPROFOR WILL REQUIRE A NATO EXTRACTION. WE BELIEVE THAT WE ARE APPROACHING PERHAPS THE FINAL CRISIS OF THE UNPROFOR MISSION IN BOSNIA. END COMMENT. MENZIES."[116]

Menzies was knocking on the OPLAN 40104 door, the one jammed shut by the Principals only a few days earlier.

The next day, May 28, Menzies briefly met Commander Smith again and heard an even sharper message from him. The machine of U.N. peace-keeping was broken and the bleak alternative was to "make war" or to become unsustainably weak. Reconfiguring or redeploying UNPROFOR "pretends that we are making war" when we are not.

Redefining the mandate of UNPROFOR would continue the "nonwar mode." Menzies reported Smith as believing that there is no real middle ground between war and the abandonment of the UNPROFOR mission. The stark decision remained, "We either fight or we don't." Menzies closed with his frank reflection: "COMMENT: SMITH HAS BEEN MAKING HIS CASE TO THE UN AND OTHERS THAT UNPROFOR IS ESSENTIALLY FINISHED. TO ATTEMPT TO WALK SOME MIDDLE GROUND BETWEEN WAR AND WITHDRAWAL IS A DELUSION. END COMMENT. MENZIES."[117]

More bad news filtered in from Bosnia: On May 28, Bosnian Foreign Minister Irfan Ljubijankić was killed when his helicopter was shot down over the Bihać region of northwestern Bosnia. Krajina Serb forces claimed responsibility. Muhamed "Mo" Sacirbey, Bosnia's ambassador to the United Nations who had intervened with Albright countless times, was named as his successor. The next day Bosnian Serb leaders announced that Pale was rescinding all agreements with the United Nations.

Prospects for the Eastern Enclaves

The summer of 1995 arrived with an intelligence report from the BTF on the prospects for the eastern enclaves—Srebrenica, Žepa, and Goražde. The entire assessment was grim, predicting an ultimate (six months to a year) Serb takeover of the enclaves in the event of an UNPROFOR withdrawal. Most of the 120,000 residents of the enclaves would flee and be driven into central Bosnia by the Bosnian Serb forces. The report noted, "The Bosnian Serbs already have begun stepping up military pressure on the eastern enclaves, launching a ground attack attempting to capture key high ground near Gorazde, pressing the frontlines at Srebrenica, and seizing UN peacekeepers. UNPROFOR Bosnia-Commander Smith believes the Serbs are embarking on a campaign to capture the enclaves."[118] But the BTF expressed caution about the timing of a Serb takeover of the enclaves. Their best guess was that it was not imminent. While the eastern enclaves were "all extremely vulnerable to a concerted [Bosnian Serb Army] offensive," they "are in relatively rugged terrain that would hinder a Serb attack and we believe the Bosnian government has substantial troops in the three enclaves." Not surprisingly, "Srebrenica is probably the most vulnerable of the three enclaves."[119]

The report did not strike fear of immediate defeat in Bosnia among policymakers. The BTF assessment of the risk of the enclaves falling had the caveat, "in the event of an UNPROFOR withdrawal." Granted, the BTF report compelled some of us to recognize that the fate of Srebrenica, Žepa, and Goradže hung in the balance and that a UNPROFOR withdrawal would greatly exacerbate the risk of Serb military takeovers of these three municipalities. But since UNPROFOR withdrawal and the closely tied OPLAN 40104 remained highly problematic on June 1, the report did not set off alarm bells in the Sit Room.

Boutros-Ghali opened the June meetings of the Security Council by presenting some options for the future of peacekeeping in Bosnia. He recommended reducing UNPROFOR's mandate, first by consolidating UNPROFOR troops and eventually reducing their numbers. That presentation set the tone for withdrawal rather than any strengthening exercise of UNPROFOR's troops. On June 2, the Bosnian Serbs shot down a U.S. F-16C fighter aircraft while it was policing the no-fly zone. It took six days for U.S. Marines to rescue the pilot, Scott O'Grady, who had evaded capture in the Bosnian forests.[120]

Meanderings

While O'Grady was still in hiding, and his fate uncertain, the Principals used their June 6 meeting in the Sit Room to little purpose other than to review inconclusive talks with Milošević (who remained stubbornly resistant to the mutual recognition plan), Deny Flight rules of engagement (reflecting concern over O'Grady's shoot-down), options for U.S. support of the U.N. Rapid Reaction Force, and how the contradictory aims of UNPROFOR strengthening and NATO withdrawal planning for UNPROFOR would be funded. Tony Lake's memorandum to Clinton on June 7 listed decisions that boiled down to review of insignificant meanderings in policymaking on Bosnia. Albright told me afterward that her takeaway was, "We do not want to change the UNPROFOR mandate!"

Lower level meetings on the Bosnian and Croat situations ensued during June 1995. They focused on monitoring developments both on the ground and in diplomatic circles. On June 9, we received an update that 146 U.N. personnel remained hostage in Bosnia: 53 in Bosnian Serb custody and 86 being prevented from leaving Goražde by Bosnian government forces. Croat Serbs were still fighting Croatian government forces with the Croatia-Bosnia border heating up with violence. Bosnian Serb teenagers were fleeing to Serbia to avoid the draft imposed by the Pale leadership. The Bosnian Serbs agreed to one UNHCR humanitarian convoy bound for Sarajevo. But Prime Minister Haris Silajdžić, visiting Washington, met a brick wall within the Clinton administration, which could not assure him of military strikes if there were a unilateral lift of the arms embargo—the old "lift-and-strike" option. The "strike" component was not even that popular on Capitol Hill anymore. The additional cost of U.S. support for deploying the European Rapid Reaction Force in Bosnia, to the tune of $300–$400 million, was not faring well in Washington. Discussions continued in New York on various drafts of a new Security Council resolution.

Two days in mid-June were packed with meetings culminating in a Deputies session on June 13. The day before, interagency and State Department meetings yielded the prognosis that OPLAN 40104 would not be ready for prime time until the end of summer or even later, in the fall. The United States would have to pay for 40–50 percent of the NATO extraction force with its up to 25,000 U.S. troops, and this on top of the normal peacekeeping assessment of 30 percent for UNPROFOR forces who would be converted to NATO duty. Thus the United States would have to pay up to 80 percent of the actual sticker price for OPLAN 40104. The State Department was thinking through how to lay the political groundwork for a post-UNPROFOR withdrawal strategy of lifting (the arms embargo), arming (the Bosniaks), but *not* striking (thus precluding U.S. air power). Another worrisome assessment was that Commander Smith had concluded that the Bosnian Serbs simply were not interested in peace talks.

Britain and France wanted to "go blue" in the Security Council on their Rapid Reaction Force (RRF) resolution. A robust RRF conceivably would deflect pressure for UNPROFOR's withdrawal and thus shelve OPLAN 40104. "Going blue" meant the resolution would be teed up for a vote. The cost for such a force remained high and that hobbled the effort, at least in Washington. Further, the Bosniaks were being asked to compromise by not initiating attacks from the safe areas so that the goal of demilitarizing those areas could be negotiated. That did not sit well in the State Department, and Albright did not like sustaining anemic rules of engagement for UNPROFOR. France's ambassador to the United Nations, Jean-Bernard Mérimée, assured her that the rules of engagement "will be more robust." But we had not yet seen the more "robust" rules.

Chirac Jumps In

In a State Department meeting that included Holbrooke, Christopher warned that the British and French resolution in New York was being rushed forward to suit the new French president, Jacques Chirac. Drafting was getting ahead of policy, Christopher warned. He said that the presumption had been that the RRF would include national forces outside direct U.N. command, but it was evolving as an UNPROFOR force. Holbrooke responded that it would be a national force but under U.N. command, with Paris insisting that command would be in the hands of UNPROFOR General Janvier and not Akashi. Christopher believed that would take considerable public relations work since the United States was committed to support the RRF. He could not imagine a sustained American commitment to the RRF without Congress approving the funds for it.

Holbrooke agreed that the United States had stated public support for the RRF. Chirac, however, would throw it back at us as a precursor of UNPROFOR withdrawal. That was not the original idea. Holbrooke recommended that Clinton speak with Chirac about this and at least get a quid pro quo of more robust rules of engagement for a more sharply defined RRF before American funding was assured. Christopher agreed and instructed aides that Chirac be advised that Clinton wanted to speak with him. He wanted any formal vote on the French resolution in New York to be put off for at least one week. Clinton and Chirac would have to work this out, so going blue in New York at the time would be premature. The imminent G-7 talks (Group of Seven largest advanced economies in the world) convening in Halifax, Canada, would need to show unity on Bosnia, but Christopher insisted on getting the formula on the RRF right, even if it meant delaying a vote before the Security Council. In hindsight, however, delays of this character meant that the RRF was still in its infancy when the Srebrenica genocide occurred less than a month later.

Christopher asked the larger question, "UNPROFOR should stay for what end?" Holbrooke answered that UNPROFOR was part of the strategy to continue to isolate the Pale leadership. Christopher's chief of staff, Tom Donilon, and negotiator Bob Frasure said the objective was to stabilize UNPROFOR and then get to an international conference. But Frasure admitted that in recent weeks the UNPROFOR mission had completely collapsed (particularly with Bosnian Serb detainment of UNPROFOR hostages). Other voices wondered anew whether the RRF would increase the chances of just muddling through, which had long been the Sit Room's favored policy choice in Bosnia.

Turning to Holbrooke at the end of the meeting, Christopher said, "You say if we withdraw from Bosnia it is a disaster for Clinton in the '96 election. But if we are still wading through the Bosnian mess in one year, then that also is a disaster for Clinton." The only way to avoid either disaster was to forge a workable short-term policy that ended the war and stabilized the situation before the election season of 1996 dominated American thinking.

Frasure and Milošević Split Up

The next day, on June 13, the Deputies meeting was preceded with interagency and other staff meetings. At the interagency gathering, we learned that UNHCR was suspending it convoys to the eastern enclaves due to the risks for staff, that the French-British resolution before the U.N. Security Council had "gone blue," and that key meetings would be held the next day in Europe on the RRF proposal. Frasure said, "We hope the British and French assure us that the RRF is not just a paper exercise for withdrawal." The U.S. aim remained fixed on the RRF being exactly what it was billed to be, namely, a rapid reaction force to deal with belligerent threats to UNPROFOR. Clinton needed to persuade Chirac the next day in

Halifax that UNPROFOR must not leave Bosnia. Milošević remained troublesome on reimposition of sanctions if the Bosnian Serbs violated any of the Contact Group plan's terms.

Then Frasure dropped a bombshell. He reported, "There's a diplomatic vacuum developing here. I cannot carry the discussion with Milošević any further." The new European Union envoy, Carl Bildt of Sweden, appeared to be the favored candidate for carrying on talks with Milošević. But the NSC's sage Sandy Vershbow, who years later became the U.S. ambassador

to Russia, balked, saying, "Milošević will take Bildt to the cleaners. He works for the EU. He's a neophyte. Do the Europeans really think Bildt will deal with the Pale Serbs?" Frasure could only respond, "It's not clear." He noted that Clinton's letter to former President Jimmy Carter, who was reinserting himself in the process, informed him that the administration would not revisit the Contact Group plan in the midst of the hostage crisis, as that would reward Pale and undercut Milošević.

The goal of demilitarizing the safe areas received sour news from the Joint Chiefs of Staff, who spoke of hundreds of square miles of mountainous terrain and the need for a large number of troops to accomplish demilitarization. Vershbow responded to complaints from Capitol Hill about poor consultations with the view that "we have to find a way to pay for the RRF." He suggested monthly briefings, saying there had to be briefings for everyone, even if not required by law, "or we're screwed." We heard word from USUN in New York that the British had agreed to delay the vote on the RRF resolution until the next Monday. We would need answers to questions about command and control, funding, and the mandate of the RRF before then. And we had to grapple with the political calculus that the RRF was viewed by many as a precursor for UNPROFOR withdrawal, which we opposed, and as political cover for governments unwilling to use the necessary military force to end the war, which certainly rang true in Washington.

Before the Deputies meeting was convened on the afternoon of June 13, USUN reported to me that the Security Council's informal meeting that morning on the French-British resolution for the RRF was "inconsequential," with a standoff between those willing to delay the vote and other nations, such as France, insisting it go forward that week or else there would be problems with the Russians, Chinese, and Serbs. Russia and China were filing weakening amendments. Council discussions were scheduled to resume the next day.

In the Situation Room, the Deputies discussed the upcoming Halifax G-7 meeting and how to avoid Bosnia as a source of dissent there. The overall funding issue for Bosnian operations remained vexing, as it always triggered the need to bring Congress on board with complex negotiations that greatly influenced what would be required for U.S. financial support. Frasure, who attended the Deputies meeting, predicted that over the next four to five days the Bosniaks would stage an offensive to secure a besieged city. Tarnoff worried that such a move could bring UNPROFOR down quickly. Slocombe said it would be difficult to defend the eastern enclaves if there were a Bosniak offensive.

Berger decided to inform French President Chirac that the United States was generally supportive of the RRF resolution but that we needed to consult with Congress, particularly given its cost implications. It was clear at the table that if the overall mission of UNPROFOR and the RRF changed, then a withdrawal of UNPROFOR would be more likely. Slocombe said that the RRF was in Bosnia to defend units of UNPROFOR, and that is the mission the United States was signing up to. Berger responded, "Let's get as much out of Chirac as we can. Will [the RRF] make UNPROFOR more effective?" The RRF had to be defensible on our terms, Berger said. He also instructed that Silajdžić be put on notice that the consequences of a Bosniak offensive would be disastrous. It could lead, Berger said, to withdrawal of UNPROFOR. No one in Sarajevo should assume that the United States would rescue the Bosniak forces or their government.

Slocombe noted that Silajdžić felt passionately about the arms lift and that the Bosniaks were entitled to U.S. air support to defend the enclaves and enforce the no-fly zone. But the chances of Congress agreeing to such American support were very low, he said. Strobe Talbott jumped in, agreeing with Slocombe and urging that the "riot act be read to Silajdžić.

The Bosnians are asking us to become allies. They want U.S. airpower while they conduct the ground war." Slocombe responded, "The Bosniaks keep asking for lift and strike," which by that point was viewed very skeptically by administration officials. General Wesley Clark proposed that the congressional legislation require that if there were a unilateral lift, and then a Bosniak offensive, there would be no strikes by U.S. air power. Berger instructed that Silajdžić be reminded of current U.S. policy, namely, that if there were UNPROFOR withdrawal and a multilateral lift of the arms embargo, the United States would offer out-of-country training to Bosniak forces.

Berger concluded the meeting with three points: First, Clinton would express to Chirac the American support for the RRF. Second, in consultations on Capitol Hill, we would defer the funding issue of the RRF to the larger funding challenge of UNPROFOR. Third, in discussions with Silajdžić, we would stress our firm opposition to a UNPROFOR withdrawal, but that if it were to occur there would be no U.S. air cover for Bosniak forces. Frasure expressed great concern over Bildt becoming the Contact Group negotiator. While he said that Bildt had American support, he did not have a mandate as such from us. The Contact Group would have to agree to his negotiating position. Frasure believed that Milošević might not be prepared to negotiate with Bildt. The only deal Milošević wanted, Bildt conceded, was with the United States. While hostages remained in Bosnia, Frasure believed that Bildt should not see anyone in Pale. Sarajevo would hate the idea of Contact Group discussions with Pale. The Germans were deeply opposed to contacts with Karadžić. Berger had the last word: The United States would not allow Bildt to be flexible on mandatory reimposition of sanctions if the Serbs failed to perform.

Advising Bildt

The next day Albright and I met with Bildt in her State Department office.[121] She was concerned over the lack of clarity in the RRF mission and whether it was being designed to add to UNPROFOR "robustness" or to its withdrawal. And what would be the consent structure for the RRF to use force? Bildt expressed his support for the RRF as a force that would act more robustly on the ground and increase options, including UNPROFOR withdrawal. That admission confirmed our fears. Albright said there was nothing worse from being mired down in Bosnia than a UNPROFOR withdrawal from Bosnia. So it was essential to get the Pale Serbs to the negotiating table. Bildt wanted to pursue the long-struggling mutual recognition and sanctions lifting options with Milošević. But Albright cautioned, "We can't give more on suspension of sanctions than we have. Milošević has walked back from our earlier bid, emboldened by the hostage-taking [of UNPROFOR troops]."

Bildt retorted, "Bad men are driven by their interests. Milošević can't be in the same situation down the road. He should be keen on sanctions relief. If we don't get a deal, which options do we have? Direct talks with the Pale Serbs? An international conference? We face a disaster on the first order." Albright observed that Milošević either could "pull the strings on the Pale Serbs or he [couldn't]." If he cannot control them, she said, why reward him? From the Bosniaks' view, the government forces' recent advances were simply to regain their original territory and thus were defensive in character. Then the fighting escalated for lack of a ceasefire. Albright advised Bildt that Milošević should not, under any scenario, get unconditional relief on sanctions: "If he's given unconditional suspension, then sanctions will never be reimposed. The Russians won't permit it."

Rapid Reaction Force

In mid-June the U.N. Security Council adopted Resolution 998 (Russia and China abstaining), which approved creation of the RRF as "an integral part of the existing United Nations peace-keeping operation, and that the status of UNPROFOR and its impartiality will be maintained." The resolution left "the modalities of financing to be determined later . . ."[122] Heavy fighting also broke out around Sarajevo as the Bosnian government forces launched probing attacks to try to lift the more than three-year siege of Sarajevo. Then a ray of light shone on June 18, when the Bosnian Serbs released the remaining 26 UNPROFOR hostages in exchange for four of their soldiers detained by the United Nations. But UNPROFOR also withdrew from the weapons collections points and observations posts around Sarajevo, which was an ominous development for the worth of the peace-keeping presence.

The Deputies convened in the Sit Room on June 19. Albright, given the centrality of discussions in the Security Council, joined the meeting by video from USUN in New York, while I sat at the table in Washington. Holbrooke joined Talbott and Frasure for the State Department. Berger said that Clinton supported creating the RRF but also saw the need to secure funding for it from Congress. Talbott considered the key issues for the RRF being its size, cost, rules of engagement, and command and control. Berger assumed all of those factors were among those being discussed with allies.

Holbrooke saw a "sea change in U.S. relations with the United Nations last week." How would we pay for the RRF when the United States "had reached the end of automatic payments for emerging U.N. operations?" He believed there needed to be a change in the consultative relationship between the United Nations and Congress and asked whether the administration would have serious high-level consultations with Congress that week. Albright, never one to let Holbrooke step too far on to her U.N. turf, described the RRF issue as a *"sui generis* problem" and that other issues, such as Presidential Decision Directive 25, which tightly regulated American policymaking on peacekeeping since May 1994, undermined U.S. flexibility at the United Nations. Holbrooke responded, "The RRF is not *sui generis*. What of Western Sahara?" The latter U.N. operation had its own peculiarities. Albright was unyielding, saying that we had to separate the RRF from UNPROFOR in all discussions. It should not affect other peacekeeping operations as it was specific only to Bosnia. She clearly had no appetite to open a whole new terrain of dialogue at the United Nations over the funding of peacekeeping operations on Holbrooke's premise that the RRF problem required special handling.

Talbott warned that time was of the essence on the RRF. Frasure explained that the next humanitarian convoy into Sarajevo would be escorted by the first RRF units by that weekend, or at least that was the plan. "If it succeeds," he said, "that will be a big plus with Congress. If it fails, that will have a big effect as well." Holbrooke stressed deploying the RRF to avoid implementing OPLAN 40104. Albright said that would require a "band aid approach" to fund RRF first in order to get it done quickly, in contrast to a grand new scheme on peacekeeping funding worked out with the United Nations, which would take much time. Berger ended the meeting with instructions to nail down options for paying the American portion of RRF costs and for working with Congress.

On June 20, NATO officials requested permission under the dual-key system for air strikes on the Bosnian Serb–held Banja Luka airport in response to violations of the no-fly zone emanating from that airstrip. The next day Clinton met with senior advisers, though not the Principals Committee, to discuss congressional approval of funding for the RRF, even if it entailed no U.S. troops, and to respond to Akashi's letter reassuring Bosnian Serbs that the RRF would not be different from UNPROFOR.

A long time coming, NATO granted provisional approval to OPLAN 40104 on June 28. The Bosnia [inter-agency working group] met that day as the humanitarian situation in the eastern enclaves, including Srebrenica, deteriorated. The NSC's Sandy Vershbow took a refreshingly tough line when he said to "get on with it" in restoring Deny Flight's credibility as we awaited a Defense Department report on that mission. A legal dispute had erupted between the State Department and the Pentagon over how to allocate the American share of the cost of the RRF within the federal government. There likely would be a voluntary fund set up with allies to finance the RRF, which would fall outside of UNPROFOR assessments. Officials also discussed how to airlift humanitarian supplies and the number of soldiers needed on the ground to serve as spotters.

The working group confronted the dilemma posed by the post-UNPROFOR withdrawal scenario—how would we avoid leaving a mess behind in Bosnia? Yet the very effort to confirm the requirements for withdrawal and a post-withdrawal conflict undermined our current policy to keep UNPROFOR in place. Such planning would force the issue as we tried to create a crystal ball of the future without UNPROFOR. The more realistic initiative would be one confirming that the allies would assist a UNPROFOR withdrawal only as a last resort and following a formal request by the Security Council. Clinton would need to issue a statement at just the right time to remind all parties that the United States would respond militarily if necessary. We knew that Milošević would never enter the war fully on Pale's side, but rather surreptitiously.

The endgame strategy devised at the working group meeting included three main elements: First, recognize the cost of any option. Second, follow through on deploying the RRF. If the RRF makes no discernible difference and the situation deteriorates on the ground, the RRF should leave. Third, if the RRF leaves, then the United States must be committed to a UNPROFOR extraction (and OPLAN 40104) and to a multilateral lift of the arms embargo. If Russia vetoes the multilateral lift in the Security Council, then Washington would use bilateral leverage against Russia: no trade, no gain, no U.S. money. We also would use sanctions leverage as our biggest weapon against the Serbs. The strategy would risk relations with Russia, face challenges with NATO partners, show we were taking sides in the military conflict, and encourage Bosniak offensive action. But we saw few other choices on the horizon as "muddling through" proved more complicated with each passing week.

The Deputies convened the next day, June 29. The challenge of preventing Bosnian Serb attacks on Sarajevo loomed large while there was some hope of breaking the siege of Sarajevo by the end of the summer. A small humanitarian convoy was enroute to Srebrenica. A French peacekeeper had just been killed by a landmine. There was fighting on all fronts in the Bihać pocket. We were pushing for voluntary funding for the RRF in addition to UNPROFOR's assessment. Encouraging news arrived from

Bonn: The German Bundestag had approved the cabinet's decision to send soldiers and fighter aircraft to support the RRF in Bosnia, which would be Germany's first potential combat mission since World War II. But this time Germany would be defending the will of the United Nations and not of a dictator.

On Capitol Hill, there was much skepticism about the RRF. Frasure believed that the RRF only had a 10 to 15 percent chance of succeeding in its mission. But it was our only chance, he said. Bosnia's new foreign minister, Muhamed Sacirbey, sent a letter to the United Nations demanding review of UNPROFOR's mandate. The latest projections for an OPLAN 40104 deployment set a much higher level of 110,000 troops and an initial cost of $3.2 billion. No one in the Sit Room embraced such an implausible price tag as June turned into July and the horrors of that fateful month redefined what is plausible.

4

Finally, Diplomacy Backed by Force July–August 1995

This war has been a long search for the magic button to bomb.

WALTER SLOCOMBE

Can we use this moment, when military action may erupt, to ignite a diplomatic track? Can we think freshly about it?

SANDY BERGER

AS THE FIRST week of July 1995 began to unfold, all was quiet in the Sit Room. There were no scheduled Deputies or Principals meetings on Bosnia. We had fallen into a rut of interagency meetings on how to finance the Rapid Reaction Force (RRF) and how to resurrect Deny Flight as an effective deterrent to Serb air attacks. Lieutenant General Howell Estes briefed Madeleine Albright and me at the Pentagon on July 7 about the increasingly implausible details of OPLAN 40104. He then described the absurdity that Deny Flight essentially had morphed into denying NATO the ability to take out Serb air defenses, including around Srebrenica, and thus grounding NATO flights, in contrast to the original mandate that NATO would deny access to the skies for Serbian aircraft, which were flying far too often.[1] The Pentagon characterized any proposal for airdrops of humanitarian supplies to the eastern enclaves as a "non-starter unless we can take out air defenses." The circularity of all options coming back to and being thwarted by the Serb air defenses captured every discussion.

The Sit Room: In the Theater of War and Peace. David Scheffer.
© Oxford University Press 2019. Published 2019 by Oxford University Press.

Srebrenica Debacle

The report of the collapse of the far eastern town of Srebrenica near the Drina River dividing Bosnia from Serbia, and the expulsion of its Muslim residents, arrived in the Sit Room with numbing clarity on July 11 and 12. Up to 25,000 Bosniaks, a large number being internally displaced and finding refuge in the safe area since 1992, were ethnically cleansed from Srebrenica by Bosnian Serb forces and herded together at Potocari, which was the UNPROFOR base just north of the town. Thousands of Bosniak men and teenage boys fled into the forests heading northwest to friendlier territory and perished, most at the hands of the Bosnian Serb forces.

In my book, *All the Missing Souls: A Personal History of the War Crimes Tribunals* (2012), I described the two emergency Deputies meetings, one on each of those critical July 1995 days, that framed Washington's policy choices as events spun out of control:

Deputies Meeting on July 11
The Serbs had threatened to unleash hell on the Dutch peacekeepers unless the NATO air strikes ended. Predictably, all NATO flights were terminated. The Dutch said that their primary responsibility was the safety of their own peacekeepers and that their evacuation must be considered. Albright reported that she had not yet been asked in New York to secure the evacuation of the Dutch peace-keepers out of Srebrenica. Indeed, Boutros-Ghali's staff thought the Dutch could get out by themselves along an eastern route. One of his aides acknowledged, "Srebrenica is gone."

    Peter Tarnoff ... conceded that there was no longer any way to retake Srebrenica, a view shared by the Pentagon. Indeed, nei-ther the French nor the British had any capability in theater to save Srebrenica. Albright wondered whether the Bosnian government would permit the enclaves to be evacuated. ... Wesley Clark ad-mitted no one could raise the Pale Serbs (meaning Karadžić) on the phone. As for the RRF, it would take at least five days before it demonstrated any capability to intervene. It would take until mid-August before the full British unit planned for the RRF could de-ploy in Bosnia. Berger asked if there were any retaliatory options, but Tarnoff responded that there would be no support for that while any Dutch peacekeepers were held hostage. Oddly, the plan-ning for Daring Lion [to militarily evacuate peacekeepers from the eastern enclaves] did not anticipate this kind of situation, where the

Bosnian Serbs already had overrun an enclave and cornered both the peacekeepers and the civilian population. Rather, Daring Lion had envisaged a threat of Bosnian Serbs taking over and an extraction of peacekeepers before the threat could be executed. . . .

Albright proposed more air cover for the enclave. The Defense Department's Walter Slocombe simply replied, "no deal." He muttered, "This war has been a long search for the magic button to bomb." Tarnoff believed we would enter the war on the side of the Bosniaks if the Deputies Committee adopted Albright's proactive suggestion. . . . General Clark added that the Dutch were not willing to risk their soldiers' lives and the British did not want to fight a war. When challenged, they backed off.

Berger wondered how to establish a firewall between Srebrenica and the towns of Goražde and Žepa. . . . Fuerth . . . asked what to do if the Serbs refused to release the Dutch peacekeepers. "What's at stake here," he said, "is an abject abdication of the institutions responsible for the security of the people."

Berger summed up by directing that we figure out what the British, French, and Dutch were willing to do to save Srebrenica. The State Department would contact Milošević and the Muslim leadership to learn what options they believed still existed in Srebrenica and the other enclaves. Evacuation scenarios would be studied. Publicly, the United States would condemn the Serb action and retain the right to force a NATO decision on close air support. We would consult with allies and express our belief that maintaining the safe area of Srebrenica was the best foundation for peace. The crisis strengthened the argument for speedy creation of the RRF. And Washington would state that NATO must be prepared to respond. Most of Berger's instructions, however, ended up in the dustbin of too little, too late.

Deputies Meeting on July 12

The British still argued that the eastern enclaves must not fall, fearing that the collapse of Srebrenica and Žepa would create a domino effect throughout Bosnia. One deputy . . . tartly barked that the British view had been overtaken by events and thus was now entirely irrelevant. Berger agreed that the United States could not alone respond to the French request for air support and airlifts for Srebrenica. But he wanted to tread carefully with the French and ask them what they were prepared to do. "We don't want to be responsible for killing any French effort to rescue Srebrenica," he said. Slocombe offered one possible outcome: that the Dutch peacekeepers and the Muslim refugees withdraw to central Bosnia while Srebrenica fell under Bosnian Serb control. It was implausible, he believed, to keep a Muslim civilian population in Srebrenica. But the Muslim-dominated government in Sarajevo was resisting the flow of refugees streaming north to Tuzla, fearing it meant the end of Srebrenica and only one more validation of ethnic cleansing by the Bosnian Serbs.

Berger ordered that a demarche be fired off to Milošević telling him to let humanitarian convoys through and permit refugees to reach Tuzla. He wanted some order to be brought to the entire U.S. diplomatic approach so that we knew who was negotiating with whom. The Bosnian government had to be told that the humanitarian necessity was to get refugees to safe havens of Goražde and Žepa. But Berger was quickly beaten back on Žepa, with even Kofi Annan conceding that the United Nations could do nothing to prevent it being taken over. There were no military options left to protect the enclaves. The State Department's John Kornblum (who soon became U.S. ambassador to Germany) lamented that the imminent fall of Srebrenica and Žepa was already being portrayed as a major defeat for the United Nations and the Bosniaks. We should focus on humanitarian issues at this point, he said. Speculation abounded at the table that the Bosnian government had allowed the fall of Srebrenica and Žepa as a reason to kick out UNPROFOR and force Washington to lift the arms embargo unilaterally.

The deputies could only "manage" the situation in Srebrenica. We needed to consult with the French and British, ensure that the Dutch peacekeepers were protected and that relief supplies got to the civilians, maintain a firebreak at Goražde, and argue that there was even more reason now to support the RRF and strengthen it. No one was yet aware of or predicting atrocities.[2]

The NSC summary of the Deputies meetings on July 11 and 12 highlighted our discussion looking beyond the Srebrenica debacle:

Deputies agreed on the need to reassert UNPROFOR's ability to carry out its humanitarian and protection missions in Bosnia, and to halt the pattern of successful Bosnian Serb military aggressiveness that has marked the past month. They also agreed that failure to reverse this pattern will result in attacks on the other enclaves and renewed strangulation of Sarajevo, precipitating the collapse of the UNPROFOR mission and initiation of a withdrawal under circumstances that will be perceived as defeat for the UN, NATO and our allies. They also expressed concern that it would accelerate passage of unilateral lift legislation by the Congress in a manner that would damage relations with our allies.[3]

The Deputies approved support for the French resolution in the Security Council "calling for the use of all available resources to restore the Srebrenica Safe Area," but we conceded that UNPROFOR could not reverse the Serb occupation of Srebrenica or prevent the fall of Žepa. We agreed to press for the safe withdrawal of the Bosniak refugees to Tuzla, which would abandon Srebrenica to Bosnian Serb occupation.

Other decisions leapt beyond the horror unfolding in Srebrenica and focused on retaining UNPROFOR in Bosnia "as the best available option for resolving the crisis short of a major Balkan war." There would be a "follow-on strategy to deter further Serb provocations and prevent the collapse of the UNPROFOR mission." This included preserving Bosniak control of Sarajevo and Goražde as the sole remaining eastern enclave resisting Serb control. Acknowledging the rapid decline of the feasibility of OPLAN 40104, the Deputies tasked the Pentagon "[t]o review the viability of U.S. and NATO quick/emergency withdrawal options as a matter of highest priority in light of the speed with which Srebrenica was overrun."[4]

Following a day of interagency and State Department meetings on July 13 as incoming reports about Srebrenica confirmed an unfolding humanitarian crisis, the Principals met in the Sit Room on July 14. Albright joined by secure video from New York accompanied on screen by Rick Inderfurth, and so he filled the Deputy seat for this particular meeting. Their engagement at the United Nations during the Srebrenica debacle was essential. I delivered a full set of recommendations to Albright and Inderfurth prior to the meeting.[5] The CIA's Interagency Balkan Task Force (BTF) advised John Deutch, who had succeeded Jim Woolsey as Director of the CIA, that the Serbs had "largely concluded the evacuation of Muslim refugees from Srebrenica. There is some fighting around Žepa, but no clear evidence of an attack underway to overrun the enclave.... Zagreb may well use this time when international attention is diverted by Bosnia to launch an attack against the Krajina Serbs."[6] That statement would prove predictive of the attack that unfolded several weeks later.

The Principals did not seek to save Srebrenica, as it was too late. But there also was no meaningful discussion about the humanitarian situation and assisting the refugees. Nor was there any reported recognition of possible atrocities at or near Srebrenica. They were still operating in the dark about much of the situation on the ground. The entire discussion focused on a future without Srebrenica and Žepa. The Principals examined "options that are militarily feasible." They deployed General John Shalikashvili, the Chairman of the Joint Chiefs of Staff, to London for a July 16 meeting with his French and British counterparts. The Principals left the fate of Goradže to a collective decision that would have to be made with "Sarajevo, London, Paris, and Kiev," with American support. The Ukrainian government was included because some of the UNPROFOR peacekeepers in Goradže were Ukrainian, so Kiev's voice was critical to their remaining deployed there. The Principals wanted America's allies meeting in London to know "that we believe such a decision would require robust use of air power and that we stand ready to provide it in conjunction with a NATO effort to restore air supremacy over Bosnia."

Priorities

The survival of Sarajevo and sustaining Bosnian government control of it remained the Principals' highest priority. They "agreed that we should not only support using the RRF to open a secure land route but measures to enable UNPROFOR to counter Serb artillery attacks on the city." Such weapons as advanced counter-battery artillery systems to defend Sarajevo were planned for the city. Senator Bob Dole's unilateral lift resolution on Capitol Hill also occupied the Principals' attention. They strategized how to amend the resolution to remove its most onerous provisions. President Bill Clinton would likely veto the resolution if left unchanged. The Principals' killer amendments reflected the imbroglio of the Bosnian conflict. They wanted congressional authorization for American participation in OPLAN 40104, which would entail a colossal price tag. Another amendment would require that the request for implementation of the lift must come from the Security Council and not just the Bosnian government, and it would have to be a multilateral lift. If the bill remained one of unilateral lift only, then it would attract Clinton's veto. Reaching agreement with Dole on such killer amendments would be an almost impossible achievement, but Secretary of Defense William Perry was tasked to try.

Finally, the Principals learned of "a new agreement that EU mediator Carl Bildt was close to concluding with Milošević to obtain a mutual recognition package between Bosnia and Serbia." They were deeply skeptical of Bildt's prospects with Milošević and "agreed that the deal would go too far in re-stricting U.S. ability to reimpose sanctions if Milošević did not live up to his commitment to seal the border." Bildt's plan "would require a majority among either the five Contact Group members or the five UNSC Permanent Members to reimpose sanctions after 9 months." That would not fly in Washington. The Principals planned for a meeting with Bildt "to explain our reservations."[7]

In his memorandum to Clinton the following day, Tony Lake wrote, "Principals agreed we should not be seen as saying 'no' to the French on efforts to make UNPROFOR more robust or their specific proposal to rein-force Goražde. But we must find ways to turn the discussion to options that are militarily feasible without falling into the trap of either having to put forces in on the ground or to be blamed for the failure of UNPROFOR." The message remained clear that no American forces would be deployed, including those that might be required to strengthen or save UNPROFOR.

Lake described the Principals' decisions to press for preemptive suppres-sion of enemy air defenses (SEAD) to support an UNPROFOR stand either at Goražde or Sarajevo; the need to eliminate the dual key in enforcing the heavy weapons exclusion zone around Goražde (and Sarajevo) to bolster the more robust posture on the ground; the need for UNPROFOR to act as though under Chapter VII provisions throughout Bosnia to reduce the like-lihood of additional hostages being taken in response to tough UNPROFOR action in Goražde. . . . the need for UNPROFOR troops assisting in the de-fense of Goražde to be effectively integrated with and supported by Bosnian government forces who would bear the primary responsibility for active de-fense of the enclave; ensuring a clear line of NATO command and control exists for any U.S. lift and/or logistical support; a commitment from the French that if we assist in redeployment of their forces to provide a more robust UNPROFOR posture, they will not turn around and withdraw from UNPROFOR anyway; and a clear signal [that] any U.S. assistance is a one-time deal that implies neither any commitment of U.S. ground forces nor willingness to engage in a similar operation again.[8]

Lake's determination to thread the needle of limiting U.S. engagement while empowering UNPROFOR and suppressing air defenses may have satisfied Clinton as Srebrenica fell. But his checklist would be eclipsed with the need for far more effective American engagement in the weeks ahead.

By July 19, when Lake next wrote to Clinton, there had been several meetings in Washington, informed by further intelligence reports, and resulting in much teeth-grinding as the Srebrenica collapse became ir-reversible. On the morning of Monday, July 17, the Principals met infor-mally for breakfast with Tony Lake in his West Wing office. NSC staffer Ivo

Daalder described this game-changer meeting in *Getting to Dayton*[9] with these prefatory words:

> Lake presented the strategy he and his staff had been working on for close to a month. Its essence was twofold. First, Lake argued that the United States needed to lead a diplomatic effort before the end of the year to get a peace settlement that would preserve Bosnia as a viable, single state composed of two entities. This required a willingness to abandon some long-standing and cherished principles regarding both territorial and constitutional provisions. Second, if this effort failed, the United States should force the issue on an UNPROFOR withdrawal in 1995, prior to the [U.S.] presidential elections. Avoiding a discussion of political calculations, Lake argued that the strategic rationale for doing so was that all sides in Bosnia would have an incentive to try to exploit perceived U.S. vulnerability to outside pressure because of the presidential campaign in 1996 to get their way either diplomatically (by asking for the unattainable) or militarily (by drawing NATO and the United States into the conflict).[10]

Bosnia Endgame Strategy

What Daalder could not reveal in 2000 when his book was published is the now declassified "Top Secret" "Bosnia Endgame Strategy" paper dated July 17, 1995, that was circulated and discussed at Lake's Monday morning breakfast. Daalder's general description of what Lake laid out to the Principals offered a snapshot. But now we can see the details. The five-page single-spaced document began with a one-paragraph summary:

> With the fall of Srebrenica and Žepa, we need to make an all-out effort in the coming weeks to restabilize the situation on the ground, restore UNPROFOR's credibility in Sarajevo, Central Bosnia and Goražde (see separate paper), and press for a realistic diplomatic settlement this year. If this effort fails, we should let UNPROFOR collapse this year and help the Bosnians obtain the military capabilities needed to level the playing field: This would be underpinned during a one-year transition period by air strikes to protect Sarajevo and the other safe areas, reinforced if possible by an UNPROFOR successor force based on a coalition of the willing. Following the transition, the Bosnians would be on their own.[11]

There was no mention of OPLAN 40104 and what requirements would accompany an UNPROFOR collapse; rather, there would be a one-year transition period, after which the Bosniaks either survived to fight on or were defeated.

The "Bosnia Endgame Strategy" provided one or two paragraph details of each strategic component. Among the significant points were the following:

(1) **Restabilization post-Srebrenica and Žepa.** "Our priority is to shore up UNPROFOR in Sarajevo and Central Bosnia by reducing its vulnerability, using the RRF to open secure routes to Sarajevo, and making more aggressive use of NATO air power (under a single key) to halt Serb artillery attacks on the exclusion zones." Washington needed "to persuade the Bosnian Government that it is in its interest to keep UNPROFOR even if this means writing off Srebrenica and Žepa and concentrating UNPROFOR's efforts in Sarajevo and Central Bosnia." (There had been lingering hope to retake the two safe areas but that was short-lived.) Bosniak forces would have to defend Goražde alongside UNPROFOR.

(2) **Pressing for a political settlement.** The paper described inducements "to break the logjam surrounding 'acceptance' of the Contact Group plan." With the loss of Srebrenica and Žepa, the Bosniaks would need to be flexible on the map, constitutional arrangements, "and possibly the Bosnian Serbs' right to secede from the Union after an initial period." The latter point directly contradicted what Lake had conveyed to Clinton days earlier. The paper continued: "We will also need to sweeten our offers to Milošević in order to encourage him to put real pressure on the Bosnian Serbs." Further details on the "Gameplan for a Diplomatic Breakthrough in 1995" revealed a willingness to renegotiate up to 10 percent of the Contact Group map, even if that meant pressing the Bosniaks to accept less than 51 percent of the territory. The new constitution would bend toward the Serbs on the "amount of autonomy their republic would have within the Union and the scope of the 'parallel special relationship' with Serbia."

Remarkably, the game plan walked over the edge to accomplish precisely what the Bosnian Serbs were fighting the war, and committing atrocity crimes, to obtain: "If necessary, we would press the Bosnians to agree that the Serbs can conduct a referendum on secession after 2–3 years, as had been agreed in the 1993 *Invincible* package. We would argue that, if the Bosnians cannot persuade the Serb population that their best future lies in reintegration, there is no point in blocking the peaceful separation of the Union along the lines of the Czechoslovak model [namely, the split into the two nations of the Czech Republic and Slovakia in early 1993]." And to top it off, the Allies and Russians would fund a post-settlement "mini-Marshall Plan" for the Balkans, including the prospect of closer ties to the European Union. So the Serbs (in Bosnia and in Serbia) would unite in one state and then get development funding to steer them toward the European Union.

The National Security Council game plan proposed getting tough with Milošević and telling him "the time has come for him to put up or shut up . . ." Unless he played ball, there would be no more sanctions relief and perhaps even a tightening of economic sanctions as well as "U.S. or NATO air strikes against the Drina Bridges [traversing the Drina River between Bosnia and Serbia] and key supply routes." If he cooperated by pressing the Bosnian Serbs to a settlement, then all sorts of sanctions relief would come his way. The sky was the limit, it seemed to me at the time, as to what would be negotiated away to end the war and validate the Serbs' years of ethnic cleansing sweeps and sieges in Bosnia.

(3) **Supporting Bosnia's survival post-UNPROFOR.** In the event the worst-case scenario unfolded with no political settlement and no stabilization on the ground, then the bogeyman of UNPROFOR withdrawal and NATO engagement under OPLAN 40104 would burden the Allies, including the United States, which would have to pay for much of it and provide tens of thousands of troops to the NATO disengagement force. Interestingly, the NSC paper preferred dealing with the issue in 1995 "rather than having to implement a messy and protracted NATO withdrawal operation in the middle of the election campaign, when the parties will have an even greater incentive to embarrass us or try to draw us into the conflict." But to avoid even the unpalatable option altogether, the United States should provide "the Bosnians with sufficient military capability to survive the immediate Serb onslaught, consolidate their authority over Sarajevo and Central Bosnia and, within a short period of time, to begin to regain territory allotted to them under the Contact Group proposal. This would make the ultimate resolution of the conflict the result of a balance of power on the ground rather than dependent on the actions of the international community."

Stated more bluntly, an effective fighting Bosniak Army would minimize international intervention and perhaps achieve a rapid implementation of OPLAN 40104 while UNPROFOR withdrew with all due haste as the Bosnian Army fought for territory. The magic wand would be lifting the arms embargo multilaterally through passage of a Security Council resolution, "perhaps part of the same resolution terminating UNPROFOR's mandate and authorizing withdrawal."

(4) **Additional support during the transition.** The one-year transition period envisaged that if the Bosniaks were left to fight into the future, there would be a plan to "[c]onduct aggressive air strikes against a broad range of Bosnian Serb military targets to protect Sarajevo (and possibly the other remaining safe areas) against Serb artillery attacks. This would preferably be done through NATO or, if our allies refused to renew the NATO mandate post-UNPROFOR, through a U.S.-led coalition of the willing. The air strikes would be based on new UNSC authority (since existing authority under 836 and 844 is tied to UNPROFOR), or, as a fallback, on a Bosnian Government request for collective self-defense."

The game plan envisaged a successor force to UNPROFOR drawn from a coalition of the willing to help defend Sarajevo, other safe areas, and Federation-controlled areas of central Bosnia. Their legal authority would be drawn either from a Chapter VII U.N. mandate to support Bosnia against Serb aggression or at the request of the Bosnian Government acting under Article 51 (collective self-defense) of the U.N. Charter. Islamic countries (other than Iran) would be invited to contribute forces alongside those UNPROFOR contributors willing to remain under new command. The deployment would last only one year unless contributing governments agreed to stay longer, with the goal to "level the playing field" and then depart and let the Bosniaks win their own war.

(5) **Keeping Belgrade out.** This goal was essential to level the playing field if fighting would become the operative way forward. The elements of the plan included offering "substantial sanctions relief to induce Milošević to stay out, fully seal the border, and accept a much larger international monitoring force [along the border with Bosnia and Croatia]." There was even flexibility to barter some of the Serb-controlled territory in Croatia, forcing the Serbs to abandon Krajina but allowing them to retain part of Sector East, the latter idea surely unacceptable to Croatian President Franjo Tudjman. However, Milošević would be warned "that, if we detect Serbian military support [of the Bosnian Serbs], we will use air power against Serbian forces operating inside Bosnia and

against the Drina bridges and other supply routes, and that we do not rule out strikes against military targets inside Serbia."[12]

Daalder's knowledge about the discussion that ensued in Lake's office after the rollout of the "Bosnia Endgame Strategy" provides important insight into the thinking that morning:

> Despite the boldness of [Lake's] presentation, however, much of the subsequent discussion among the principals was as staid and business-as-usual as previous ones on Bosnia. Albright was fully supportive of the effort, including the particulars. [Warren] Christopher warned that the United States did not have any leverage over the allies or the parties. The risks of failure therefore loomed larger than the possible benefits of trying something new. Lake disagreed, arguing that the United States needed to go for broke, because the risks of not trying a new approach were by now outweighed by the risks of failing if they did try. Lake also rejected Christopher's preference for diplomatic half-measures. He argued that the administration needed to "leap-frog" the obstacles in order to get an integrated approach to the problem. . . . Christopher, Perry, and Shalikashvili showed minimal interest in the ideas Lake had laid before them, preferring instead to return to the immediate issues at hand. . . . Christopher and Perry in particular were not enthralled by yet another policy review. As usual, preoccupation with immediate tactical considerations was crowding out consideration of long-term strategy. And past policy review had hardly been fruitful.[13]

Daalder also recounted in his book that toward the end of the meeting, Clinton walked in. " 'I don't like where we are now,' Clinton said. 'This policy is doing enormous damage to the United States and to our standing in the world. We look weak.' Without a change, more trouble lay ahead. '[I]t can only get worse down the road. The only time we've ever made any progress is when we geared up NATO to pose a real threat to the Serbs.' He called on his advisers for new ideas that would get them out of the rut the administration was in, and then left." Lake, bolstered by Clinton's intervention, asked the Principals to study the "Bosnia Endgame Strategy," consider where the United States should be in six months on its Balkans policy, and then get their own ideas to him.[14]

The "Bosnia Endgame Strategy" became the critical first step toward Dayton. Many of its elements never found traction as both violence and diplomacy veered in unpredictable directions over the coming weeks. The document's willingness to explore huge concessions to the Serbs in exchange for peace would have fundamentally altered the future in the Balkans if ever implemented, perhaps for the better but probably for the worse. Those concessions would have validated the aggressive use of atrocity crimes to homogenize and seize territory. But we needed a template to work with and the "Bosnia Endgame Strategy" became a sounding board for policymakers.

Albright passed the "Bosnia Endgame Strategy" over to me and others on her staff to study. I joined an interagency group tasked with coordinating the drafting of each agency's "ideas" paper. Daalder wrote, "The group was chaired by Sandy Berger and included Sandy Vershbow from the NSC; James Steinberg, Peter Tarnoff, and Bob Frasure from the State Department; Walter Slocombe and Joseph Kruzel from the Defense Department; and David Scheffer from the Washington office of Ambassador Albright. They met almost daily over the next two weeks to ensure that the papers presented the president with the real policy options."[15] Daalder summarized the major papers, including Albright's that I worked on, which were submitted to Berger by early August 1995.[16] But first, much occurred over the two weeks following the July 17 meeting in Lake's office that merits full disclosure to understand the views expressed in the agency papers backed by the Principals.

Albright, her U.S. Mission to the United Nations (USUN) advisers, and I discussed on July 18 how to "melt" the dual key for use of air power that was held by U.N. Secretary-General Boutros Boutros-Ghali. We concluded that authority existed under standing Security Council resolutions and in NATO's own principle of collective self-defense to recalibrate how air power against the Bosnian Serbs could be unleashed. We would need to persuade Boutros-Ghali to delegate his turning power on the key to a local UNPROFOR commander who would be more sensitive to the need for it in real time. We were not aiming at obtaining fresh Security Council approval, as that would prove extremely difficult not only with Russia but perhaps also with the French and British, who had troops deployed in UNPROFOR and thus at risk during any air strike.

The BTF reported on July 18 that the "Bosnian Army defense of Srebrenica collapsed because of a combination of material shortcomings, the light infantry composition of the defenders, a lack of effective command and control, and an underlying reliance on UNPROFOR and NATO to deter Bosnian Serb attacks against the enclave." The BTF concluded, "When it became obvious that outside intervention was not going to save Srebrenica, there was no last-ditch fallback plan and it was too late for the defenders to do anything but try to escape."[17]

A second report by the BTF on July 18 assessed the fate of Goražde: "The Bosnian government almost certainly will make a determined effort to defend Goražde with the forces available in the enclave. The Bosnian Government, however, has little ability to reinforce or assist its forces in Goražde, except possibly by mounting offensives elsewhere to relieve pressure on the city. In the long run, the isolated Bosnian Army forces in Goražde probably would be unable to withstand a strong [Bosnian Serb Army] offensive."[18] These reports painted a grim picture of Bosniak military capabilities in the days ahead.

A Killer Amendment

Lake wrote to Clinton on July 19 about the latest Contact Group initiative and its "decisive phase" with Milošević and the Bosnian Serbs. One killer amendment that Lake anticipated from the Serbs would be "a constitutional provision establishing a right for the Serbs to secede after two years following a referendum. This is a non-starter for us and for the Bosnian Government: it would make the agreement a way-station on the road to the dismemberment of Bosnia-Herzegovina and the establishment of a Greater Serbia. Our goal from the start has been to get a reasonable deal for the Bosnian Government, which means preserving Bosnia as a single union, albeit a loose confederation." He continued with a candid assessment of other governments' views: "Serb efforts to insert a right of secession will likely be viewed sympathetically by the Russians, and perhaps by the French and British, who have always been inclined to impose a settlement on the Muslims. We will need to hold firm, citing our partners' previous commitment to Bosnia's territorial integrity and the need for the international community not to legitimize the change of borders by force. The Serbs' right to establish practical links with Serbs is the most we can offer."[19]

Lake also feared that the Russians would press for a "front-loaded approach to sanctions relief as a sweet[e]ner for the Serbs." This the United States would firmly oppose, "since it will be hard to reestablish tight enforcement of the sanctions regime once its main elements are suspended." Lake warned Clinton that if an agreement were achieved by July 30 with the Serbs, then immediate action would be required on Capitol Hill and in NATO to follow through with the military requirements of such an agreement. That would include convincing Congress to support, including financially, the deployment of as many as 20,000 U.S. troops to Bosnia to implement the settlement. If there were no agreement—the likelier scenario—then we would face the challenges of "tightening of economic sanctions; extension of exclusion zones to the other safe areas; and stricter enforcement of the exclusion zones by NATO aircraft." Lake feared that "our Allies are already showing some hesitation about following through on the air strike threats, citing the limited effectiveness of air power and the risks of Serb retaliation against UNPROFOR. They and the Russians may seek to defer decisions and prolong negotiations past July 30."[20]

The national security adviser was not prepared to let matters string out indefinitely. "But at some point," he wrote, "we will need to tell the Allies and the Russians that our credibility is on the line and remind them of the irresistible pressures we will face to lift the arms embargo if the Contact Group fails to make good on its previous warnings." Clinton handwrote on Lake's memorandum, "am in general agreement with yr. analysis . . . if Europe & Russia balk—Cong will move on embargo." What if the Serbs balk? Lake wrote in his missive to Clinton that "[i]f the Serbs have still not relented and agreed to the peace plan, our Contact Group partners have agreed that a UNSC decision to lift the arms embargo 'could be unavoidable.'"[21] Lake's was a rare view that the Security Council might execute a multilateral lift of the arms embargo if pushed far enough by the Serbs. So whoever might balk—the Serbs, our European allies, or Russia—lifting the arms embargo either unilaterally or multilaterally seemed like a plausible outcome on that midsummer day.

The London Conference

The London conference of July 21 created a new benchmark for Bosnia policy. Secretaries Warren Christopher and William Perry and Chairman of the Joint Chiefs of Staff John Shalikashvili represented the United States while their counterparts in Britain and France also attended. The Americans arrived with a robust set of proposals that essentially would unshackle NATO air power in Bosnia and serve to deter further Serbian aggression. Daalder described the outcome:

In the end, the London conference was a success. Three key agreements were reached that, once fully operationalized by NATO in subsequent discussions, would fundamentally alter the scope and extent of NATO air power in Bosnia. First, NATO would respond to an attack against Goražde with a significant air campaign, which could include targets throughout Bosnia, not just limited strikes in the immediate vicinity of the "safe area." Second, NATO could respond in this manner not only when the Bosnian Serbs attacked the

Goražde enclave as they had Srebrenica and Žepa, but as soon as it was clear that they were preparing to do so. Third, the command-and-control arrangements were streamlined. Authority for calling in NATO close air support to protect individual peacekeepers or units would rest with the local commander of the unit, while authority for more extensive NATO air strikes to deter attack against Goražde would rest with General Smith, the UNPROFOR commander. The agreement provided the basis for the first sustained NATO air campaign in Bosnia, Operation Deliberate Force, which was to commence on August 30, 1995.[22]

Despite the seeming clarity of the London conference mandate, differing interpretations of the mandate and the allies' discordant views about the use of air power in Bosnia clouded the way forward to confront the Serbs.[23]

Berger scheduled a Deputies meeting in the aftermath of London, for Saturday afternoon, July 22. The BTF's Norman Schindler advised the CIA Deputy prior to the meeting that the senior leaders' conference in London on July 21 achieved "general agreement to give the Serbs a warning that attacks on Goražde would be met with strong NATO air strikes. U.K. Foreign Secretary Malcolm Rifkind told a news conference, however, that UN commanders on the ground would continue to have an effective veto over use of air power." But there appeared to be "no real movement on the issue of bolstering UNPROFOR forces in Goražde." Schindler argued for "maintaining some international presence in Bosnia" to deter Bosnian Serb action against Sarajevo and to bolster the Croat-Muslim Federation. But he continued: "On lifting the arms embargo, we believe that the eventual prospect of Serbian intervention would more than outweigh the benefits the Muslims would derive from new weapons shipments. Ultimately, we believe a political settlement is in the best interests of the Muslims, and achievement of one will require a diplomatic initiative that moves in the direction of the Serbs."[24] This fortified the concessions to the Serbs set forth in the "Bosnia Endgame Strategy."

Predictions About Croatia

The BTF also circulated a Top Secret Intelligence Report on July 21 that predicted a Croatian offensive as early as midsummer to seize major portions of UN Sectors North and South, although a time frame of autumn 1995 for the Croatian offensive seemed more plausible as Zagreb "currently plans to order a major offensive. . . . this autumn." The BTF predicted "substantial success" by the Croatian Army but doubted it could "completely defeat the Krajina Serbs if the Bosnian Serb and 'Yugoslav' Army lend substantial support."[25] The Intelligence Report's suggestion of sooner than later proved true very quickly, indeed within two weeks, as the Croatian Army swept through the Serb-held sectors of Croatia within a matter of days in early August, facing almost no resistance from either the Bosnian Serbs or the Yugoslav Army.

At the time, however, the report's title, "Croatia: Major Conflict Likely This Autumn," and most of its content left the impression that this was a threat more likely to unfold two or three months later, when a peace settlement might have been achieved that would change the calculus for Zagreb and thus undermine the prediction of an offensive. The report noted, "Zagreb almost certainly will give its key Western allies—the US and Germany—limited warning before launching a major offensive. . . . Croatian Army units can quickly mobilize, limiting our ability to predict the exact timing of an attack."[26]

Debate: Unilateral Lift and OPLAN 40104

When Deputy National Security Adviser Sandy Berger convened the Deputies meeting on July 22, he informed us that Clinton posed three sets of questions that required discussion: First, what would be our strategy on Senator Bob Dole's amendment to force a unilateral lift of the arms embargo? Second, what would we do if UNPROFOR collapses; do we bomb, and what happens as refugees stream out of Bosnia? Third, what would be our diplomatic strategy if European envoy Carl Bildt's efforts failed, as seemed likely? All of these questions brought to the forefront the "Bosnia Endgame Strategy."

Berger worried about the inevitability of a unilateral lift, but for the time being thought it could be stalled as long as UNPROFOR took measures it had agreed to take to protect safe areas and open up access roads to Sarajevo, Goradže, and elsewhere. If "London fails," meaning NATO would remain constrained in its ability to unleash air power over Bosnia, he wanted to seek a multilateral lift first and fall back to a unilateral lift as the final option. The circumstances could unfold, he said, where a unilateral lift gained irreversible traction.

Albright joined this critical Deputies meeting, so I sat against the Sit Room wall as her "plus-one." She attended a number of Deputies meetings in July and August 1995 as the officials she so often interacted with—Strobe Talbott, Peter Tarnoff, Richard Holbrooke, Wesley Clark, Sandy Berger, Walt Slocombe—attended the Deputies meetings, and she could wield her own considerable influence face to face with them. She responded to Berger's introductory remarks by pushing back on unilateral lift: "If we go unilateral, we lose the French on Iraq [where we needed French support to sustain the sanctions regime against Saddam Hussein]." Talbott cautioned that any move to lift the arms embargo "must not strain the alliance." Tom Donilon, Christopher's chief of staff, warned that any congressional progress on a unilateral lift would undermine the London talks, where Christopher and his counterparts were striving to maintain UNPROFOR's presence in Bosnia, seeking a negotiated delivery of humanitarian aid to Sarajevo, and ensuring that Goražde not fall. Talbott cautioned that a "unilateral lift could endanger the President's national security interests in NATO."

The NSC's Sandy Vershbow, echoing the "Bosnia Endgame Strategy," said that if the London talks failed to produce a path to peace and UNPROFOR left Bosnia, then we should seek a multilateral lift, and if that failed, then the last resort would be a unilateral lift. Under Secretary of State for Political Affairs, Peter Tarnoff, suggested using Article 51 of the U.N. Charter to claim collective self-defense for Bosnia, a legal argument I had long championed in the Sit Room, and in this instance would legitimize a multilateral or if necessary unilateral lift of the arms embargo.

Berger ran through some hypotheticals of UNPROFOR collapsing because of a renewed NATO bombing campaign or because the United States pursued a unilateral lift of the arms embargo, or because the London talks collapsed and OPLAN 40104 covered an UNPROFOR withdrawal. He mused about a "lift, train, strike, reconstitute UNPROFOR, save a central rump Bosnian state" scenario. Talbott responded, "I can't see us getting from here to there. We speak of the 'coalition of the willing.' We may have a 'coalition of the non-willing' that would be larger. What was central to our success in Haiti [in 1994] is that the United States was it. For Bosnia, we would have to have troops on the ground." Tarnoff agreed, saying "Are we going to sustain Bosnia bilaterally and then others follow our example? That is not a coalition of the willing."

Donilon, who many years later became President Barack Obama's national security adviser, cautioned not to pull the switch immediately to activate OPLAN 40104 if Goražde were to fall. How long would we keep UNPROFOR in central Bosnia and would its withdrawal altogether be a

"soft" or "hard" withdrawal while we were punishing the Serbs? What level of support would the United States provide? Admiral William Owens, the Vice Chairman of the Joint Chiefs of Staff, answered Donilon by advising that NATO could do much more with reconnaissance and air strikes. The Serbs would come in over four roads. So while UNPROFOR withdrew, the necessary air strikes would focus on those roads. But the air strikes would essentially be an element of neutrality to permit a safe withdrawal of UNPROFOR troops. After UNPROFOR withdrew, we could get weapons to the Bosniak covertly or "keep the lever in our hands with air strikes" against the Serbs.

Fuerth digested Owens' remarks and concluded that OPLAN 40104 required "major revision." Talbott complained that the London talks addressed only the fate of Goradže and no other safe area. Bosnian Serb General Ratko Mladić was certain to "go after other areas." Tarnoff cited Tuzla and Bihać as areas that we needed to decide how to defend. The U.S. position in London was to defend all of the enclaves while the British and French focused only on Goražde. Bihać, we learned, probably was Mladić's next target.

Berger asked the key question: "Can we use this moment, when military action may erupt, to ignite a diplomatic track? Can we think freshly about it?" He must have had the "Bosnia Endgame Strategy" in mind. He proposed harder thinking about blocking unilateral lift (meaning the Dole amendment) but contemplating an end state of unilateral lift and what we wanted if that were to happen. He asked us to deconstruct what would happen if UNPROFOR failed and what to do about Bildt's diplomatic efforts.

Berger began to summarize the Deputies' discussion: As long as the London strategy was working and Goradže and any other enclave did not fall, and provided UNPROFOR stayed in Bosnia, then there should be no lifting of the arms embargo. If London failed, any enclave fell, and if UNPROFOR withdrew, then the United States would have to lead the evacuation of UNPROFOR (OPLAN 40104) and in that capacity we would provide the necessary support to the government and people of Bosnia to strengthen their capacity to exercise a legitimate right of self-defense. Any contingency plan, including OPLAN 40104, must bring enough support to bear to be successful. The president would reserve the right to determine that the Security Council was no longer maintaining or re-storing international peace and security. The withdrawal of UNPROFOR would constitute a failure to maintain or restore international peace and security. The introduction of any NATO force into Bosnia in connection with a UNPROFOR withdrawal would trigger the unfettered right of self-defense. For an extraction of UNPROFOR to be successful, it must not be followed by civilian losses and territorial losses by the Bosniaks.

The Deputies did not venture into more of the details of the "Bosnia Endgame Strategy" that day as the fate of the London talks hung in the balance. If the strategy explored in London worked, then that would de-flate some of "Strategy" 's urgency.

Tarnoff shortly thereafter convened the first daily Bosnia meeting in his spacious office on the seventh floor of the State Department. The dual key on use of air power over Bosnia remained alive in Paris, so there was much strategizing on how to break down French resistance to liberating the decision-making process. The French and British support for the London package was linked to securing U.S. backing of the Bildt diplo-matic deal with Milošević, which would make reimposition of sanctions very unlikely even if the Serbs reneged on the negotiated framework.

Holbrooke, who attended the Tarnoff meeting, warned that we should agree to the Bildt reimposition formula only if we achieved a very clear understanding of the air-strike policy. Since the British and French were challenging efforts to dismantle the dual-key procedure, what was the point of the exercise? "We'll never re-impose sanctions once they are lifted," warned Holbrooke. He complained, "We need to know what the [air-strike] targets are in Bosnia! Why don't we know? Any graduated re-sponse is a bad idea. We have to be briefed." Holbrooke, in characteristic mode, focused on the thorniest issue and sought to bring it out in the open to expose Bildt's formula for what it was—a huge concession to Milošević—while demonstrating the weakness of our own knowledge of how we would achieve a viable air-strike policy as part and parcel of giving Milošević what he wanted on sanctions.

I weighed in with a self-defense rationale that remained consistent with Security Council resolutions but would require a revision of OPLAN 40104. I summarized my proposal in a memorandum to Inderfurth to prepare him for Security Council discussions:

I argued that we could erect numerous barriers to trigger the lift op-tion (London or RRF failure, UNPROFOR withdrawal), regard the

Federation as the successor to perform the duties of UNPROFOR, utilize the NATO extraction operation as a means by which to provide weapons and equipment to the Federation, and use the authority of Resolution 743 [of February 21, 1992, establishing UNPROFOR], which permits delivery of weapons and equipment for the sole use of UNPROFOR, as sufficient grounds to arm the Federation as the successor of UNPROFOR on the ground. In this manner we would not have to embrace unilateral lift, but rather enhance existing UNSC authorities. (And we'd block any effort in the Council to dispute, by vote, our interpretation of Resolution 743.)

Frasure thought my plan would rip apart the alliance; OSD said it would require a major change in OPLAN 40104, and there's not time before the Dole bill. Fair points, but Dole's bill will rip apart the alliance if it's veto-proof. The alliance may find my option more attractive than the Dole Bill. While Dole's does not obligate the U.S. to arm the Federation, we know the allies will pull out [of] UNPROFOR if his bill is adopted and that the United States will get drawn in. My proposal limits the arms transfer to the extraction operation and confirms our responsibility to help the Federation defend itself by getting arms (and associated training) in immediately with the extraction operation—a gutsier move then Dole's. But we would not necessarily continue arming the Federation after our extraction force is removed. (If our rationale on 743 holds, though, we could keep arming the Federation.)[27]

I also cautioned Inderfurth about what would be raised the next day, July 24, at the Deputies meeting in the Sit Room, as he needed to know what was planned in Washington while he held forth in New York. Annex I of the "Bosnia Endgame Strategy" would be on the table, namely, the "Gameplan for a Diplomatic Breakthrough in 1995," which proposed a referendum on Bosnian Serb secession. I wrote, "Caution on any referendum on secession for the Serbs. It's a very slippery slope. The Serbs have seized enormous territory through ethnic cleansing, and then we hold a 'democratic' referendum to confirm such aggression? A very transparent act of appeasement."[28]

Albright and I attended the Deputies meeting. Berger informed us that the Deputies would convene every day "from now on" to address the Bosnian issues. Under Clinton, the Deputies had never before focused that intensively, each day, on any other foreign policy issue. One way or another, the status quo, or muddling through, was no longer an option. Berger announced that the president would be speaking with French President Jacques Chirac about Bosnia literally within the next five minutes. Albright reported that Boutros-Ghali was refusing to meet with the British and French ambassadors and herself until he received a "nonpaper" on NATO planning. The Deputies arranged for a joint U.K.-French-American non-paper to reach Boutros-Ghali in time for his 5 p.m. meeting with his aides that day. Albright noted that Boutros-Ghali seemed genuinely confused about what was happening beyond the fate of Goražde, and thus the non-paper would help him understand. He was holding onto his institutional prerogatives to control the dual key on air strikes, and he refused to delegate his power to turn the key over to UNPROFOR Bosnia Commander Rupert Smith.

Cities Under Threat

The discussion at the Deputies meeting turned quickly to the fate of Bihać in northwestern Bosnia. "[T]he Croatian government had notified [U.S.] Ambassador [Peter] Galbraith of its intention to launch an attack into the Bihać sector during the early morning of July 25. [The Deputies] agreed that, given the deteriorating military situation in Bihać and the inability immediately to apply the London agreement to Bihać, it would be inappropriate to attempt to dissuade the Croatians from their plans."[29] An area of 125 square kilometers in Bihać had been captured by the Bosnian Serbs during the preceding week. We were advised that any defeat there would be more significant than defeat in Goradže. Berger wanted to obtain a North Atlantic Council (NAC) decision on use of NATO power to defend Bihać underpinned by existing authorities to legitimize the decision. James Steinberg, the brainy head of Policy Planning at the State Department who later became Deputy National Security Adviser during Clinton's second term, aptly noted that for Goražde we had long sought to ensure a viable deterrent to Serb aggression, while in Bihać we needed to deter the Serbs who were on the march.

Talbott raised the fate of the Croatian city of Knin, held by Krajina Serbs and a clear target for the Croatian Army if and when Tudjman decided to retake Sector South, Krajina. "We can't demarche Tudjman. We are winking at Croatia on this," Talbott said. The Pentagon's Walter Slocombe interjected, "If Tudjman attacks Knin, he will likely set off a major fight, risking a confrontation with Belgrade." Talbott responded, "We can't turn this off." Slocombe believed it "would be easier to secure European support on Bihać if Tudjman stands back from Knin." So the Deputies decided "that the Croats should be warned against taking this opportunity to launch an attack against Knin, with the accompanying risk of a multi-front campaign and possibly drawing Serbian Government forces into the conflict."[30]

London at Risk

Berger intervened with a read-out of the president's just completed phone call with Chirac, the notes of which had been rushed into the Sit Room. Clinton "made all of our points," Berger said. These included that Commander Smith was the right level of decision for the dual key as a matter of sound military practice and that Washington and Paris needed to jointly sell the idea to Boutros-Ghali. Chirac considered Smith as appropriate for ongoing decisions for close air support and the protection of Goražde. But he said that French General Bernard Janvier, who was the theater commander for UNPROFOR and was Smith's superior, should make the initial decision. Boutros-Ghali should retain power over the dual key for decisions on a countrywide air campaign, but Chirac believed he would agree to turn the key. The French leader described his view to Clinton as representing that of the many troop contributors to UNPROFOR.

The Deputies reacted immediately at the table, arguing that "several key elements of what had apparently been agreed in London now seemed to be coming undone." We had to restore the London consensus. Berger told us that we would have to work the dual-key issue at levels below Chirac "and play this out." Talbott cautioned that we were up against a strong view that the dual key should remain in a civilian U.N. official's control. Berger responded, "We will stand for Rupert Smith."

Talbott then linked Chirac's resistance on the dual key to the Croatia situation. He said, "A setback for Chirac would make it unlikely to get Tudjman to hold back now. We don't want to turn this into a wider war."

The Dole resolution calling for unilateral lift of the arms embargo on Bosnia still raised the specter of the president having to cast a veto that might not be sustained in Congress. The Deputies endorsed seeking a series of amendments to the Dole resolution that would "(1) change the triggering mechanism to ensure that the Bosnian government could not unilaterally start the clock on a requirement for the U.S. to lift the embargo; (2) endorse the efforts to strengthen UNPROFOR through the RRF and the London Conference; and (3) change the requirement from unilateral lift to multilateral lift." If Dole insisted on unilateral lift, the Deputies would recommend that Clinton veto the resolution.[31]

Berger turned the Deputies' attention to the "Bosnia Endgame Strategy" and what had been launched at the Principals' July 17 meeting in Lake's office. Frasure said that Holbrooke and he had met with Bildt only two hours earlier in Washington. It was a "bad conversation," he recalled. He even wondered whether Bildt would resign his post as European envoy to the Balkans. Bosnian Prime Minister Haris Silajdžić was no longer interested in working with Bildt. Frustrated at the lack of progress in the talks with Milošević, Frasure proffered the idea of peeling back a good number of the sanctions on Serbia in order to make some headway in Bosnia.

This gave Berger an opportunity to move past such details and stress, "The President is looking for a broad strategy on diplomacy. Take Annex I of the *Bosnia Gameplan Strategy* [laying out the diplomatic plan] and add some ideas to it." Talbott demurred, saying, "No, we need to subtract from the Annex I diplomacy." Frasure added, "On the ground it is much more complicated. It's illusory to structure a diplomatic strategy." But Berger pushed back, "When slippage stops, where do we go? We need to game out a new diplomatic package!" So the Deputies "considered the need to look at multiple diplomatic options and tracks given the fluid nature of the current environment and the need to move thinking beyond the current 'Milošević track.'"[32]

Endgame Thinking

The Deputies met on July 25, convening in the middle of intensive NAC negotiations at NATO Headquarters that stretched deep into the evening in Brussels. Tarnoff declared, "We have to try to save London." He meant the agreed outcome of the London conference. Ironing out what approvals would be required under the dual-key formula proved maddeningly difficult as the Americans, British, French, and Boutros-Ghali squared off among themselves, with each arguing their own variation to the common theme of how to authorize NATO air power over Bosnia under various options, ranging from Option 1 covering the most obvious Bosnian Serb military targets to Option 3 covering a broader range of strategic targets. The Deputies would have little or no impact on the NAC talks at this late stage of the day, but they agreed "to the French proposal that UN authority for Option 1 and 2 air strikes be delegated to the UNPF theater commander, General Janvier, with the expectation that he would delegate authority for close air support to the local commander [namely, Commander Smith]. They agreed that, in light of French opposition to delegating authority for Option 3 air strikes to Janvier, we would agree to defer a NAC decision on the modalities for UN-NATO coordination until the time Option 3 authority was sought. This would be without prejudice to the U.S. position that a decision by UN Secretary General Boutros-Ghali was not required."[33]

The NAC finally agreed after lengthy discussion to the essential elements of the London consensus.[34] Then, in relatively short order, the NAC extended such fresh proactive NATO air power beyond the aim of defending Goražde to the remaining safe areas on August 1. On August 10, Admiral Leighton "Snuffy" Smith, the commander of the U.S. AFSOUTH forces covering the Balkans, and General Janvier "signed a memorandum of understanding on the circumstances for NATO air strikes in case of a threat or attack against any UN 'safe area' and the targets to be struck in case such strikes were deemed necessary."[35] The stage was set for the use of NATO air power in late August when a Sarajevo market place came under Bosnian Serb shelling.

On July 25, the Deputies also discussed the rather dyspeptic Bildt negotiations with Milošević. Frasure would be attending a Contact Group meeting the next day and needed instructions on how to handle the package that Bildt had negotiated with Milošević. The Deputies "agreed that we should not endorse or provisionally accept the Bildt-Milošević package but that we needed to take a sufficiently positive stance to encourage continued UK/French support for serious NATO military action." Frasure would signal U.S. support for continued efforts by Bildt, but Bildt would need to consult more closely with the Bosnian government "to address their concerns." Also, Bildt would need to understand that the United States remained opposed both to "de facto lifting of sanctions in the guise of suspension" and to giving Milošević nine months before reimposition could be initiated. Fuerth argued that it "was clear that lift for nine months means that it's permanent." We also needed to see more from Milošević on closing the Serbian-Bosnian border and accepting more international monitors.[36]

Frasure pondered what an actual closing of the border would look like. "We can't move ahead with Milošević," he lamented, "as long as Mladić is on an aggressive binge and playing out his Attila the Hun mode." Fuerth said, "It's absurd to proceed with further concessions for Milošević until London is saved." Talbott countered, "We have to keep the talks with Milošević going in order to keep the allies on board." Frasure observed,

"We are a long way from consummating any deal with Milošević." Berger concluded, "We are prepared to continue working on this, but we can't commit to what Bildt is negotiating while so many other factors are on hold." The Deputies agreed that "the negotiations must proceed in tandem with genuine restabilization and de-escalation by the Bosnian Serbs; otherwise it would [be] politically untenable for us to move ahead with a deal with Milošević."[37]

The Deputies meeting on July 26 focused almost exclusively on the "Bosnia Endgame Strategy." Berger set up the initial questions: What is the level of U.S. engagement after UNPROFOR is withdrawn? What will trigger a UNPROFOR withdrawal? Should the United States be neutral during the extraction of UNPROFOR? What is our policy if UNPROFOR comes under attack while withdrawing? Would the London agreement collapse?

Slocombe postulated that if we reached September having muddled through, there would be a deteriorating situation to confront. We might conclude at that point that UNPROFOR could not be saved. Bihać might be under large-scale attack. The RRF and the London package might not have fixed the situation, leaving UNPROFOR with little choice but to withdraw. Berger asked about U.S. goals during a UNPROFOR withdrawal: Minimize U.S. casualties? Minimize UNPROFOR casualties? Get out as quickly as possible? Demonstrate a posture of neutrality?

Admiral Owens warned that if we executed unilateral or multilateral lift after UNPROFOR withdraws, then that would give a green light to the Serbs to attack. Wesley Clark pondered aloud whether the Serbs had the intention to oppose a UNPROFOR withdrawal. I noted the difficulty of the NATO force sustaining a nonbelligerent status with so many objectives to achieve in a limited period of time. The principle of neutrality comes with a lot of baggage under international law.[38] Berger nodded and asked about such options as arming the Bosniaks overtly or covertly, training their forces, launching air strikes to defend them, and what to do if the Croatian Army moved against the Serbs in Sectors North and South.

Slocombe saw the endgame as one of containment of the Serbs and not having the United States committed militarily on the ground. What kind of Bosnia would emerge? A unitary state with a central government, a sort of Balkanized Switzerland? Or a largely Muslim state within its current borders? He argued for holding the current territory that the Bosniaks control, not using air support or arming of the Bosnian Army to reconquer territory, and preparing to guarantee a territorial solution with the Bosnian government accepting the current borders.

Berger stated firmly that we would not ratify ethnic cleansing and not ratify aggression. He agreed with Slocombe that the Bosniaks must defend what they now held as a matter of self-defense. The next option was for the negotiating track to roll back the Serbs from any territory they currently held. But negotiations would be the only way to accomplish that.

Admiral Owens cautioned that we might be underestimating what it took for the Bosniaks to defend themselves. "It will be very hard," he said. If we do not defend the Bosnian state, then we would have to see what could be accomplished to negotiate a "rump state." The most plausible option might be to lift, arm, train, and strike but only to the extent that the Bosniaks accepted the status quo on territorial control.

Berger returned to the basic worst-case scenario: How does this end? How do we get out of the house before it collapses, and we are able to blame someone else? Are we a nonbelligerent withdrawing from Bosnia? The Serbs surely would not be neutral as we retreated. He described the basic objectives as not putting U.S. combat forces into Bosnia, containing the Bosnian Serbs, maximizing the viability of the Bosniaks, rejecting aggression and ethnic cleansing, preserving the larger objective of Bosnian statehood (even if as a rump state), and providing humanitarian relief.

Berger told us that Clinton asked whether there was any diplomatic game other than one that engaged Milošević. Could Bildt's collapse in his talks with Milošević provide an opening? Fuerth intervened with the maxim that we had to be prepared to use military force to back up our diplomacy. Tarnoff proposed that the United States take the leading role on diplomacy, which in fact would be realized shortly in August when Richard Holbrooke took over the negotiating duty. Tarnoff proposed that we tell Bildt to go home and inform the Contact Group to back off as Clinton took the lone lead. Indeed, the Allies might be relieved if the United States took the lead. But we had to accept the risk of failure if we were to lead.

Fuerth argued that the United States, if it took the helm, could offer an alternate vision of a reconstituted Bosnia rather than a destroyed country. We could spearhead spending money to rebuild Bosnian cities. Tarnoff echoed Fuerth's words, saying we would be there to help the Bosniaks get the best possible deal, just as we did for Israel. The United States certainly was not going to break with the Bosniaks. We would try to get them the best possible deal. Slocombe quickly agreed. Owens chimed in that if we wanted to make sure Bosnia was preserved, we must use the necessary force.

Berger summarized that the Deputies were leaning toward a self-defense strategy for existing Bosniak territory and using the negotiating track to roll back some Serb gains. There would have to be a major U.S. diplomatic push if and when UNPROFOR withdrew. But such diplomacy must be linked to the willingness to use military force. The options for UNPROFOR were total withdrawal, partial withdrawal, staying in Bosnia over the winter, or staying only in Croatia and Macedonia. There remained a clear option to arm the Bosnian Army during or after a UNPROFOR withdrawal, but the latter would encourage the Serbs to act aggressively immediately. Between neutrality and a nonbelligerent status, the United States would favor a nonbelligerent status. The meeting ended with Berger stating flatly that "diplomacy has to be associated with force."

Croatia's Army on the Move

The next day, July 26, produced two critical developments. First, Boutros-Ghali delegated his dual-key power for air strikes to General Janvier, which seemed like a progressive move except that now we had an equally obstinate U.N. official, Janvier, to persuade to activate air strikes. Second, the U.S. Senate voted to lift the arms embargo on Bosnia if the United Nations decided to withdraw UNPROFOR from the theater.[39] That possibility remained highly problematic.

The Deputies met to address, among other items, the defense of Goražde and the unfolding crisis in Bihać on July 27. Lake, Perry, and Christopher were talking with their British counterparts about the "zone of action" and likely targets around Goražde if air strikes were required to defend it. Discussions were underway in the NAC to extend agreed procedures for use of air power to other safe areas. Berger wanted coverage for Tuzla, Sarajevo, and Bihać. Ambassador Galbraith reported in from Zagreb about his discussions with the Croat defense minister. By the following week there would be a strong Croat force deployed around Bihać. Even if we declared a "zone of action" it would probably not deter the Croats, concluded Galbraith. The Croats, we learned, were planning to attack the Krajina Serbs on August 1, thus revising the CIA's earlier estimate of mid-autumn.

If the Croat forces stalled in their advances, then we feared that Milošević would intervene with Yugoslav forces. U.S. personnel already stationed in Zagreb and Split, Croatia, would be exposed to risk when the expected military push began. If we could not assure the Croatians that there was some kind of protection for Bihać, then we would not be able to dissuade them. Tarnoff warned not to oversell our ability to influence the Croats. Slocombe said he would delay Assistant Secretary of Defense Sarah Sewall's trip to visit the Federation so as to avoid feeding suspicions that it would be tied to what the Croats were planning.

The Bildt plan with Milošević looked increasingly at risk as well. Berger advised that we focus on the "Bosnia Endgame Strategy" and move beyond Bildt. The strategy paper, Berger reminded everyone, addressed three scenarios: the house collapsing, withdrawing UNPROFOR and the post-withdrawal strategy, and quickly launching a diplomatic initiative. He needed our views, soon.

The next day we learned that the Croatian Army was on the move near Krajina, capturing a key town. The Krajina Serbs were retreating. Croatian MiG-21 flights violated the no-fly zone. There was no shelling of Bihać yet. Reports from Zagreb confirmed the August 1 date for an attack on Krajina. At the interagency working group meeting on the morning of July 28, Sarah Sewall categorically denied any supply of arms to the Croatian Army, noting that the arms embargo was still part of U.S. federal law, which prohibited retransfers of arms into Croatia or Bosnia. The British were opposed to using NATO air power around Bihać, including extending Goražde defensive rules to Bihać. We considered the option of creating another exclusion zone around Bihać as Pentagon officials cautioned not to let another safe area fall as that could tilt the overall strategic balance against the Bosniaks.

The Deputies convened later in the day on July 28. A massive attack by the Croatian Army, numbering about 250,000 troops, to take both Sectors North and South appeared imminent. Berger wanted to caution the Croats about stoking a wider conflict. Fuerth responded, "It would be an irrelevant message. An intense war is designed to produce results in the shortest period of time." Tarnoff agreed with Berger, though, that a message to Zagreb should seek to discourage a larger conflict. Fuerth speculated that Croatian President Tudjman was beyond the point of no return. Tarnoff reported that Galbraith believed the "go/no go" decision would be made by Tudjman on Sunday evening, July 30.

Fuerth recommended that maximum international pressure be brought to bear against the Serbs to stand down in order to avoid a wider conflict. Berger asked for Christopher to call Kozyrev with that message. Tudjman also should be made aware of our efforts to defuse the looming military conflict, particularly our contacts with Moscow. The Joint Chiefs of Staff believed that aiding Bosniaks in Bihać was a pretext for moving the Croatian Army through Sectors North and South. U.S. troops in Zagreb and U.N. Confidence Restoration Operation in Croatia (UNCRO) peace-keeping forces would be at risk. The United States had genuine interests—the safety of American troops—in talking to Tudjman.

Berger summarized that Christopher would call Kozyrev to urge a Serbian stand-down; Galbraith would go back to Tudjman to warn against going beyond Bihać, which would stoke a much wider conflict; the Pentagon would position U.S. troops in Zagreb and Split and our embassy staff in Zagreb in safe positions. Regarding the "Bosnia Endgame Strategy," I reported that Albright's paper would be circulated soon, and that was done on August 3.

Albright's "Greatest Hit"

Albright's secret memorandum to Lake, on which years later was scribbled "Greatest Hits" by the declassifier, aimed "to examine how to shift from a European-led plan to an American-led plan." The reality pointed to an Americanized outcome anyway as policymakers had been discussing deploying American ground forces either to cover the extraction of UNPROFOR or to implement a peace plan. "Muddle through is no longer an option." Albright argued "that the issue has become bigger than Bosnia." Bosnia could no longer be viewed as "primarily a European responsibility . . ." She feared that Bosnia, like Haiti a year earlier, would overshadow Clinton's entire first-term accomplishments.

Albright coyly extrapolated from the premise of the European failure to resolve Bosnia and the "serious erosion in the credibility of the NATO alliance and the United Nations" to state the obvious truth:

> Worse, our continued reluctance to lead an effort to resolve a military crisis in the heart of Europe has placed at risk our leadership of the post Cold War world. President Chirac's comment—however self-serving—that "there is no leader of the Atlantic Alliance" has been chilling my bones for weeks."

"We have also failed," she wrote, "to take into account the damage Bosnia has done to our leadership outside Europe. . . . [W]e must stop thinking of Bosnia as a 'tar baby.' Instead. . . . our Administration's stewardship of foreign policy will be measured—fairly or unfairly—by our response to this issue. That is why we must take the lead in devising a diplomatic and military plan to achieve a durable peace. If we agree that American troops will be in Bosnia sooner or later, why not do it on our terms and on our timetable?"

Albright observed, "The essence of any new strategy for Bosnia must recognize the one truth of this sad story: our only successes have come when the Bosnian Serbs faced a credible threat of military force. Hence, we must base our plan on using military pressure to compel the Pale Serbs to negotiate a suitable peace settlement." But she cautioned, "If despite our best efforts, UNPROFOR becomes unsustainable, then a modified form of lift and strike remains the best way to promote an acceptable peace over the long term." She called for primarily air power "to help the Bosnians by changing the balance of power." Albright held out little hope for a negotiated peace settlement under then current conditions. She feared that UNPROFOR's "window of credibility" would begin to shut "as the Europeans lose their stomach for military action." The Serbs' motivation to negotiate then would wane. A UNPROFOR withdrawal, of course, would see American troops pour into Bosnia probably by the spring or summer of 1996 to cover the peacekeepers' backs.

The Albright plan rested on three pillars: set a deadline for the Bildt-plus diplomatic track to work by some time in fall 1995; if that track failed in the short term, withdraw UNPROFOR before the end of 1995 and insert a multinational force (that likely would include European UNPROFOR troops remaining in Bosnia under the new multinational force) to train Federation forces and identify target acquisition for the air campaign; concurrently lift the arms embargo on Federation forces to strengthen their self-defense capabilities and make "a credible commitment to the decisive use of air power against the Serbs to prevent a collapse of Sarajevo and other Federation territory before new arms can be integrated into the Bosnian army." The multinational force would have a small U.S. contingent, serving "as a magnet for European participation, thus avoiding the possible all-Muslim army scenario many fear." She noted, "With U.S.-led air power and training for the Bosnians, this transition can be accomplished with a minimum exposure for the United States. The effect would be a new balance of power that provides the only real chance of concessions by the Bosnian Serbs as well as new leverage for us to play a decisive diplomatic role with all sides."

Then, Albright tested her own moral compass. Though contingent on Bosnian government advance approval, she suggested two concessions to the Bosnian Serbs in order to reach a peace settlement. The first would be a "more forward-leaning" posture with the Bosnian Serbs to secede peacefully from Bosnia and join a "Greater Serbia." Albright seemed to be hedging her bets that secession would fail as an option. The second, and more realistic, concession would be trading Federation territory for Serb-held territory. "The principle would be quality not quantity," she wrote. "For example, Goražde or Federation territory around the Posavina corridor might be exchanged for territory around Sarajevo and in Central Bosnia." She sought "reasonable objectives" to contain the conflict "over the long-term."

Finally, the Russians were "the prime diplomatic obstacle," particularly in terms of their support for Serbia and opposition in the Security Council to lifting the arms embargo. Albright argued for a "high-level diplomatic effort" to avoid a Russian veto. She felt that Russia might be swayed with support for a lift from Britain and France and Muslim countries and the legal consequences of a withdrawal of UNPROFOR that would strip the arms embargo of a rationale. But, she also noted, "we may need a parallel lifting of sanctions on Serbia."[40]

Operation Storm

The Croatian Army launched "Operation Storm" on August 4 to retake their lands in Croatia from the Serbs. The Croatian Army captured the Krajina Serb capital of Knin on August 5. Over the course of three days, a total of about 200,000 ethnic Serb civilians and troops were expelled, or ethnically cleansed, into Serbia and across the border into Bosnia. On August 7, the Bosnian government, spurred by Operation Storm's assault on Serbs, took control of Bihać that had been under siege by the Serbs. Croatian Minister of Defense Gojko Šušak announced that day as well that all military operations in Sectors North and South in Croatia had been completed. The lightning speed of Operation Storm had shown how weak the Serb occupation of Croatian territory really had been for years.

Planning vacations for August while in public service can be risky as foreign crises always erupt in that month. But I tried to be a normal person that summer by planning (way back in May) for a long-awaited vacation during the first two weeks of August. Despite the war clouds gathering in Croatia and continuing work on the "Bosnia Endgame Strategy," Albright allowed me to remain faithful to my plans as James O'Brien, whose expertise on Bosnian diplomacy was unparalleled in the office, would cover

meetings and advise her. Holbrooke also was on vacation in Colorado and thus was absent during the endgame strategizing.

The best account of what transpired at the August 7, 8, and 9 Principals meetings was written by Ivo Daalder in his book, *Getting to Dayton*:

Lake led off the meeting [on August 7 with Clinton and Gore attending], going over the major points in the papers. He said everyone agreed that muddling through no longer was a credible option. Instead, they accepted that a last-ditch effort to reach a diplomatic settlement should be made by exploiting NATO's newfound resolve and engaging directly with the Pale leadership. All agreed that U.S. leadership would be indispensable, but they realized that even then the effort might not succeed. Finally, there was consensus that if no settlement could be reached soon, or if UNPROFOR's credibility did not improve, "we should pull the plug on UNPROFOR, lift the arms embargo, and agree on a post-UNPROFOR withdrawal strategy." However, there was no agreement on what the content of such a strategy should be.

Lake then went over the differences dividing the president's major foreign policy advisers. . . . Christopher and Perry argued that the United States should help the Bosnians consolidate the territory they controlled at the time of a cease-fire and perhaps make some marginal territorial additions thereafter. . . . Albright and Lake . . . argued that the United States could not depart in any substantial way from the essence of the Contact Group plan of a single Bosnian state, consisting of two entities, each with about fifty percent of the territory, give or take five percentage points.

The second major difference among the principals, Lake pointed out, related to the interests at stake and the risk the United States should be willing to run to safeguard those interests. State and Defense believe that the limited U.S. interest involved did not warrant running the grave military risks that a defense of a unified Bosnia would entail.

State believed that U.S. interests would be best served by an end to the violence, and that this should be the primary aim. The Pentagon was most concerned about avoiding a sustained military involvement, and saw in arm, train, and strike the shades of Vietnam. Lake noted that he and Albright had a quite different view. They maintained that the stakes went far beyond the particulars in Bosnia. The issue was not one state or two, three, or none. Rather, the issue was U.S. credibility as a world leader, its credibility in NATO, the United Nations, and at home. That credibility would be enhanced, moreover, if Washington were clearly prepared to go the extra mile to get a settlement. This included adopting a "tough love" approach toward the Bosnians and making clear that U.S. support was conditioned on their adopting a constructive attitude in the talks.

Following Lake's summary. . . . the president indicated support for Albright's argument. "I don't agree with every one of her prescriptions, but I agree with her paper," Clinton said. "We should bust our ass to get a settlement within the next few months," the president added, indicating that he liked the specifics of Lake's diplomatic approach. "We've got to exhaust every alternative, roll every die, take risks." If the situation were not resolved soon, Clinton feared the decision to engage would be "dropped in during the middle of the campaign."[41]

Clinton attended the next Principals meeting on August 8 and instructed Lake to head to Europe with the endgame strategy and to sell it to the Europeans. Lake departed on August 9 on a flight with his staffers Sandy Vershbow and Peter Bass, State's Peter Tarnoff and Bob Frasure, and the Pentagon's Wesley Clark and Joe Kruzel.[42]

The Deputies met on August 11 and 14 to consider a host of essentially procedural issues in preparation for the next Principals meeting on August 15. The situation in Croatia, where government forces had routed the Serbs from Croatian territory in a matter of days, dominated these discussions. The Deputies plotted the handoff of the "Bosnia Endgame Strategy" from the Lake mission to the Holbrooke team. Perry would seek to restrain further Croatian military movements and ensure civil treatment of Serbian refugees. USUN was tasked to manage U.N. discussions about the future of UNCRO to ensure that no action was taken to draw down UNCRO, at least not yet. NATO would be advised not to knock out air defense systems threatening enforcement of the no-fly zone, at least not yet. The 1992 Kosovo warning might have to be reiterated if the Serbs sought to forcibly move more Krajina Serb refugees from Croatia to Kosovo, as several thousand already were arriving in Kosovo.[43]

In preparation for the Deputies meeting on August 18, the Defense Department produced a secret paper entitled, "Implementing a Balkan

Peace Settlement," the principles of which were adopted by the Deputies the next day. The paper assumed acceptance of a peace plan by the war-ring parties and a cessation of hostilities, and aimed to train and equip Federation forces (for which there was a separate planning paper) and in-ject a NATO force to implement the peace plan. It assumed no U.N. in-volvement in military decision-making for the operation, authorization for UNPROFOR withdrawal, and U.S. ground forces as part of the NATO-led Peace Implementation Force (PIF). The tasks of the PIF would be: deter violations of the ceasefire, monitor and enforce compliance by all parties with the peace agreement, ensure self-defense and freedom of movement of the PIF, facilitate the provision of humanitarian aid in Bosnia and be prepared to secure convoys, and employ NATO air power in support of peace enforcement operations and in defense of peace implementation forces. The desired end state in the paper dictated that "[t]he mission of the PIF will be complete when the terms of the peace plan have been im-plemented by all parties and the Federation has enhanced its self-defense capability relative to the Bosnian Serbs."

Among the issues that required more discussion before planning com-menced was the precise nature of the UNPROFOR withdrawal, namely, the "UN-organized withdrawal of those elements of UNPROFOR which will not transition to the PIF while the other elements of the PIF are deploying into the region . . ." There would have to be a rapid transition from UNPROFOR to the PIF "to minimize the risk of early violation of the peace plan." A diplomatic effort to secure forces for the PIF would be required, and that included Russian and Islamic nation participation. Importantly, the proper U.N. Security Council and North Atlantic Council mandates would need to be voted in New York and Brussels, including rules of engagement authorized under Chapter VII of the U.N. Charter. U.S. funding for the PIF would have to be secured with new appropri-ations and approvals by Congress.[44]

PIF to the Rescue

The Deputies' meeting lasted two hours. The BTF had advised the Deputy Director of Central Intelligence beforehand that the Bosnian government was cool to any territorial division, such as the Bosnian Serbs receiving Goradže, and various constitutional provisions in the new American plan. The BTF memorandum also stated, "Tudjman's response clearly appalled Holbrooke and Ambassador Galbraith. . . . A confident Tudjman openly revealed his desire to carve up Bosnia and warned of the dangers of Islamic fundamentalism. Galbraith has recommended that the US respond sharply to Tudjman's statements, reminding him of our support for the Croat-Muslim federation." Given Tudjman's views, "The Muslims would face a desperate situation if forced to confront both Serb and Croatian forces . . ."[45]

When the Deputies convened in the Sit Room, we considered the Peace Implementation Force, with its wimpy acronym PIF ("PIF, the magic dragon!") dreamed up in the Pentagon, and how it would be deployed largely on Federation territory with the possible exception of delivering humanitarian aid in Bosnian Serb territory, if that proved necessary. Berger summarized that the mandate of the NATO-led PIF should include all necessary use of force in self-defense, whether through air power or other means. "If there is a massive attack against the Federation, the PIF will respond," he said. "So if there is any attack against PIF, we will respond with air power. If there is an attack on Bosniak positions by Serb shelling, we will respond robustly by air," Berger stated with confidence. But some Deputies mumbled that the subject would require further consideration.

Principles of reciprocity were scarce at the table. If the Bosnian Army violated the terms of the settlement by launching major offensives to gain strategic advantage, the PIF would have to leave. But if the Serbs were the violators of the agreement "by launching major campaigns to gain strategic advantage, the PIF would undertake actions that moved up a pre-established ladder of escalation." Thus, the PIF would be distinguished from UNPROFOR by having the will and mandate to fight back to protect itself. Berger said that while the PIF would be deployed to separate warring forces, the Serbs would have to honor the ceasefire, and if air power did not enforce that point, then ground troops might have to do so.

Strobe Talbott returned to reciprocity and asked whether the PIF would be a pro-Bosniak and anti-Serb mission, as that would become very tricky with Russia. Or would it be a mission of even-handedness between the warring parties? Berger responded that there would be different remedies with different violations. Bosniak and Serb forces would need to move, and if anyone shot at the PIF, then "we shoot back." The State Department's John Kornblum added that we had to better define consensual and breakdown issues. Berger saw the PIF as a mission to separate forces and enforce a zone of separation. The goal would be some degree of parity. That would mean pressuring the Serbs to build down so that we didn't have to build up Bosnian government forces very much. There would need to be heavy weapons exclusion zones and a narrow 1,000-meter demilitarized zone (DMZ) as another buffer. UNCRO and U.N. Preventive Deployment Force (UNPREDEP) would continue under U.N. auspices and would not be incorporated into the PIF. The United Nations would continue to operate civilian functions like U.N. Civilian Police and the U.N. High Commissioner for Refugees (UNHCR) in the PIF area of responsibility.

The Deputies agreed on a rapid initial deployment of the PIF, which could include leaving in theater thousands of UNPROFOR troops from NATO member states. A NATO command and control headquarters would be set up on the ground. NATO's OPLAN 40104, designed for a UNPROFOR withdrawal, might be retooled to plan the initial deployments of the PIF, while UNPROFOR units that were not a part of NATO and not remaining to join the PIF would be withdrawn securely.

The exit strategy for the PIF elicited several views about how long the PIF could remain in theater. The Defense Department had estimated a nine-month commitment to Bosnia, noting that using OPLAN 40104 provided guidance on how to draw down the PIF itself when the time came. Others at the table predicted a longer period of the PIF deployment. Berger was prepared to say that there was a finite period for the PIF. Kornblum, always the realist at the table, envisaged NATO receiving a request from the United Nations to go in for a period of time. But when NATO, namely, the PIF, left Bosnia, much would remain to be done. "What we are doing," Kornblum said, "is preparing the NATO element of a long-term reconstruction plan for Bosnia."

Once the Principals endorsed the Defense paper on planning for the PIF, the Deputies recommended that key allies in NATO should meet to refine the plans and arrange for the NAC to "bless" an updated version of OPLAN 40104 encompassing the implementation of a peace settlement—and thus deployment of the PIF—as well as ultimate withdrawal of the PIF. They also approved key elements of arming and training the Federation forces, including the United States attempting to lead a multilateral effort to build up the core defensive capabilities of the Bosnian Army and counterbalancing the strengths of the Bosnian Serb Army. The arm-and-train planning would have to proceed, as it would be required even more so if no peace plan was implemented.

Lake Briefs the Diplomats

Meanwhile, Tony Lake briefed foreign diplomats in Washington on August 18 about his and Holbrooke's efforts to advance the peace process.

He reported that the results of his mission to Europe were very positive, indicating strong support for the American initiative. Holbrooke would be traveling to the region. While not insisting that any side give up any particular piece of territory, the Americans believed that each party would have to show flexibility if a settlement were to be achieved. Lake described being "guided by several enduring principles and interests: maintaining American relationships with allies, maintaining the credibility of NATO and the UN, avoiding conflict with Russia that could undermine reform and international cooperation, and preventing the escalation of the Bosnian conflict into a wider war that could destabilize southeastern Europe and lead to a greater humanitarian tragedy."[46] Lake said that Washington remained committed to Contact Group principles of a single Bosnian state, equitable territorial arrangements that did not reward the Serbs for ethnic cleansing, and a constitutional framework. Any settlement falling short of these standards would be a defeat for the NATO alliance and for the West.

Lake reaffirmed to the foreign diplomats that Clinton remained committed to contributing American ground forces to a NATO-led operation after congressional consultation. Clinton had recently vetoed the Dole bill, which called for unilaterally lifting the arms embargo.[47] Lake noted that the administration had long argued that unilaterally lifting the arms embargo would lead to a new escalation of the conflict. It would force the United States to take responsibility for protecting the Bosnians before they were able to defend themselves and would obligate Washington to help NATO extract UNPROFOR under hostile conditions. A unilateral lift also would cause major rifts with allies, possible confrontation with Russia, and undermine support for U.N. sanctions against Iran and North Korea, sanctions that protect vital U.S. interests.

Lake, seeking to defend past policy, said that from the outset, the United States had consistently worked to relieve the human suffering in Bosnia, contain the war, and bring about a peaceful settlement. American efforts had saved many lives, brought an end to fighting between Muslims and Croats through formation of the Bosnia-Croat Federation, and prevented the war from spreading. In a cable to U.S. embassies describing the Lake briefing, Christopher offered this answer to any question that might arise about atrocities:

I HAVE ASKED AMBASSADOR ALBRIGHT TO PRESENT INFORMATION WE HAVE ON ATROCITIES TO THE U.N. SECURITY COUNCIL. AT OUR URGING, THE U.N. SECURITY

COUNCIL IS EXPECTED TO ADOPT RESOLUTIONS CONDEMNING CRIMES ON ALL SIDES, HIGHLIGHTING BOSNIAN SERB ATROCITIES AGAINST REFUGEES FROM SREBRENICA AND ŽEPA. THERE MUST BE JUSTICE, AND THOSE WHO HAVE VIOLATED INTERNATIONAL HUMANITARIAN LAW MUST BE HELD ACCOUNTABLE. WE WILL CONTINUE TO WORK WITH THE INTERNATIONAL WAR CRIMES TRIBUNAL FOR THE FORMER YUGOSLAVIA AND URGE THAT IT PROSECUTE THOSE SUPSECTED OF WAR CRIMES, CRIMES AGAINST HUMANITY, AND GENOCIDE. SUCH CRIMINAL ACTIONS MUST NOT AND WILL NOT REMAIN UNPUNISHED.[48]

Mount Igman's Wrath

The next day, Saturday, August 19, the Holbrooke mission was climbing Mount Igman southwest of Sarajevo in U.N. vehicles so as to reach the city to discuss the peace plan with Bosnian government officials. I have driven that road, known as "the most dangerous road in Europe," and it is treacherous and unpredictable one turn after another. But it was the more certain way of getting to Sarajevo without risking an air flight over the Bosnian Serb forces encircling most of the city and the usual high winds that often prevented aircraft from landing on the U.N.-controlled air strip. I have often been prevented from landing in Sarajevo and taking off from the airport due to those high winds. Indeed, once my Austrian Airlines flight into Sarajevo had reached the city but had to turn back to Vienna for the night due to inclement weather. So driving into the city, despite Mount Igman's hazards, would have appeared the surer bet.

But on August 19 the gods did not favor the Holbrooke mission. The French armored personnel carrier vehicle in which Joe Kruzel, Bob Frasure, and Nelson Drew were seated tipped over the ledge of the narrow dirt road and tumbled down the mountain face. Munitions inside the vehicle exploded, and when it finally came to rest in the dense forest, all three men had perished. Years later I visited the site. No one could have survived that descent and explosive outcome. A stark memorial at the site where the vehicle halted its descent commemorates those who died, including the driver, a French corporal.

I had known Kruzel since my Harvard days when he used to swim at the indoor pool where I had a student job as a lifeguard. He was a muscular sharp-edged fellow, who often would stop to talk with me about

 my studies, as he was a graduate student in the same field as mine—government—at the time. He voiced pride about his service in the U.S. Air Force and his determination to pursue a policy job in foreign affairs. When we reconnected in the Clinton administration, primarily in the Sit Room, we were both pursuing our professional dreams and shared a few smiles about our dialogues of long ago.

I came to know Bob Frasure in the Sit Room, where his negotiations with Milošević were some of the most interesting and important briefings we ever absorbed. Frasure's integrity was framed with an honest and thorough grasp of every issue and every player on the chessboard of the Balkans. He was the consummate diplomat, and I for one felt a sudden blindness when I learned he would no longer be there to guide us. Nelson Drew I knew from the Sit Room as well, always providing fact-based information from the National Security Council and perspectives to guide the discussions. They were honest, fair-minded, and professional men who did not die in vain.

I was in the State Department that Saturday and rushed to the Operations Center to learn as much detail as possible. Not only was it unclear whether the Bosnian Serbs had triggered the mishap, but we knew the fate of the peace plan hung in the balance. Holbrooke and Wesley Clark, who had been on the road with the armored vehicle carrying their colleagues, immediately tried to go to their aid on the mountainside, but to no avail. It would be several days, which included return of the bodies to the United States, before the peace initiative could be resumed. But the tragedy had the effect of fortifying the will of everyone to push forward even harder. The same goals remained, and we had to forge ahead in memory of those who sacrificed their lives in pursuit of peace in Bosnia.

The Principals met without the Deputies on August 22. The aim of the meeting was to hear from Holbrooke about the continuation of his mission in the wake of the Mount Igman tragedy, so it was mostly a dialogue between Holbrooke and Lake. The controversial topic of Goražde's fate arose, with Perry bluntly stating that the city could not be included in Bosnian territory as it would be "too expensive" for the peace plan. Holbrooke pushed back, as any such outcome would have to be worked jointly with the Bosniaks who had publicly insisted on including Goražde in Federation territory. Lake appeared to straddle the issue. Holbrooke sought authority to proffer a $500 million figure to the Bosnians as an initial contribution to economic reconstruction of the region. But Christopher and Office of Management and Budget Director Alice Rivkin refused, as more consultation with Congress would be required.

The CIA summary of the meeting recorded: "Holbrooke presents the Bosnian Serbs as the tough sell, and downplays the difficulties of bringing the Bosnian government into the agreement. Balkan Task Force analysis is the reverse—Bosnian Serbs are ready to deal and Bosnian government will be the problem."[49]

Tough Questions

The Deputies also gathered on August 23 for several grueling hours of deliberation. Berger set out what the Deputies had agreed during the prior week about the mandate and mission of the PIF. Many questions remained to be answered, and that was the task before the Deputies that day. General Wesley Clark, representing the Joint Chiefs of Staff (JCS), pondered what were the incentives for the warring parties to work together. There certainly needed to be enough protection for the Federation, but that might entail positioning no PIF troops on Bosnian Serb territory and it was not clear the Serbs would tolerate such a presence anyway. He argued for a minimalist approach to what constituted enforcement of the peace agreement. Talbott shot back, saying that the purpose of the PIF was to enforce the agreement, the key to which was security and viability of the peace deal. "We are an interposition force," he said, which I took to mean would entail a range of enforcement capabilities and interventions whatever the views of the Bosnian Serb leadership.

Fuerth stressed that first there would be the political agreement and then the deployment of the PIF. That would occur in the aftermath of a civil war, and both sides would insist on the right to bear arms for their own self-defense. Berger noted that there would be a Bosnian state and a Bosnian government with a Bosniak and Croat Federation and a Bosnian Serb entity represented in it. He even suggested there would be the right of the Bosnian Serbs to secede in the future.

Slocombe interjected, "How much more than nothing will we make the unitary part of Bosnia? The Vance-Owen Plan sought to create a new Switzerland in Bosnia. That puts a huge burden on a U.N. or NATO force. We should go more modest." He had no interest in creating "a U.N.-supervised mid-wife" to police anything. Berger responded, "It is not partition. Words matter." He stressed that there would be a central government to preserve a unitary Bosnian state, and that the Bosniaks would seek a more genuine central authority. The enforcement of the peace agreement would focus on the ceasefire, as Kornblum emphasized, and the exchange of territory.

Berger tasked the State Department to draft in two sentences a mission statement in a way that did not endorse self-determination and committed to enforcing the peace agreement within limits, and to do so in understandable language. The two primary mission tasks would be separation of warring parties and enforcement of the ceasefire. Clark countered that he already had specified NATO tasks from Shalikashvili. Berger stopped him, saying this must be an integrated process in drawing up such tasks. He tasked Clark to be prepared to set out boundaries between the Federation and the Bosnian Serbs as required by the peace plan. The JCS would need to incorporate decisions from the Deputies Committee.

What would constitute more than a minimalist mission for the PIF? Clark spoke skeptically about disarmament and cantonment of weapons, but more positively about escorting humanitarian convoys and helping people move back to their homes (the latter two objectives certain to be required by the U.N. Security Council). Fuerth wondered whether there was any workable solution for Sarajevo and how municipalities could be shared jurisdictions without separating populations. Kornblum cautioned that we should not assume all of these functions had to be done by military force. Berger agreed, pointing to a political, economic, and military framework for peace, similar to what had been created for Haiti. Clark, however, said that the more DMZs and separation areas were created, the harder it would become to withdraw the PIF once deployed. Berger said that at the end of the day, we might need to keep Goradže in Federation control and that could be a deal-breaker. He tasked a paper from Defense on what would be involved if Gorazde were retained as Federation territory. Deputy Secretary of Defense John White agreed to include that analysis, but it would be one based on some assumptions about how to militarily deploy and then withdraw with Goradže in the mix. Clark offered to design an option for Goražde for nine months as secure Federation territory, but to leave its future thereafter to the Bosnian Army.

Fuerth said that if Serbs and Bosniaks actually learned to live safely among each other in Sarajevo, and the negotiations insisted on a unified Bosnian state, then there must be a way to allow people to stay where they were in Sarajevo without displacing them.

Berger worried about low-intensity warfare from either party. Should the PIF respond on the ground to such warfare? Clark said that the PIF must respond decisively with the first violation, and it should not allow a tit-for-tat pattern of attacks to continue. The ground commander must have the authority to use the forces available to him, and he must have overwhelming authority.

The arms limitation component of the peace plan risked being counterintuitive: At the same time as the PIF supervised a Bosnian Serb drawdown, we would be arming the Bosnian Army. The Bosnian Serbs would be presented with a choice: either we build up the arms for the Bosnian Army or the Bosnian Serbs build down their arms. Berger asked, "What is this concept? What is the realistic notion of a builddown and a buildup?" He tasked the State Department to figure it out.

Berger proposed an exit date for the PIF of end of 1996. He asked that we try to define the benchmarks of military, political, and economic progress. Talbott suggested we "red team" the approach—how would the Bosniaks and the Serbs try to manipulate the process? The Deputies finally agreed on a late 1996 exit strategy for the PIF.

The Deputies turned to the command of the PIF. NATO would have to control it. Talbott exclaimed, "No keys! No vetoes! No Security Council obstructions!" He added, "At some point we have to figure out some way to use post–Cold War NATO add-ons [the newly liberated countries seeking NATO membership through the Partnership for Peace (P4P)]." General Clark responded, "If the add-on is only cosmetic, there will be inefficiencies in the field. No P4P partners have trained for this kind of duty." Berger suggested that 75 percent of the PIF would be drawn from NATO members and 25 percent from non-NATO countries (although some aspiring to become members). Slocombe cryptically asked, "So how will real command and control be exercised?" Fuerth answered that this would be an out-of-area NATO operation, and we would have to figure out command and control. The Deputies struggled with permitting non-NATO participants in the PIF and how command and control would be established, especially as American troops would be a significant part of the PIF. What would be the entry criteria for non-NATO forces? How would the costs of the PIF be shared, perhaps with each country paying its own way?

The Deputies then discussed the political superstructure that would operate on top of the implementation force. Would it be the North Atlantic Council? Kornblum interjected with characteristic bluntness: "Is there a U.N. superstructure to implement the political elements of this plan? No!

So let's not let any U.N. creep get his hands on it. The political side must understand that it doesn't fuck around with the military side, provided we all know what the military objectives are."

As for the return of displaced populations and refugees, who were largely Bosniaks, the Deputies discussed whether part of the PIF's mission would be to protect civilian and aid convoys. I sought specific guidance for the PIF on how to interact with UNHCR and facilitate displaced and refugee returns. Was it part of the PIF mission to protect UNHCR returnees? Clark suggested that such duties would constitute a more general mission of the PIF, which would be prepared "to protect as necessary." But such protection would not be viewed as a routine function. A PIF contingent would not accompany every convoy returning displaced and refugees to their homes. I realized this was not as much protection as my colleagues in New York were seeking, but it was better than none at all. I was relieved that the Deputies agreed at least to these principles.

The issues of economic sanctions and economic reconstruction then dominated the Sit Room discussion. Clinton was forward-leaning on providing reconstruction aid to the Bosnian government. Holbrooke was seeing Alija Izetbegović the next Monday and wanted to put something forward, between $500 million and $1 billion of economic assistance over five years. But could such an amount be offset within the federal budget? Talbott said it would be unrealistic to try to offset any such commitment by sacrificing some other part of the State Department, or for that matter anything else in the federal budget. "Our cupboard is bare at State," he said. Berger responded, "No, we are not talking about a supplemental. Rather, when the budget comes crashing down, we will cover this with a reconciliation [expedited spending] bill, not a supplemental." Slocombe added that the military cost would be very large. If the United States committed 20,000 troops to the PIF, the cost could run well over $1 billion. Holbrooke emphasized that he was looking for "earnest money" to sway the Bosnian government, and he needed to demonstrate that Clinton was prepared in good faith to ask Congress for an economic reconstruction program over a term of years. Talbott quipped, "You only get it if you ask for it."

The economic sanctions against Serbia raised other issues regarding how to control any partial lifting of sanctions in exchange for Pale's and Belgrade's cooperation, how to sustain veto power over extending any lift of sanctions, and how to reimpose sanctions at the request of any Security Council permanent member (such as with three out of five votes from the

five major powers). The "outer wall" of sanctions related directly to cooperation by Belgrade on war crimes matters and the Yugoslav Tribunal, and
required much attention to sustain.

Implementing a Peace Deal

Five days later, on August 28, the Deputies met for more than two
hours in the Sit Room to labor over implementation of the proposed
peace deal. Treasury, Office of Management and Budget, and Agency for
International Development representatives joined us. Holbrooke was in
the middle of his negotiating rounds in the region. A catastrophic shell
had just hit the Sarajevo Markale food market that day, killing at least 37
and wounding 85 civilians.[50] The first such shelling of Markale had occurred on February 5, 1994, setting in motion the peace initiative of that
year. (I visited the site of the shelling years later, and it remains a bust-
ling market, just as it was on that fateful day. There is a memorial inside
the market, seemingly lost among the crowds of Sarajevo shopping for
vegetables and fruits, walking past the memorial without a moment's
pause.) Talbott argued for a prompt and meaningful response. General
Smith held the key, as General Janvier had delegated it to him recently.
The Sarajevo massacre was thought to be caused by an artillery shell from
a Bosnian Serb position overlooking the besieged city. A logical response
would be to target Serb artillery positions around Sarajevo. Silajdžić called
for a suspension of Holbrooke's diplomatic mission, and Izetbegović kept
that option open.

Berger said the aim of the meeting was to finalize a memorandum to
the Principals in order to move the peace plan forward. An NSC paper entitled "Additional Tasks for the PIF" was on the table. The relationship of
the PIF to the Eastern Slavonia problem in Croatia had to be resolved or
identified to the Principals as a significant issue. Talbott said that Eastern
Slavonia would only be resolved diplomatically. As for additional tasks for
the PIF in Bosnia, White and Slocombe were negative on any "police function" and argued that the PIF should engage in civil affairs only if they
related to the military mission. The PIF would not do border patrols per
se; that would be the job of monitors. And humanitarian relief would be
the job of aid organizations, not the PIF, although White and Slocombe
were willing to leave that issue vaguely stated. In short, they were negative on most additional taskings beyond the ceasefire and force separation
objectives.

Kornblum reminded everyone that the PIF would be part of a political settlement structure. Someone had to carry out humanitarian assistance and policing of communities. Berger argued that such additional
functions must be incidental to the military mission of the PIF if NATO
soldiers were to engage in them. He tasked State to figure out who would
undertake the nonmilitary tasks.

The Deputies ultimately agreed that the PIF should only play a limited
role, as essential to the conduct of its core mission, in such areas as civil
works, population movements, and relief support. Some of the possible additional functions, such as border demarcation and monitoring and arms
control implementation, should be conducted by civilian authorities. State's
paper would examine how to integrate the political with the military functions in the political counterpart that would have to be created alongside the
military's PIF. The fate of Goražde hung in the balance for further discussion.

There then ensued a debate over how air power would be used in conjunction with the PIF. Would Deny Flight continue after the PIF completed
its mission and withdrew? Berger asked whether the use of air strikes
should cease at the end of 1996, when the PIF was expected to withdraw.
Talbott questioned whether they should end at that time and suggested
we be ambiguous about the issue. In his view, NATO air strikes were the
equalizer for both the pre-PIF and post-PIF eras. So Berger tasked JCS to
draft a paper on continuation of air support beyond the PIF deployment.

Holbrooke remained fixated on dangling the carrot of economic reconstruction before the Bosnian government. The World Bank estimated that
$2 billion to $3 billion would be required to start reconstructing the devastated country. The CIA reported at the meeting that $16 billion over the next
15 years would be required. The Deputies authorized Holbrooke to inform
Izetbegović that Clinton in good faith would press for a multimillion dollar,
multiyear, and multiparty deal on reconstruction assistance, but Holbrooke
should not reveal specific numbers. The Principals would have to decide
whether Holbrooke could disclose Clinton's willingness to ask Congress for
$250–$500 million as the American share. While the United States would
serve as a catalyst in the effort, we looked to the European Union to take the
lead, with Japan and Islamic states pitching in with funding.

Following an inconclusive discussion about sanctions relief as part of
the negotiating package with Milošević, the Deputies decided that non-
PIF personnel, namely, private contractors, would train the Bosnian Army.
They also agreed to further consider key questions about "arm and train"
at the next Bosnia meeting.[51]

The final days of August were a rush of State Department and interagency meetings as the Holbrooke mission plodded forward in Europe. On August 29, American diplomat John Menzies reported in from Sarajevo that Commander Smith had been forward-leaning in activating air power and had turned the key irrevocably. But General Janvier had returned and was reviewing target lists, which made Menzies nervous about the will of U.N. commanders again. Menzies asked that the moment Janvier started to cause any problems, namely, hesitancy with air power, to let him know (unless he found out first). However, even Smith was backing off on use of artillery in response to the Sarajevo massacre. Talbott said, "Our view is that something needs to happen soon, like in the next few hours. What about artillery?" The United Nations, I reported, already had announced Bosnian Serb responsibility for the market attack.[52]

Holbrooke was in Paris negotiating with Izetbegović. He was rolling out economic reconstruction numbers with the Bosnian president, although Izetbegović thought the amount being offered was paltry. The political advisers in the U.N. Secretariat were taking a hands-off approach, which was fine as no one in Washington wanted Boutros-Ghali, in the words of one State official at the meeting, "to stick his nose into the matter. The United Nations has done precisely what it wants done. It has determined beyond a reasonable doubt who was responsible for the market attack. Kofi Annan did not resist the U.N. turning the key." The State meeting concluded with one participant complaining about the Carter Center (former President Jimmy Carter's think tank in Atlanta) meddling in Bosnian policy again by proposing that the Bosnian Serbs offer to assist in the investigation of the market attack.

Sarajevo Shelling Unleashes Air Strikes

An interagency meeting on Bosnia followed quickly on the heels of the early-morning gathering. We learned of shelling in Sarajevo the night before. Convoys of humanitarian relief to Sarajevo had been canceled. Janvier had returned to Zagreb, and Smith's key was turned. Fighting had sprung up in Dubrovnik, where the war had essentially started years earlier. Milošević met with Radovan Karadžić and Ratko Mladić in Belgrade over the weekend. The Bosnian Serb Parliament welcomed the peace initiative, presumably to stave off retaliation. The defense of Goražde would require increased force levels. Lake asked that we think hard about the worth of defending Goražde. Would it be economically viable for the Bosnian government to sustain control of Goražde? The time frame for PIF deployment veered between nine and fourteen months. If a multilateral lift of the arms embargo were not achieved, the NATO air support might need to extend beyond the departure of the PIF. Nonetheless, Berger wanted a date certain for the end of U.S. involvement in the PIF. After that date, the Bosniaks would be responsible for their own self-defense, even though they still would not have their own air force.

We talked about convening a multinational conference to build the coalition necessary for the PIF and for arm and train. There was a major diplomatic battle underway between the British and the French over whether to use air power or artillery in response to the Sarajevo massacre. The British wanted to wait while the French were ready to act immediately with artillery shelling of Bosnian Serb positions. The French were convinced that to sustain the peace effort, NATO had to strike quickly with air power. The Germans urged rapid action with their Tornadoes. The JCS advised it was too difficult to use the artillery assets in Sarajevo. The only viable option was air power and that would take time as it would entail a major squabble with the British over the security of their UNPROFOR troops. But soon the air strikes commenced.

In fact, a fourth wave of air strikes was under way on August 30 when I convened with other State officials in Talbott's seventh-floor conference room. Holbrooke was in Belgrade, and we had received no word yet of the outcome of his talks with Milošević. Talbott said, "Today, we shift the emphasis back to diplomacy and resume the business of peace." Force was backing up diplomacy. The British and French were annoyed with press reports that the air-strike operation in the wake of the Sarajevo massacre was an American operation. There needed to be a greater emphasis on it being a joint operation. We wanted Holbrooke to say something in Belgrade about the fact that "we are back on the peace initiative." Kornblum cautioned there was catch-up to do with the Russians, but we should be totally nonapologetic when approaching them. The Russians would be pressed to use their influence with the Serbs to redouble diplomatic efforts.

Menzies reported in from Sarajevo that there were 17 minutes of sustained explosions from an ammunition depot north of Sarajevo. Someone delivered a bouquet of flowers to Menzies' driver at 6 a.m. that morning as an expression of thanks for the NATO air strikes.

True to form, and emblematic of Kornblum's concern, Sergey Lavrov, the Russian ambassador to the United Nations, called for an immediate cessation of air operations when the Security Council covened later on August

30. He said that NATO was destroying the military infrastructure of the Bosnian Serbs and that would make a political settlement less likely. The Russians also had approached the U.N. Secretariat and NATO with their interest in seeking a peace conference and their complaint that they had been informed but not consulted about the bombing campaign. The Russian diplomat dodged a question whether the continued air operation would effectively dismantle the Contact Group.

The bombing campaign was beginning to wake up the Serbs. Both Pale and Belgrade announced that a joint negotiating team, led by Milošević, would consider the U.S. peace plan. But Bosnian Serb forces also shot down a NATO French Mirage 2000 near Goražde, with the French pilots' immediate fate unknown.

The next day, on August 31, during Talbott's usual 8 a.m. morning meeting with top State officials, we learned that CNN was reporting a disagreement between the political and military sides of the administration about whether to continue the bombing campaign. The reality was pressure coming from outside Washington. Bosnian Foreign Minister Muhamed Sacirbey sought "unrelenting continuation" of the air strikes until Sarajevo was free of further risks of shelling. The British were seeking a pause even without any political decision so as to give Holbrooke and the peace plan some breathing room. Albright, in New York, told me, "I don't like this." Holbrooke did not ask for any letup in the air strikes as they gave him greater leverage, and Albright was not about to agree to any cessation when her long-argued position to use air strikes was finally in motion and working. Holbrooke was scheduled to remain in Belgrade on August 31 and see Milošević at 7 p.m. Then he would be in Bonn and Brussels on Saturday to brief NATO ambassadors.

Later, the Holbrooke team reported that Karadžić did not think he needed to go to Belgrade. Fine, the team responded, they did not want Karadžić or Mladić in the room with Milošević. But if Mladić in particular were to enter the room, Holbrooke would have to deal with the dynamics of the meeting as he saw best.

We were all entering a new, and final, phase of the Bosnian imbroglio. Would we continue using air power to compel a peace agreement? What would be the fate of UNPROFOR? Would NATO offer a credible alternative? Would there be endgame peace talks, and if so, when and where and who should attend? Who would draw the final map of ethnic cleansing in Bosnia in the quest for peace? The answers were within reach.

5

Forging Peace
September–December 1995

Revealingly, he [Milošević] has never expressed even the smallest concern for the people who might be killed or wounded in these attacks.

RICHARD HOLBROOKE

Remain amazed at their [Milošević, Tudjman, Izetbegović] ability to turn on charm socially while spouting venom in negotiations.

DONALD KERRICK

THE FINAL MONTHS of the search for peace in Bosnia and Croatia were high-risk acrobatics that left everyone scrambling to reach the next stage of diplomatic and military engagement. NATO's air campaign against the Bosnian Serbs, which commenced on August 30, 1995, as "Operation Deliberate Force," paused briefly on September 1 in order to facilitate a meeting between UNPROFOR Commander Bernard Janvier and Bosnian Serb General Ratko Mladić in Zvornik. Richard Holbrooke held forth in Slobodan Milošević's dacha that day. In Washington, we viewed this as a strictly military pause authorized by NATO command to allow the Janvier and Mladić meeting to take place. It lasted thirteen grueling hours. The generals failed to reach a deal.

Janvier reiterated his three key demands in a letter to Mladić shortly thereafter, for which failure to comply would trigger a resumption of the air campaign:

(1) there must be no attacks on Sarajevo or other safe areas,
(2) Bosnian Serb heavy weapons must be withdrawn from the 20 km exclusion zone around Sarajevo without any delays, and

The Sit Room: In the Theater of War and Peace. David Scheffer.
© Oxford University Press 2019. Published 2019 by Oxford University Press.

(3) the United Nations and authorized international humanitarian agencies must be granted complete freedom of movement and unrestricted use of the Sarajevo airport.

Mladić refused to withdraw the heavy weapons and showed no appetite for Janvier's final conditions. So on the morning of September 5, Janvier and the theater NATO commander, Admiral Snuffy Smith, agreed to resume the air operations.[1]

"Eyes Only"

Holbrooke planned to return to Washington to give his team some rest. His talks in Serbia during the pause had been discouraging. Indeed, on September 4, prior to his return to Washington, Holbrooke sent a secret cable to the White House Situation Room communications center addressed "eyes only" to Strobe Talbott, Willliam Perry, Tony Lake, Madeleine Albright, and General John Shalikashvili. For that reason, I never saw the cable until it was declassified years later. The following extracts portray Holbrooke and his team conveying strongly held views at a critical moment in both the negotiations and in the use of air power against the Bosnian Serbs:

2. ... WHILE WE HAVE CREATED A PUBLIC IMPRESSION OF PROGRESS, WHICH IS ALSO USEFUL IN CREATING PRESSURE FOR GENUINE MOVEMENT, WE HAVE MADE VIRTUALLY NO HEADWAY ON THE FUNDAMENTAL ISSUES DIVIDING THE ADVERSARIES. NEITHER SIDE HAS SHOWN ANY WILLINGNIESS TO COMPROMISE ON THE CORE ISSUES, ESPECIALLY THE POLITICAL AND CONSTITUTIONAL ONES.

3. BOTH SARAJEVO AND BELGRADE WILL HAVE TO SHOW A FLEXIBILITY THEY HAVE SO FAR RESISTED. WE DO NOT BELIEVE THAT RHETORIC AND VERBAL PRESSURE WILL BE SUFFICIENT TO ACHIEVE THIS. THEREFORE, WE HAVE CONCLUDED THAT A RESUMPTION OF THE BOMBING TONIGHT IS AN ESSENTIAL COMPONENT OF OUR NEGOTIATING STRATEGY. WE RECOGNIZE— AND INDEED I WILL CONTINUE TO ASSERT PUBLICLY— THAT THE BOMBING [WAS] NOT DESIGNED FOR THE NEGOTIATIONS, BUT WAS, RATHER, A NECESSARY RESPONSE TO THE OUTRAGEOUS ATTACK IN SARAJEVO.

BUT ITS VALUE IN BOTH BEGRADE AND SARAJEVO IS BECOMING INCREASINGLY CLEAR.

4. THIS IS NOT A RECOMMENDATION FOR A LINEBACKER-TYPE CAMPAIGN. INDEED, THERE WILL UNDOUBTEDLY COME A TIME WHEN, FROM A POLITICAL/DIPLOMATIC POINT OF VIEW, SUSPENDING THE BOMBING WILL BE MORE USEFUL THAN CONTINUING IT. BUT THAT TIME IS DEFINITELY NOT TODAY.

5. OF COURSE, IF MLADIĆ GIVES US EVERYTHING JANVIER REQUESTS TODAY WE MAY HAVE NO CHOICE BUT TO STOP BUT ANYTHING SHORT OF FULL—REPEAT, FULL—COMPLIANCE SHOULD BE REJECTED. AND THAT IS THE MOST LIKELY COURSE PALE WILL TAKE TODAY—OFFERING ABOUT SEVENTY-FIVE PERCENT OF THE JANVIER DEMANDS AND TRYING TO PROLONG THE PAUSE.

6. WHY DO WE TAKE SUCH A POSITION? FIRST, SARAJEVO. THIS IS FAIRLY OBVIOUS. THE FLEXIBILITY WE NEED FROM SARAJEVO ON VARIOUS ISSUES REQUIRES MORE THAN VERBAL PRESSURE. BOMBING HELPS US; ITS ABSENCE STIFFENS THEIR FRACTIOUS POLITICAL PROCESS. THIS IS NOT THEORY; WE HAVE HAD AMPLE ANECDOTAL EVIDENCE OF IT.

7. BELGRADE IS MORE COMPLICATED, BUT THE CONCLUSION IS THE SAME. MILOŠEVIĆ RAISES THE BOMBING FREQUENTLY AS AN IMPEDIMENT TO PROGRESS AND SOMETHING THAT COULD MAKE PALE MORE INTRANSIGENT. AT THE SAME TIME, HE HAS YET TO INVEST THIS ISSUE WITH THE SAME DEGREE OF EMOTION OR HIGH RHETORIC THAT MARKS HIS COMMENTS ON SAY, KARADJIĆ'S CRAZINESS, SANCTIONS RELIEF, OR THE FUTURE BALKAN ECONOMIC ZONE. HIS HIGHLY THEATRICAL (AND FREQUENT) TRIPS UPSTAIRS TO TELEPHONE MLADIĆ—AND LAST NIGHT, FOR THE FIRST TIME IN OUR PRESENCE, (HE SAID) KARADJIĆ—ARE NOT SIMPLY THEATRE; HIS FRUSTRATION WITH MLADIĆ IS GROWING VISIBLY AND HE NOW FREELY ADMITS THAT THE GENERAL WHOM I BELIEVE HE'S SCARED OF, IS A MAJOR OBSTACLE TO HIS GOALS AS WELL AS OURS. (HE FLIRTED WITH THE IDEA OF OUR MEETING MLADIĆ FACE-TO-FACE TODAY TO MAKE CLEAR THE

U.S. POSITION BUT EVEN BEFORE IT BECAME APPARENT THAT MLADIĆ WOULD NOT COME TO BELGRADE YET, WE HAD MADE CLEAR THAT WE WERE NOT GOING TO BECOME AN INTERMEDIARY IN THE JANVIER-MALDIĆ CHANNEL.)

8. MOST IMPORTANTLY, MILOŠEVIĆ HAS NOT YET LINKED THE BOMBING TO ANY OTHER ISSUE—GENEVA, SANCTIONS, THE MAP, ETC. HE MAY DO SO LATER, BUT NOT YET. I SUSPECT THAT HE AT LEAST HALF HOPES THE BOMBING WILL WEAKEN BOTH KARADJIĆ AND MLADIĆ AND STRENGTHEN HIS HAND AGAINST THE BOSNIAN SERBS. (REVEALINGLY, HE HAS NEVER EXPRESSED EVEN THE SMALLEST CONCERN FOR THE PEOPLE WHO MIGHT BE KILLED OR WOUNDED IN THESE ATTACKS.)

9. IF WE READ HIS BODY LANGUAGE HERE CORRECTLY, THE BOMBING—IN ITS CURRENT PHASE, AT LEAST— WILL GAIN US MORE ON THE MAP ISSUES THAN WE ORIGINALLY SUSPECTED—BECAUSE MILOŠEVIĆ DOESN'T CARE AS MUCH AS WE THOUGHT ABOUT THE MAP. IT WILL BE LESS LIKELY TO GAIN MUCH ON THE POLITICAL ISSUES, PRECISELY BECAUSE HE DOES CARE ABOUT THEM MORE—THEY SET THE STAGE FOR HIS LONG TERM GOAL WHICH HE HAS NOW DEFERRED FOR A FUTURE DATE, BUT WHICH HAS NOT CHANGED.

10. IN CONCLUSION, BOMBING THIS WEEK WHILE WE GO TO GENEVA WILL BE A PLUS IN THE TALKS THEMSELVES, IN STRENGTHENING OUR OVERALL IMAGE IN EUROPE, WITH SARAJEVO, AND IN PARTIALLY RESTORING SOME OF THE EVENTS OF RECENT YEARS. IT WILL GIVE US A BETTER CHANCE FOR PROGRESS AND PERHAPS—IF THE UN AND NATO CAN BE MANAGED CORRECTLY—A FUTURE BARGAINING CHIP.

11. THIS RECOMMENDATION SHOULD NOT BE READ AS A CALL FOR A SUSTAINED AND PROLONGED CAMPAIGN. WE ARE NOT SARAJEVO'S AIR FORCE AND THIS IS NOT "ROLLING THUNDER." WE WOULD RESERVE ANY JUDGMENT ON THE LARGER ISSUES.[2]

Back to the Drawing Board

As Operation Deliberate Force resumed with bombing of Bosnian Serb targets, the Principals met on September 5. Rick Inderfurth, beaming in securely from the U.S. Mission to the United Nations (USUN), sat in for Albright while I held forth in the Sit Room along with Jim O'Brien. The Interagency Balkan Task Force (BTF) memorandum prepared for CIA Director John Deutch illuminated the current state of thinking about the fate of Goražde:

> The Administration appears to have backed off of its initial plan to propose that the Bosnian Government give up Goražde in exchange for territory around Sarajevo. Maintaining Goražde—and a corridor to the enclave—as part of the federation, however, will require a significant augmentation of the peace implementation force, not to mention a significant bolstering of federation forces to defend it once the implementation force leaves. OSD and JCS do not believe Goražde is worth this effort. . . . There is agreement that the implementation force should complete its mission by 31 December 1996, and that this date should be announced in advance to build political support for the dispatch of US troops. There is disagreement, however, over whether NATO air assets may continue to be made available for a period after the implementation force is withdrawn to assist the federation.[3]

John Shalikashvili, deep into his final year as Chairman of the Joint Chiefs of Staff, briefed the Principals on the air campaign, which, consistent with Holbrooke's recommendation, resumed that morning with 200 sorties hitting command and control targets and supply and ammunition depots. Weather had caused a slowdown, but Shali expected the pace to pick up again by nightfall. NATO aimed to continue to pound its current target list until there were significantly more weapons removed from the Sarajevo Exclusion Zone. If they ran out of targets near Sarajevo—since the NATO air campaign responded most directly to the August 27 Bosnian Serb attack on the Sarajevo marketplace—then NATO could open up the targets to a larger area of Bosnian Serb operations. That would require fresh North Atlantic Council (NAC) authority, however. Inderfurth reminded everyone that Boutros Boutros-Ghali would have to "turn the key" for the broadest range of targets in Bosnia (Category 3). Lake said, "We are prepared to bomb, pause or no pause, until the objectives are met."

Sandy Berger posited that if heavy weapons were not removed from the Sarajevo exclusion zone, the bombing should continue. Lake agreed, but said that would not rule out pauses along the way. Deputy Defense Secretary John White noted that some Category 2 targets were not targeted yet because of civilians in the areas and the targets might appear too far afield from Sarajevo. Lake did not want the Bosnian government to take advantage of the bombing of Bosnian Serb targets, but Talbott assured him that Holbrooke and he had reminded Bosniak officials of that demand all the time. Admiral William Owens confirmed that the Bosniaks also assured him they would not take advantage of the bombing for tactical objectives. Shali interjected that there was agreement between the U.N. Secretariat and NATO on the sequencing of targets (Category 1, then 2, then 3) and advised handling issues informally with SACEUR General George Jouwan and thus not try to change the system, which was working well.

The Principals agreed to support the continuation of NATO air strikes, as agreed by the U.N. and NATO commanders, as long as the Bosnian Serbs failed to comply with U.N. and NATO conditions. If they retaliated, the Principals agreed to support further escalation by NATO.[4]

As for the American diplomatic initiative, Owens concluded that Bosnian Serb leaders Radovan Karadžić and Momčilo Krajišnik had become nonplayers. Milošević and Mladić were the real powerbrokers on the Serbian side. But Mladić had "gone underground" the day before; he was protecting his own skin and avoiding any arrest strategy keyed to the Yugoslav Tribunal indictment against him. Deutch reported that Karadžić and Mladić remained more coordinated but were making themselves scarce. The Serbian military had more links to the Bosnian Serbs, and hence Mladić's greater influence. Lake said, "Mladić just gets pissed." I took this to mean "pissed" with bouts of drunkenness.

The forthcoming meeting in Geneva of the Contact Group was aimed at producing an agreement on general principles for a political settlement and Serbia's recognition of Bosnia. There already was speculation of where the "big talks," namely, the final peace talks among the warring parties, would be held in the United States. Options included Camp David, Williamsburg, and somewhere in New York. (The ultimate site was Dayton, Ohio.) The Principals agreed not to provide further sanctions relief for Serbia in return for interim steps such as mutual recognition. Belgrade's cooperation with the Yugoslav Tribunal would be required in the peace settlement agreement. And they noted the importance of maintaining the outer wall of sanctions contingent on Serbian cooperation with the Yugoslav Tribunal.

The critical decision that day was to approve the concept for military implementation of the peace plan. Finally, we had all come to our senses and renamed the Peace Implementation Force (PIF) as the multinational Implementation Force, or IFOR. That was a far more credible acronym for the significant combat-ready force that would be entering Bosnia following a peace agreement. I almost wanted to pound the Sit Room table with a Bravo salute the first time I heard "IFOR." Now we could get serious and let the wordsmith in the Pentagon who came up with "PIF" take a cold shower.

A decision sheet would be drafted for the North Atlantic Council so that NATO military authorities could be tasked. They also agreed that the exit strategy summarized in the Deputies Committee memorandum should be clarified to state that IFOR would withdraw when the Bosnian Federation was capable of defending itself, but in any case no later than 12 months from its initial deployment. But the Principals recognized that time was wasting on the political side of the equation, and that a U.S. position on the political framework for implementation of a settlement had to be drawn up quickly. Finally, we had to figure out what to do with the Russians who were objecting to NATO heading up IFOR.[5]

Equip and Train

The contentious issue of equipping and training the Federation armed forces, the subject of endless study papers, arose again at the Principals meeting on September 5. While they agreed that the United States should take the lead in coordinating a multinational effort to equip and train Federation forces, they preferred a more modest American role while other states provided the bulk of the Federation's needs. But such assistance from Washington would be contingent on excluding radical states like Iran from equipping and training the Bosniaks, and that would require an explicit agreement with the Bosnian government. The difficulties with allies and the Russians also did not escape the Principals.[6] Lake conceded the idea "was very difficult with the Europeans. For them, it is counter-intuitive: how do we negotiate a peace agreement and simultaneously agree to send arms to one of the parties?" In frustration he admonished one Principal who still spoke of "PIF" with a sharp correction: "It's IFOR, not PIF!"

Shali noted that if equip and train were critical to making the peace plan work, then the United States should be the leader. But should Washington really be in the lead to arm and equip the Bosnian Army? he asked. Under Secretary of State for Political Affairs Peter Tarnoff suggested taking the lead in concept but "without flooding them ourselves" with arms. Shali clearly was cool to the entire concept and suggested that an interagency working group collaborate with other governments to develop arm-and-train components, an idea that Talbott quickly endorsed. Leon Fuerth cautioned, though, that the peace agreement without arms control would be "looney." It had to be structured so as not to stimulate an arms race. Lake and Shali finally agreed that the United States would retain the lead in developing the concept for arming and training the Federation and mostly Bosniak Army, but would not necessarily arm and train the army itself—others should be brought into the mission. Talbott reminded them that it would be hard to get support for economic reconstruction if we "dropped the ball" on arm and train, as donors would want to know that the Federation army was capable of defending whatever was reconstructed. The European Union wanted to take the lead on economic reconstruction, while Japan begged off.

The time had come for the Principals to intensify consultations with Congress, which had been on August and Labor Day recesses. The NATO air strikes and U.S. diplomatic initiative and planning for peace implementation clearly had to be briefed to members of Congress. Funding the various components of the peace plan would be Topic A. For starters, the full Senate would be briefed on September 6 and the relevant House committees on September 7.[7] Talbott speculated that the typical Hill inquiry would be, "Who is Janvier?" Lake said that the administration would have to be frank: Peace is going to have a price. Alice Rivlin, the petite in body and huge in mind budget director, noted that there was no expectation on the Hill that the United States would get this deeply involved in a peace deal. Shali closed the meeting stating a simple fact: "We have no funds budgeted to drop bombs or to continue Deny Flight past October 1."

Foreign Policy Team Briefing

Early in the morning on September 8, President Bill Clinton and Vice President Al Gore met with their foreign policy team at the White House. Inderfurth sat in for Albright, who was otherwise committed. The other Principals—Lake, Shalikashvili, Perry, Christopher, and Deutch—joined him with Clinton. The meeting was largely a briefing for Clinton and

Gore. In preparation for the Deputies meeting later in the day, Inderfurth briefed me on a few developments at the foreign policy meeting.

Perry said the bombing campaign would last another four or five days and then an assessment might kick it into Category 3 targets. Shali agreed that Category 3 might be required. Inderfurth cautioned that Category 3 was not a done deal yet, as the Security Council would have to weigh in. Christopher and Lake had urged the Bosnian government not to take advantage of the bombing campaign. There had to be some way to assure the Bosnian Serbs as a predicate to reaching a peace agreement.

Clinton had called Russian President Boris Yeltsin. Inderfurth mentioned the last Security Council meeting where Sergey Lavrov, Russia's permanent representative to the United Nations, held forth with strong points of view. Clinton asked whether the Chinese had spoken, and Inderfurth said no, they appeared to be looking for a face-saving way to engage. Inderfurth stressed that there had to be found ways to deal with the Russians on Bosnia, as their leverage in the Security Council was considerable.

IFOR at the Helm

Later in the day the Deputies met, with Inderfurth joining me in the Sit Room. At this meeting the political implementation mechanism of the peace agreement was finally settled among the Deputies. Before any details were discussed, Berger announced to the Deputies what the Principals already had digested: the death of "PIF" and the use thereafter of "IFOR," a suitably hefty acronym to describe the NATO-led military "Implementation Force" that would enter Bosnia upon conclusion of the peace agreement. Berger quipped that in Brussels some at NATO Headquarters were trying to advance "NIFORE" (NATO Implementation Force) as the alternative, and he instructed the Pentagon to kill this lame effort, which they did. "NIFORE" sounded like some acidic medication we

were all supposed to ingest to induce sleep. Who concocts such banalities?

The political implementation mechanism was no easy structure to erect. Would it be a freestanding entity or part of the United Nations? What would be its mandate authority and bureaucratic character? Should an American be the senior person? The State Department's John Kornblum, working with Holbrooke in the

European affairs bureau, argued for a person of sufficient stature and authority with whom all must touch base, but not along classic lines of authority. There would need to be considerable interaction among authorities high and low. Berger saw the challenge as one of coordinating rather than controlling, which required a strong political person. But whether it was U.N.-based or self-standing was a tough question. Fuerth argued the individual should be chartered as part of the peace agreement. He or she had to endure beyond IFOR. Jim Steinberg from the State Department's Policy Planning Bureau cautioned that it would not simply be coordination, as stressed by Berger, but also arbitration over disputes.

Berger held firm that the political mechanism must not control IFOR. Its first mission would be to coordinate and its second mission would be some top-level control, depending on the function in question. Horizontally it must pull together international agencies, but vertically it must deal with the Bosnian government. It doubtless would require a strong political person. He agreed that the mechanism would endure beyond IFOR, be self-standing, and hopefully blessed by the Security Council.[8]

Inderfurth and I agreed to do a paper on the various options on civilian peace implementation, and this became a major effort on my part in following weeks. The paper would address

- managing plans for reconstruction,
- adjudicating property disputes,
- creating an appellate investigative body regarding human rights violations,
- whether the mechanism would have a role to play with atrocity crimes,
- who would be charged to make sure elections occur, and
- how we would supervise negotiation of an arms control agreement.

Berger added that the mechanism needed to coordinate, exercise some controlling authority in particular functions, be led by a strong international diplomat, and be authorized by agreement as freestanding, blessed by the Security Council, and lasting beyond IFOR.

The Deputies continued to bicker over equip and train, with tension over the degree to which the United States should lead any such effort. Talbott dryly noted that we did not know yet where the handle was on equip and train. "This is some Balkan version of the Adam Smith invisible hand," he concluded. Fuerth thought it absurd to enter into a peace agreement for the purpose of arming the Bosnian Army. He suggested radically revisiting the issue in terms of any peace agreement. He feared the Bosnian Serbs would sign an equip-and-train deal with Belgrade.

Negotiating Tactics

Meanwhile, at a September 10 State Department meeting, the Bosnia team learned that General Janvier was trying to understand what Mladić would accept in a peace deal. The Bosnian Serb general had taken a hard line in his meeting with Janvier, threatening to attack U.N. troops and expressing no interest in Janvier's assurances. Nonetheless, Janvier conceded that Mladić was more reasonable than in prior encounters. Serbia had recently provided some supplies to the Bosnian Serbs, and it was clear that Milošević was trying to isolate himself from Karadžić in particular. The Bosnian Serbs would take a hard line on giving up any territory around Sarajevo and actually were less interested in acquiring Goražde. The Bosnian Serbs still controlled 62 percent of Bosnian territory, less than their greatest seizure of territory at up to 70 percent in the past.

Holbrooke attended the meeting and informed us of his impending trip to Belgrade and Zagreb. He wanted "early rewards" for Milošević in his talks, namely, a longer extension of existing sanctions relief to 180 days, but Albright still needed to weigh in on that proposal. Holbrooke said he would make recommendations from the field on where to hold the international conference, but he definitely rejected Geneva. On the bombing campaign, the Category 2 targets needed to be exhausted before assessing additional targets falling into Category 3.

Later in the day, updates arrived about the sanctions relief option to incentivize Milošević. Several Contact Group members favored a 100-day extension of sanctions relief, although Germany wanted less and the Russians were indefinite. Albright leaned toward a 100-day rather than the 180-day extension favored by some.

In a memorandum to Clinton on September 11, 1995, Lake briefed the president for a drop-in on the Principals meeting that would occur that day and which Albright and I attended. The diplomatic initiative scored high marks in Lake's memorandum, because there was relatively good news from the Geneva meeting the week before among the foreign ministers of Bosnia, Croatia, and Serbia and the Contact Group representatives. Lake wrote that the Geneva group "produced agreement on 'Basic Principles' of a settlement in Bosnia, including: preservation of Bosnia-Herzegovina as a single state within its present borders; the 51:49 parameter as the basis for the territorial division between the Federation and the Serb Republic, but with adjustments possible by mutual agreement; rights for both entities to establish 'parallel special relationships' with Croatia and Serbia consistent with the sovereignty and territorial integrity of Bosnia-Herzegovina; and agreement in principle on mechanisms for dealing with displaced persons, human rights abuses and dispute resolution."

Lake continued, "The preservation of Bosnia as a single state represents an important concession on the part of the Bosnian Serbs, who were present at the meeting but operating under Belgrade's proxy. Bosnian Government agreement to the term 'Republika Srpska,' on the other hand, confers a degree of legitimacy on the Bosnian Serbs that Sarajevo has been reluctant to grant. Additionally, significant is the fact that ranking Serbian leaders met for the first time with Bosnian Government officials and agreed to statements that come close to recognition of Bosnia."[9]

Holbrooke joined the Principals and their "plus-ones" for the meeting in the Sit Room on September 11. He briefed us on the state of play in the negotiations, and started with a blunt assessment: "We have gotten five percent of the job done. Everything that we achieved on Thursday night last week unraveled. [Alija] Izetbegović this morning announced a positive step towards peace: The Serbs had to accept and recognize Bosnia and Herzegovina. The Bosniaks had to accept the Serb Republic. Both sides have to end the war." In Belgrade,

Milošević made a strategic move for peace. He's had it with the Bosnian Serbs. He's a guy we might be able to deal with. But he does not have control over Karadžić. Nor perhaps over [Momčilo] Perišić [Chief of General Staff of the Yugoslav Army and later prosecuted by the Yugoslav Tribunal]. Any agreement is not implementable if Mladić is commander-in-chief in the field. Milošević says he does not want Goradže. But we cannot put NATO forces in there because the Bosnian Serb Army will fight. Mladić is the most dangerous man in Europe since Stalin's death. When we negotiate with Belgrade, it is only one person we negotiate with. So long as Mladić remains in the mix, don't sign a peace agreement. Milošević understands that Mladić is unacceptable.

Lake resisted Holbrooke's argument that as long as Mladić was a player, the peace agreement would not be implemented. Holbrooke did not respond to that point, but went on to say that the bombing "clearly helped us so far. The bombing should continue through the current package of targets, as long as possible in the present context. We got an agreement without sanctions relief and with bombing going on. The bombing has weakened the Bosnian Serb Army politically and given us flexibility to negotiate."

Holbrooke urged unilateral acts to lift sanctions for substantially longer periods of one year to entice Milošević. He wanted at least something low-key to give to Milošević. He thought it was a mistake for Clinton to give so little latitude on sanctions relief in the president's letter to Senator Dole. Inderfurth counterproposed knocking down the relief period from one year to 180 days. Christopher seemed to agree, complaining that Belgrade was giving too much aid to the Bosnian Serbs.

Holbrooke was cynical about the Contact Group process and particularly including non–Contact Group countries, like Italy, in consultations as the peace negotiations progressed. Lake pushed back, saying the Italians were very important, particularly if the peace plan collapsed and the U.S. military airbases in Italy became even more important. He said a meeting in Rome should be the model for all that follows for expanded meetings of the Contact Group. "Politics is the act of inclusion," he flung at Holbrooke across the Sit Room table.

On September 14, the NATO air strikes were suspended for 72 hours (and then extended to 114 hours) to facilitate ceasefire talks and Bosnian Serb withdrawal of heavy weapons from the Sarajevo exclusion zone. On September 20, Operation Deliberate Force ended as the Bosnian Serbs were deemed to be complying with U.N. conditions regarding their military forces.

The French Are Coming

The Deputies convened by Secure Video Teleconference System (SVTS) on September 15 to prepare for meetings with the French on post-settlement implementation issues a few days later at the State Department. I was deeply engaged in drafting the plans for the peace settlement political structure and thus looked forward to arriving at some decisions prior to the talks with the French. The central issue was the relationship between the new political entity and IFOR. There were some key differences between the French opening position and American thinking in the Sit Room.

Berger described the French position, so far, which proposed a lot of links between IFOR and U.N. commanders and the U.N. Secretary-General. That was anathema to Berger, who stressed that the United Nations must have no retained authority over IFOR, that the U.N. Secretary-General could not be the sole nominator of the civilian high representative, and that the Contact Group would exercise control over that nomination. Neither the United Nations nor NATO would have direct control over the individual, who would be a coordinator with degrees of authority over particular functions ironed out in the peace agreement. Berger rejected the French proposal of referring disputes regarding the civilian high representative to the U.N. Secretary-General for resolution.

The designated name of the civilian high representative went through many variations in the months ahead. For purposes of clarity, I will hereafter use the term that was most descriptive and popular: Senior Implementation Coordinator, or SICOR.

Admiral Owens of the JCS interjected that SICOR would not be in a consultative role with NATO, but would communicate through a liaison. "IFOR does not need to consult with the [SICOR] to get any job done," he bluntly stated. Berger said that Washington should be able to live with a non-American in the SICOR role "but we ought to get a lot for it. How we play that card will be tactical."

The Deputies saw potential areas of agreement with the French on seven requirements of the political implementation structure: Settlement documents should establish the political implementation structure and its mandate; the United Nations should give approval for the structure through a Security Council resolution; there should be a senior civilian head; the head should be charged with coordinating among the various actors responsible for post-settlement programs; the head should serve as an interface with the parties; the NAC would oversee military implementation by the IFOR; and the commander of IFOR and NATO'S Commander in Chief, Allied Forces Southern Europe would maintain liaison with the head of the political implementation structure and with the United Nations.

As to what the United States could not compromise on in the talks with the French, the Deputies identified four key issues: IFOR and its force commander would not take political guidance or be required to coordinate with the United Nations or any entity other than the NAC, through SACEUR; we would reject the French suggestion that disputes in the NAC about Bosnia would be referred to the U.N. Security Council; the United Nations would not be permitted to select the head of the political implementation structure, although we would want the United Nations to approve the choice made by the Contact Group; while we could agree that a French officer (the present U.N. Peace Forces Commander) could become the Deputy Force Commander of the IFOR and retain operational control over residual U.N. forces in Croatia and Macedonia, we could not agree that the same person should also be the Land Force Commander, as the French proposed. We continued to favor making NATO's Ace Rapid Reaction Corps (ARRC) Commander the Land Force Commander for IFOR.[10]

On two other issues, the Deputies put down firm markers: The French proposed that the head of the political implementation structure be a European Union state national, a position that Washington ultimately could accept but first sought European concessions on other implementation issues before so agreeing. Also, non-NATO (including Russian) troops interested in participating would need to be integrated into IFOR under NATO operational control, but how that would be done still needed to be explored.

The meeting with the French in Washington lasted the entire day of September 18, and it proved to be a turning point in how the peace agreement could be pressed forward in later weeks with a high degree of confidence. We knotted the political objectives together with the emerging military objectives so that a coherent peace deal could be negotiated. Getting there, however, was not so easy and required an enormous amount of skillful negotiation by all of us in one of the State Department's more ornate conference rooms in deference, I assumed, to French expectations for proper ambience. On the American side of the table sat Kornblum, Alexander Vershbow, Walter Slocombe, and myself. The French had Quai d'Orsay and Defense Ministry officials representing their views. We reached basic agreement on the vital issues of the independent status of SICOR and IFOR's freedom of military command and operation divorced from any U.N. control other than an initial Security Council resolution.

Holbrooke in Washington

The next day, September 19, Holbrooke met with the early-morning Talbott group in the State Department and complained about the Franjo Tudjman and Izetbegović problems and that the U.S. team was spending a lot of time trying to buttress the Federation. But fighting in western Bosnia continued. The Croats drove toward Banja Luka to get an advantage over the

Bosniaks. The Croat offensive began to slow down, though. Holbrooke threatened that air strikes against the Serbs would be called off if the Croat offensive continued. We also discussed the Russian resolution at the U.N. Security Council and whether Albright could delay it while Holbrooke talked with Tudjman and Izetbegović. Kornblum thought the resolution would be a disaster, but Holbrooke would try to use it as leverage. A re-writing of the resolution had to condemn the Bosnian Serb offensive.

The situation on the ground in Bosnia on September 20 was still fairly chaotic. The NATO air strikes were ended that day as the Bosnian Serb target lists were practically exhausted anyway. All sides were trying to con-solidate their positions to be in control of territory they sought before any negotiating process began. Holbrooke had held firm with Milošević re-garding indicted fugitives Karadžić and Mladić—that they would receive no immunity if they traveled to the United States or to any European country. The Yugoslav Tribunal indictments were non-negotiable and of no value as pawns in the negotiations. Holbrooke's tough position in fact aided Milošević as it strengthened his power as the Serbian negotiator. We all agreed that there would be no immunity for Karadžić and Mladić.

Beth Jones, who worked in Holbrooke's State Department bureau, briefed the Bosnia team that the NAC agreed to accept the U.S. language for an indefinite suspension of the air strikes as opposed to a termination of them. Boutros-Ghali had sought a cessation and threatened to take the key away from General Janvier. But Holbrooke insisted on an indefinite suspension instead. Meanwhile, the Bosniaks were focused on how war crimes would be fit into the peace plan. A linkage needed to be sustained, including the outer wall of sanctions.

At the Bosnia SVTS meeting on September 21, right after the suspension of the bombing campaign, there were questions about where the Bosnian Serbs' heavy weapons had gone. The Bosniaks and Croats were bickering over Banja Luka and who would have what power in the Federation following a peace agreement. We all wondered where Yasushi Akashi had come up with a 9 percent compliance figure for the parties. There was some nasty speculation about amnesty floating into the peace negotiations, and every-one was told that the State Department's seventh floor leadership opposed amnesty and there was a memorandum to that effect. Later in the day I met with Assistant Secretary of State for Democracy, Human Rights, and Labor John Shattuck to discuss atrocity crimes. Holbrooke confirmed his own statements regarding the indicted fugitives: They likely would be arrested if they traveled. He had raised the issue with Milošević, who had made a pro forma appeal for immunity for Karadžić and Mladić. That would include immunity for travel or perhaps even broader. Holbrooke told Milošević that if they traveled to any European country or to the United States, they would be arrested.

I received a call on September 21 from the Yugoslav Tribunal Prosecutor Richard Goldstone. He had spoken with Holbrooke and, he claimed, had a "good" conversation. Goldstone reported that Yugoslav Tribunal President Antonio Cassese had sent a letter to Belgrade requesting that the Serbs hand over Mladić. Milošević replied that day, saying he had been informed by Pale that Mladić had left Bosnia. He did not say whether Mladić, by then presumably in Serbia, would be turned over to the Tribunal.

The Principals and Deputies convened in the Sit Room on September 22. Holbrooke attended and was the Energizer man driving the process forward. The Washington lawyer who was special adviser to the U.S. delegation engaged in the talks, Bob Owen, said the negotiating team had put together a new, second package that superseded what had emerged from the basic Geneva Principles. "We believe it's acceptable to Milošević, but it will be a hard sell to the Bosnian Serbs," he reported. The team hoped to obtain Bosnian Foreign Minister Muhamed Sacirbey's agreement for the Bosniaks by the next day. The superstructure of the new government needed to be finalized as the Presidency, Parliament, and Constitutional Court. All three branches must be responsive to the risks of partition. "All of the connective mechanisms will be in place," Owen said. "Veto powers are customary in the Balkans, but we have watered them down so they are considerably weakened. There will be three entities."

Holbrooke announced that diplomat Chris Hill, Jim O'Brien, and Bob Owen would fly to Belgrade shortly and hopefully return on Sunday evening with an agreement. Christopher was scheduled to meet with the foreign ministers of the three parties in the Waldorf-Astoria Hotel in New York on Monday of the next week, but there would be no such meeting unless the negotiating team first succeeded at lower levels. Then, Holbrooke said, there would be a Contact Group political directors' meeting in Geneva on Tuesday, where "[w]e will try to keep the Russians on the reservation." On Wednesday and Thursday there would be unpublicized bilaterals in New York, particularly on the fate of Eastern Slavonia.

Holbrooke alerted the Principals: "There are growing tensions in the Federation. I had a frantic call with Sacirbey today. He claims Tudjman is on such a high that he's really dangerous. Tudjman starting ripping into Izzie." He proposed that Christopher send immediate instructions to Ambassador

Peter Galbraith in Zagreb and John Menzies at the U.S. embassy in Sarajevo, saying that they must prevent the Federation from squabbling like this between themselves. "All we got two days ago from Tudjman was not to attack Banja Luka. We have to shine bright flashing red lights on any actions against Banja Luka and Eastern Slavonia." Holbrooke was leaving the impression that land grabs elsewhere by Tudjman or Izetbegović might be tolerated. Lake interjected, "Wait, Dick. We have a clear public message of no further movements being tolerated. Don't implicitly encourage anyone to take more territory." Holbrooke shot back: "But you can't publicly tell them to stop taking land that had been ethnically cleansed!!"

Albright sought to calm down the exchange. "The Russians are pressuring us in New York on what assurances we have given, particularly to the Bosniaks." Christopher chimed in, "It's been stabilizing on the battleground. So stick with our line [that the parties not take more territory]." Deutch added, "Huge numbers of Serbs are being displaced out of these areas." Holbrooke: "This may be the moment to go for a ceasefire." Lake: "How about proposing a one month halt for Sarajevo?" Holbrooke: "That's an interesting idea."

At that point Holbrooke told the story about his latest meeting in Belgrade with Milošević as the central character: "There were many ironies. Eleven hours with Milošević, Karadžić, and Mladić . . . stunning hours. Mladić was everything Hollywood would typecast. He looked like a beaten man. He erupted twice to engage in verbal matches with us. But we never spoke directly to him. Karadžić became the group facilitator. Milošević came in and out of the room. Their references to NATO were endless; they did not like the Tomahawks! The Tomahawk attack was a masterstroke, a stunning event. The results reflected 50 percent NATO strikes and 50 percent the negotiations. These are whining, self-defeating people. So the threat of resumption of air strikes is essential."

Shali took up Holbrooke's bid for more air strikes: "Admiral Smith still has the NATO key. He's uncertain whether Janvier still has the U.N. key." Albright confirmed: "Kofi told me that Janvier still has the key." Holbrooke observed: "Milošević is willing to open the airport and roads into Sarajevo, but Smith and Janvier refuse to test the meaning of his proposal. The United Nations is not letting Bosnian civilians openly travel on those roads. It's the U.N., not the Serbs, preventing the testing of what 'unimpeded' means! The U.N. is still scared—a lot of old thinking. The U.N. is still being too timid. We have not tested access to Sarajevo yet!" Albright: "Yes, the British, French, and Russians are pushing Kofi [Annan] and Boutros-Ghali to be too cautious." Holbrooke: "Our greatest frustration has been the reluctance of Smith and Janvier to test the limits." Shali added, "Admiral Smith believes Janvier remains on board for more air strikes if that proves necessary. Maybe we just need to pressure Janvier to test the access to the roads."

Albright cautioned: "But the British and French don't want the Bosniaks to gain any strength at all." Lake responded, "We should test it. The British and French logic seems to be that if we insist on broad, unimpeded access, then anything less than being afforded that access will trigger more NATO bombing." Holbrooke intervened: "We are not committed to resumption if there is one attack on the road. Personally, I would bomb if there is a single violation. It's the best thing for the peace talks. This is about Milošević and [Army Chief of Staff] Perišić keeping their word. My greatest fear is getting lulled into an arrangement followed by Anschluss." Holbrooke was referring to Hitler's annexation of Austria in 1938 with strong-arm tactics before the beginning of World War II. He did not want to see Milošević and friends do the same with Serb-dominated and even Federation territories of Bosnia.

On Eastern Slavonia, Holbrooke was unsparing: "As the war has progressed, Tudjman is reverting to Nazism. He won't agree to anything unless he gets Eastern Slavonia. We're hesitant to move toward an international peace conference because of Eastern Slavonia. Tudjman would invade as the preferable option over a multi-year peace process. So what is our leverage? Do we forget sanctions relief as a bargaining chip for recognition?"

Deutch reported that the Serbs had pulled back from Eastern Slavonia, which presented a "big problem" because it left it exposed to a Croatian takeover, which could ignite Serb opposition to a peace deal at a time when forging the peace agreement was vital. Chris Hill said, "We need to get Tudjman's attention. He needs to understand the importance of the Federation and support for it, and not only Eastern Slavonia. We could flag a hint of sanctions, which would help people like [Croatian Foreign Minister] Granić." Lake immediately arranged for a message to be sent from Gore to Granić.

The territorial control had changed dramatically since August. There was a 50/50 split on territory held by the Federation and the Bosnian Serbs. Milošević was willing to grant a corridor between Sarajevo and Goradže, but the width of it had not yet been negotiated. We knew that the Bosniaks would not give up Goradže after the Srebrenica debacle. The fate of Sarajevo would be the final key to the peace process.

The Principals pondered when the first elections could be scheduled after a peace deal was signed. The Bosniaks were insisting that no elections be held until the war criminals had been removed. Then Lake shifted to Italy: "Consultations with the Italians . . . they have gone loonier. Any additional allied deployments to Italy to implement the peace agreement will be approved in Rome only if Italy is satisfactorily involved in the negotiations and peace talks. They have no better friend than us. This is really stupid."

Holbrooke and Lake explored a middle way: A wider meeting in the talks would be held in Rome, with a large group "to be as inclusive as possible." Holbrooke noted, "Other than needing the Canadians, who comes from Europe to such a meeting is a European problem." Shali reinforced the Italian imperative: "You can't conduct any military operation without Italy." Lake concluded, "OK, so Rome next, and then Moscow for meetings. The politics of Rome are more important than the politics of Italy at this point." Albright added, "Italy will want to attend the Contact Group meeting in New York next week." Lake and Holbrooke, in unison, burst out, "No!," and Holbrooke explained, "It's a negotiating session." Albright continued, "Well, keep in mind that the United Nations wants [EU envoy Thorvald] Stoltenberg in the room with only the Contact Group and Bildt." Holbrooke said the French had proposed the Contact Group and the Islamic states. Vershbow suggested a "quint meeting" with the Germans and Italians participating. Slocombe reminded us that the Italians needed to be part of IFOR in order to provide the real estate needed for deployment into the theater. Lake concluded, "Let's push for a quint meeting with the Italians and press them on IFOR access."

Albright shifted to the Russians. "At lunch the Russians said, 'Are you fooling us about the size of the IFOR force, if the peace agreement will be so successful?'" Shali delivered a textbook answer to the Principals: "NAC instructed military authorities to get on with the planning. The force size will be determined by tasks we want it to accomplish. The tasks are about right. But how do we end up with the map in the peace agreement? Because every 'we assure' we make on the map requires more forces." Shali further reported that the IFOR brigades would be made up of American, French, and British forces and brigades from other nations as well. "Non-NATO members of IFOR won't have a problem working with NATO, except Russia. We have to have a structure that won't violate the NATO chain of command." He continued, "The force has to be large enough so it's not challenged. We can use the Haiti model—once IFOR has established its bona fides we can start reducing the force. But it has to be large enough to forestall challenges early on when tensions run high."

Shali continued, "We have to set the time period for the new borders within Bosnia. And we need a time period to permit movement of forces. If thereafter there is no required movement of warring forces, then it will be up to IFOR to nudge them out." Holbrooke said that the "chapeau document must contain language that affords maximum discretion to IFOR. That is critical!"

The Principals turned to the stabilization plan. Shali admitted, "I'm treading water on the arming part of this plan. We need an assessment team to figure out what is needed. Less is better than more."

Holbrooke concluded, "The Yugoslav Tribunal has proven more valuable than we thought. It gives Milošević an excuse to keep Karadžić and Mladić out of the peace conference. Their travel is non-negotiable." Christopher was circumspect, having been burned in 1993: "There seems to be an unjustified tide of optimism. We have to be careful about the rhetoric. This deal is not anywhere near done." He identified problems as the content of the Constitution and the map, from which "all ugliness will flow again." He continued, "Implementation is premature and hypothetical. Don't' talk about any numbers yet."

Lake referred to the Security Council draft resolution as "unbalanced." There needed to be some inclusion of the Serbs in the resolution to warn them to stop their fighting. Lavrov, in his view, was on a "suicidal path" with the resolution. In addressing the needs of Congress, Christopher said, "We have not made it yet." Lake wanted to stress U.S. strength: "We should hype the leadership so far." Berger agreed, saying, "We have a rare opportunity now to consult with Congress early enough, so let's do that."

European Talks on the Peace Agreement

I left Washington on September 24 in a military aircraft along with Slocombe, Wesley Clark, and Kornblum to discuss with NATO allies how the peace agreement could be structured in both military and peace implementation terms. We were bound for London, Paris, Rome, and Brussels. Slocombe and Clark focused on IFOR. Kornblum and I took the lead in the nonmilitary components of peace implementation phase following the signing of the peace agreement. We all huddled together flying across the Atlantic to finalize our opening positions.

The basic framework of peace would settle on a 51/49 division of territory between the Federation and the Bosnian Serbs, recognizing that the
Bosniaks were seeking more than 51 percent. But a final verdict of 49 percent of Bosnian territory under Bosnian Serb control would claw back a
chunk (but only some) of the territory seized by them during the war and
redraw the ethnic map of Bosnia. The political entities of the Federation
(and its components of the Bosniaks and the Croats) and Republika Srpska
would each have considerable autonomy and be self-supporting. The Serbs
would have to pull back from Sarajevo, Goradže, and the Posovina Corridor.
There would be strictly enforced zones of separation. IFOR would be run
by NATO and would operate neutrally. The mission of IFOR would be to
oversee and enforce the withdrawal of warring forces behind new internal
borders inside Bosnia. If there were a total breakdown in the process and
war erupted again, then IFOR would withdraw. But if the forces moved behind the borders set in the peace agreement, zones of separation would be
established, and they would be monitored by IFOR, which would respond to
violations of the borders, and monitoring of the separation of forces would,
in Clark's words, "be very tough." But other types of violations within the
autonomous regions would not fall to IFOR to respond to or enforce. For
example, IFOR would not patrol the roads within the regions. IFOR would
remain deployed for only one year. The IFOR chain of command would
flow from the NAC, then SACEUR, and then the theater commander.

On the civilian implementation side, Kornblum and I examined how
reconstruction, humanitarian assistance, and management of refugees
would be addressed with flexible but narrowly defined taskings. The responsibilities of SICOR would flow from the peace agreement as agreed
to by the signing parties.

These were intensive days in each city as we entered often difficult
discussions with our European allies and Russia's envoy to NATO, Vitaly
Churkin, in Brussels. Some of our allies sought to place SICOR under
U.N. authority and control and even IFOR under some higher political
control, prospects that we opposed during the talks. Kornblum and I held
firm to our position that SICOR would be created by the peace agreement
itself and not by the U.N. Security Council or the U.N. Secretary-General.
Many international institutions would need to work together for this to
succeed. SICOR would not be a U.N. civil servant. His or her role could
be validated by the United Nations, but SICOR would fulfill an exclusive
mandate. He or she would liaise with NATO military commanders but
have no responsibility as a coordinator of military activity.

As a practical matter, the Clinton administration would not receive congressional approval to back SICOR if there were any whiff of a U.N. role in the operations, which had be minimized. So SICOR must be a function of the peace settlement itself. It was important that the parties themselves accept the individual's authority. Yes, there should be a Security Council resolution, and we wanted the concurrence of the U.N. Secretary-General in naming the person. But the SICOR mandate must arise through the peace settlement. And we would expect the NATO Secretary-General to be regularly briefed by SICOR.

Kornblum and I spoke during these meetings of the unique structure required for the political implementation of the peace agreement. Kornblum summarized our view during the Rome session: "The sides don't necessarily want anyone telling them what to do, wearing a U.N. badge. There are widely-varied tasks, with a combination of specific tasks given to agencies, and that requires a coordinator." Examples would be the European Union–led agency for economic reconstruction and the Organization for Security and Cooperation in Europe's human rights monitoring and rudimentary confidence-building measures. "None of this should be decided by the United Nations," Kornblum added. "It all should emerge from the peace agreement and annexes of details. An overall mandate would be given by the United Nations. SICOR would be an international person of stature. But not sent by the United Nations, rather arising from the peace agreement. And not a representative of the Secretary-General. A Security Council resolution would grant authority to him but not exercise it. The Special Representative (SICOR) would be supported by NATO and by all of us. There would be an international coordinating committee to support him. This would all transpire with the parties rather than imposed upon them." Heads nodded, but the final views of the British, French, and Italians still had to play out in coming weeks.

As we flew out of Rome, bound for Brussels on September 27, I wrote down a list of 32 issues to follow up on in light of our European talks. That list revealed continued tension among the United States and its allies as to how to stitch together the peace agreement and deploy IFOR. It did not get any easier in Brussels.

The administration team met with Russian Ambassador Vitaly Churkin, who was concerned that the Bosnian Serbs might fail to accept a peace deal. Clark assured him that "Milošević has shown he can deliver. No single piece of paper will guarantee this. It will be gauged in terms of power each time." Churkin thought the enforcement concept "very messy" and wondered what would happen when IFOR pulled out.

Clark responded, "Karadžić was happy as he wants the bombing stopped. The only hardliner was Mladić, who is still emotional. But he did not sign any delegation of authority to Milošević."

Clark and Churkin then tussled. Churkin wanted the entire military and political operation done under one chapeau of authority. He accused Clark of being too optimistic, citing problems with deployment of the Rapid Reaction Force (RRF) and with humanitarian convoys. Clark shot back, "There will be a minimum of situations where either side, once separated, will be dependent on the other. This is not Somalia." Churkin objected, saying it would be more difficult than Somalia with fractured lines of authority. But Clark would not have any of it. "We have to address military effectiveness problems. The United Nations cannot communicate well in the field. We had sad experiences with the U.N. on application of the use of force. The U.N. simply can't deal with any time-sensitive issue of orders."

"So, after Bosnia, are you [NATO] going to run all military operations!?" Churkin acidly remarked. Slocombe jumped in: "Some things the U.N. does well—like traditional peacekeeping. The problem is that in order to carry out the Security Council mandate, it makes sense to charge NATO to create an international military force. Where combat power is needed, this will work better. The new dynamic is that we need to send in a substantial military force that hopefully will operate peacefully but if necessary will have to be prepared to use military force." After more prodding by Churkin, Slocombe assured him that IFOR's deployment "is not indefinite. If it fails, we've done our part. All are eager to get out. We've set 12 months for IFOR in Bosnia." Slocombe told Churkin, "We're not setting up a U.N. government or trusteeship for Bosnia. We prefer 'Special Coordinator' responsible for implementation of the civil side who would interface with the military. He would not be a traditional U.N. Secretary-General Special Representative. Reconstruction duties would be up to the European Union, and the refugee operation up to the UNHCR. The Special Coordinator would be coordinating, not giving orders."

Churkin was deeply skeptical. "How will IFOR be even-handed? The U.S. attitude is a matter of historical record. You're not perceived as being even-handed." Slocombe responded frankly, "Almost all of the territorial back-steps will be by Bosnian Serbs. We admit it is a problem to use force against Bosniak forces. We have more leverage over the Sarajevo government. If the Bosnian Government signs, it's because it's a very good deal for them. We've spent a lot of political capital in the last few weeks pressing the Bosniaks not to continue the offensive."

"You'll only take care of Serb transgressions," Churkin scolded. Slocombe paused and then said, "If the Bosniaks don't pull this off, all bets are off on the other goodies. The Bosniaks are prepared to accept the Contact Group map." Churkin blurted out, "But they are irrational!" Slocombe responded, "If they shoot at IFOR, they are in trouble. We have to find a way for Russia to play a role. We're prepared to be flexible and imaginative in ways we normally would not." Clark noted that SACEUR Jouwan was prepared to host a Russian three-star general as part of his staff to coordinate, as well as officers of lesser rank on his and theater staff.

Churkin was still concerned about U.N. effectiveness for the long term, whether everything always would fall under NATO command, about even-handedness and how the process would work against Bosnian Serbs and Croats, about the limited duration of operations, especially if the U.N. structure has been dismantled by the time IFOR withdrew, that the domestic difficulties for Washington were no greater than they were in other capitals, and about seeing a Russian contingent subordinated to NATO command. He asked, "Why can't the whole thing be done under U.N. command with a U.S. general in charge in the theater? The U.N. would be a good chapeau for the operation. I'm concerned about a disaster in December 1996, after IFOR pulls back and things may deteriorate rapidly."

We departed from Brussels recognizing that the Russian component of our grand peace plan was anything but stable. It was rattling the entire edifice.

Drawing Down UNPROFOR

I held many consultations, including with Albright, on September 30 about the state of play in New York. The prospect of the drawdown of UNPROFOR loomed over all discussions. Albright had spoken to Boutros-

Ghali about it and Kofi Annan had been briefed. The U.N. Secretary-General's views about how to manage the peace process and IFOR deployment were being mocked in New York. Holbrooke had briefed Boutros-Ghali the prior Monday evening. Annan pulled Inderfurth aside and told him he was drawing down UNPROFOR. Boutros-Ghali had "broke" on September 18 and wanted UNPROFOR out. Janvier, Smith, and Holbrooke believed there were too many forces in UNPROFOR anyway. Annan was consulting bilaterally with countries about reducing their forces.

The Deputies met during the last days of September to address some of the stickiest issues in the peace process. First to bat was what to do with the Russians. Talbott suggested that Minister of Foreign Affairs Andrei Kozyrev persuade Yeltsin to order his defense minister to sit down with Perry and get to "yes." Russian units under NATO command probably would not work, but Talbott did not rule it out. Berger floated the idea of a Russian zone in Bosnia. Tarnoff pushed back and said the Bosniaks would object, while Slocombe chirped, "Even the Serbs would object to a Russian zone." Talbott cautioned not to leave the Russians alone in any area. Berger noted that we wanted Russia to participate in IFOR with certain functional responsibilities. Could the fallback be that the Russians would report to Janvier?

Berger further posited that we had to explain to Congress in two sentences the unity of command of a NATO-led operation in Bosnia. We want the Russians in the tent, but how? We had to work this out both in terms of IFOR operations and the United Nations. Fuerth said, "We need to convince the Russians that NATO is not U.S.-owned." Berger cautioned that, in order to persuade Congress, the role of the United Nations had to be limited.

Then we turned to the stability pact, which involved lifting the arms embargo and training. "Equip and train" needed to be more robust, Berger advised. "Stability is some balance of restraint and arms. We need to lift but also stabilize." He called for a new paper exploring a minimalist lift and a maximalist lift on the arms trade with Bosnia.

Later that day I spoke with Albright, who had just met with Annan. The numbers on withdrawals of national contingents from UNPROFOR were growing, with Bangladesh, Pakistan, and Malaysia already thinning out their troops. The Canadians also were planning to withdraw. How such downsizing would mesh with IFOR deployments still required study. I briefed Albright about the European trip, that the Russians obviously remained at odds with us over the peace process, and that we were still ironing out the role and relationship of SICOR, particularly with the United Nations.

I flew to New York on October 2 to meet with Annan and other U.N. Secretariat officials, joined by a group of U.S. officials from Washington and USUN to discuss the details of IFOR planning. The objective was that by the end of October we should have IFOR planning completed for an early November deployment. Annan was concerned about Janvier being rehatted as deputy of IFOR for a brief period. What would he do without any troops? Annan anticipated a transition period for UNPROFOR converting into IFOR and for UNPROFOR units to be withdrawn. In his view, once UNPROFOR was withdrawn, Janvier would have no military role. Annan understood that SICOR would not oversee the IFOR commander and there would be no dual key. But how would he undertake all of the civilian tasks? "We need ideas," Annan pleaded. "We need to know the civilian pieces as soon as possible. There will be a big tie-in with U.N. agencies." Sashi Tharoor, Annan's aide and future Indian politician, asked whether a decision had been made to cut loose UNPROFOR at the end of November if the peace agreement failed. Inderfurth responded with an emphatic, "No."

Annan said he acted as chief administrative officer of UNPROFOR and could save funds without affecting the efficiency of the operation. The generals already believed there were too many peacekeepers on the ground. The United Nations also had introduced large numbers of RRF troops. There were proposals for withdrawing more Bangladeshi, Canadian, Dutch, Pakistani, British, Malaysian, Nordic, Spanish, and Turkish forces. The total number of repatriated units, including Canadian, stood at 4,211 peacekeepers. UNPROFOR was being cut down to a total force of 22,000 troops. Annan did not view this as impacting effectiveness. None of the logistics units were reduced. "So it's a thinning out concept." He would begin further withdrawals that week. The meeting with Annan seemed encouraging.

Critical Decisions

The Principals, absent their Deputies, met on the morning of October 4 in the Sit Room as fighting continued in Bosnia to discuss four issues: no-fly zone violations, a ceasefire and proximity talks, Russian participation in IFOR, and military stabilization. The BTF had reported the day before that "by all accounts, the Serbs are making limited gains against the Muslims in western Bosnia. The Croatians/Bosnian Croats continue to sit on their hands, not taking any action to help relieve pressure on the Muslims. This inaction promises to further burden the federation. . . . Holbrooke continues to tour the region at a blistering pace. . . . It is still not clear how much—if any—progress is being made in negotiating a cease-fire and narrowing differences over the territorial division of Bosnia."[11]

The Principals delayed any decision on enforcing the no-fly zone against the Bosnian Serbs at the Banja Luka airport, deciding that they "would not make a cease-fire a precondition for the convening of proximity talks or an international conference," and that the venue for the proximity, or peace, talks would be a secluded location in the United States but easily reachable from Washington or New York for senior American officials to drop in. They agreed on how to handle the Russians in IFOR:

> If the Russians are prepared to accept NATO operational control for their forces, a Russian brigade could be integrated into one of the three Allied divisions likely to comprise the IFOR. The Russian brigade commander would report to the division commander. At the political level, Russia (and other non-NATO troop contributing nations) would participate in a planning/coordination group that would advise and consult with the NAC, but not make decisions; decision-making would remain with the NAC. Russian liaison officers could be established at various levels in the NATO chain of command. If the Russians are not prepared to participate on the above basis, then we would suggest that they not engage in the military operation, but instead provide military forces to perform specific civilian tasks that would be under the purview of the Senior Implementation Coordinator.

Finally, on military stabilization, the "Principals reaffirmed that our goal should be to ensure that there is a rough balance of power between the Federation and the Bosnian Serbs by the end of the one-year peace implementation period. They endorsed a military stabilization plan that would involve both arms control/confidence-building measures and a program to equip and train Federation armed forces." They further agreed to "develop a military assistance package that would provide the Federation with the minimum capability necessary to create a balance of power without stimulating a regional arms race." The Principals determined that the United States should "lead in organizing the equip-and-train effort so that we can exercise control over the types of weapons provided to the Federation and limit the involvement of Iran and other radical states." But Washington would do so "in a low-profile manner—e.g., quiet bilateral approaches to potential contributors rather than hosting a multilateral donors' conference."[12]

These were critical decisions at the time as all of us engaged at the highest levels of policymaking for the Bosnian situation needed to know whether a ceasefire had to precede convening the talks, where the location of the talks would be, how to handle the Russians with clear guidance, and how equip and train would be implemented.

The Deputies followed up two days later, on October 6, with a Sit Room meeting that focused exclusively on developing detailed principles for Russian participation in IFOR and calculating IFOR's role during the local elections that would follow (at some point) the peace process. As backdrop, the long-awaited ceasefire across Bosnia had been announced on October 5, set to go into effect the following week, provided utilities were restored to Sarajevo. The BTF reported: "The Bosnian Government signed the [ceasefire] agreement only under great pressure from Holbrooke. . . . Fighting continued today in western Bosnia, with the Serbs making some gains and the Croatians reintroducing a limited number of forces, probably to limit the Serb advance. Fighting also continued south of Sarajevo, with the Muslims making gains."[13]

The Deputies looked at two options relating to Russian participation following the underlying decision of the Principals on October 4: either the Russians would operate *in* IFOR or *with* (in cooperation with) IFOR. Slocombe insisted there be no geographical area of responsibility for the Russians. Berger set forth the operating principles:

(1) The best option for Russian participation would be within IFOR and under the NATO operational control (OPCON).
(2) We oppose the Russians having a separate geographic area of responsibility.
(3) If Russians take on functional responsibility outside IFOR, they do so in "cooperation with" IFOR.
(4) Where Russians take on non-core functions outside IFOR responsibilities, they should report to SICOR.
(5) Only the NAC would make decisions for and provide political guidance to IFOR; any NAC + 1 arrangement would not enable the Russians to interfere in that decision-making and guidance, but would be limited to consult, advise and/or inform the NAC.
(6) Russia would not have any veto over relations with or participation in IFOR by other non-Allies.[14]

Talbott added, "Our goal, our trick, is to trap the Russians into doing something we think is good for them. They can cooperate in a circumstantial and probational way. The Russian goal seems to be to establish a relationship with NATO. But equality and veto—we can't give that to them."

Berger responded, "The fact is we'll do this without the Russians if necessary. Our relationship will survive either way. Not everything is riding on this." Talbott objected, "But that's not true. If this goes off the rails, it will be difficult to keep Hyde Park [the Clinton-Yeltsin talks to be held at Hyde Park, New York, on October 23, 1995] on the tracks." Slocombe said that if the Russians agree to fulfill some designated functions only, namely, cooperation with IFOR, "we could live with it." Kornblum added, "Lots of non-NATO nations will want to associate with IFOR. There can be no veto by Russia on IFOR relationships with other non-NATO contributors."

The prospect of IFOR providing security during the elections in Bosnia came under attack, with Holbrooke not wanting to rule it out and the Pentagon strongly opposing the responsibility, arguing instead that by IFOR fulfilling its primary functions, that would help create the secure conditions for elections. No formal decision emerged.

The Deputies "agreed that we continue to prefer that the Senior Implementation Coordinator (SICOR) be appointed as part of the peace settlement, with enhanced international authority conferred by the UN Security Council. Deputies agreed that we may ultimately need to accommodate the position of our allies and the Russians that the SICOR be appointed by the UNSC or the UN Secretary General but deferred a decision on this question."[15] Our view about SICOR was open to some compromise by that stage, but we also knew that we were going to continue to press hard for SICOR's independence in the upcoming peace talks and, as it turned out, that independence was sustained.

On October 11, we learned that the ceasefire never took hold. The Bosniaks were not willing to stop fighting due to Sarajevo's electricity problems. They used 40 megawatts as a standard, but only 28 megawatts was flowing. The Bosnian Serbs were willing to agree to the ceasefire at first, but then their internal authority to sign lapsed as the fighting continued.

Kornblum sent a memorandum to Talbott on October 12 entitled, "A Multilateral Framework for Bosnian Peace Implementation." He succinctly summarized U.S. interests as including several requirements: complete autonomy for NATO as the organizer of IFOR, an indirect link to the United Nations but absent requirements for U.N. oversight of either the military or civilian components, a means of integrating non-NATO participants, especially Russia, into the IFOR, on the basis of NATO command and control, and a credible central civilian implementation structure that did not become embroiled in the politics of the United Nations, European Union, or other organizations.[16]

The Deputies meeting for October 16 focused, once again, on the Russians and requirements for their relationship with IFOR. These were unremarkable discussions about how essentially to sit the Russians at the IFOR table. The Deputies also "reaffirmed that the negotiating team had no authority to offer interim sanctions relief to [Serbia] prior to signature of a peace agreement but that the option would be reviewed if requested by the negotiating team."[17]

Annan's Washington Talks

I spent October 17 shepherding Annan around Washington for meetings with key Washington figures for detailed discussions about Bosnia. We first met with Tarnoff at the State Department. Annan complained that the negotiating team needed to let him know more about what was going on. We needed to come to grips with the overall architecture of the military (very fast track) and the civilian (important too) implementation. The role of SICOR would be key. Tarnoff agreed that the military planning was ahead of the civilian-role planning.

Annan explained, "The question of the U.N. role is bothering a lot of governments. There is concern that the U.S. Government would try to hide the U.N. role in order to avoid civil war in Washington. The more that is done, the more it will provoke governments. We need to find some medium ground." Tarnoff responded, "This is an opportunity to work with the United Nations. We must, though, have unity of command and control for IFOR. But we also need to establish a meaningful relationship for SICOR and the United Nations." Annan asked, "Who decides what needs to be done among all of the components? No one. So it's becoming quiet urgent. How do you see post-1996?" Tarnoff answered, "We need to establish a military equivalent during the 12 month IFOR deployment. Lift the arms embargo. Possibly use U.N. monitors for arms control. Try to restrain some of the arms supplies. There may be a need for a follow-on force. Foreign officers would need to be there to train."

Annan and I met with Berger at the White House. Annan reiterated his point that "[w]e don't have much time to bring the military and civilian components together and develop the role of [SICOR]. The civilian side needs time to organize." He said, "There's a feeling that the U.S. is trying to kick the U.N. aside. The U.N. needs to be seen to know the status of the negotiations. If it works, we have to do a lot together. If it does not work, we're left holding the bag at the U.N." Berger said there should be a SICOR but we did not know yet how that person would be selected. Who will have the most legitimacy with the parties? "IFOR must be in a strictly NATO box." Annan agreed. Berger said that if there were no agreement, we would hope that UNPROFOR stayed through the winter. The ceasefire would be very unstable in the absence of a peace agreement. And there would be enormous pressure to lift the arms embargo. But Annan responded, predictably, that if the arms embargo were lifted, the British and French peacekeepers would pull out.

Our next stop was Capitol Hill to meet with Senator John Warner, the imposing, tall Republican chairman of the Senate Armed Services Committee (and once married to actress Elizabeth Taylor). Warner said that Congress would debate the peace process and that Clinton "ought to seek a formal approval from Congress." Other key senior senators endorsed this view, he said. "I want the strongest measure of public opinion to back up the President," Warner opined. "I'm not sure I'll be there. There's a fervor out there: 'Don't get us involved!'" Annan responded, "There will be casualties. You should factor this in the debate." (Annan's prediction proved unfounded.) Warner concluded the meeting, "I'm not anti-U.N. I'd vote tomorrow for money we owe to the United Nations."

The Joint Chiefs of Staff told Annan their best estimate was that Milošević would not intervene in Eastern Slavonia. The winter weather would not be a show-stopper for IFOR. Washington intended to send a robust, all-weather force into Bosnia. General Jouwan had proposed that a three-star general be a direct liaison with SICOR. Also, the United Nations might have to take on additional civilian responsibilities. Who would appoint SICOR? the military brass pondered. We would need clear lines of authority. SICOR had to be able to have a bird's-eye view of what is going on in theater. Annan left Washington with eyes wide open as to Washington's perspective and the critical role of the United States during the weeks ahead.

More Planning in Washington

The Deputies gathered in the Sit Room on October 18 to discuss Bosnian reconstruction and IFOR planning. They endorsed some numbers and concepts for economic reconstruction for a strategy paper destined for the Principals:

– Humanitarian assistance, with the U.S. share for 1996 at roughly $100 million for food, shelter, and relocation.

- Premature repatriation of 550,000 refugees abroad could pose many difficulties for repatriation. I stressed the need for a systematic plan for the right of return.
- The European Union would be responsible for coordination of assistance, but leaving a prominent role for the international finance institutions, which Congress would insist upon anyway.
- An American aid assessment team would visit Bosnia later in October.
- The G-7 nations agreed to look favorably at reducing Bosnia's sovereign debt by 50 to 100 percent.
- Estimates of reconstruction needs were $4 billion over three years for the territory the Federation held before August 15 and $1.2 billion for additional territory captured since then, as well as $800 million for Bosnian Serb territory.
- After accounting for expected international institutional financing, the Bosnia reconstruction gap over the next four years would be $1 billion in the first year, $0.8 billion in the second and third years, and $400 million during the fourth year.

What if Milošević asked for assistance for Serbia? Deputies agreed he would have to reach a quick and fair settlement on the successor state issues. And he would be told that Serbia is not reforming its economy enough to qualify for assistance.[18]

Kornblum viewed "the prospect of economic reconstruction as key leverage with the parties. There is real tension, though, between this and Congressional funding. Holbrooke wants to iron this out before the proximity talks." Berger responded that "[w]e will need to set up an EXCOM [Executive Committee] on Bosnia with daily management responsibility and an IWG [inter-agency working group] on economic reconstruction." Kornblum continued, "We need a Serbia policy, including the war crimes tribunal, with conditions on admission to international organizations and reconstruction aid."

On IFOR, there was concern that a gap was widening between IFOR planning in NATO and the negotiations on the ground. Holbrooke seemed to be promising a more activist role for IFOR than that being considered by NATO. Further, NATO planners appeared to have different views about what to do if either side violated the terms of the agreement. The United States would treat Serb and Muslim violations differently, and yet NATO would treat them the same.[19]

It was basically agreed that IFOR would have the authority to intervene but exercise discretion in each case. "There are questions in several areas of IFOR implementation that need resolution. One example discussed is what to do if there are reports of atrocities in Banja Luka."[20]

The Joint Chiefs of Staff had originally conceived of a one- or two-kilometer separation zone. "The Deputies need to decide whether they want a 20-kilometer heavy-weapon exclusion zone, and, if so, whether they intend to enforce it. They also wondered what to do when both sides make unreasonable demands and whether we intend to enforce such demands."[21]

"We need to flush out 'even-handedness,'" posited the Principal Under Secretary of Defense for Policy Jan Lodal. The North Atlantic Council favored even-handedness. They believed that IFOR should respond to sporadic violence. For serious assaults, there may be a different reaction. If the Muslims assaulted the Bosnian Serbs, then IFOR would depart. If the Serbs assaulted the Muslims, then we would unleash the F-16s on them.

General Howell Estes reported that 16,000 of 24,000 UNPROFOR peacekeepers would remain in Bosnia under IFOR. Up to eight non-NATO troop contributors of UNPROFOR had asked to join IFOR. He also noted, "Since IFOR will be stationed on the Federation side, it will be more difficult for Muslims to aggregate at the border aggressively. Whereas if the Serbs aggregate, then we'll react quickly."

The Deputies left unresolved critical issues "regarding mission creep, use of force, zones of separation, and states, required Presidential decisions, and the coordination of U.S. policy, negotiations, NATO decisions and military planning. JCS, State and NSC had to provide answers for immediate Deputies' consideration by the end of the week.[22]

The next day, on October 19, we learned that the Rapid Reaction Force was in disastrous straits. Only $3.5 million of the $115 million voluntary funding had been collected. It seemed the RRF simply was not a viable solution to the enormous challenges facing us.

IFOR Guidance

The Deputies convened on October 20 for one of their most important meetings of the year. It would be the 73rd meeting in 1995 alone of Deputies or other high-level officials in key agencies (often joined by various Deputies, like myself) about the Balkans.[23] The BTF reported beforehand, "Sandy Berger and the other Deputies are becoming increasingly apprehensive that a disconnect is developing between what NATO planners anticipate for IFOR and what is being negotiated. NATO planners seem to be taking a minimalist approach on the mission of the force while the US negotiators seem to be taking a broader approach to the mission which could even include some police function." Continuing, "Yesterday JCS briefed the President on IFOR. He was surprised to learn that the JCS thought the civilian structure needed to be in place when the troops arrive. The President indicated: —He wants to avoid mission creep. He wants to maintain unity of command. He does not want IFOR to operate as a police force."[24]

The Deputies agreed to a long list of policy stances prior to finalizing positions for the Dayton proximity talks.[25] In flushing out these points, the Deputies noted that some of our allies believed any significant use of force by IFOR would need prior NAC approval. They also wondered what would be the IFOR reaction to a serious breach of the ceasefire. While cross-border firing would be a violation eliciting IFOR action, there was no rule of engagement for Serb-on-Bosniak violence. General Clark admitted, "We need guidance on this." Berger concluded, "We're not creating a civil order function for IFOR except in reaction to gross human rights violations and refugee problems." Shalikashvili objected to deploying IFOR forces on Bosnian Serb territory while Holbrooke disagreed, arguing that election security depended on an IFOR presence throughout the country.

We learned from Berger that Clinton's message to us was clear: Before he agreed to a 12-month IFOR deployment, he wanted to see the terms of the peace settlement and NATO's updated plan for deployment. Then there was the disagreement between the Pentagon and Holbrooke that emerged during the Deputies meeting: The Deputies for JCS and Defense believed elections must not be a precondition to withdrawal, while Holbrooke argued that the key to an IFOR exit would be a successful round of elections in Bosnia.

The Deputies met on October 24 for almost three hours to examine resolved and unresolved issues pertaining to IFOR. For starters, however, Talbott briefed the Deputies on Clinton's just-concluded meeting with Russian President Boris Yeltsin at Hyde Park. "Clinton turned Yeltsin around 180 degrees," he said. The Russians would have two battalions operating throughout Bosnia. Their tasks would be logistics support, demining, and airlift duties. The Russian relationship would be a liaison with IFOR, not one directly under NATO, a point Clinton reiterated at the Hyde Park lunch. Yeltsin consented, but he wanted more functions for his troops and some Russian pride of place in the command structure. There was no real discussion between them about the United Nations' role and authority. "So, the Russians will be supine," Talbott predicted. Yeltsin's caveat was: Don't put us in second class, and so the Russians should not be characterized as "support" or "secondary" forces but rather "special operations." Clinton agreed. Semantics were very important. Yeltsin pushed hard for the Moscow summit on the peace plan to take place on October 30 before the proximity talks in Dayton. Clinton agreed to press Izetbegović and Tudjman to attend what we foresaw as a short and largely symbolic meeting in Moscow.

Talbott spoke of the "positive" meeting at Hyde Park. The two leaders even discussed the Yugoslav Tribunal extensively and committed to enable access by "media and the international organizations," presumably meaning the Yugoslav Tribunal as well, to all places where atrocity crimes were thought to have been committed.

The following issues provoked the most discussion among the Deputies, as summarized in a memorandum by Rear Admiral Dennis Blair at the CIA:

a. IFOR response to violence: DoD and JCS reps want IFOR limited to stopping violence in plain view. State representatives want IFOR to provide on-call protection for international organizations.
b. Preconditions for deployment of IFOR. JCS and DoD representatives want fundamental conditions for peace (ceasefire, start of withdrawal, etc.) in Bosnia to be confirmed prior to IFOR deployment. State representatives are afraid that if the preconditions are too stringent, rejectionist elements in Bosnia can cause enough incidents to prevent IFOR from being deployed.
c. Movement of IFOR throughout Bosnia. DoD and JCS representatives want IFOR to be in Republic of Serbsca [sic] only to protect IFOR lines of supply. State representatives want IFOR to be enough of a presence in Republic of Serbsca [sic] to impress the Bosnian Serbs.
d. Movement of warring armed forces back into cantonments. The negotiating team is pursuing the idea of treaty language restricting Bosnian Serb, Bosnian government and Bosnian Croat armed forces to garrisons. DCI and other representatives question the practicality of verifying such movements and the force requirements to enforce them.[26]

Annan Returns to Washington

Kofi Annan returned to Washington on October 25 while the Principals were meeting again in the Sit Room. I accompanied him on his rounds. At his primary meeting with Holbrooke and Talbott in the State Department, Annan stressed, "We are racing against the clock! We must look at the comparative advantage of who can get work done efficiently, not just who wants to do it." He added that SICOR would need a secretariat with deputies assisting him. If there were gross violations, cut off economic reconstruction aid. Who would referee conflicts between SICOR and the military, and between humanitarian agencies and the military? There should be daily meetings between SICOR and the military.

Annan continued by pointing to "Mostar, with its two totally separate forces, Muslim and Croat. They've never been integrated. That's the problem. We will want international monitors working side-by-side. We should use the presence of experienced international police to show by example. . . . We have to convince European governments not to push refugees back into Bosnia too quickly. . . . We should emphasize the return of talented, professional people. I would guess about 800,000 potential returnees for Bosnia."

The police force was, in Annan's view, a very tough problem. "I don't see it," he said. "Who finances it? It's a big project, spread over a large area, with logistics and communications requirements. It's very difficult for OSCE even for small operations. . . . So the real problem is the political decision of who is going to do what, and how to coordinate it. At some point, the UNHCR will lift the temporary protection shield over Bosnian refugees throughout Europe. Then, they are no longer refugees and presumably must go home."

Holbrooke finally spoke. SICOR would report to neither the Security Council nor to the U.N. Secretary-General. "We're 100 miles from a peace agreement. . . . But we are very interested in the police function," he said. Annan focused on SICOR's authority—what would be his reporting lines and his relationship with the military? "This will be a very complex and difficult task." He would have to be appointed by some group. "If he's not appointed by the United Nations or the Security Council, that raises the question of legitimacy and authority," Annan counseled.

Talbott described SICOR as a "*sui generis* creature. The individual is a product of the negotiating process and represents implementation of the London conference. We would look for a Security Council resolution validating this." Holbrooke jumped in with the blunt observation that "SICOR is not on any party's mind." He continued, "Enforcement authority is very tricky for any police force. We can't have international police doing enforcement work."

"Since London," Talbott interjected, "the operating principle has been diplomacy backed by force. The international community is contracting NATO to take this on." He predicted that the Serbs would most likely be on the receiving end of force, as they were the most credible threat. The Russians were politically unable to operate under NATO command. The United States, though, insisted that IFOR be a NATO operation. "Can we reconcile these views?" Talbott asked. "Maybe." The solution might be the Russian willingness to conform to noncombat tasks, such as reconstruction, engineering, and airlift. They would not have to be under direct NATO control. But it also could look second-class for them. No Russian could be in Bosnia with either real or potential combat functions without being under NATO command. So at a minimum, Russians would perform noncombat duties. We were taking a very hard line against a Russian sector in Bosnia. The Russians would not be free to conduct assignments that IFOR considered nonconducive to objectives. The Russians wanted another dual key, but that was "no way" with Clinton. So Washington was gravitating toward a Security Council resolution like in the Gulf War: a grant of authority and an invitation to report.

Holbrooke said there would be three co-chairmen at Dayton: Holbrooke, Russian diplomat Igor Ivanov, and European Union envoy Carl Bildt. Lavrov, he noted, was a more contentious diplomat, but the Russians got their Moscow mini-summit agreed to, so that should calm the waters. Once the peace agreement was behind us, Holbrooke advised, then IFOR, SICOR, and U.N. senior representatives must all be headquartered in Sarajevo.

Annan agreed, but he was visibly angered, complaining, "The United Nations has not been invited to the proximity talks! The British and French will invite us. We need the parties to know we are in this all together." Holbrooke shot back, "No! A U.N. representative at the talks does not make sense right now. If the East Slavonia talks heat up, then sure, send in [Thorvald] Stoltenberg. But you'll have a continuous up-date on Dayton from Albright and Scheffer. When U.N. issues come up, you'll be briefed." Annan relented but acidly remarked, "Remember, someone has to assign tasks in Bosnia after Dayton, so that has to be part of the talks."

Debate Over Easing Sanctions

The Principals met on October 25, with the Deputies joining them, and approved the recommendations contained in the Deputies Committee Memorandum to Principals of October 24, 1995, which included our agreement on issues pertaining to IFOR. Thus, for the first time, there was full agreement on IFOR's mandate.[27]

However, considerable debate ensued in the Sit Room over the critical issue of whether and how to ease sanctions on Serbia as the peace talks unfolded with Milošević participating. Christopher started with his view that "[w]e should suspend during the course of the negotiations and then reverse gears if the talks break down. We have flexibility with Congress on this. We should aim for what will best achieve a peace agreement. So let's suspend everything but the frozen assets."

Holbrooke reinforced Christopher, saying, "The goal is success in Dayton. Now the suggestion is suspension for signing and lift for implementation. Milošević is way ahead of us. He wants suspend now, then lift at signing. We should suspend for the duration of the talks. If there's a break down in the talks, then the suspension is off, unless the Security Council votes to continue the suspension. So the Security Council resolution on sanctions would be automatically reimposed unless the Security Council votes to continue suspension." He continued, "We're using sanctions to propel Dayton. It should be an incentive to reach a deal, not as pressure on Milošević."

Perry cautioned, "We have to have the ability to turn it off. If there's a break down in the talks and it's Milošević's fault, then we have to automatically reimpose the sanctions." Lake interjected, "What if the 'break down in the talks' is ambiguous?" Milošević could easily claim no responsibility for the collapse of the talks and insist on continued sanctions relief. Holbrooke responded, "It's our decision." Lake cynically remarked, "We'll be marginalized. The Russians will be pleased with us."

Then Albright weighed in. "The negotiations ought to have latitude," she started. "First, Milošević has gotten a great deal by just coming here, to Dayton. Second, there would be a lot of ambiguity in sanctions suspension—a lot of questions. We need some breathing space. Third, we should aim for an omnibus resolution in New York, one that blesses the peace accord and then ties together sanctions lifting with the lifting of the arms embargo. The two lifts have to be coupled together. Otherwise, we're giving leverage away. And unless the Bosnians are on board, you can't get it through a Security Council vote." Christopher added, "So we turn to the lawyers to ensure automaticity for reimposition and the need for Council affirmative vote to continue the suspension."

Holbrooke responded, "The Bosnian government will go along with this. We need to use the sanctions regime as leverage on Milošević. It's the single best incentive. Milošević has internal domestic problems. Reimposition would be automatic if Dayton breaks down."

Albright countered, "Why give in now, making us appear directly opposed to Sarajevo? If Milošević knows that at the end of the Dayton talks, he gets suspension, that should work. He'll be received in Dayton, and that's a big deal for him." Dennis Blair, the CIA Deputy, agreed: "Sanctions relief is not the goal right now. It won't make much difference for him at home."

Holbrooke resisted, saying, "There's no incentive for him to stay [at Dayton] because there's nothing punitive if he leaves." Lake clarified, "If Milošević leaves [Dayton], he doesn't get sanctions suspended, or lifted."

Holbrooke returned to an earlier point. "Look, I don't agree with Dennis on the domestic impact for Milošević. I don't believe the President's letter to Senator Dole is determinative. It would be suspension only for [the duration of] Dayton." But Berger disagreed. "It will be inconsistent with the Dole letter. We'll be seen as making a concession, right at the beginning, a concession to the worst actor in the Balkans." Holbrooke exclaimed, "We are trying to act for peace! The American public will support anything that gets us there. It's a suspension for the duration of Dayton only."

Christopher veered toward Holbrooke's position. "The suspension threat is real pressure on Milošević. If he walks out, he's responsible for reimposition of sanctions. We would suspend for just the negotiations." Lake, though, was concerned. "In two or three weeks, he could stockpile oil."

Holbrooke dug in. "Milošević argues that this would strengthen his case against Tudjman and Izetbegović."

Albright dug in deeper. "We should adopt a U.N. Security Council resolution," she stated, "that suspends sanctions at the *end* of the peace talks, and tie such suspension to the success of the talks." Holbrooke retorted, "I don't like it." Shalikashvili pondered, "There is a linkage between suspension of sanctions and eventual lifting of the arms embargo. We'd be pushing back arms embargo and thus extend the life of IFOR because there would not be enough time to improve the Federation force's defensive capabilities."

Albright exclaimed, "If the sanctions are suspended, we lose all the advantages! We need to dangle the carrot at the end. This will be the incentive to finish talks rapidly and successfully." Perry showed his cards: "I have misgivings for this proposal. The points raised by Madeleine and Sandy [Berger] are good. But I consider it imperative to support our negotiator. I accept his judgment over mine."

Christopher added, as seeming support of Holbrooke, "Milošević will not be pleased with his treatment in the States. He'll be an unhappy camper there." Fuerth, our sanctions expert, took a different tact: "It's difficult to find words for automatic reimposition of sanctions. Once suspended, even if reimposed, they won't function anymore. Once the front-line states get a taste of trade, it's very hard to shut it down. We won't be able to get performance out of front-line states."

Lake tried to reach closure, saying, "I don't think the case for sanctions suspension has been made, with all of its psycho drama and how it supports the negotiations. I'm torn." Holbrooke fought back: "Peace is only possible if Milošević delivers on the Pale Serbs. Suspending the sanctions would

- strengthen Milošević against domestic forces,
- pressure him not to leave Dayton,
- pressure Izzie not to leave Dayton,
- strengthen Milošević with the Pale Serbs,
- strengthen our hand with the Contact Group, and
- send a signal to Tudjman, which he richly deserves."

Berger looked across the Sit Room table at Holbrooke and said dourly, "You can't say any of that publicly." To which Holbrooke said: "No, the public line is that suspending the sanctions will help bring peace." Lake sighed with exasperation, "Let's decide this on Monday."

The Sit Room discussion briefly turned to IFOR. Holbrooke began by saying, "At Dayton, we need to achieve separation of forces, cantonment [of forces], and no reinforcement of partition. But IFOR needs to go beyond the military aspects of the peace agreement. The issue is whether we seek cantonment on Day One." Shali responded: "SACEUR says he can't enforce cantonments with existing troops. They can be confidence-building measures, but I can't enforce them." Holbrooke shot back, "But the zone of separation unintentionally promotes partition. We want it to act like a U.S. state line, not the Korean DMZ [demilitarized zone]! We have to get forces off that line."

Shali rebutted Holbrooke, "But that works only if you get the forces secured in cantonments. Don't give IFOR a mission to enforce unless you give them the resources to do it." Everyone departed the Sit Room silently with despondent faces.

The Principals met for almost two hours on October 27 to revisit what had been left unresolved two days earlier. On the prior day, the BTF advised the Director of Central Intelligence about the joust on sanctions suspension and lift: "[T]he Principals remain split over Holbrooke's proposal.

State argues that it is necessary that he have bargaining freedom before the negotiations. In his opinion this would keep the talks going. Several of the Principals oppose this as rewarding Milošević, causing problems in Congress, and lessening pressure on Milošević. One of the issues is that Holbrooke argues that Milošević is under heavy pressure internally and needs this benefit. We don't see that he is under that much pressure, but that he could use the opportunity to import a lot of oil and strategic materials even in a short period." Then, in talking points, the BTF wrote, "We don't see the connection between suspension of sanctions on Serbia and Milošević being able to pressure the Bosnian Serbs although that is what Milošević would like the West to believe. Milošević's main clout over them is through his ability to control the flow of material support." Another talking point read, "Reimposing sanctions after the proximity talks will be hard. The frontline states will be loathe to start up again and it will be hard to maintain an international monitoring regime during a suspension."[28]

Discussion about sanctions relief at the Principals meeting on October 27 proved to be relatively short. Holbrooke, in attendance with Christopher, reported, "Milošević said that he wants relief before he gets to Dayton. Izetbegović was willing to do a partial sanctions suspension if he could get the Goražde road open. Sacirbey has hardened. Izzie's view is that he get something for it and then he'll consider." Lake replied, "We have no choice but to hold off [on sanctions suspension]; it's too much water to carry. We've got to assume Milošević will attend Dayton. Sanctions suspension is designed to put pressure on him to stay, not to arrive there. We will reconsider it as necessary over the coming days." The NSC summary of the meeting concluded, "Principals agreed that sanctions against Serbia should not be suspended prior to the proximity talks, but agreed they would be prepared to revisit the issue of sanctions relief later, if requested by the negotiator."[29] Albright had prevailed.

Unresolved IFOR Issues

The Principals then turned to unresolved issues on IFOR, and the duel between Shali and Holbrooke resumed. Shali reiterated, "Don't structure tasks for IFOR they can't meet." Holbrooke argued, "IFOR can skip the 20 kilometer exclusion zone and go straight to cantonments but only if cantonments are mandatory. I oppose partition. We have a line on a map today. That line has to be adjusted for Posavino, Sarajevo, and Goražde. The Bosnian Serbs need to be forced to withdraw from these areas. Cantonments would reduce the risk to IFOR forces."

Shali dryly remarked, "Annex A (Cessation of hostilities) language [in the draft peace agreement] already has the right for IFOR to force troop movements into cantonments." Wesley Clark interjected, "IFOR would have the right to respond by force but not the obligation to do so." Shali continued, "I don't object to cantonments in exchange for a 20 km exclusion zone. That could be negotiated at Dayton. IFOR would have the right to do it, but not be obligated to do it if the parties are resisting." Lake asked, "How do you force them into cantonments, at your discretion?" Shali responded, "I reserve the right when they are outside cantonments to push them back."

Berger explored another point, saying, "It's not IFOR's mission to deal with humanitarian convoys or civilian issues. If a UNHCR convoy is calling for assistance, then yes, atrocities can be responded to within the IFOR commander's capacity to make the decision." Shali added, "In the instance of killings, we should authorize IFOR to act when in plain sight or close proximity of the atrocities. But I am leery to investigate each incident." Albright suggested, "Why not create a force within IFOR of volunteers to meet humanitarian threats?" Shali answered, "It's not a question of risks. You can't successfully accomplish those tasks. Civilian police make a big difference. Law and order are the responsibility of police forces."

I always marveled at the fact that atrocities and humanitarian calamities would be caused by a military force—in this case the Bosnian Serb Army—but our response to such threats often rested on the "police." Why the military could not confront the military for the security and survival of civilians typically escaped the Pentagon's reasoning.

Berger continued, "Where there are reports of massive atrocities, the only one who can make a determination is the ground or local commander." Holbrooke shifted the focus: "What's at stake is what happens in Serb territory. The key event in 12 months will be an election. We have to get rid of Karadžić. The Bosnian Serbs will test IFOR's rules of engagement. Will IFOR keep Goražde road open?"

Albright responded, "UNPROFOR had the authority but did not use it."

Holbrooke continued, "The right of return is the toughest issue in New York today. Sacirbey claims that the Muslims of Banja Luka have the right to return. But what if the transport of refugees gets hung up by the Serbs?"

Shali bluntly stated, "IFOR won't guarantee safe passage for all." Lake clarified, "We are in favor of the right of return. But we can't guarantee it." Shali continued: "IFOR can't do blanket security. We must expect police to do their utmost to provide security. If there's a major incident, IFOR may react, particularly if the police force is overwhelmed. The existing police force consists of 14–16,000 policemen, but they are often the abusers. We need to replicate what's in Haiti: police monitors."

Albright reinforced Shali's point. "Exactly, we need to form something like what the U.N. has in Haiti—human rights monitors and police monitors." Lake pushed back, "That's not a function of IFOR. IFOR will have a presence on external borders." Shali clarified, "I want to do it, but only in six or seven spots. We need enough soldiers in each spot and they must be very visible." John White thought it might be a bridge too far: "We never planned a substantial force in [Bosnian] Serb territory."

Holbrooke grimaced, "I never said 'substantial'."

The Principals meeting reached several conclusions, as summarized by the National Security Council's note taker:

Principals agreed that, at a minimum, IFOR would enforce a 4-km all-weapons-free zone along the zone of separation. They requested that agencies study further whether IFOR could effectively establish and enforce a 20-km heavy-weapons-free zone, an all-weapons-free zone that would be broader than 4-km in selected areas, and/or cantonment areas for the parties' forces in support of the implementation of a peace settlement. They agreed to have State, JCS, and OSD develop options for Principals' consideration prior to the proximity talks.

Principals agreed that the IFOR commander at the Corps level should have the authority to act, on the basis of his own judgment, against reported "over the horizon" gross violations of human rights and/or attacks on international civilian agencies, in situations of urgent and serious humanitarian needs or attacks, and where NATO forces have the means and opportunity to stop violence to life and persons and where it will not adversely affect the IFOR mission.

Principals agreed that the IFOR should provide a presence on the external borders of Bosnia at crossings where heavy traffic in support of the IFOR mission occurs (6 or 7 sites). Principals also agreed that JCS should prepare options for principals' decision about how IFOR can provide a more significant presence early in the operation in Serb territory, such as through regular IFOR patrols that traverse Serb areas.[30]

The Deputies gathered on November 1 to discuss the nuts and bolts on economic reconstruction and military stabilization. From this point forward, the meetings in the Sit Room assumed a strictly operational character of how to facilitate the Dayton talks and implement the results into documents that could be signed by all parties in Paris on December 14.

Dayton Place

The Dayton talks began on November 2. There would not be another Deputies Committee meeting on Bosnia until November 13, and the next Principals meeting on Bosnia occurred on November 15. The Dayton talks are well recorded elsewhere[31] while the purpose of this book has been to illuminate the Sit Room meetings. However, the recently declassified Situation Reports ("SITREPS") of Donald Kerrick on Holbrooke's delegation provide vibrant new insights into what occurred at Dayton during those historic negotiations. I recite extracts of the Kerrick SITREPS in the endnotes.[32]

In a memorandum to Secretary Christopher on November 14, Holbrooke downplayed the prospects for success at Dayton. He was distressed that the talks had fallen behind schedule, where Day 14 should have been Day 8 or 9. "Most disturbingly, we have had a series of emotional map discussions in which the Bosnians constantly changed their mind. While the Bosnians are the sort of friends that try one's patience, Milošević has often lied outright about factual data or changed his position after we thought we had locked something in. As for Tudjman, he is fast becoming the King of Dayton (well, only after Strobe [Talbott] moved to Cleveland, of course)."

Holbrooke continued:

> By [late that night], our entire delegation was fed up with the Bosnians, led by Mad Dog [Haris Silajdžić], who has been moving forward on the parallel track of constitutional issues. Yet Haris [Silajdžić] told me that today has been the best day of Dayton so far, that peace was within sight, and so on. I thought he must be on some controlled substance, since it seemed to me that the tortoise of our progress was being outrun by the hare of the calendar. But he was serious, and perhaps he is right. It is true that we made gains today even in the territorial field, with Milošević giving up a few key areas of the map. But those were ones that were in Federation hands anyway, and he had always intended to relinquish them.
>
> Beyond that, however, we hit the wall on many key issues. The Bosnians were still fighting with the Croats over many issues, and Tudjman was skillfully playing one side off against the other

while slicing off pieces of land for his people. Izzy was in a terrible mood today, and refused to see either Milošević or Tudjman, while Tudjman refused to see Milošević. That is why they call these proximity talks, of course, but it did constitute retrogression.

All the parties want peace, but they still don't know how to get it. They look forward to your helping them stop killing each other—and so do we.[33]

Holbrooke's additional "Secret" memorandum to Christopher on November 17 illuminated the turbulence in the Dayton talks near their conclusion:

A fierce argument over sanctions, in which I think Tony [Lake] advanced policy significantly. After facing a front assault from Slobo [Slobodan Milošević], Tony explained our policy, stressing that while suspension would come with initialing, lift could only accompany implementation. To our pleasant surprise, Slobo accepted this concept and dropped away from his previous insistence on lift with signing. Clearly he now sees that in real terms it is suspension, not lift, that make[s] a difference to the people of Yugoslavia. We then argued over what constituted implementation, with Milošević trying to get us to agree that 'implementation' should be defined as the moment when the BSA [Bosnian Serb Army] pulls back to the inter-entity boundary line. I said that while we needed to study this issue before making a decision it would certainly not be possible to consider anything in the sequencing earlier than pulling back the two kilometers from either side of the entity boundary line. Milošević seemed to buy this, but balked when I pushed on to the next level, pull-back to cantonments. My real goal here would be elections, but this issue requires a decision at the PC [Principals Committee]. This issue has now become urgent. You have promised Milošević a look at the sanctions resolution prior to the final agreements in Dayton, but in New York all, or almost all, is confusion. Madeleine [Albright] today stopped a messy and damaging process in the mid-levels of the bureaucracy on this subject, but she must have guidance and finish the job even before you land so we can discuss it with Milošević. Tony agrees, and further agrees not to drop the previous idea of an omnibus resolution. He now favors, as I do, dividing the resolutions into at least two packages, one solely

on sanctions, the other on lifting the arms embargo and other matters. . . . After almost two hours of computer travel over the hills and
valleys of the Goražde area, a trip made far livelier by the substantial
amount of scotch consumed by many of the group, Wes Clark and
the team managed to eke out a minor concession—the widening of
the land corridor from Goražde to Sarajevo from three kilometers to
a wider corridor which would vary based on terrain features.

. . . Interestingly, Milošević asked for [Christopher's chief of
staff] Tom Donilon by name, presumably to ask Tom to run his next
campaign (this is one even Tom probably couldn't screw up).

. . . The Bosnians still wish us to believe that they are getting a
lousy deal. But they know it is not only a good deal but the best
they will ever get. Logically, therefore, they must accept. Yet the dynamic of their delegation, plus their internal thinking processes,
make this a very close call. Izzy spent nine years of his life in jail,
and is not a governmental leader so much as a movement leader.
He had no understanding of, or interest in, economic development
or modernization—the things that peace can bring. He shows remarkably little concern for the suffering his people have endured;
after all, he has suffered greatly for his ideals. To him, Bosnia is
an abstraction, not several million people who overwhelming want
peace. Haris [Silajdžić], on the other hand, is more modern and focused heavily on economic reconstruction, something Izzy never
mentions. If Haris did not have such an unpredictable personality,
he would have played the hare here; we still have hopes he will do so.
Mo [Sacirbey] is driven by several contradictory motives: he wants to
be liked by the Americans (he is, after all, one of us), but his primary
goal seems to be to undermine Haris at all times. We are constantly
looking for ways to deal with this problem, and may call on several
of you to give Dutch-uncle talks to either one of them.

. . . Milošević seems to be enjoying himself here at Dayton Place,
although he likes to try to bully people. Standing up to him when he
attacks is the key; he respects and likes people who act as tough as
he does. He is always testing us. In order to move him, we must lay
down very firm markers and not move them unless we know exactly
what we are getting in return.[34]

The General Framework Agreement for Peace in Bosnia and Herzegovina
was initialed on November 21, 1995, in Dayton, Ohio. The formal signing

of the peace deal would occur several weeks later in Paris, with Milošević, Izetbegović, and Tudjman committing for their respective countries and with the leaders of the Contact Group, namely, the United States, Russia, Germany, United Kingdom, and France, signing as witnesses.[35]

Surveying the Dayton Results

But before Paris, the Principals alone met with Clinton in the Sit Room on November 22 for one hour to survey the Dayton results and address four questions that he posed.

First, could Milošević deliver the Bosnian Serb leadership to support Dayton? Shalikashvili said that Washington would demand statements from Bosnian Serb leaders (those designated by Milošević) supporting the peace plan (including its all-important military annex governing IFOR) and guaranteeing the safety of IFOR troops, including American forces.

Second, what commitments had the United States made to arm and train Bosniak forces (which some in Congress, Clinton observed, saw as sacrificing our objectivity and impartiality in the conflict)? Deutch stressed some arm-and-train effort was needed in exchange for serious Bosniak efforts to send their allied Iranian fighters home. Berger argued that the U.S. arm-and-train initiative was essential to "build down" the military forces of all parties. Clinton accepted that rationale, stressing that we should present arm-and-train as part of a comprehensive arms-reduction package.

Third, what was the Iranian threat to U.S. forces and what would be our response? Deutch summarized what our intelligence revealed about Iranian activities in Bosnia. He stated that the Bosnian government now lacked the resources to control the activities or guarantee the withdrawal of the Iranian fighters. Holbrooke, who had been invited to the Principals meeting, agreed that the Iranians posed a here-and-now real problem. But he argued that the threat would decline quickly as we made solid progress with the three parties to the conflict. Nonetheless, the Principals agreed that the United States needed to develop more initiatives to get the Iranians out of Bosnia.

Fourth, when would the Dayton agreement be officially signed in Paris? The date in December had not yet been specified. Shali described the military and political approvals needed at NATO early that week. Holbrooke cited several preliminary steps to be taken to get Milošević to deliver, to properly brief the Allies and Congress, and to pin down details on the Sarajevo provisions of the Dayton agreement.

Clinton told the Principals that he wanted briefers from the Pentagon to present their information on Capitol Hill truthfully in the weeks ahead. He was concerned about reports that some from the Pentagon were letting personal opinions critical of him and administration policy creep into their briefs. He asked all such individuals be appropriately disciplined.[36] I had experienced a similar impression two years earlier while part of an interagency team led by the National Security Council to forge a new policy on U.N. peacekeeping. I listened to some Pentagon mid-level officers disparage Clinton, saying they would never follow his orders. I also heard them cater to the most cynical questioning by Republican staffers in Congress during our monthly peacekeeping briefings.

The Principals tasked Holbrooke to instruct the U.S. chargé d'affaires in Belgrade, Larry Butler, to meet Milošević's incoming plane. Butler would tell Milošević to contact the Russians and urge them to back down on opposing immediate lifting of the arms embargo. The Security Council resolution that day, November 22, would first lift the arms embargo and then suspend economic sanctions against Serbia. Yeltsin had sent a letter to Clinton suggesting deferral of the arms lift until the Russian-sponsored summit was held prior to Paris. Christopher called Kozyrev during the Principals meeting to stress Washington's position.

Holbrooke concluded that Milošević, for all his warts, had carried the day in Dayton. Tudjman could be trusted to "carry out his part." However, Holbrooke awarded Izetbegović the prize for being the most unreasonable and uncooperative at the table, and in Holbrooke's view perhaps he would be the least trustworthy during the months ahead.[37] As the primary victim of the conflict and the party that had to compromise the most in the aftermath of ethnic cleansing of their people and a de facto partition of Bosnia and Herzegovina rewarding Bosnian Serb and Bosnian Croat land grabs, the Bosniaks and their leader, Izetbegović, could be forgiven for being the toughest customer to please at Dayton and its immediate aftermath.

The signing ceremony in Paris, which I did not attend, was anticlimactic. We Deputies had done our job, however frustrating the process and results at times, and I felt rather battle-scarred after almost three years of strategizing in the Sit Room that led to that moment on December 14, 1995, in Paris. The mettle of our work would begin to be tested, particularly in the wartorn nation of Bosnia. There would follow a full year of Deputies and Principals meetings that I attended to implement the Dayton Agreement, but that is a different story about sustaining the fragile peace we had helped forge.

Epilogue

A result from which "all ugliness will flow again."
WARREN CHRISTOPHER

THE BOSNIAN WAR took three years of intensive diplomacy to end, while combat and atrocities were unremitting. The talking phase of armed conflicts has veered wildly from days to decades in recent history, and often failed completely when one side fought to achieve outright military victory. There were no negotiations to end World War II; only total defeat of the Axis Powers sufficed. The Korean War ended in a stalemate absent any substantive talks, and the United States and North Korea remained, technically, at war, for decades thereafter. Negotiations to end the Vietnam War began in 1968 and continued into the next decade only to be eclipsed by the total victory of North Vietnamese and Viet Cong forces in 1975. The catastrophic Syrian conflict began in 2011 and continued unabated despite years of U.N.-sponsored talks in Geneva. The Colombian government and the indigenous guerilla group, Revolutionary Armed Forces of Colombia–People's Army (FARC), finally ended their civil war in 2016 with a peace agreement after 26 years of on-again, off-again negotiations.

I often think back to those days in 1993, 1994, and 1995 when so many of our Sit Room meetings on Bosnia seemed utterly detached from the horrors unfolding there and yet were so critical to finding a way out of the conundrum. We kept reaching for the brass ring, only to find our hands slipping from one oily rope to the next. The personalities of both allies and adversaries dominated discussions as we tried to discern the true thinking of the politicians, generals, and diplomats who populated the daily calculus of action and inaction. While Bob Frasure and Richard Holbrooke had interesting insights into the psyche of their counterparts in the region, and Tony Lake and Madeleine Albright had penetrating observations for years, the Sit Room could have had a seat occupied occasionally by

The Sit Room: In the Theater of War and Peace. David Scheffer.
© Oxford University Press 2019. Published 2019 by Oxford University Press.

professionals of the mind. Psychologists, psychiatrists, and social anthropologists should have advised the Principals and Deputies how to evaluate the rhetoric and actions of minds steeped in evil or influenced by the vicissitudes of Balkan history and culture. Policymakers at the highest level need that input periodically.

If I had to do it all over again in the circumstances confronting us, but with hindsight my ally, I posit that the challenges could have been managed differently if Albright's point of view had prevailed in the Sit Room in 1993, we had forced the Serbs' hand with NATO-led air strikes, and we had exercised political will in Washington to transform UNPROFOR with American troops deployed with it or alongside it and strengthened with enforcement mandates to effectively protect civilians *and* compel the Bosnian Serb Army not only to end its ethnic cleansing operations but roll them back. Given how quickly the Bosnian Serbs and Slobodan Milošević capitulated to negotiate during and after Operation Deliberate Force in late August and September 1995, one can only imagine what might have been a different outcome in 1993 and how many lives could have been saved and municipalities spared ethnic cleansing and destruction.

The Sit Room embodies the risk and hope for peace before, during, and after war. Of course, the primary objective of Sit Room meetings is to prevent war from ever breaking out. There can be a tendency in the Sit Room to avoid information or proposals that would ignite fierce debate or instinctive ridicule among agency representatives at the table. But very few ideas should be banned from the Sit Room, however bold, academic, legalistic, theoretical, or unconventional they may seem at the time. To walk down the path of least resistance defies the very purpose of that historic room. Granted, the goal is to forge consensus among the national security agencies to arrive at a decision the president can support. But there were times during the Bosnian war when the Principals and Deputies tried to muddle through without factoring in, at least seriously enough, the immediate fate of civilians on the ground and of defeating ethnic cleansing with its consequences for human rights, democracy, economic survival, and peace. While some voices spoke of morality at times in the Sit Room, that dimension of our deliberations and decisions rarely took center stage. I only trust, in retrospect, that morality implicitly guided us every day.

Another issue that cropped up frequently in the Sit Room, but in a narrow, American-centric way, was the cost of the Bosnian war. The budgetary impact of policy choices focused exclusively on the federal budget and what it would cost to commit American forces or to cover the U.S. share of the bills for UNPROFOR or OPLAN 40104 or the Rapid Reaction Force, or to provide America's portion of humanitarian or reconstruction aid. Never did we discuss the totality of costs for everyone, including what might be gained by investing funds in timely actions that could prevent much larger appropriations of funds in the future if the war dragged on or if a de facto partitioned Bosnia would require extraordinary commitments of assistance to sustain fractured populations for generations. Ideally, we should have had rolling estimates of costs as the months and years tolled by, with such looming figures reflected in monetary terms as well as lives at risk, lives lost, property devastated or at risk of destruction, and updated calculations of what restoring the infrastructure of Bosnian and Croatian societies would cost the international community and the peoples of these two countries when peace finally arrived. The CIA sometimes created helpful data in this respect, but not systematically or thoroughly and not in ways that should have influenced more deeply the decisions of policymakers. Without such empirical information, muddling through can be the easiest, albeit ultimately the costliest, option to embrace in the Sit Room.

There were some moments in the Sit Room when it seemed that the United States would sell the farm to achieve the acquiescence of the Bosnian Serbs and their benefactors and enablers in Belgrade. I was no fan of false equivalency where one denies important raw facts of what occurred in the Balkans during the early 1990s and suspends critical judgment in order to distribute responsibility for violence and death equally among the warring parties. The Yugoslav Tribunal prosecuted perpetrators of atrocity crimes from all sides in the conflict, and while the judgments of conviction or acquittal have attracted fierce criticism from whichever party feels aggrieved or wronged when justice is rendered, the evidence presented over more than two decades at the Yugoslav Tribunal overwhelmingly lays the primary responsibility at the doorstep of the Bosnian Serbs, and sometimes to Serbian officials in Belgrade.

The bogeyman of secession for the Bosnian Serbs, which would sanctify their ethnic cleansing campaign with the reward of partition from Bosnia and union with neighboring Serbia, reared its head occasionally. But the Dayton Agreement made the prospect of secession extremely difficult to realize and preserved a sovereign, although still deeply divided, nation of Bosnia and Herzegovina. One can debate the merits of that outcome to this day, but from my perspective, the idea that in the last decade of the twentieth century we would reward the crime of ethnic cleansing with an easy pathway to secession still strikes me as deeply immoral.

I held the same view about the bargaining that emerged over how much territory the Federation would control under a negotiated peace deal. The bottom floor of 51 percent for the Federation and the top floor of 49 percent for the Bosnian Serbs sadly validated much of the ethnic cleansing that occurred during the war. By the time we were approaching the Dayton talks, with the recent gains achieved by Federation forces under the air strikes of Operation Deliberate Storm, the seesaw had tipped against the Bosnian Serbs on territorial control.

But the 51/49 formula held firm under the final agreement. Goražde remained on the chopping block for handover to the Bosnian Serbs during months of negotiations until the very end, when Alija Izetbegović insisted at Dayton on the city remaining under Bosniak control. In the Sit Room, Goražde kept appearing as a likely bargaining chip with Milošević even though its gratuitous loss would have represented a triumph for Bosnian Serb bullying and intimidation. Territory for peace became the trade-off that dominated the Dayton talks, whatever the illegalities and cultural upheavals preceding the final deal.

Warren Christopher's fear that "all ugliness will flow again" when implementing the new Constitution and the Dayton map came to pass in Bosnia, which struggles with both negotiated outcomes to this day. The entire region is also crippled with the mindset of denial, particularly by the Serbs and Bosnian Serbs over vast bodies of proven evidence of atrocity crimes revealed by the jurisprudence of the Yugoslav Tribunal. My hope is that future generations will understand the truth if they are given the chance to study authentic history untainted by the propaganda of denial.

There also arose the stark prospect of the looming presidential election of 1996 in the United States, when Bill Clinton would have to defend his Bosnia policy and we hoped be able to promote it as a principled success. His expected rival, war hero Senator Bob Dole, was a hawk on Bosnia and we knew would be a fierce opponent. Although strategizing based on the forthcoming politics of the election was discouraged in the making of Bosnia policy, everyone in the Sit Room knew throughout 1995 that Clinton's re-election bid was the bloated elephant sitting in the corner (behind Lake!). The pressure was on, implicitly, to make a deal and resolve the Bosnian conflict, particularly if it meant U.S. soldiers would be deployed to implement a peace agreement rather than fight toward one. This confluence of war and politics during the final year of the Bosnian nightmare worked to the benefit of all, as it helped spur Washington into action, particularly after the Srebrenica genocide. We needed to redeem ourselves for that debacle and ensure that Clinton was not crippled by a destabilizing Bosnian crisis during his 1996 campaign.

Another outcome that drove decision-making was the prospect that a fresh military deployment to Bosnia, namely, the NATO force destined for OPLAN 40104 or in later planning for IFOR, presumed a maximum one-year commitment for any such deployment. Thereafter, the Bosniaks were on their own to win or lose any resulting flare-up of the war. This was the convenient short-term perspective that enabled all other decisions to be reached. One more year of this mess with total U.S. engagement, including on the ground, and we could call it quits just before Clinton's second term. Whatever the fate of the Bosniaks thereafter, it would not be Washington's responsibility. This proved to be an utterly unrealistic view as the Bosnian situation, despite the relative peace achieved at Dayton, could not be sufficiently stabilized after only one year. Those countries committed to a peaceful Bosnia could not just walk away. The NATO-commanded Stabilization Force, or SFOR, technically replaced IFOR in late 1996 and laid the foundation for continued NATO troop presence in Bosnia for several more years, followed by the European Union picking up the torch for a continuous multinational presence on the ground. Thankfully, the Bosniaks did not have to fight for their survival again despite Sit Room speculation that we would abandon them to their next war.

I conceived of this book as Syria descended into atrocities, vicious warfare, and despair while the Western world, including the United States and its NATO allies, essentially stood by, and then European nations reeled under the onslaught of millions of refugees. I wondered whether discussions in the Sit Room during the Obama administration resembled at all the meetings we had during the Clinton administration and our own Syria crisis, namely, Bosnia. It is too early to unearth the historical record of the Syrian debacle, but I fear that the sophisticated strategizing that I experienced in the Sit Room, with its often futile consequences for Bosnia until the summer of 1995, may have repeated itself during the Syrian crisis and perpetuated an awful failure of the human potential to overcome evil and save hundreds of thousands of lives sooner than later.

Then there is today. The American republic is pummeled with foreign policy by tweets and bombastic rhetoric from a president who may precipitate unnecessary conflict and divisiveness in the world rather than act to prevent such outcomes. We also risk, under such erratic leadership, rendering the United States irrelevant on the global stage. I hope that in the realm of America and the world, men and women of high character will studiously absorb briefing papers and intelligence reports, recall the lessons of history, and then deliberate in the Sit Room with courage for the fate of humanity.

Acknowledgments

THERE ARE INDIVIDUALS and institutions that truly helped me launch this book and bring it to closure. First and foremost, I express my deep appreciation to the American Academy of Berlin and its outstanding staff for affording me the opportunity to begin the research and writing of this book in the fall of 2013. Having received the Berlin Prize, I was the Bosch Public Policy Fellow at the Academy during four months of intellectual discourse and intensive work on *The Sit Room*, which arose from my proposal for the fellowship. That is why this book is dedicated to the Academy, which was founded by Richard Holbrooke while he was the American ambassador to Germany, and of course he is a central figure in the book.

I heartily acknowledge the support of many individuals who, during my several years of toil, assisted me in bringing this book to reality: my superb editors at Oxford University Press, namely, Blake Ratcliff and David Lipp, the anonymous peer reviewers, project manager Balamurugan Rajendran, and copy editor Mary Rosewood; Melody Dernoceur (my law student whose early meticulous research proved invaluable), Gregory Townsend, Dr. Caroline Kaeb, Samuel Halter, Eben Saling, the librarians of the Pritzker Legal Research Center, my dear friends in Santa Fe (Gordon Harris, Beau Borrero, Holly Davis, Bruce Velick, Denise Filchner, Curtis Freilich, and Richard Martinez) who never wavered in their belief of this book, and Anne V. Barbaro and Behar Godani at the U.S. Department of State, whose skill and efficiency in achieving clearance at the State Department and marshalling the book through clearance at the National Security Council and the Central Intelligence Agency earned my sincere gratitude.

The Sit Room: In the Theater of War and Peace. David Scheffer.
© Oxford University Press 2019. Published 2019 by Oxford University Press.

The portraits of the main characters of the book were drawn by Julie Murphy, an illustrator in Chicago. I deeply appreciate the enthusiasm and skill with which she took up the challenge. I also gratefully acknowledge support from the Northwestern University Pritzker School of Law Faculty Research Program in connection with the writing of this book.

Finally, I warmly thank my dear wife, Michelle Huhnke, and my daughter, Kate, and son, Henry, whose unyielding love and support for so many years gave me the strength and will to forge ahead.

Notes

INTRODUCTION

1. Peter Baker, Maggie Halberman, and Glenn Thrush, "Trump Removes Steve Bannon from National Security Council Post," *New York Times*, April 5, 2017, https://www.nytimes.com/2017/04/05/us/politics/national-security-council-stephen-bannon.html?_r=0.
2. Darlene Superville, Associated Press, "Obama Recites Love Poem to Wife on National Television," *Seattle Times*, February 12, 2016, http://www.seattletimes.com/nation-world/nation-politics/obama-recites-love-poem-to-wife-on-national-television/.
3. "Bosnian Declassified Records" Collection, Clinton Digital Library, https://clinton.presidentiallibraries.us/collections/show/37.

SETTING THE STAGE

1. *See* Morton H. Halperin and David J. Scheffer with Patricia L. Small, *Self-Determination in the New World Order* (Washington, D.C.: Carnegie Endowment for International Peace, 1992).
2. Speech by Slobodan Milošević at Gazimestam, Kosovo, June 28, 1998, http://www.slobodan-milosevic.org/spch-kosovo1989.htm.
3. For an extensive examination of many of the atrocity crimes committed during that period, see, for example, International Criminal Tribunal for the former Yugoslavia, "Judgment," *Prosecutor v. Ratko Mladic* (November 22, 2017), 176–1583
4. Population Loss Project 1991–1995 (Sarajevo: Research and Documentation Centre, 2007).
5. "Refugees and Displaced Persons in the Former Yugoslavia," *REF/RL RESEARCH REPORT*, vol. 2 (15 January 1993): 1–4.

The Sit Room: In the Theater of War and Peace. David Scheffer.
© Oxford University Press 2019. Published 2019 by Oxford University Press.

6. Sarina Ramet, *Social Currents in Eastern Europe: The Sources and Consequences of the Great Transformation* (Durham NC: Duke University Press, 1995), 407–408.

7. Ramet, *Social Currents in Eastern Europe*, 406–407.

CHAPTER 1

1. Mulholland to Kanter, Memorandum, January 11, 1993 (declassified), in *Bosnian Declassified Records*, https://clinton.pesidentiallibraries.us/collections/show/37.

2. "1993-01-22, Presidential Review Directive 1 re U.S. Policy Regarding the Situation in the Former Yugoslavia," *Clinton Digital Library*, accessed September 28, 2017, https://clinton.presidentiallibraries.us/items/show/12299.

3. Ibid.

4. "Crisis in the Balkans; Statements of United States' policy on Kosovo," *New York Times*, April 18, 1999, New York edition.

5. Colin Powell, "U.S. Forces: Challenges Ahead," *Foreign Affairs*, Winter 1992, vol. 71, Issue 5, 32–45.

6. Madeleine Albright, *Madame Ambassador* (New York: Miramax, 2003).

7. "Sandy Berger Fined $50,000 for Taking Documents," CNN, September 8, 2005, http://www.cnn.com/2005/POLITICS/09/08/berger.sentenced/.

8. "1993-01-29 BTF Memorandum re Principals Committee Meeting on the Former Yugoslavia January 28, 1993," *Clinton Digital Library*, accessed September 28, 2017, https://clinton.presidentiallibraries.us/items/show/12303.

9. Ibid.

10. Ibid.

11. Ibid.

12. Michael Gordon, "Powell Delivers a Resounding No on Using Limited Force in Bosnia," *New York Times*, September 28, 1992, http://www.nytimes.com/1992/09/28/world/powell-delivers-a-resounding-no-on-using-limited-force-in-bosnia.html.

13. "1993-02-04, BTF Memorandum re Principals Committee Meeting on Yugoslavia February 3, 1993," *Clinton Digital Library*, accessed September 28, 2017, https://clinton.presidentiallibraries.us/items/show/12306.

14. Ibid.

15. "1993-02-05, Minutes of the Principals Committee Meeting on Bosnia, February 5, 1993," *Clinton Digital Library*, accessed September 28, 2017, https://clinton.presidentiallibraries.us/items/show/12307.

16. United Nations Security Council, Resolution 770, August 13, 1992.

17. Ibid.

18. *Legal Encyclopaedia on the Yugoslav Crisis; Volume 6; The United Nations Resolutions and Documents*, eds. Graham Greene and Sabine de Haardt (Tilburg, The Netherlands, Global Law Association, 2002).

19. Warren Christopher, "New Steps toward Conflict Resolution in the Former Yugoslavia," Opening statement by the secretary of state at a news conference, February 10, 1993. Reprinted in *Dispatch*, vol. 4 (February 15, 1993), 81. For

reactions to the statement, see "1993-02-19B, BTF Memorandum re Reactions to Secretary Christopher's February 10 Announcement of U.S. Policy toward the Former Yugoslavia," *Clinton Digital Library*, accessed September 28, 2017, https://clinton.presidentiallibraries.us/items/show/12311.

20. "Conflict in the Balkans: Christopher's Remarks on Balkans: 'Crucial Test,'" *New York Times*, February 11, 1993.

21. "1993-02-19A, BTF Memorandum re Principals Committee Meeting on Airdrops in Bosnia," *Clinton Digital Library*, accessed September 28, 2017, https://clinton.presidentiallibraries.us/items/show/12310.

22. Ibid.

23. United Nations Security Council, Resolution 781, October 9, 1992.

24. United Nations Security Council, Resolution 786, November 10, 1992.

25. U.N. Secretary-General letter, S/24783, November 6, 1992.

26. United Nations Security Council, Resolution 808, February 22, 1993.

27. United Nations Security Council, Resolution 827, May 25, 1993.

28. "1993-03-01, BTF Memorandum re Deputies Committee Video Conference on the Former," *Clinton Digital Library*, accessed September 28, 2017, https://clinton.presidentiallibraries.us/items/show/12314.

29. Ibid.

30. Ibid.

31. Ibid.

32. U.S. Embassy in Zagreb, Cable 00731 ("Human Rights Abuses in B-H: Mass Killing, Female and Male Rape at Luka Camp—Case of V.G."), March 3, 1993 (declassified).

33. Ibid.

34. "1993-03-09, BTF Memorandum re Deputies Committee Video Conference on Bosnia March 4, 1993," *Clinton Digital Library*, accessed September 28, 2017, https://clinton.presidentiallibraries.us/items/show/12315.

35. *See* Tony Lake's memorandum of February 19, 1993, to President Clinton recommending U.S. engagement with the humanitarian endeavor that became known as Operation Provide Promise, at "1993-02-19C, Anthony Lake to President Clinton re Presidential Decision on Humanitarian Air Drops for Bosnia," *Clinton Digital Library*, accessed September 28, 2017, https://clinton.presidentiallibraries.us/items/show/12312.

36. "1993-03-10, Office of European Analysis Memo re March 9 Deputies Meeting on Bosnia," *Clinton Digital Library*, accessed September 28, 2017, https://clinton.presidentiallibraries.us/items/show/12316.

37. Madeleine Albright, "Current Status of US Policy on Bosnia, Somalia, and UN Reform," *US State Department Dispatch*, vol. 4, no. 14, article 7 (1993), http://dosfan.lib.uic.edu/ERC/briefing/dispatch/1993/html/Dispatchv4no14.html, (accessed October 23, 2017).

38. United Nations Security Council, Statement by the President (S/25426), March 17, 1993.

39. "1993-03-23A, BTF Memorandum re Evaluation of Revised OSD Paper on Lifting Siege of Sarajevo," *Clinton Digital Library*, accessed September 28, 2017, https://clinton.presidentiallibraries.us/items/show/12317; "1993-03-23B, BTF Memorandum re Serb War Aims," *Clinton Digital Library*, accessed September 28, 2017, https://clinton.presidentiallibraries.us/items/show/12318; "1993-03-23C, BTF Memorandum re Establish Safe Havens Around Srebrenica and Other," *Clinton Digital Library*, accessed September 28, 2017, https://clinton.presidentiallibraries.us/items/show/12319; "1993-03-23D, BTF Memorandum re Likely Consequences of Warnings of Air Strikes," *Clinton Digital Library*, accessed September 28, 2017, https://clinton.presidentiallibraries.us/items/show/12320; "1993-03-23E, BTF Memorandum re Likely Consequences of Partially Lifting the Arms Embargo in Conjunction with Air Strikes," *Clinton Digital Library*, accessed September 28, 2017, https://clinton.presidentiallibraries.us/items/show/12321; "1993-03-23F, BTF Memorandum re Likely Consequences of Fully Lifting the Arms Embargo on Bosnia," *Clinton Digital Library*, accessed September 28, 2017, https://clinton.presidentiallibraries.us/items/show/12322; "1993-03-23G, BTF Memorandum re Likely Consequences of Aggressive Delivery of Relief Supplies," *Clinton Digital Library*, accessed September 28, 2017, https://clinton.presidentiallibraries.us/items/show/12323.

40. "1993-03-23A, BTF Memorandum re Evaluation of Revised OSD Paper on Lifting Siege of Sarajevo," *Clinton Digital Library*, accessed September 28, 2017, https://clinton.presidentiallibraries.us/items/show/12317.

41. "1993-03-23B, BTF Memorandum re Serb War Aims," *Clinton Digital Library*, accessed September 28, 2017, https://clinton.presidentiallibraries.us/items/show/12318.

42. "1993-03-23E, BTF Memorandum re Likely Consequences of Partially Lifting the Arms Embargo in Conjunction with Air Strikes," *Clinton Digital Library*, accessed September 28, 2017, https://clinton.presidentiallibraries.us/items/show/12321.

43. Ibid.

44. "1993-03-23F, BTF Memorandum re Likely Consequences of Fully Lifting the Arms Embargo on Bosnia," *Clinton Digital Library*, accessed September 28, 2017, https://clinton.presidentiallibraries.us/items/show/12322.

45. "1993-03-23G, BTF Memorandum re Likely Consequences of Aggressive Delivery of Relief Supplies," *Clinton Digital Library*, accessed September 28, 2017, https://clinton.presidentiallibraries.us/items/show/12323.

46. Ivo Daalder, *Getting to Dayton: The Making of America's Bosnia Policy* (Washington, D.C.: Brookings Institution Press, 2000), 12 (hereafter "Daalder").

47. Ibid.

48. United Nations Security Council, Resolution 815, March 30, 1993.

49. United Nations Security Council, Resolution 816, March 31, 1993.

50. "1993-04-09, DDCI Memo re Debrief of Principals Meeting on Bosnia April 9, 1993," *Clinton Digital Library*, accessed September 28, 2017, https://clinton. presidentiallibraries.us/items/show/12325.

51. Ibid.

52. Ibid.

53. Ibid.

54. Ibid.

55. "1993-04-14, Ambassador Madeleine Albright to National Security Advisor re Options for Bosnia," *Clinton Digital Library*, accessed September 28, 2017, https://clinton.presidentiallibraries.us/items/show/12326.

56. "Nothing in the present Charter shall impair the inherent right of individual or collective self-defence if an armed attack occurs against a Member of the United Nations, until the Security Council has taken measures necessary to maintain international peace and security. Measures taken by Members in the exercise of this right of self-defence shall be immediately reported to the Security Council and shall not in any way affect the authority and responsibility of the Security Council under the present Charter to take at any time such action as it deems necessary in order to maintain or restore international peace and security." United Nations Charter, Article 51.

57. United Nations Security Council, Resolution 770, August 13, 1992.

58. Ibid., para. 2.

59. United Nations Security Council, Resolution 771, August 13, 1992.

60. Ibid., para. 7.

61. United Nations Security Council, Resolution 816, March 31, 1993.

62. Chronology of the Bosnian Conflict 1990–1995, Netherlands Institute for War Documentation, 113, https://niod.nl/sites/niod.nl/files/XIII%20-%20 Chronology%20of%20the%20Bosnian%20conflict%201990%20-%201995. pdf.

63. Michael R. Gordon, "12 in State Dept. Ask Military Move Against the Serbs," *New York Times*, April 23, 1993, http://www.nytimes.com/1993/04/23/world/ 12-in-state-dept-ask-military-move-against-the-serbs.html?pagewanted=all&mc ubz=1.

64. Daalder, 14.

65. Ibid., 14–15.

66. United Nations Security Council, Resolution 819, April 16, 1993.

67. United Nations Security Council, Resolution 820, April 17, 1993.

68. United Nations Security Council, Resolution 821, April 28, 1993.

69. United Nations Security Council, Resolution 1326, October 31, 2000.

70. Daalder, 15.

71. Dayton History Project, Interview with Madeleine Albright, October 28, 1996, 2–3.

72. Daalder, 16.

73. Elizabeth Drew, *On the Edge* (New York: Simon and Schuster, 1994), 157.

74. Warren Christopher, *In the Stream of History* (Stanford: Stanford University Press, 1998), 347.

75. Daalder, 18.

76. "Remarks by the President in a Photo Opportunity with the Cabinet" (White House, Office of the Press Secretary, May 21, 1993).

77. NBC News, "Meet the Press," May 2, 1993, https://search.alexanderstreet.com/preview/work/bibliographic_entity%7Cvideo_work%7C3223153?ssotoken=anonymous.

78. United Nations Security Council Resolution 824, May 6, 1993.

79. U.S. Mission to the United Nations, Cable 02248, May 7, 1993 (declassified).

80. United Nations Security Council, Presidential Statement, May 7, 1993.

81. Roger Cohen, "Europeans Reject U.S. Plan to Aid Bosnia and Halt Serbs," *New York Times*, May 11, 1993.

82. "1995-09-01B, BTF List re Balkan Crisis Chronology of International Response, Significant Events," *Clinton Digital Library*, accessed October 29, 2017, https://clinton.presidentiallibraries.us/items/show/12527, 11.

83. Daalder, 19.

84. "1993-06-03, BTF Memorandum re Deputies Committee Meeting on the Former Yugoslavia May 26–27, 1993," *Clinton Digital Library*, accessed September 28, 2017, https://clinton.presidentiallibraries.us/items/show/12329.

85. United Nations Security Council, Resolution 836, June 4, 1993.

86. Ibid., paras. 4 and 5.

87. Ibid., paras. 9 and 10.

88. Snell to Prince Alexander, letter, U.S. State Department, June 23, 1993, https://foia.state.gov/searchapp/DOCUMENTS/foiadocs/54f6.PDF.

89. United Nations Security Council, Resolution 838, June 10, 1993.

90. "NAC Final Communique," *US State Department Dispatch*, vol. 4, no. 25, article 5 (1993), http://dosfan.lib.uic.edu/ERC/briefing/dispatch/1993/html/Dispatchv4n026.html, (accessed October 22, 2017).

91. Warren Christopher, "U.S. Leadership After the Cold War: NATO and Transatlantic Security." (Intervention at NAC Ministerial, Athens, Greece, June 10, 1993), Indiana University, http://webapp1.dlib.indiana.edu/virtual_disk_library/index.cgi/4233379/FID396/SPEECHES/WCSPCH93.PDF, 148–53.

92. Daalder, 19.

93. Ibid., 19–20.

94. Daniel Williams, "U.S. at Impasse in Bosnia," *Washington Post*, July 22, 1993, https://www.washingtonpost.com/archive/politics/1993/07/22/us-at-impasse-in-bosnia/1692e26f-36f5-465d-8352-71702dc68f31/?utm_term=.75934a68c64b

("Secretary of State Warren Christopher, all but ruling out use of force to rescue besieged Sarajevo, said yesterday the United States had reached the limit of its active involvement in Bosnia. 'That's a tragic, tragic situation in Bosnia, make no mistake about that,' Christopher said with an unusually forthright air of resignation. 'It's the world's most difficult diplomatic problem, I believe. It defies simple solution. The United States is doing all it can consistent with our national interest.' With those words he seemed to be saying what other administration officials have been acknowledging privately in recent weeks: the Clinton administration has reached a virtual dead end in Bosnia. Potentially cataclysmic events like the fall of Sarajevo spotlight the shortcomings of U.S. policy, which continues to operate on the margins of the Bosnian conflict by assisting international relief efforts.").

95. "1993-08-02, BTF Memorandum re Deputies Committee Meeting July 26, 1993," *Clinton Digital Library*, accessed September 28, 2017, https://clinton. presidentiallibraries.us/items/show/12332.

96. Bob Dole, "Bosnia: It's Not Too Late," *Washington Post*, August 1, 1993, C7. Proquest Historical Newspapers (140835727).

97. "Press Statement by the Secretary General," following the Special Meeting of the North Atlantic Council (Brussels: NATO Headquarters, August 2, 1993), quoted in Daalder, 22.

98. "1993-08-05, NIC Memorandum re Likely Allied Reactions to Unilateral U.S. Actions in Bosnia," *Clinton Digital Library*, accessed September 28, 2017, https://clinton.presidentiallibraries.us/items/show/12333.

99. Anthony Lewis, "Abroad at Home; Tragedy and Farce," *New York Times*, August 9, 1993, http://www.nytimes.com/1993/08/09/opinion/abroad-at-home-tragedy-and-farce.html.

100. International Criminal Tribunal for the former Yugoslavia, "Judgment," *Prosecutor v. Ratko Mladić* (November 22, 2017).

101. "1995-09-01B, BTF List re Balkan Crisis Chronology of International Response, Significant Events," *Clinton Digital Library*, accessed October 29, 2017, https://clinton.presidentiallibraries.us/items/show/12527, 14.

102. Ibid., 15.

103. Ibid.

104. "1993-08-25, Anthony Lake to President Clinton re Bosnian End-Game Strategy," *Clinton Digital Library*, accessed September 28, 2017, https://clinton. presidentiallibraries.us/items/show/12334.

105. Mark Bowden, *Black Hawk Down: A Story of Modern War* (New York: Grove Press, 1999).

106. "1995-09-01B, BTF List re Balkan Crisis Chronology of International Response, Significant Events," *Clinton Digital Library*, accessed October 29, 2017, https://clinton.presidentiallibraries.us/items/show/12527, 19.

CHAPTER 2

1. Carol J. Williams, "Frustrated U.N. Troops Humiliated in Bosnia: Balkans: Top Military Officials Say the Mission Is Caught Between Lofty Resolutions and Hostile Forces," *Los Angeles Times*, January 16, 1994, http://articles.latimes.com/ 1994-01-16/news/mn-12508_1_hostile-forces.

2. Julia Preston, "Boutros-Ghali, U.N. General Widen Rift," *Washington Post*, January 12, 1994, https://www.washingtonpost.com/archive/politics/1994/01/ 12/boutros-ghali-un-general-widen-rift/c6fce7fd-c23b-4d8b-a452-3213ab27f81e/ ?utm_term=.eee73a7f1870; Roger Cohen, "Dispute Grows Over U.N.'s Troops in Bosnia, *New York Times*, January 20, 1994, http://www.nytimes.com/1994/01/ 20/world/dispute-grows-over-un-s-troops-in-bosnia.html.

3. Robert Block and Christopher Bellamy, "Croats Destroy Mostar's Historic Bridge," *Independent*, November 10, 1993, http://www.independent.co.uk/ news/croats-destroy-mostars-historic-bridge-1503338.html. Many years later the Appeals Chamber of the Yugoslav Tribunal confirmed the Bosnian Croat military origin of the shelling of Mostar Bridge but acquitted several defendants of war crimes in striking the bridge. *See* International Criminal Tribunal for the former Yugoslavia, "Judgement," *Prosecutor v. Prlić et al.* (November 29, 2017), paras. 405–426, http://www.icty.org/x/cases/prlic/acjug/en/171129-judgement-vol-1.pdf.

4. *Mrkšić* et al. (IT-95-13/1) "Vukovar Hospital," International Criminal Tribunal for the former Yugoslavia, http://www.independent.co.uk/news/croats-destroy-mostars-historic-bridge-1503338.html.

5. *Prosecutor v. Tihomir Blaškić* (IT-95-15-A), Judgement (Appeals Chamber), July 29, 2004, http://www.icty.org/x/cases/blaskic/acjug/en/bla-aj040729e.pdf.

6. ICTY Press Briefing, 8 November 2000, http://www.icty.org/sid/3414.

7. Philip Shenon, "Admiral, in Suicide Note, Apologized to 'My Sailor,'" *New York Times*, May 18, 1996, http://www.nytimes.com/1996/05/18/us/admiral-in-suicide-note-apologized-to-my-sailors.html?pagewanted=all&src=pm.

8. "1995-09-01B, BTF List re Balkan Crisis Chronology of International Response, Significant Events," *Clinton Digital Library*, accessed October 29, 2017, https:// clinton.presidentiallibraries.us/items/show/12527, 23.

9. United Nations Security Council, Presidential Statement, February 3, 1994, Chronology of the Bosnian Conflict 1990–1995, Netherlands Institute for War Documentation, 159, https://niod.nl/sites/niod.nl/files/XIII%20-%20 Chronology%20of%20the%20Bosnian%20conflict%201990%20-%201995. pdf.

10. Daalder, 24.

11. Ibid.

12. Ibid., 24–25.

13. John Kifner, "66 Die as Shell Wrecks Sarajevo Market," *New York Times*, February 6, 1994, http://www.nytimes.com/1994/02/06/world/66-die-as-shell-wrecks-sarajevo-market.html?pagewanted=all&mcubz=1.

14. U.S. Embassy in Belgrade, CABLE 01037, February 9, 1994 ("SERBIAN PROPAGANDA MACHINE GEARS UP; ACCUSES MUSLIMS OF STAGING SARAJEVO MASSACRE") (declassified), https://foia.state.gov/searchapp/DOCUMENTS/foiadocs/5516.PDF.

15. *Prosecutor v. Stanislav Galić*, Trial Chamber Judgement and Opinion (IT-98-29-T), December 5, 2003, http://www.icty.org/x/cases/galic/tjug/en/gal-tjo31205e.pdf; upheld on appeal, *Prosecutor v. Stanislav Galić*, Appeals Chamber Judgement (IT-98-29-T), November 30, 2006, http://www.icty.org/x/cases/galic/acjug/en/gal-acjudo61130.pdf.

16. Daalder, 25.

17. United Nations Security Council, Resolution 820, April 17, 1993.

18. Ibid., para. 31.

19. "1994-02-14, DDCI Memo re Deputies Committee Meeting on Bosnia Serb Sanctions February 9, 1994," *Clinton Digital Library*, accessed September 29, 2017, https://clinton.presidentiallibraries.us/items/show/12338.

20. Madeleine Albright, Interview by Tim Russert, "Meet the Press," NBC, transcript, February 13, 1994, http://search.alexanderstreet.com/preview/work/bibliographic_entity%7Cvideo_work%7C2408895.

21. "1995-09-01B, BTF List re Balkan Crisis Chronology of International Response, Significant Events," *Clinton Digital Library*, accessed October 29, 2017, https://clinton.presidentiallibraries.us/items/show/12527, 25.

22. Daalder, 17.

23. "1994-03-22, BTF Memorandum re Results of Principals Committee Meeting on Bosnia," *Clinton Digital Library*, accessed September 29, 2017, https://clinton.presidentiallibraries.us/items/show/12339.

24. United Nations Security Council, Resolution 908, March 31, 1994.

25. United Nations Security Council, Statement by the President, April 6, 1994 (S/PRST/1994/14).

26. David Usborne, "NATO Jets Bomb Bosnian Serbs: Rose Calls in Strike by US F-16s to Prevent Imminent Fall of Besieged Gorazde Enclave," *The Independent* (April 10, 1994); Thomas W. Lippman and John Lancaster, "Clinton Team Committed to Airstrikes," *Washington Post*, April 12, 1994.

27. "1995-09-01B, BTF List re Balkan Crisis Chronology of International Response, Significant Events," *Clinton Digital Library*, accessed October 29, 2017, https://clinton.presidentiallibraries.us/items/show/12527, 27.

28. "Remarks and an exchange with reporters," Weekly Comp. Pres. Doc., April 18, 1994, 771+.

29. "1994-04-13, BTF Memorandum re Principals Committee Meeting on Bosnia April 10, 1994," *Clinton Digital Library*, accessed September 29, 2017, https://clinton.presidentiallibraries.us/items/show/12344.

30. Ibid.

31. Madeleine Albright, "Bosnia in Light of the Holocaust: War Crime Tribunals." (Address at the U.S. Holocaust Memorial Museum, Washington, D.C., April

12, 1994), Indiana University, http://webapp1.dlib.indiana.edu/virtual_disk_library/index.cgi/4233379/FID2741/STATEPDF/DISV5N16.PDF, 1–4.

32. United Nations Security Council, Resolution 913, April 22, 1994.

33. United Nations Security Council, Statement by the President of the Security Council (S/PRST/1994/31), June 30, 1994.

34. "1994-07-26D, BTF Memorandum re Principals Committee Meeting on Bosnia July 27, 1994," *Clinton Digital Library*, accessed September 29, 2017, https://clinton.presidentiallibraries.us/items/show/12362.

35. U.S. Mission to NATO, CABLE 02771, July 23, 1994 (declassified).

36. Mark Heinrich, "Serbs Flout U.N. Weapons-Free Zone," *Reuters*, August 2, 1994.

37. "1994-08-12A, BTF Memorandum re Principals Committee Meeting on the Balkans August 10, 1994," *Clinton Digital Library*, accessed September 29, 2017, https://clinton.presidentiallibraries.us/items/show/12364.

38. Ibid.

39. "1994-08-12B, BTF Memorandum re Principals Committee Meeting on Bosnia September 13, 1994," *Clinton Digital Library*, accessed September 29, 2017, https://clinton.presidentiallibraries.us/items/show/12365.

40. "1994-09-14, Anthony Lake to President Clinton re Principals Committee Review of Bosnia Policy," *Clinton Digital Library*, accessed September 29, 2017, https://clinton.presidentiallibraries.us/items/show/12366.

41. United Nations Security Council, Resolution 941, September 23, 1994.

42. United Nations Security Council, Resolution 942, September 23, 1994.

43. United Nations Security Council, Resolution 943, September 23, 1994.

44. John Diamond, "Congress Urges Stepped Up Efforts on Bosnia," Associated Press, Aug. 12, 1994, https://apnews.com/6967696bff11ce47bec182a2cecf35cb.

45. Michael R. Gordon, "President Orders End to Enforcing Bosnian Embargo," *New York Times*, November 11, 1994, p. A1.

46. For a fascinating account of how the indicted fugitives of the International Criminal Tribunal for the former Yugoslavia were brought into custody, *see* Julian Borger, *The Butcher's Trail: The Secret History of the Balkan Manhunt for Europe's Most-Wanted War Criminals* (New York: Other Press, 2016).

47. "1994-11-21, BTF Memorandum re Principals Committee Meeting on Bosnia November 18, 1994," *Clinton Digital Library*, accessed September 29, 2017, https://clinton.presidentiallibraries.us/items/show/12378.

48. "1994-11-29, BTF Memorandum re Principals Committee Meeting on Bosnia November 28, 1994," *Clinton Digital Library*, accessed September 29, 2017, https://clinton.presidentiallibraries.us/items/show/12383.

49. Ibid.

50. "1994-12-02, BTF Memorandum re Principals Committee Meeting on Bosnia," *Clinton Digital Library*, accessed September 30, 2017, https://clinton.presidentiallibraries.us/items/show/12386.

51. "1994-12-09, BTF Memorandum re Principals Committee Meeting on Bosnia December 12, 1994," *Clinton Digital Library*, accessed September 30, 2017, https://clinton.presidentiallibraries.us/items/show/12387.

52. Ibid.

53. Ibid.

54. "1994-12-13, Anthony Lake to President Clinton re Principals Review of Bosnia Policy," *Clinton Digital Library*, accessed September 30, 2017, https://clinton.presidentiallibraries.us/items/show/12388.

55. Ibid.

56. "1994-12-19, BTF Memorandum re Deputies Committee Meeting on Bosnia December 19, 1994," *Clinton Digital Library*, accessed September 30, 2017, https://clinton.presidentiallibraries.us/items/show/12390.

57. Ibid.

58. Daalder, 36.

CHAPTER 3

1. "1995-01-13, Anthony Lake to President Clinton re Update on Bosnia and Croatia," *Clinton Digital Library*, accessed November 25, 2017, https://clinton.presidentiallibraries.us/items/show/12395.

2. "01-11B, Summary of Conclusions of Deputies Committee Meeting on Bosnia and Croatia January 11, 1995," *Clinton Digital Library*, accessed September 30, 2017, https://1995-clinton.presidentiallibraries.us/items/show/12394.

3. "1995-01-18, BTF Memorandum re Report on Deputies Committee Meeting January 11, 1995," *Clinton Digital Library*, accessed September 30, 2017, https://clinton.presidentiallibraries.us/items/show/12396.

4. "1995-01-13, Anthony Lake to President Clinton re Update on Bosnia and Croatia," *Clinton Digital Library*, accessed September 30, 2017, https://clinton.presidentiallibraries.us/items/show/12395.

5. Ibid.

6. "1995-01-27, BTF Memorandum re Report on Deputies Committee Meeting January 25, 1995," *Clinton Digital Library*, accessed September 30, 2017, https://clinton.presidentiallibraries.us/items/show/12398.

7. "1995-02-02, Summary of Conclusions of Deputies Committee Meeting on Bosnia and Croatia February 2, 1995," *Clinton Digital Library*, accessed September 30, 2017, https://clinton.presidentiallibraries.us/items/show/12400.

8. Ibid.

9. "1995-02-01, BTF Memorandum re Report on Deputies Committee Meeting February 2, 1995," *Clinton Digital Library*, accessed September 30, 2017, https://clinton.presidentiallibraries.us/items/show/12399.

10. "1995-02-06, BTF Memorandum re Principals Committee Meeting on Bosnia February 7, 1995," *Clinton Digital Library*, accessed September 30, 2017, https://clinton.presidentiallibraries.us/items/show/12401.

11. Ibid.

12. "1995-02-07B, Summary of Conclusions of Deputies Committee Meeting on Bosnia and Croatia February 7, 1995," *Clinton Digital Library*, accessed September 30, 2017, https://clinton.presidentiallibraries.us/items/show/12403.

13. Ibid.

14. "1995-02-13A, BTF Memorandum re Principals Committee Meeting on Bosnia February 13, 1995," *Clinton Digital Library*, accessed September 30, 2017, https://clinton.presidentiallibraries.us/items/show/12405.

15. "1995-02-13B, Summary of Conclusions of Principals Committee Meeting on Bosnia and Croatia February 13, 1995," *Clinton Digital Library*, accessed September 30, 2017, https://clinton.presidentiallibraries.us/items/show/12406.

16. Ibid.

17. "1995-02-20B, BTF Memorandum re Principals Committee Meeting on Bosnia February 21, 1995," *Clinton Digital Library*, accessed September 30, 2017, https://clinton.presidentiallibraries.us/items/show/12408.

18. "1995-02-21, Summary of Conclusions of Principals Committee Meeting on Bosnia and Croatia February 21, 1995," *Clinton Digital Library*, accessed September 30, 2017, https://clinton.presidentiallibraries.us/items/show/12409.

19. Ibid.

20. "1995-03-07, BTF Memorandum re Deputies Committee Meeting February 22, 1995," *Clinton Digital Library*, accessed September 30, 2017, https://clinton.presidentiallibraries.us/items/show/12419.

21. Ibid.

22. "1995-02-22, Summary of Conclusions of Deputies Committee Meeting on Bosnia and Croatia February 22, 1995," *Clinton Digital Library*, accessed September 30, 2017, https://clinton.presidentiallibraries.us/items/show/12410.

23. Ibid.

24. "1995-03-07, BTF Memorandum re Deputies Committee Meeting February 22, 1995," *Clinton Digital Library*, accessed September 30, 2017, https://clinton.presidentiallibraries.us/items/show/12419.

25. Ibid.

26. Ibid.

27. Ibid.

28. Ibid.

29. "1995-02-28, Summary of Conclusions of Deputies Committee Meeting on Bosnia and Croatia February 28, 1995," *Clinton Digital Library*, accessed September 30, 2017, https://clinton.presidentiallibraries.us/items/show/12414.

30. "1995-03-02B, BTF Memorandum re Probable Principals Committee Meeting March 3, 1995," *Clinton Digital Library*, accessed September 30, 2017, https://clinton.presidentiallibraries.us/items/show/12416.

31. "1995-02-28, Summary of Conclusions of Deputies Committee Meeting on Bosnia and Croatia February 28, 1995," *Clinton Digital Library*, accessed September 30, 2017, https://clinton.presidentiallibraries.us/items/show/12414.

32. "1995-03-02A, Summary of Conclusions of Deputies Committee Meeting on Bosnia and Croatia March 2, 1995," *Clinton Digital Library*, accessed September 30, 2017, https://clinton.presidentiallibraries.us/items/show/12415.

33. Ibid.

34. "1995-03-02B, BTF Memorandum re Probable Principals Committee Meeting March 3, 1995," *Clinton Digital Library*, accessed September 30, 2017, https://clinton.presidentiallibraries.us/items/show/12416.

35. "1995-03-03, Summary of Conclusions of Principals Committee Meeting on Bosnia and Croatia March 3, 1995," *Clinton Digital Library*, accessed September 30, 2017, https://clinton.presidentiallibraries.us/items/show/12417.

36. Ibid.

37. "1995-03-06, Anthony Lake to President Clinton re U.S. Participation in Step Two of NATO," *Clinton Digital Library*, accessed September 30, 2017, https://clinton.presidentiallibraries.us/items/show/12418.

38. Ibid.

39. Ibid.

40. "1995-03-08A, BTF Memorandum re Deputies Committee Meeting March 9, 1995," *Clinton Digital Library*, accessed September 30, 2017, https://clinton.presidentiallibraries.us/items/show/12420.

41. "1995-03-09, Summary of Conclusions of Deputies Committee Meeting on Bosnia and Croatia March 9, 1995," *Clinton Digital Library*, accessed September 30, 2017, https://clinton.presidentiallibraries.us/items/show/12422.

42. "1995-03-16A, BTF Memorandum re Principals Committee Meeting March 17, 1995," *Clinton Digital Library*, accessed September 30, 2017, https://clinton.presidentiallibraries.us/items/show/12425.

43. Ibid.

44. "1995-03-16A, BTF Memorandum re Principals Committee Meeting March 17, 1995," *Clinton Digital Library*, accessed September 30, 2017, https://clinton.presidentiallibraries.us/items/show/12425.

45. "1995-03-16B, NSC Paper re Discussion Paper for Principals Committee March 17, 1995," *Clinton Digital Library*, accessed September 30, 2017, https://clinton.presidentiallibraries.us/items/show/12426.

46. Ibid.

47. Ibid.

48. Ibid.

49. "1995-03-17, Summary of Conclusions of Principals Committee Meeting on Bosnia and Croatia March 17, 1995," *Clinton Digital Library*, accessed September 30, 2017, https://clinton.presidentiallibraries.us/items/show/12427.

50. Ibid.

51. Ibid.

52. "1995-03-18, Anthony Lake to President Clinton re U.S. Participation in Step Two of UNPROFOR Withdrawal from Bosnia," *Clinton Digital Library*, accessed September 30, 2017, https://clinton.presidentiallibraries.us/items/show/12428.

53. Ibid.

54. Ibid.

55. "1995-03-18, Anthony Lake to President Clinton re U.S. Participation in Step Two of UNPROFOR Withdrawal from Bosnia," *Clinton Digital Library*, accessed September 30, 2017, https://clinton.presidentiallibraries.us/items/show/12428.

56. Ibid.

57. Ibid.

58. Ibid.

59. U.S. Embassy in Belgrade, "MILOŠEVIĆ ON BOSNIA RECOGNITION: NO," CABLE 01773, April 12, 1995 (declassified).

60. Ibid.

61. Ibid.

62. Ibid.

63. "1995-04-13A, BTF Memorandum re Principals Committee Meeting on Bosnia and Croatia April 14, 1995," *Clinton Digital Library*, accessed September 30, 2017, https://clinton.presidentiallibraries.us/items/show/12432.

64. "1995-04-13B, Joint Chiefs of Staff Paper re UNPROFOR Information Paper," *Clinton Digital Library*, accessed September 30, 2017, https://clinton.presidentiallibraries.us/items/show/12433.

65. Ibid.

66. "1995-04-13C, Joint Chiefs of Staff Paper re OPLAN 40104 Information Paper," *Clinton Digital Library*, accessed September 30, 2017, https://clinton.presidentiallibraries.us/items/show/12434.

67. Ibid.

68. "1995-04-14A, Department of State Paper re Bosnia Going for a Small War," *Clinton Digital Library*, accessed September 30, 2017, https://clinton.presidentiallibraries.us/items/show/12435.

69. "1995-04-14B, Department of State Paper re Croatia," *Clinton Digital Library*, accessed September 30, 2017, https://clinton.presidentiallibraries.us/items/show/12436.

70. "1995-04-27C, BTF Report re UNPROFOR Watchful Waiting," *Clinton Digital Library*, accessed September 30, 2017, https://clinton.presidentiallibraries.us/items/show/12442.

71. "1995-05-05, BTF Memorandum re Deputies Committee Meeting April 27, 1995," *Clinton Digital Library*, accessed September 30, 2017, https://clinton.presidentiallibraries.us/items/show/12453.

72. "1995-04-27A, Summary of Conclusions of Deputies Committee Meeting on Bosnia April 27, 1995," *Clinton Digital Library*, accessed September 30, 2017, https://clinton.presidentiallibraries.us/items/show/12440.

73. "1995-05-05, BTF Memorandum re Deputies Committee Meeting April 27, 1995," *Clinton Digital Library*, accessed September 30, 2017, https://clinton.presidentiallibraries.us/items/show/12453.

74. Ibid.

75. Ibid.

76. Ibid.

77. "1995-04-27A, Summary of Conclusions of Deputies Committee Meeting on Bosnia April 27, 1995," *Clinton Digital Library*, accessed September 30, 2017, https://clinton.presidentiallibraries.us/items/show/12440.

78. "1995-05-05, BTF Memorandum re Deputies Committee Meeting April 27, 1995," *Clinton Digital Library*, accessed September 30, 2017, https://clinton.presidentiallibraries.us/items/show/12453.

79. "1995-04-28A, Summary of Conclusions of Principals Committee Meeting on Bosnia April 28, 1995," *Clinton Digital Library*, accessed September 30, 2017, https://clinton.presidentiallibraries.us/items/show/12444.

80. "1995-04-30, NSC Memorandum re Principals Tasking on Sarajevo Situation," *Clinton Digital Library*, accessed September 30, 2017, https://clinton.presidentiallibraries.us/items/show/12446.

81. "1995-04-28A, Summary of Conclusions of Principals Committee Meeting on Bosnia April 28, 1995," *Clinton Digital Library*, accessed September 30, 2017, https://clinton.presidentiallibraries.us/items/show/12444.

82. Ibid.

83. "1995-05-02, Anthony Lake to President Clinton re Principals Review of Bosnia April 28, 1995," *Clinton Digital Library*, accessed June 13, 2018, https://clinton.presidentiallibraries.us/items/show/12450.

84. Ibid.

85. Ibid.

86. Ibid.

87. Ibid.

88. International Criminal Tribunal for the former Yugoslavia, "Judgement," *Prosecutor v. Milan Martić* (October 8, 2008), http://www.icty.org/x/cases/martic/acjug/en/mar-ajo81008e.pdf.

89. "1995-05-04A, BTF Memorandum re Deputies Committee Meeting on Bosnia and Croatia May 4, 1995," *Clinton Digital Library*, accessed September 30, 2017, https://clinton.presidentiallibraries.us/items/show/12451.

90. "1995-05-04B, Summary of Conclusions of Deputies Committee Meeting on Bosnia and Croatia May 4, 1995," *Clinton Digital Library*, accessed September 30, 2017, https://clinton.presidentiallibraries.us/items/show/12452.

91. "1995-05-15B, BTF Memorandum re Deputies Committee Meeting on Bosnia and Croatia May 9, 1995," *Clinton Digital Library*, accessed September 30, 2017, https://clinton.presidentiallibraries.us/items/show/12460.

92. Ibid.

93. "1995-05-08, BTF Memorandum re Deputies Committee Meeting on Bosnia and Croatia May 9, 1995," *Clinton Digital Library*, accessed September 30, 2017, https://clinton.presidentiallibraries.us/items/show/12455.

94. "1995-05-09, Department of State Memorandum re Bosnia Diplomatic Strategy Sarajevo Airport," *Clinton Digital Library*, accessed September 30, 2017, https://clinton.presidentiallibraries.us/items/show/12456.

95. "1995-09-01B, BTF List re Balkan Crisis Chronology of International Response, Significant Events," *Clinton Digital Library*, accessed October 29, 2017, https://clinton.presidentiallibraries.us/items/show/12527, 54.

96. "1995-05-15B, BTF Memorandum re Deputies Committee Meeting on Bosnia and Croatia May 9, 1995," *Clinton Digital Library*, accessed September 30, 2017, https://clinton.presidentiallibraries.us/items/show/12460.

97. "1995-05-12A, Office of the Secretary of Defense Joint Chiefs of Staff Memorandum re Proposed U.S. Policy Principals During NATO-led UNPROFOR Withdrawal," *Clinton Digital Library*, accessed September 30, 2017, https://clinton.presidentiallibraries.us/items/show/12457.

98. "1995-05-12B, Department of State Memorandum re Contact Group Consensus in Frankfurt," *Clinton Digital Library*, accessed September 30, 2017, https://clinton.presidentiallibraries.us/items/show/12458.

99. U.S. Embassy in Zagreb, CABLE 1822, May 17, 1995 (declassified).

100. "1995-05-16, Department of State Paper re Bosnia Formulating a Post-UNPROFOR Withdrawal Strategy," *Clinton Digital Library*, accessed September 30, 2017, https://clinton.presidentiallibraries.us/items/show/12461.

101. Ibid.

102. Ibid.

103. "1995-05-17, NSC Paper re Bosnia Strategic Choices," *Clinton Digital Library*, accessed September 30, 2017, https://clinton.presidentiallibraries.us/items/show/12462.

104. Ibid.

105. Ibid.

106. United Nations Security Council, Resolution 994, May 17, 1995.

107. "1995-05-19A, Summary of Conclusions of Principals Committee Meeting on Bosnia May 19, 1995," *Clinton Digital Library*, accessed October 8, 2017, https://clinton.presidentiallibraries.us/items/show/12464.

108. "1995-05-19A, Summary of Conclusions of Principals Committee Meeting on Bosnia May 19, 1995," *Clinton Digital Library*, accessed September 30, 2017, https://clinton.presidentiallibraries.us/items/show/12464.

109. "1995-05-25, Ambassador Madeleine Albright to Anthony Lake re The FRY and the Outer Wall of Sanctions," *Clinton Digital Library*, accessed September 30, 2017, https://clinton.presidentiallibraries.us/items/show/12468.

110. "U.S. Lifts Yugoslav Sanctions," CBSNEWS.com, January 19, 2001, https://www.cbsnews.com/news/us-lifts-yugoslav-sanctions/.

111. "1995-05-22, BTF Memorandum re Principals Committee Meeting on Bosnia and Croatia May 23, 1995," *Clinton Digital Library*, accessed September 30, 2017, https://clinton.presidentiallibraries.us/items/show/12466.

112. "1995-05-23, Summary of Conclusions of Principals Committee Meeting on Bosnia May 23, 1995," *Clinton Digital Library*, accessed September 30, 2017, https://clinton.presidentiallibraries.us/items/show/12467.
113. Ibid.
114. Akashi, UNPF-HQ, Zagreb, CABLE UNPROFOR Z-86B, May 26, 1995.
115. "1995-05-27, Department of State Cable re I've Broken the Machine," *Clinton Digital Library*, accessed October 23, 2017, https://clinton.presidentiallibraries. us/items/show/12469.
116. Ibid.
117. "1995-05-28, Department of State Cable re Smith 'We Either Fight or We Don't,'" *Clinton Digital Library*, accessed October 23, 2017, https://clinton. presidentiallibraries.us/items/show/12470.
118. "1995-06-01B, BTF Report re Prospects for the Eastern Enclaves Following a UN Retrenchment," *Clinton Digital Library*, accessed September 30, 2017, https://clinton.presidentiallibraries.us/items/show/12473.
119. Ibid.
120. Scott Grady and Jeff Coplon, *Return with Honor* (New York: Doubleday, 1995).
121. David Scheffer, *All the Missing Souls* (Princeton: Princeton University Press, 2012), 89–90.
122. United Nations Security Council, Resolution 998, June 16, 1995.

CHAPTER 4

1. Scheffer, *All the Missing Souls* (Princeton: Princeton University Press, 2012), 91–92.
2. Scheffer, *All the Missing Souls*, 94–97.
3. "1995-07-11, Summary of Conclusions of Deputies Committee Meetings on Bosnia July 11-12, 1995," *Clinton Digital Library*, accessed October 1, 2017, https://clinton.presidentiallibraries.us/items/show/12491.
4. Ibid. "Beyond these immediate actions, Deputies also agreed on the need to work with allies on the development of a follow-on strategy to deter further Serb provocations and prevent the collapse of the UNPROFOR mission (Action: NSC/State/OSD):
    • At a minimum, this strategy must preserve Bosnian government presence in and access to Sarajevo, and it must sustain UNPROFOR deployments in Federation territory so as to continue maintaining peace where it exists.
    • To this end, we will support robust use of the existing elements of the RRF to secure overland access to Sarajevo using the Mt. Igman route and possibly to restore control over Sarajevo airport.
    • Given the political imperative not to be seen as abandoning all of the eastern enclaves and the fact that NATO credibility is engaged in Gorazde, the strategy should include a commitment to protect this safe area, even if protection of Žepa proves unfeasible." Ibid., 2–3.

5. Scheffer, *All the Missing Souls*, 100–101.

6. "1995-07-13A, BTF Memorandum re Principals Committee Meeting on Bosnia July 14, 1995," *Clinton Digital Library*, accessed October 1, 2017, https://clinton.presidentiallibraries.us/items/show/12492.

7. "1995-07-14, Summary of Conclusions of Principals Committee Meeting on Bosnia July 14, 1995," *Clinton Digital Library*, accessed October 1, 2017, https://clinton.presidentiallibraries.us/items/show/12494.

8. "1995-07-15, Anthony Lake to President Clinton re Principals July 14 Conclusions on Bosnia," *Clinton Digital Library*, accessed October 1, 2017, https://clinton.presidentiallibraries.us/items/show/12495.

9. Daalder, 99–101.

10. Ibid., 99.

11. "1995-07-20A, NSC Paper re Bosnia Endgame Strategy," *Clinton Digital Library*, accessed October 1, 2017, https://clinton.presidentiallibraries.us/items/show/12499.

12. Ibid.

13. Daalder, 100–101.

14. Ibid., 101.

15. Ibid., 102.

16. Ibid., 102–106.

17. "1995-07-18A, BTF Report re The Bosnian Army in Srebrenica: What Happened?," *Clinton Digital Library*, accessed October 1, 2017, https://clinton.presidentiallibraries.us/items/show/12496.

18. "1995-07-18B, BTF Report re The Bosnian Army's Defense of Gorazde," *Clinton Digital Library*, accessed October 1, 2017, https://clinton.presidentiallibraries.us/items/show/12497.

19. "1995-07-19, Anthony Lake to President Clinton re Bosnia Next Steps," *Clinton Digital Library*, accessed October 1, 2017, https://clinton.presidentiallibraries.us/items/show/12498.

20. "1995-07-19, Anthony Lake to President Clinton re Bosnia Next Steps," *Clinton Digital Library*, accessed October 1, 2017, https://clinton.presidentiallibraries.us/items/show/12498.

21. Ibid.

22. Daalder, 75.

23. Ibid., 77.

24. "1995-07-21A, BTF Memorandum re Deputies Committee Meeting on Bosnia July 22, 1995," *Clinton Digital Library*, accessed October 1, 2017, https://clinton.presidentiallibraries.us/items/show/12501.

25. "1995-07-21B, BTF Report re Croatia Major Conflict Likely This Autumn," *Clinton Digital Library*, accessed October 1, 2017, https://clinton.presidentiallibraries.us/items/show/12502.

26. Ibid. [Useful maps of Bosnia and Croatia in the 21 July 1995 BTF report].

27. "Weekend discussions on Bosnia, Talking Points for Quad and CG Meetings on July 24," Scheffer memorandum to Inderfurth, July 24, 1995 (declassified).

28. Ibid.

29. "1995-07-24, Summary of Conclusions of Deputies Committee Meeting on Bosnia July 24, 1995," *Clinton Digital Library*, accessed October 1, 2017, https://clinton.presidentiallibraries.us/items/show/12504.

30. Ibid.

31. Ibid.

32. Ibid.

33. "1995-07-25B, Summary of Conclusions of Deputies Committee Meeting on Bosnia July 25, 1995," *Clinton Digital Library*, accessed October 1, 2017, https://clinton.presidentiallibraries.us/items/show/12506.

34. *See* Daalder, 77–79.

35. Ibid., 79.

36. "1995-07-25B, Summary of Conclusions of Deputies Committee Meeting on Bosnia July 25, 1995," *Clinton Digital Library*, accessed October 1, 2017, https://clinton.presidentiallibraries.us/items/show/12506.

37. Ibid.

38. George Sher, *Beyond Neutrality: Perfectionism and Politics* (Cambridge: Cambridge University Press, 1997), 20–44.

39. Bosnia and Herzegovina Self Defense Act of 1995, S. 21, 104th Cong. (1995).

40. "1995-08-03B, UN Ambassador Memo re Bosnia Endgame Strategy," *Clinton Digital Library*, accessed October 1, 2017, https://clinton.presidentiallibraries.us/items/show/12511.

41. Daalder, 107–109.

42. Tony Lake's presentation in Europe is described in Daalder, 112–113.

43. "1995-08-03B, UN Ambassador Memo re Bosnia Endgame Strategy," *Clinton Digital Library*, accessed October 1, 2017, https://clinton.presidentiallibraries.us/items/show/12511; "1995-08-14A, Summary of Conclusions of Deputies Committee Meetings on Bosnia August 14, 1995," *Clinton Digital Library*, accessed October 1, 2017, https://clinton.presidentiallibraries.us/items/show/12514.

44. "1995-08-18B, NSC Memorandum re Deputies Committee Meeting on Bosnia, August 18, 1995," *Clinton Digital Library*, accessed October 1, 2017, https://clinton.presidentiallibraries.us/items/show/12519.

45. "1995-08-17, BTF Memorandum re Deputies Committee Meeting on Bosnia and Croatia August 18, 1995," *Clinton Digital Library*, accessed October 1, 2017, https://clinton.presidentiallibraries.us/items/show/12517.

46. Secretary of State, "OFFICIAL—INFORMAL NO. 116," CABLE STATE 197630, August 18, 1995 (declassified).

47. Todd S. Purdum, "Clinton Vetoes Lifting Bosnian Arms Embargo," *New York Times*, August 12, 1995, http://www.nytimes.com/1995/08/12/world/clinton-vetoes-lifting-bosnia-arms-embargo.html.

48. Ibid.

49. "1995-08-23, Memo re Principles [sic] Committee Meeting on Bosnia, August 22, 1995," *Clinton Digital Library*, accessed October 1, 2017, https://clinton. presidentiallibraries.us/items/show/12522. At this critical juncture in the peace initiative, the BTF summarized the views of the four parties—Serb interests in Belgrade and, separately in Pale, Bosniak interests in Sarajevo, and Croatian interests in Zagreb—in a grid entitled "Warring Parties' Views on US Peace Initiative." Ibid.

50. BBC News, *Sarajevo: Another Massacre*, April 4, 2012, http://www.bbc.com/ news/av/uk-17402772/sarajevo-another-market-massacre.

51. "1995-08-28A, Summary of Conclusions of Deputies Committee Meeting on Bosnia August 28, 1995," *Clinton Digital Library*, accessed October 1, 2017, https://clinton.presidentiallibraries.us/items/show/12523.

52. Rick Atkinson and John Pomfret, "NATO Hits Bosnian Serbs with Massive Air Raid," *Washington Post*, August 30, 1995.

CHAPTER 5

1. "Annex A, Note to Mr. Annan, 6 September 1995, NATO Air Operation," Outgoing Code Cable No. 2939, Annan to Akashi, 6 September 1995, CNZ 868 CYZ 865 (declassified).

2. U.S. Embassy in Athens, "BELGRADE TALKS," CABLE ATHENS 007875, September 4, 1995 (declassified).

3. "1995-09-04, BTF Memorandum re Principals Committee Meeting on Bosnia September 5, 1995," *Clinton Digital Library*, accessed October 1, 2017, https:// clinton.presidentiallibraries.us/items/show/12528.

4. Ibid.

5. Ibid.

6. Ibid.

7. Ibid.

8. "1995-09-08, Summary of Conclusions of Deputies Committee Meeting on Bosnia September 8, 1995," *Clinton Digital Library*, accessed October 1, 2017, https://clinton.presidentiallibraries.us/items/show/12533.

9. "1995-09-11C, Anthony Lake to President Clinton re Drop-by at the September 11 Principals Meeting on Bosnia," *Clinton Digital Library*, accessed October 1, 2017, https://clinton.presidentiallibraries.us/items/show/12537.

10. "1995-09-15, Summary of Conclusions of Deputies Committee Meeting on Bosnia September 15, 1995," *Clinton Digital Library*, accessed October 1, 2017, https://clinton.presidentiallibraries.us/items/show/12538.

11. "1995-10-03, BTF Memorandum re Principals Committee Meeting on Bosnia October 3, 1995," *Clinton Digital Library*, accessed October 1, 2017, https:// clinton.presidentiallibraries.us/items/show/12552.

12. "1995-10-04, Summary of Conclusions of Principals Committee Meeting on Bosnia October 4, 1995," *Clinton Digital Library*, accessed October 1, 2017, https://clinton.presidentiallibraries.us/items/show/12553.

13. "1995-10-05, BTF Memorandum re Deputies Committee Meeting on Bosnia October 6, 1995," *Clinton Digital Library*, accessed October 1, 2017, https://clinton.presidentiallibraries.us/items/show/12554.

14. "1995-10-06B, Summary of Conclusions of Deputies Committee Meeting on Bosnia October 6, 1995," *Clinton Digital Library*, accessed October 1, 2017, https://clinton.presidentiallibraries.us/items/show/12556.

15. Ibid.

16. "1995-10-12A, Department of State Memorandum re A Multilateral Framework for Bosnian Peace," *Clinton Digital Library*, accessed October 1, 2017, https://clinton.presidentiallibraries.us/items/show/12558.

17. "1995-10-16, Summary of Conclusions of Deputies Committee Meeting on Bosnia October 16, 1995," *Clinton Digital Library*, accessed October 1, 2017, https://clinton.presidentiallibraries.us/items/show/12562.

18. "1995-10-18B, BTF Memorandum re Deputies Committee Meeting on Bosnia October 18, 1995," *Clinton Digital Library*, accessed October 1, 2017, https://clinton.presidentiallibraries.us/items/show/12564.

19. Ibid.

20. Ibid.

21. Ibid.

22. "1995-10-18A, Summary of Conclusions of Deputies Committee Meeting on Bosnia October 18, 1995," *Clinton Digital Library*, accessed October 1, 2017, https://clinton.presidentiallibraries.us/items/show/12563.

23. "1995-10-19B, BTF Memorandum re Deputies Committee Meeting October 19, 1995," *Clinton Digital Library*, accessed October 1, 2017, https://clinton.presidentiallibraries.us/items/show/12566.

24. Ibid.

25. The list of issues included:
    "– IFOR will not provide for civil order, and State should prepare a paper addressing the outstanding issues of establishing a police force and the implications for a peace settlement if no viable police force exists.
    – State should prepare a paper on a possible IFOR role in implementing a settlement in Eastern Slavonia.
    – Russian forces should not have a separate zone.
    – IFOR will create secure conditions for elections by completing its primary tasks; OSCE should be solicited as the lead organization in the electoral component of the overall implementation effort.
    – There should be indicators of seriousness in the framework agreement that the parties should commit to fulfill between initialing and signature of the

peace agreement, but their fulfillment would not be a precondition for rapid deployment of IFOR.

- Until we have a final peace agreement and final implementation plan, we will preserve our flexibility on the exact duration of IFOR's mission while continuing to use 12 months as the planning figure.
- Entities firing from one territory to another across the zone of separation is a violation of the peace agreement and the IFOR commander will judge when and what force will be used to enforce the settlement.
- IFOR forces should be authorized to stop deliberate violence to life and person against international civilian personnel and indigent population, and to act against gross humanitarian violations where NATO forces are present or have the means and opportunity to act.
- IFOR will not be responsible for investigating past incidents of attacks, atrocities, or human rights violations.
- IFOR will not provide protection for relief convoys and civilian movements.
- IFOR will not evict civilians from newly found homes nor bring prior residents back.
- Although IFOR will recognize the right of displaced civilians to return to their homes, it will not become involved and has no role in movement of refugee population.
- NAC will ultimately define "total breakdown" based on the situation and the advice of military commanders.
- The IFOR commander will coordinate his actions with SICOR and can talk to the civilian heads of each entity concerning military matters.

Those issues left unresolved and to be decided by the Principals were:

- Under what circumstances will IFOR use force against the Federation, in keeping with the principle of impartiality adopted by NATO?
- Will IFOR pull out if the Serbs unilaterally withdraw "strategic consent?" Will IFOR use force to compel Serb acceptance before pulling out as the option of last resort?
- What does IFOR do about reported "over the horizon" violations of the peace agreement or gross violations of human rights?
- Do we want a 20 km heavy-weapons-free zone and/or a 2 or 4 km all-weapons-free zone along the zone of separation?
- What is the nature of IFOR presence in Bosnian Serb territory besides free access?
- What is an acceptable end state for the U.S. when IFOR leaves?"

See "1995-10-20B, Summary of Conclusions of Deputies Committee Meeting on Bosnia October 20, 1995," *Clinton Digital Library*, accessed October 1, 2017, https://clinton.presidentiallibraries.us/items/show/12568.

26. "1995-10-24A, Memo re Deputies Committee Meeting on Bosnia October 24, 1995," *Clinton Digital Library*, accessed October 1, 2017, https://clinton.presidentiallibraries.us/items/show/12570.

27. "1995-10-25, Summary of Conclusions of Principals Committee Meeting on Bosnia October 25, 1995," *Clinton Digital Library*, accessed October 1, 2017, https://clinton.presidentiallibraries.us/items/show/12573. Appended to this Summary of Conclusions is a ten-page "MEMORANDUM FOR PRINCIPALS" on the subject of "IFOR Issues," authored by Sandy Berger. This was a critical guiding document for Principals and Deputies in the weeks ahead.

28. "1995-10-26B, BTF Memorandum re Principals Committee Meeting October 27, 1995," *Clinton Digital Library*, accessed October 1, 2017, https://clinton.presidentiallibraries.us/items/show/12575.

29. "1995-10-27, Summary of Conclusions of Principals Committee Meeting on Bosnia October 27, 1995," *Clinton Digital Library*, accessed October 1, 2017, https://clinton.presidentiallibraries.us/items/show/12577.

30. Ibid.

31. *See, e.g.*, Richard Holbrooke, *To End a War* (231–314); Daalder, 117–189; Elizabeth Cousens and Charles Cater, *Toward Peace in Bosnia: Implementing the Dayton Accords* (Boulder: Lynne Rienner Publishing, Inc., 2001); Derek Chollet, *The Road to the Dayton Accords* (New York: Palgrave Macmillan, 2005); Christopher R. Hill, *OUTPOST: Life on the Frontlines of American Diplomacy: A Memoir* (New York: Simon & Schuster, 2015), 67–111.

32. Extracts from the Kerrick SITREPS follow:

SITREP # 1, NOVEMBER 2

"Day one of serious negotiations complete. Described as 'typical' day one by state pros. Atmospherics remain positive. Even lighthearted. Will take several days or even full week to see if positive steps today lead anywhere. All seem willing to deal—even anxious to do so." "1995-11-02, Don Kerrick to Tony Lake re Dayton SITREP #1 November 2, 1995, 900pm," *Clinton Digital Library*, accessed October 1, 2017, https://clinton.presidentiallibraries.us/items/show/12579.

SITREP #2, NOVEMBER 4

"Dreary, cold skies over Dayton on day three. Parties remain warm and receptive to one another, but showing almost no movement on key issues—yet." "1995-11-04, Don Kerrick to Tony Lake re Dayton SITREP #2 November 4, 1995, 1020pm," *Clinton Digital Library*, accessed October 1, 2017, https://clinton.presidentiallibraries.us/items/show/12580.

SITREP #3, NOVEMBER 7

"All going well—just unclear where all is going."

"Talks at all levels continued Monday. Parties continue talking to each other—atmosphere continues to improve. Positive tone evident at Talbott dinner last night where Milošević and Izetbegović told jokes to each other in native language. They may be enjoying each others' company too much. No evidence anyone—parties or Euros—want to close deal. Intend to ratchet up pressure today." "1995-11-07, Don Kerrick to Tony Lake re Dayton SITREP #3 November 7, 1995, 900am," *Clinton Digital Library*, accessed October 1, 2017, https://clinton.presidentiallibraries.us/items/show/12581.

SITREP #4, NOVEMBER 8

"While short of outright rejection, Bosnians clearly see current IFOR concept as implying future partition. Will not accept without change. Surprise is length of time it took Bosnians to recognize . . . Will surely require PC or other high level review fairly soon."

"Map slugfest continues. Painful process with little forward movement."

"Dick Holbrooke (at encouragement of Strobe and Jan Lodel) will provide regular update to Principals and Deputies. Despite daily reports by Jim Pardew and LTG. Wes Clark, OSD apparently felt insufficient information from head of delegation contributed to panic in Pentagon over Eastern Slavonia, etc. Not clear additional report will make issues any easier." "1995-11-08, Don Kerrick to Tony Lake re Dayton SITREP #4 November 8, 1995, 100am," *Clinton Digital Library*, accessed October 1, 2017, https://clinton.presidentiallibraries.us/items/show/12582.

SITREP #5, NOVEMBER 9

"In scene reminiscent of the Godfather, two families (don Slobo and outcast Bosnian Serbs, don Izy and Federation) held truly remarkable six-hour map marathon. Despite hours of heated, yet civil exchanges, absolutely nothing was agreed. Astonishingly, at one moment parties could be glaring across table, screaming, while, at another moment minutes later they could be seen smiling and joking together over refreshments. Nevertheless, not clear Sarajevo solvable. Completely different views." "1995-11-09, Don Kerrick to Tony Lake re Dayton SITREP #5 November 9, 1995, 200am," *Clinton Digital Library*, accessed October 1, 2017, https://clinton.presidentiallibraries.us/items/show/12583.

SITREP #6, NOVEMBER 10

"Intense shuttling between Serbs and Bosnians residences dominated Thursday in Dayton. Full court press underway on constitution, elections, and map. Both Milošević and Izetbegović fully engaged. Some progress, but no agreed decisions. Shuttle efforts continue overnight and into Friday."

"In fascinating exchange with Milošević over lunch, he told me: 'General Kerrick, while America's professional prestige is on the line, my head and life are at stake—literally.' He wants us to believe that Krajišnik and others are capable and willing to remove him if he goes [too] far. [Israeli Prime Minister Yitzhak] Rabin remains fresh memory."

In handwriting: "Late Breaking News: Bosnians (Izy) totally rejected Serb counterproposal on map . . . Clearly, Bosnians have chosen not to seriously engage on map—yet." "1995-11-10, Don Kerrick to Tony Lake re Dayton SITREP #6

November 10, 1995, 130am," *Clinton Digital Library*, accessed October 1, 2017, https://clinton.presidentiallibraries.us/items/show/12584.

SITREP #7, NOVEMBER 11

"Parties mood remains positive. Still enjoying each others company, but more they see each other, more they seem to be willing to chuck it all and return to war. Convinced, our optimism on chances for success directly linked to tidal Potomac. Every twelve hours sure we will fail only to find real chances for success at next high tide."

"After ten days of negotiations, map talks at full stop. No progress. Bosnians yet to fully engage. Bosnian Serbs, while theatrically engaged, have yet to seriously present rationale proposal. Efforts now underway to jump-start map talks. Saturday is day of maps." "1995-11-11, Don Kerrick to Tony Lake re Dayton SITREP #7 November 11, 1995, 910am," *Clinton Digital Library*, accessed October 1, 2017, https://clinton.presidentiallibraries.us/items/show/12585.

SITREP #8, NOVEMBER 11–13

"Weekend very discouraging. Despite good news on Eastern Slavonia, map talks are going nowhere. Both sides dug in over their heads. Shouts, anger; highlight talks. . . . We are preparing a U.S. map which will make no one happy and may drive Izy public—which he has threatened to do." "1995-11-13B, Don Kerrick to Tony Lake re Dayton SITREP #8 November 11–13, 1995, 1030am," *Clinton Digital Library*, accessed October 1, 2017, https://clinton.presidentiallibraries.us/items/show/12587.

SITREP #9, NOVEMBER 14

"Hectic pace on all fronts. Tudjman hosted dinner last night for his two amigos (Izy, Slobo) at officers club. Remain amazed at their ability to turn on charm socially while spouting venom in negotiations. Izy inability to bring his delegation to united position threatens Dayton success."

"Brcko emerging as territorial issue most likely to spiral Dayton into failure. Bosnians clearly prepared to return to war. No real signs of progress, but sides have begun to negotiate seriously through U.S. delegation." "1995-11-14E, Don Kerrick to Tony Lake re Dayton SITREP #9 November 14, 1995, 110am," *Clinton Digital Library*, accessed October 1, 2017, https://clinton.presidentiallibraries.us/items/show/12592.

SITREP #12, NOVEMBER 17

"Last night, after your departure, spent bizarre two hours with Milošević in our map room looking in great detail over Goražde. After four scotches, Milošević offered up more forthcoming corridor to Sarajevo. Falls short of Contact Group proposal, but better than previous offer. Initial reaction from [Haris Silajdžić] this morning is cautiously favorable. Details now being examined by Bosnian map experts.

"Milošević has invited U.S. delegation to another feast tonight . . . Spirou hosted. We have accepted—someone has to do it.

"Walt Slocombe says Speaker (Gingrich) himself has suggested joint session of Congress for all three Presidents to welcome peace and ask for U.S. troops. Never cease to be amazed." "1995-11-17, Don Kerrick to Tony Lake re Dayton SITREP #12 November 17, 1995, 1110am," *Clinton Digital Library*, accessed October 1, 2017, https://clinton.presidentiallibraries.us/items/show/12597.

33. "1995-11-14E, Don Kerrick to Tony Lake re Dayton SITREP #9 November 14, 1995, 110am," *Clinton Digital Library*, accessed October 1, 2017, https://clinton.presidentiallibraries.us/items/show/12592.

34. "1995-11-17, Don Kerrick to Tony Lake re Dayton SITREP #12 November 17, 1995, 1110am," *Clinton Digital Library*, accessed October 1, 2017, https://clinton.presidentiallibraries.us/items/show/12597.

35. General Framework Agreement for Peace in Bosnia and Herzegovina, B.A.-H.R.-YU., December 14, 1995, 35 *International Legal Materials* 75.

36. "1995-11-27, DDCI Memo re Principals Committee Meeting on Bosnia November 22, 1995," *Clinton Digital Library*, accessed October 1, 2017, https://clinton.presidentiallibraries.us/items/show/12603.

37. Ibid.

Index